GLACIER NATIONAL PARK

BECKY LOMAX

Contents

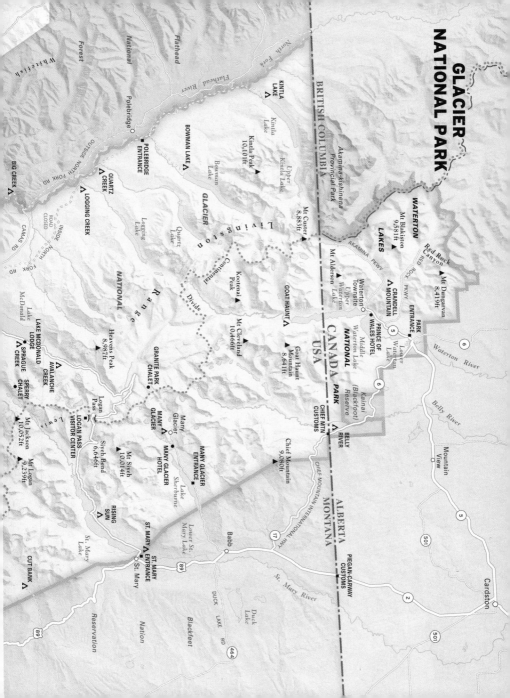

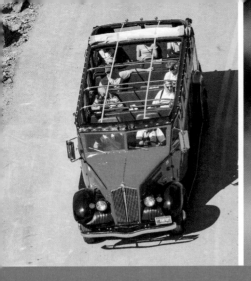

DISCOVER

Glacier National Park

Glacier National Park is the undisputed "Crown of the Continent." It's a place where the earth's forces have left their imprints on the landscape with jagged arêtes, red pinnacles, and glacier-carved basins. Acres of lush green parkland plunge from jagged summits. Waterfalls roar, ice cracks, and rockfall echoes in scenery still under the paintbrush of change.

In this rugged 1 million acres (0.4 million hectares), indigenous grizzly bears and wolves top the food chain. Mountain goats prance on precarious ledges. Wolverines romp in high glacial cirques. Bighorn sheep graze in alpine meadows while pikas shriek nearby. Only two animals present in Lewis and Clark's day are missing: the woodland caribou and the bison.

The Continental Divide splits Glacier into the west side and the east side. They differ in character, yet are wrought from the same geologic building blocks. Two Wild and Scenic Rivers splash along park boundaries, converging at 3,150 feet (960 m) in elevation, while six peaks surpass 10,000 feet (3,048 m). Mount Cleveland is the tallest, its north face one of the highest vertical walls in the United States.

Slicing through the park's heart, the historic Going-to-the-Sun Road twists

---

Clockwise from top left: red tour bus; yellow columbine; hikers on top of the Continental Divide at Swiftcurrent Lookout; bighorn sheep at Logan Pass; hiking through wildflowers in Preston Park; Red Rock Falls in Many Glacier.

and turns on a narrow cliff climb. Tunnels, arches, and bridges lead sightseers over precipices where seemingly no road could go. Visitors overlook ice-abraded valleys, thundering cascades, mammoth lakes, and serrated peaks.

More than 700 miles (1,130 km) of trails wind through Glacier's remote wilderness. Hikers walk up verdant valleys, beneath frigid waterfalls, and over high passes. Peak panoramas and blue-green lakes are strung like pearls along trails in places of solitude.

Designated a Biosphere Reserve by the United Nations Educational, Scientific, and Cultural Organization (UNESCO), Glacier hosts a rich diversity of wildlife and has a wealth of natural attributes, boasting a tremendous geological heritage, plus a cultural history as sacred Indigenous land. Glacier National Park, combined with Canada's Waterton Lakes National Park, is the world's first International Peace Park and has also been declared a World Heritage Site by UNESCO.

The park's glaciers fuel North America's major rivers, with crystal-clear water tumbling to Hudson Bay, the Gulf of Mexico, and the Pacific. But those glaciers will soon meet their demise. That change will repaint the scenery once again.

Glacier preserves some of the nation's wildest country. Welcome to this rugged slice of nature's best.

Clockwise from top left: St. Mary Fall; multi-colored rocks in Lake McDonald; Sexton Glacier on Siyeh Pass Trail; playing in Upper Kintla Lake.

10 TOP
EXPERIENCES

1 **Cruise Going-to-the-Sun Road:** Traveled by **car** (page 109) or an iconic **red bus** (page 107), this stunning road cuts through immense cliffs and glacier-carved mountains dripping with waterfalls. For avid **cyclists** (page 133), the climb rates as one of the best in the country, especially in spring, when the road is closed to cars.

2 **Touch the Continental Divide at Logan Pass:** While you're there, you can climb the boardwalk to Hidden Lake Overlook or take a commemorative photo (page 116).

3 **Go Backpacking:** Explore the rugged, remote backcountry over **Boulder Pass** (pictured; page 88) or the **Northern Circle** (page 166). For a shorter trip, try the **Dawson-Pitamakin Loop** (page 197).

4 **Soak Up the Ambience at a Historic Park Lodge:** Visit **Many Glacier Hotel,** a classic example of Parkitecture, in an idyllic lakeside setting surrounded by jagged peaks (page 157).

5 **Hike to Grinnell Glacier:** The park's glaciers have only a few years left. Hike to Grinnell Glacier, which is the most accessible one (page 161).

6 Paddle Lakes: Canoe, kayak, or paddleboard in remote solitude at **Kintla Lake** (pictured; page 79) or **Bowman Lake** (page 79). For easier access, float **Lake McDonald** (page 56).

>>>

7 Stay at Granite Park Chalet: It's rustic and simple, but Granite Park Chalet perches on a knoll above the treeline with a 360-degree mountain view. Reach it by hiking the Highline Trail (page 140).

<<<

8 Relish Summer Wildflowers: See meadows of wildflowers blooming in Preston Park on the **Piegan Pass** and **Siyeh Pass trails,** along **Many Glacier Road,** and in many other places throughout the park (page 318).

>>>

9 **Watch Wildlife:** See mountain goats, bighorn sheep, bears, and moose (page 34). Two of the best places are the Hidden Lake Overlook Trail at **Logan Pass** (page 116 and **Many Glacier** (page 157).

10 **Explore the Park in Winter:** Even when snow buries and closes park roads, you can still snowshoe or cross-country ski to **Bowman Lake** (page 79), **McGee Meadows** (page 81), **Rocky Point** (page 59), or on **Going-to-the-Sun Road** (page 136).

Planning Your Trip

Where to Go

West Glacier and Apgar

West Glacier and Apgar form the park's western portal. Divided by a nationally designated **Wild and Scenic River,** the pair attracts a frenzy of visitors with **white-water rafting, horseback riding, fishing, paddling, boating,** and **hiking.**

WHY GO

West Glacier is the rafting capital of Glacier, and Apgar lays claim to camping and water sports at the foot of Lake McDonald, the largest lake in the park. The pair make good bases for venturing into the North Fork and Two Medicine, plus driving Going-to-the-Sun Road. Avid hikers will want to go to Huckleberry Lookout.

North Fork

Head to the remote North Fork on Glacier's west side for real rusticity, not just the look of it. Bumpy dirt roads lead to **Polebridge Mercantile** and **Northern Lights Saloon.** Farther along are scenic **Bowman** and **Kintla Lakes.**

WHY GO

The North Fork is a place to decompress, since its dirt roads deter many visitors. With no cell reception, your brain can disconnect from the electronic world.

Going-to-the-Sun Road

Glacier's biggest attraction and the only road bisecting the park leads drivers on a skinny cliff

rental and tour boats at Two Medicine Lake

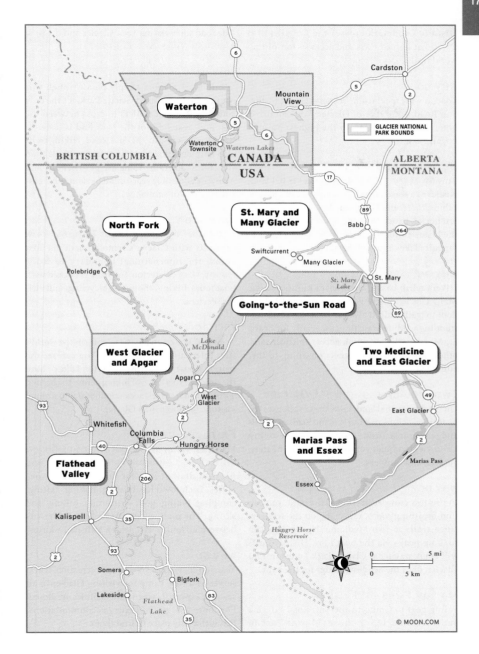

Cardston

Mountain View

Waterton

Waterton Townsite *Waterton Lakes*

BRITISH COLUMBIA **CANADA**

USA

GLACIER NATIONAL PARK BOUNDS

ALBERTA
MONTANA

St. Mary and Many Glacier

Babb

North Fork

Swiftcurrent

Many Glacier

Polebridge

St. Mary Lake St. Mary

Going-to-the-Sun Road

West Glacier and Apgar

Lake McDonald

Apgar

West Glacier

Two Medicine and East Glacier

East Glacier

Whitefish

Columbia Falls

Hungry Horse

Marias Pass and Essex

Marias Pass

Flathead Valley

Essex

Kalispell

Hungry Horse Reservoir

Somers

Bigfork

Lakeside *Flathead Lake*

0   5 mi

0   5 km

© MOON.COM

shimmy into the craggy alpine. The National Historic Landmark crosses the **Continental Divide** at **Logan Pass** and accesses top-of-the-world trails.

WHY GO

Loaded with spectacular scenery, Going-to-the-Sun Road is the core of Glacier. You can drive, bike, or ride a tour bus to the highest point at Logan Pass.

St. Mary and Many Glacier

Tiny **St. Mary,** located on Blackfeet tribal land, bustles as a seasonal hub of campgrounds, lodges, cabins, cafés, and Going-to-the-Sun Road's eastern portal. Inside the park, **Many Glacier** holds the historic **Many Glacier Hotel,** plus trails to sapphire lakes and high passes.

WHY GO

Hikers relish basing themselves in ultra-scenic Many Glacier, where you can walk right out the door to trailheads. It also has boat tours and outstanding wildlife-watching, especially for bears. St. Mary works for quick access to trailheads, other park locales, and scenery on Going-to-the-Sun Road.

Two Medicine and East Glacier

On Blackfeet tribal land, **East Glacier** houses the historic **Glacier Park Lodge** and loads of motels and restaurants. Inside the park, **Two Medicine Lake** yields a quiet contrast for hikers, boaters, anglers, and campers.

WHY GO

In this less crowded section of the park, you can find breathing room, especially on the scenery-laden trails at Two Medicine. Non-hikers can soak up peaks via the boat tour. History buffs will enjoy staying at Glacier Park Lodge in East Glacier, once the headliner lodge for the park.

Marias Pass and Essex

Paling next to Going-to-the-Sun Road's drama but still scenic, U.S. 2 crosses **Marias Pass** in the fastest route over the **Continental Divide.** The road squeezes between Glacier and the **Bob Marshall Wilderness Complex.**

WHY GO

While most visitors simply pass through this southern route around Glacier Park, it's the only route for RVs and trailers to cross between the east and west sides of the park and is faster to drive than Going-to-the-Sun Road. Hiking trails also have benefits: Most have fewer people than the Sun Road trails, some are pet-friendly, and many are accessible year-round by donning cross-country skis or snowshoes.

Waterton

In Canada, **Waterton Lakes National Park** connects with Glacier's remote north via boat across the international boundary to **Goat Haunt, USA.** Waterton Townsite is packed with boat tours, hiking, shopping, bicycling, and visitor services.

WHY GO

Together, Waterton and Glacier form the world's first International Peace Park. You can see the pair on a boat tour across Waterton Lake or have the unique experience of hiking across the border. This Canadian park sees about 500,000 annual visitors, far fewer than Glacier.

Flathead Valley

Flathead Valley is the **gateway to Glacier. Whitefish, Columbia Falls, Kalispell,** and **Bigfork** draw visitors for their unique personalities. Each town has boating, fishing, rafting, camping, biking, golf, swimming, hiking, and skiing. The main **airport** serving Glacier sits between all four towns, with a Kalispell address.

WHY GO

Year-round, Flathead Valley has recreation. It also serves as a base camp for visiting Glacier in all seasons, especially when park facilities are closed. For those who prefer luxury accommodations, this is the only place to find them.

If You're Looking for...

BICYCLING

- For road cyclists, the big prize is the demanding climb of **Going-to-the-Sun Road.** Ride it in spring before vehicles are permitted.

BOAT TOURS

- In summer, historic wooden boats cruise **St. Mary Lake, Lake McDonald, Two Medicine Lake, Swiftcurrent** and **Josephine Lakes,** and **Upper Waterton Lake.**

FISHING

- Cast a line for wild trout into the **North Fork** or **Middle Fork of the Flathead River,** which form boundaries of the park.

GLACIERS

- Take your binoculars to see **Jackson and Blackfoot Glaciers** from Going-to-the-Sun Road. Hikers can see glaciers from the **Siyeh Pass Trail** and **Grinnell Glacier Trail.**

HIKING

- In summer, the most popular and crowded trails are located in Many Glacier (**Iceberg Lake, Grinnell Lake,** and **Grinnell Glacier**) and at Logan Pass (**Hidden Lake Overlook** and **Highline Trail**). Two Medicine offers more solitude on the **Dawson-Pitamakin Loop** or **Cobalt Lake Trails.**

HORSEBACK RIDING

- Hop on guided horse rides in **Many Glacier, Apgar, West Glacier, East Glacier, Lake McDonald,** and **Waterton.**

LAKES

- Giant glaciers dug **Lake McDonald** and **St.**

rafting the Middle Fork of the Flathead River

Mary Lake, the park's two largest lakes flanking Going-to-the-Sun Road. Drive paved roads to smaller subalpine lakes at **Two Medicine** or **Many Glacier** or follow dirt roads to **Bowman** and **Kintla Lakes.**

RIVER RAFTING

- Four rafting companies based out of West Glacier guide white-water, scenic float, or overnight trips on the **North Fork** and **Middle Fork of the Flathead River.**

WATERFALLS

- Enjoy copious waterfalls on **Going-to-the-Sun Road.** In Two Medicine, see the unique **Running Eagle Falls.** In Many Glacier, hike to **Red Rock Falls.** In Waterton, stroll across town to soak up **Cameron Falls.**

When to Go

High Season (June-Sept.)

Summer attracts crowds when **lodges, campgrounds,** and **trails** are open. **Going-to-the-Sun Road** is generally open **mid-June to mid-October,** with peak visitation and the best weather crammed into July and August. Mosquitoes descend in early summer, and snow buries some trails into July before wildflowers peak in late July and huckleberries ripen in August. Wildfire season is late July through September.

At low elevations on the west side, summer **temperatures** usually average 70-85°F (21-29°C) during days and 45-49°F (6-9°C) at night. St. Mary and Many Glacier see the same range of high temperatures, but low temperatures range more widely at 40-49°F (4.5-9°C). At higher elevations, you will encounter temperatures about 10-15°F (6-8°C) cooler. Summer temperatures in Two Medicine, East Glacier, Browning, and Essex average 65-80°F (18-27°C) during days and 40-43°F (4.5-6°C) at night. In Waterton Townsite, temperatures usually average 65-85°F (18-29°C) during summer days, dipping to 40°F (4.5°C) or cooler at night.

Off-Season (Oct.-May)

Although saddled with unpredictable weather, off-season offers less-hectic visits. Low-elevation trails are usually snow-free in May and October, but **minimal commercial services** are open. When **Going-to-the-Sun Road is closed to vehicles,** bikers and hikers tour it without cars in spring and fall.

In **spring,** May-June rains intersperse with cobalt-blue skies. In **fall,** warm bug-free days and cool nights usher in the larch and aspen turning gold. Peak-top snows descend in September. In **winter,** snow closes most park roads, which become quiet snowshoeing and cross-country ski trails.

On the west side, winter **temperatures** waffle between 0°F (-18°C) to 35°F (2°C). At St. Mary Lake and Lake McDonald, temperatures can range from above freezing to -10°F (-23°C) with wind chills much lower. On the east side and in Essex, temperatures range -10°F up to 35°F (-23°C to 2°C). In Waterton Townsite, winter temperatures range between -40°F (-40°C) and 50°F (10°C).

Before You Go

Park Fees and Passes

Entrance passes are valid for seven days. Vehicle entrance costs $35 ($25 winter), motorcyclists pay $30 ($20 winter), hikers and bicyclists pay $20 ($15 winter). **Annual passes** include the Glacier National Park Annual Pass ($70) or the America the Beautiful National Parks and Federal Recreational Lands Passes ($80, free for military and fourth graders). Lifetime passes are available for U.S. seniors ($80). To speed through the entrance lines, you can buy Glacier-only passes in advance online (www.recreation.gov).

Free admission is on Martin Luther King Day (Jan.), first day of National Park Week (Apr.), the National Park Service's birthday (Aug. 25), Public Lands Day (Sept.), and Veterans Day (Nov. 11).

Entrance Stations

Glacier has eight entrance stations:

- **West Glacier** from U.S. 2; west portal for Going-to-the-Sun Road and Lake McDonald (open year-round)

Tips for Dodging Crowds

In recent years, Glacier has seen record-breaking crowds in summer. About 80 percent of the park's annual visitors show up mostly in July and August when Going-to-the-Sun Road opens. Parking fills up at Logan Pass and some trailheads. Some overcrowded trails see long lines of hikers, and shuttles pack out with riders. In addition to being patient and flexible, what can you do to have a more enjoyable trip?

- **Visit in June or September.** Avoid the ultra-crowded season between July 4 and Labor Day. Because June still has snow in the high country, precluding access to Logan Pass and some trails, plan for potential limitations pending road plowing and weather. Early season visitors can bicycle Going-to-the-Sun Road while it's closed to vehicles, an exceptional experience. September brings more breathing space with access to Logan Pass and high-elevation trails, but be ready for schizophrenic weather bouncing between sunny days and snow and potential wildfire smoke during dry years.

- **Buy your entrance pass before you arrive.** Get your entrance pass digitally online (www.recreation.gov) in advance to whisk through entrance lines faster.

- **Use Glacier's dashboard.** Make use of the Glacier dashboard (www.nps.gov/applications/glac/dashboard/), also known as the Recreational Access Display, for the real-time status of campgrounds, weather, road access restrictions, and parking lot congestion in order to adjust your plans and destination accordingly.

- **Drive Going-to-the-Sun Road early or late.** Once it opens for the season, you can drive Going-to-the-Sun Road 24/7. Plan to catch the sunrise or sunset, and you'll encounter fewer people. Plus, early morning and evening yield better lighting for photography. In the extended daylight of June and July, you can hike Hidden Lake Overlook in the evening (but finish by dusk). Hang in the parking lot after dark to soak up views of the Milky Way.

- **Hike off the beaten path.** Avoid the heavily used trails along the Going-to-the-Sun Road corridor and in Many Glacier. Instead, hike trails in Two Medicine (Scenic Point, Cobalt Lake, Dawson-Pitamakin), Cut Bank (Triple Divide, Medicine Grizzly Lake), or the North Fork (Glacier View, Numa Lookout).

- **Plan ahead for backpacking.** Apply in mid-March for an advance reservation for a summer backpacking permit to get to those idyllic backcountry havens.

- **Camp and stay put.** Rather than fighting for a new campsite in a new campground every morning, select a campground to use as home base. Then, drive to other locations as day trips. Make reservations six months ahead for campgrounds at St. Mary, Fish Creek, Many Glacier, and Waterton Townsite.

- **St. Mary** on U.S. 89; east portal for Going-to-the-Sun Road (open May-Oct.)

- **Many Glacier** from U.S. 89; goes to Many Glacier and Swiftcurrent (open mid-May-early Nov.)

- **Two Medicine** from MT 49; goes to Two Medicine Lake (open late May-Oct.)

- **Polebridge** via Outside North Fork Road; access to Bowman and Kintla Lakes (open late May-Oct.)

- **Camas** via Outside North Fork Road; goes to Apgar and West Glacier (open mid-May-Oct.)

- **Cut Bank** from U.S. 89; dirt road leads to Cut Bank Campground and trailhead (open June-Sept.)

- **Goat Haunt** by boat or trail from Waterton Lakes National Park (open late May-mid-Sept.)

Reservations

Advance reservations for all in-park lodgings are **imperative,** especially for July and August. Contact **Xanterra** (855/733-4522, www.glaciernationalparklodges.com) 13 months in advance for Many Glacier Hotel, Lake McDonald Lodge, Rising Sun Motor Inn, Swiftcurrent Motor

Be a Responsible Traveler

Traveling sustainably in Glacier means assuming care for and respecting the landscape and wildlife. Here are some tips to help you leave as little an impact as possible.

- Protect sensitive park features and follow **Leave No Trace** principles (www.lnt.org).

- Bring a **refillable water bottle** to use at the park's water stations instead of multiple plastic bottles.

- Buy **locally made** products to support the communities near Glacier. Look for the **Made in Montana** label.

- Sign up for adventure tours with **local guide companies**, and support **Blackfeet businesses.**

- Ditch the car. Take **shuttles** or **bus tours** whenever possible. Hike, bike, paddle, or ski to be more intimate with the scenery and lessen your **carbon footprint.**

- Protect **wildlife** by maintaining appropriate distance at all times.

- Shoot **wildflower photos** from a safe stance on solid rocks or logs rather than in meadows.

- Adjust your schedule to accommodate visiting crowded sites at **less crowded times** or seasons. If a trailhead parking lot is full, bypass it in favor of hiking at one less crowded.

spring biking on Going-to-the-Sun Road

- Always **have a Plan B, C, and D** in case crowds, weather, or wildfires preclude your Plan A.

- Bring your own health kit with **hand sanitizer,** sanitizing wipes, face masks, and **cleaning supplies.**

Inn, and Apgar Village Inn. Make reservations 13-16 months ahead with **Pursuit Glacier Park Collection** (844/868-7474, www.glacierparkcollection.com) for Apgar Village Lodge and Motel Lake McDonald. For Granite Park Chalet and Sperry Chalet, make reservations in early January through **Belton Chalets** (406/387-5654 or 888/345-2649, www.graniteparkchalet.com, www.sperrychalet.com).

Most of Glacier's 13 campgrounds are **first-come, first-served.** Reservations (877/444-6777, www.recreation.gov) are accepted for **Fish Creek, St. Mary,** and **Many Glacier** starting six months in advance. Reserve group campsites 12 months in advance for **St. Mary** and **Apgar.** For backpacking, secure an advance reservation ($40) for a **backcountry permit** ($7 pp per day) starting mid-March.

Lake McDonald Lodge

In the Park

Visitors Centers

Glacier National Park has tiny visitors centers. On Going-to-the-Sun Road, **Apgar Visitor Center** (year-round, weekends only in winter) anchors the west entrance and **St. Mary Visitor Center** (late May-early Oct.) at the east entrance, while **Logan Pass Visitor Center** (mid-June-mid-Sept.) perches at the apex.

Campgrounds

The park houses 13 campgrounds. To plan your arrival, check fill times online (www.nps.gov/glac) for previous days and for the same month in previous years.

Getting Around

The **free Going-to-the-Sun Road shuttles** (www.nps.gov/glac, July-early Sept.) transport visitors to multiple locations on Going-to-the-Sun Road, including Logan Pass, trailheads, campgrounds, and lodges. Fee-based shuttles outside the park are run by **Pursuit Glacier Park Collection** (844/868-7474, www.glacierparkcollection.com) and **Xanterra** (855/733-4522, www.glaciernationalparklodges.com).

In summer, historic **red buses** (855/733-4522, www.glaciernationalparklodges.com) and Blackfeet-owned **Sun Tours** (406/226-9220, http://glaciersuntours.com) take passengers on guided tours of Going-to-the-Sun Road.

Weather, rockfall, fire, snow, floods, and construction can close the Sun Road. Check on current conditions for driving all park roads (406/888-7800, www.nps.gov/glac).

In-Park Lodging

	Location	Price	Season	Amenities
Apgar Campground	Apgar	$20	Apr.-Oct.	tent sites, unserviced RV sites
Fish Creek Campground	Apgar	$23	June-early Sept.	tent sites, unserviced RV sites
Apgar Village Lodge	Apgar	$120-335	late May-late Sept.	motel rooms, cabins
Apgar Village Inn	Apgar	$185-320	late May-mid-Sept.	motel rooms
Logging Creek Campground	North Fork	$10	July-mid-Sept.	tent sites
Quartz Creek Campground	North Fork	$10	July-Oct.	tent sites
Bowman Lake Campground	North Fork	$15	late May-Oct.	tent sites
Kintla Lake Campground	North Fork	$15	mid-June-Oct.	tent sites
Sprague Creek Campground	Going-to-the-Sun Road	$20	early May-mid-Sept.	tent sites, unserviced RV sites
Lake McDonald Lodge	Going-to-the-Sun Road	$118-515	late May-late Sept.	hostel, lodge, and cottage rooms, restaurants
Motel Lake McDonald	Going-to-the-Sun Road	$180-200	early June-mid- Sept.	motel rooms
Avalanche Campground	Going-to-the-Sun Road	$20	mid-June-mid- Sept.	tent sites, unserviced RV sites
Granite Park Chalet	Going-to-the-Sun Road	$82-120 pp	July-early Sept.	backcountry hostel
Sperry Chalet	Going-to-the-Sun Road	$160-240	early July-early Sept.	backcountry chalet
Rising Sun Motor Inn	Going-to-the-Sun Road	$182-200	mid-June-mid-Sept.	cabins, motel rooms, restaurant
Rising Sun Campground	Going-to-the-Sun Road	$20	mid-June-mid-Sept.	tent sites, unserviced RV sites
St. Mary Campground	St. Mary	$23	Apr.-Oct.	tent sites, unserviced RV sites
Many Glacier Campground	Many Glacier	$23	late May-Oct.	tent sites, unserviced RV sites
Swiftcurrent Motor Inn	Many Glacier	$120-200	mid-June-mid-Sept.	cabins, motel rooms, restaurant
Many Glacier Hotel	Many Glacier	$220-590	mid-June-mid-Sept.	hotel rooms, suites, restaurant
Cut Bank Campground	Cut Bank Valley	$10	early June-late Sept.	tent sites, unserviced RV sites
Two Medicine Campground	Two Medicine	$20	late May-Oct.	tent sites, unserviced RV sites

Best of Glacier National Park

Spend four days in Glacier to experience the best of the park. Stay in historic park lodges by making reservations 13 months in advance. If you have time, add on three more days to make a full week.

Day 1

Start your Glacier adventure by enjoying **Lake McDonald,** the park's largest lake. Rent a **paddleboard** or **kayak** to ply the waters around Apgar.

Drive **Going-to-the-Sun Road** up the west side to the historic **Lake McDonald Lodge** and leave your bags. Catch the late afternoon **red bus tour** up the alpine section of the Sun Road to **Logan Pass.** After returning, dine late in **Russell's Fireside Dining Room** topped by strolling the lakeshore at sunset.

Day 2

With a 7am start and a packed lunch, go to **Avalanche** to hike **Trail of the Cedars** and **Avalanche Lake.** After hiking, drive up the west side of Going-to-the-Sun Road, stopping at **Big Bend** to eat lunch on the rocks overlooking McDonald Valley. Then, cross the **Continental Divide** and drop down the east side of Glacier.

If time and energy permit, hike to **St. Mary Fall** and **Virginia Fall.** Otherwise, go to **Sun Point** to soak up the blue hues of **St. Mary Lake.** Drive outside the park to swing around north into **Many Glacier** to check into the historic **Many Glacier Hotel** for two nights.

Day 3

In the morning, hop the first boat across **Swiftcurrent Lake** and **Lake Josephine** to hike to turquoise **Grinnell Lake.** For a different (and tougher) option, follow a park naturalist up through cliffs and moraine to **Grinnell Glacier** and **Upper Grinnell Lake.**

If time allows when you return, rent a canoe to **paddle Swiftcurrent Lake.** After dinner, watch

Wild Goose Island in St. Mary Lake

Best in One Day

Glacier's biggest attraction is the 50-mile (81-km) **Going-to-the-Sun Road.** From West Glacier or St. Mary, the drive on the historic road over Logan Pass yields a taste of the park's grandeur, with waterfalls, immense glacier-carved valleys, and serrated peaks. To beat the crowds at Logan Pass, go there first thing, and then tour the west and east sides of the road. Pack a lunch to spend your time in the scenery, and plan to drive over and back for the full experience.

LOGAN PASS

Depart by 6am from West Glacier and 6:30am from St. Mary to drive directly to **Logan Pass,** since the parking lot often fills by 8am. At the pass, nab a photo of the Continental Divide sign, tour the small visitors center, and walk the paved self-guided interpretive trails. Climb the boardwalk and trail to **Hidden Lake Overlook** for views of Hidden Lake.

Bus Tour Option

If you want to avoid the stress of getting a parking spot at Logan Pass, take a **red bus tour** (www.glaciernationalparklodges.com) or the Blackfeet-led **Sun Tour bus** (www.glaciersuntours.com) from West Glacier, Apgar, or St. Mary. You can soak up the scenery rather than focusing on driving the narrow, cliffy road. Plus, tour buses are **guaranteed parking** at Logan Pass.

DESCENDING THE WEST SIDE

After departing the pass, pull over at **Oberlin Bend Overlook** to take in the views of the road's west side. Stop at **Big Bend** to see waterfalls, and **The Loop** to photograph **Heavens Peak.** Drop through the **West Side Tunnel** and fol-

East Side Tunnel on Going-to-the-Sun Road

low **McDonald Creek** downstream. Visit historic **Lake McDonald Lodge** and walk to any of the beaches from pullovers along Lake McDonald.

DESCENDING THE EAST SIDE

On the descent east of Logan Pass, enjoy burbling **Lunch Creek** before driving through the **East Side Tunnel,** which frames Going-to-the-Sun Mountain at the exit. Use binoculars to see **Jackson Glacier** in the distance from **Jackson Glacier Overlook.** Stop at **Sun Point** for the view of **St. Mary Lake.** Finish by touring the **St. Mary Visitor Center.**

the **sunset** over the Continental Divide from the back deck of Many Glacier Hotel.

Day 4

Get up early to take a dawn drive on **Many Glacier Road.** It's prime time to see wildlife, including **moose, bears,** and **bighorn sheep.**

After returning and enjoying a leisurely breakfast at the hotel, hop on **horseback** for a trail ride with **Swan Mountain Outfitters** before departing.

With More Time

- If you have **one day** more, tack on a hike up

Hidden Lake Overlook Trail

Swiftcurrent Valley to Red Rock Lake, Bullhead Lake, or farther up Swiftcurrent Pass and Lookout. Look for beargrass in July, huckleberries in August, and moose around the lakes.

- If you have three extra days, add on one day of hiking to Iceberg Lake in Many Glacier.

For the second day, drive to Two Medicine to take a boat tour on Two Medicine Lake, a mountaintop hike to Scenic Point, or both. Drive over Marias Pass to spend the night in West Glacier before celebrating your last day rafting on the Middle Fork of the Flathead River.

Best Hikes

Waterton-Glacier International Peace Park is a hiker's paradise, with more than 700 miles (1,130 km) of trails. Summer shuttles accommodate point-to-point hiking on Going-to-the-Sun Road and in Waterton.

Family-Friendly Hikes (Under 5 mi/8 km)

GRINNELL LAKE
A scenic boat ride across **two lakes** whittles this hike down to 2 miles (3.2 km) to see the turquoise lake fed by a **giant waterfall.** Kids love the **swinging bridge** and wading in the frigid lake.

RED ROCK CANYON AND BLAKISTON FALLS
In Waterton, loop 0.6-mile (1-km) around a colorful **red-rock gorge** with places to reach the **waterfall** splashing at its lower end. Extend the adventure 1.2 miles (1.9 km) round-trip to see Blakiston Falls.

HIDDEN LAKE OVERLOOK
Stand atop the **Continental Divide** at Hidden Lake Overlook on this 2.6-mile (4.2-km) round-trip adventure from Logan Pass, where you might spot **baby mountain goats.**

ST. MARY FALLS AND VIRGINIA FALLS
This 3.4-mile (5.5-km) trail takes in **two waterfalls.** One gushes through a rocky slot while the other sprays in a veil.

TRAIL OF THE CEDARS AND AVALANCHE LAKE
A 1-mile (0.6-km) trail tours an **accessible boardwalk,** bridges, and hard surface through **ancient cedars** that look like a gnome-land. Families can add on a 3.8-mile (6.1-km) round-trip walk up to a pretty **subalpine lake** fed by several waterfalls.

Day Hikes (5-10 mi/8-16.1 km)

SCENIC POINT
Switchbacks ascend a **rocky slope** with sparse vegetation to crest a windswept knoll. **Views** plummet down to Two Medicine Lake and shoot miles across the plains on this 5.8-mile (9.3-km) round-trip trail.

GRINNELL GLACIER
A **boat ride** clips mileage off the route to Grinnell Glacier, dropping it down to 7.8 miles (12.6 km) round-trip. It's the shortest route to see a glacier up close.

PIEGAN PASS
An 8.8-mile (14.2-km) round-trip trail climbs through **forest** and **wildflower meadows** to crest through a talus basin to a pass tucked under the Continental Divide.

SIYEH PASS
From Siyeh Bend on Going-to-the-Sun Road, this point-to-point trail circles 10 miles (16.1 km) around **Going-to-the-Sun Mountain.** View **colorful wildflowers** in Preston Park en route and two **glaciers.**

ICEBERG LAKE
A 10.4-mile (16.7-km) round-trip trail terminates at a lake where you can **swim with icebergs** in August.

Butt-Kickers (Over 10 mi/16.1 km)

HIGHLINE TRAIL AND GRANITE PARK CHALET
Beginning at Logan Pass, the stunning 11.4-mile (18.3-km) point-to-point walk tiptoes along the **Continental Divide** to historic Granite Park Chalet before dropping to The Loop. Hikers often see **mountain goats, bighorn sheep, bears,** or **wolverines.**

Fun for Kids

For a successful Glacier trip with kids, prepare for hikes and drives by bringing water, snacks, and lunch; places to fuel kids up are few and far between inside the park. Take along layers to don in case the weather sours. Have kids, even little ones, carry their own packs even if they only tote a sweatshirt.

LEARNING

- Stop at a ranger station or visitors center to pick up the **Junior Ranger** booklet. Complete activities to receive a Glacier badge.

- Visit the **Apgar Nature Center** for hands-on learning about wildlife, plants, and rocks.

- Hone in on wildlife through the **ranger spotting scope** in the Swiftcurrent parking lot at Many Glacier.

- Learn about wildlife survival in the alpine with hand-cranked narration and kid-targeted panels on the paved interpretive loop at **Logan Pass.**

ENGAGING

- Take older kids for a **trail ride on horseback** in Apgar, West Glacier, East Glacier, Many Glacier, Lake McDonald, or Waterton.

- Rent a canoe or kayak for **paddle fun** on Lake McDonald, Swiftcurrent Lake in Many Glacier, Two Medicine Lake, or Waterton Lake.

- Pedal through the Waterton Townsite on a **two-person surrey bike.**

- **Raft** the Middle Fork of the Flathead River with one of the companies in West Glacier. Older kids will love the white water, and younger kids can do the **scenic float.**

- **Fish** Lower McDonald Creek.

kid-friendly interpretive panels at Logan Pass

- Go **stargazing** at Logan Pass, St Mary Visitor Center, or Apgar Visitor Center.

HIKING

- Hike from **Logan Pass** to **Hidden Lake Overlook** to see mountain goats and walk on the **Continental Divide.**

- Hop the **double boat ride** across **Swiftcurrent Lake** and **Lake Josephine** in Many Glacier to hike to **Grinnell Lake,** crossing a river on a **swinging bridge.**

- Hike to **Avalanche Lake** to wade at its foot or fish at its head.

PTARMIGAN TUNNEL

An 11.4-mile (18.3-km) round-trip trail climbs past **Ptarmigan Lake** to switchback up to a hiker-and-horse tunnel cut through an arête to look down on **Elizabeth Lake.**

CARTHEW PASS

In Waterton, an 11.2-mile (18-km) point-to-point trail climbs from **Cameron Lake** over windy Carthew Pass to drop past **Alderson Lake** before reaching the Waterton Townsite.

Oberlin Bend just below Logan Pass

CRYPT LAKE

In Waterton, a **boat ride** and switchbacks ascend to a **ladder, tunnel,** and **cliff walk** to reach a hanging valley containing an idyllic lake on this 10.8-mile (17.4-km) round-trip hike that includes multiple **dramatic waterfalls.**

DAWSON-PITAMAKIN LOOP

Starting or finishing with a **boat ride** at Two Medicine, this 15.3-mile (24.6-km) loop crosses three passes on a narrow top-of-the-world trek through **bighorn sheep** summering range.

Glacier Road Trip

From popular stops to remote places of solitude, this road loop stitches together touring with iconic scenery. Enjoy this seven-day tour by staying in motels and park lodges.

Day 1
Kalispell to East Glacier
112 MILES (180 KM); 2.5 HOURS
From **Kalispell,** hop on U.S. 2, which skirts the south end of Glacier National Park. Stop at **Izaak Walton Inn** for lunch and to explore railroad history. Pull into the **Goat Lick** to peer down to mineral seeps that attract white shaggy goats.

To enjoy a bit of the **Middle Fork of the Flathead River,** roll into **Bear Creek River Access.** Take in the interpretive site at **Marias Pass** to learn about its discovery, geology, and history. Enter Blackfeet tribal land and bypass East Glacier for now, continuing farther to **Browning** to visit the **Museum of the Plains Indian.** Return to **East Glacier** to spend two nights at historic **Glacier Park Lodge.**

Day 2
Day Trip to Two Medicine
28 MILES (45 KM)
ROUNDTRIP; 1 HOUR
Pack a lunch for a day at **Two Medicine.** After entering Glacier National Park, walk the nature trail to **Running Eagle Falls** on the way to **Two Medicine Lake.** At the lake, rent a kayak to **paddle** or hop on the **tour boat.**

Afterwards, walk to **Aster Park** for views overlooking the lake or climb **Scenic Point** to get higher before returning to East Glacier.

Day 3
East Glacier to Waterton
112 MILES (181 KM); 4 HOURS
From East Glacier, drive north on the curves of MT 49 and U.S. 89. On the final hill descending

into **St. Mary,** stop at the **St. Mary Overlook** to explore the interpretive site and take in the view of the park. Then continue through St. Mary to **Chief Mountain Highway.**

After crossing into Canada, stop at the overlook of **Waterton Lakes National Park.** From the park entrance road, drive scenic **Red Rocks Parkway** to walk the loop and admire **Red Rocks Canyon.** Then, continue on to the **Waterton Townsite.** Stroll through the townsite, feast on dinner, and walk along the **Waterton Lakeshore path** to watch the alpenglow on the peaks before spending the night.

Day 4
Waterton to Many Glacier
50 MILES (80 KM); 2 HOURS
In the morning, hop aboard the *International* for a scenic boat tour on **Upper Waterton Lake.** Then, head back across the border to **Many Glacier.** Saunter around **Swiftcurrent Lake** and pop over the moraine ridge to **Lake Josephine** for the view of Mount Gould. After dinner at historic **Many Glacier Hotel,** enjoy bear-watching from the deck followed by the sunset over the Continental Divide and a good night's sleep.

Day 5
Many Glacier to Lake McDonald
60 MILES (97 KM); 2 HOURS
With a 6am start and a to-go lunch, head south to drive the **Going-to-the-Sun Road.** Stop briefly at **Wild Goose Island** overlook for a classic photo of **St. Mary Lake.** Then drive straight to **Logan Pass** to get a parking spot. Tour the visitors center and hike to **Hidden Lake Overlook.**

Descend westward, stopping at **Oberlin Bend** and **The Loop** to gaze at **Heaven's Peak.** Walk into the rainforest of **Trail of the Cedars** before overnighting at **Lake McDonald Lodge** for two nights.

Glacier is the ancestral land of the Blackfeet, Salish, and Kootenai. It served as a source for seasonal hunting and gathering needs plus it was a place where groups performed spiritual ceremonies and dances. The Blackfeet have an especially strong connection with Glacier because the western boundary of their reservation included the eastern side of the park (up to the Continental Divide) until the 1890s. Today, the Blackfeet share part of their western boundary with Glacier National Park.

Here are some of the ways you can learn about this area's Indigenous people and their heritage:

- Attend an evening **Native America Speaks** program at a campground, lodge, or locations on the Blackfeet Reservation.

- Visit the **Museum of the Plains Indian** in Browning.

- Stay overnight in a tipi at the **Blackfeet Culture Camp** in Browning.

- Tour Going-to-the-Sun Road with Blackfeet guides on **Sun Tours.**

- Attend **North American Indian Days** in early July in Browning.

North American Indian Days on the Blackfeet Reservation

Day 6
Day Trip to Bowman Lake
102 MILES (164 KM)
ROUND-TRIP; 4 HOURS

This is a dirt-road adventure day. Drive up the **Camas Road** and the rugged **North Fork Road.** Stop at the **Polebridge Mercantile** for fresh-baked cookies and sandwiches to go. Then enter the park and jounce along the bumpy **Inside Road** to **Bowman Lake** for a picnic. Walk along the shore to enjoy the views. On your return, sit outside at **Northern Lights Saloon** for a brew with a view. Return to Lake McDonald Lodge.

Day 7
Lake McDonald to Whitefish
51 MILES (82 KM); 1.25 HOURS

After yesterday's rugged road trip, today is easy. Take your time saying farewell to the park by stopping in **Apgar.**

Hit the road to **Whitefish.** Drive up to **Whitefish Mountain Resort** ride the chairlift to the **summit of Big Mountain** to soak up the panorama of Glacier peaks, plus overlook **Flathead Valley.** Descend via chairlift or hiking before heading to downtown Whitefish to celebrate your adventure.

Geologic Wonders

With some of North America's oldest exposed rock, a landscape created from moving earth, and the carving action of ice, Glacier National Park is filled with captivating scenery. Enjoy sinking into iconic Glacier landscapes by touring roads, but then don your hiking boots, for the best of Glacier's features are seen up close from trails.

Rock Features

The geologic landscape of Glacier National Park is like no other. Tremendous forces shaped the scenery.

First, an ancient, shallow, inland sea gave Glacier its **multicolored rocks.** At **Logan Pass,** hike to **Hidden Lake Overlook,** examining the rocks along the trail. Ripple marks and mud cracks show evidence of the **Belt Sea.** Look for layers of many colors on **Mount Clements,** created from various sediments deposited in the sea.

Second, a shifting of the earth's **tectonic plates** made the Pacific Plate's older rock slide over the Continental Plate's younger rock. Go to **Marias Pass** to see where geologists discovered the **Lewis Overthrust Fault.** Hike to **Firebrand Pass** to see the older mountains drop to the younger plains as you gain elevation.

Third, ancient **rivers of ice** followed by a smaller, shorter ice age shaped Glacier's mountains and valleys. Even though **Two Medicine** no longer has glaciers, find their footprints in the **U-shaped valley,** Pumpelly Pillar **arête,** and Flinsch Peak **horn.**

Glacial Features

Glacier National Park's glaciers from the Little Ice Age are melting. So where can you see them before extinction?

For drivers on Going-to-the-Sun Road, **Jackson Glacier Overlook** and the next two **pullouts** east offer the best views of glaciers. Use **binoculars** to scope out the glacial basin across the valley.

rippled rock from an ancient seabed

Jackson Glacier

Wildlife-Watching Hot Spots

Glacier has 60 mammal species and more than 260 species of birds; bring binoculars to aid in watching wildlife.

INSIDE ROAD
Spot elusive **gray wolves** on this uncrowded dirt road at dawn or dusk.

MCGEE MEADOWS
McGee Meadows bustles with **snipes, soras, red-tailed hawks,** and many species of **songbirds.**

AVALANCHE PATHS
In early spring, **grizzly bears** prowl for carcasses on avalanche slopes on Mount Cannon and the Glacier Wall on Going-to-the-Sun Road.

LOGAN PASS
Mountain goats and **bighorn sheep** circle the Logan Pass parking lot and frequent the Hidden Lake Overlook and Highline Trails.

TWO DOG FLATS
In spring and late fall, **elk** feed in early morning at Two Dog Flats near Rising Sun while aspens attract **woodpeckers, flickers,** and **owls.**

ST. MARY AND VIRGINIA FALLS
These two waterfalls create perfect habitat for dark, bobbing **American dippers.**

MOUNTS ALTYN AND HENKEL
Grizzly and **black bears** feed on huckleberries on these two peaks in Many Glacier in late summer.

SWIFTCURRENT VALLEY
A gentle hike runs through **moose** country to Red Rock and Bullhead Lakes. Listen for **white-crowned sparrows, loons, Clark's nutcrackers,** and **golden eagles.**

grizzly sow and cubs

GOAT LICK
On U.S. 2, the natural mineral lick attracts **mountain goats** in early summer.

WATERTON LAKES
Waterton's Maskinonge and Linnet Lakes wetlands abound with **ospreys, swans,** and **kingfishers.**

BISON PADDOCK
The Waterton **bison** paddock houses a small herd of shaggy bovines that once roamed wild.

Hikers can reach the closest glacier by climbing to **Grinnell Glacier.** The toe of the glacier is melting into a frigid **iceberg-filled lake.** On the jagged wall above the lake perch the tiny **Salamander Glacier** and **Gem Glacier,** both of which have shrunk to **static snowfields.**

Other trails take in views of nearby glaciers. The **Siyeh Pass Trail** offers views of **Piegan Glacier** and **Sexton Glacier.** A trail from **Sperry Chalet** climbs up through tranquil lake shelves and the rock-hewn stairway at **Comeau Pass** into the scoured basin that houses **Sperry Glacier.**

Water Features

Glacier is one of the most water-filled parks in the nation, due to depressions left from ancient glaciers. Experience a few of the park's most notable **762 lakes,** all footprints of glaciers.

Take **boat tours** on **Lake McDonald, Two Medicine,** or **St. Mary.** In Many Glacier, a double boat ride crosses **Swiftcurrent Lake** and **Lake Josephine.** In **Waterton Lakes National Park,** take a two-nation tour that crosses from Canada into the United States on **Upper Waterton Lake.**

Paddle park lakes. Rent **canoes** and **kayaks** on **Lake McDonald, Two Medicine Lake, Swiftcurrent Lake** in Many Glacier, and **Upper Waterton Lake.** Escape up the North Fork to remote **Bowman Lake** or **Kintla Lake** for day paddles or overnights in wilderness.

Hike to milky turquoise glacial lakes. In Many Glacier, go to **Grinnell Lake** or **Cracker Lake.**

Waterton Lake

West Glacier and Apgar

Sitting 2 miles (3.2 km) apart, West Glacier and Apgar span Glacier National Park's southwestern boundary, marked by the Middle Fork of the Flathead River.

While West Glacier sprouted up outside the park along Great Northern Railway tracks, early trapper and logger homesteads dug in a foothold at Apgar on Lake McDonald as the port to the park's wild interior before Going-to-the-Sun Road was built. Connected by the "new bridge," the park entrance road, and a 2-mile (3.2-km) paved bicycling and walking path, the pair are doorways for exploring Glacier. As such, they throng with cars and visitors in summer; 60 percent of visitors access the park via this west entrance. The communities also launch sightseers in two different directions: to the untrammeled

Highlights

Look for ★ to find recommended sights, activities, dining, and lodging.

★ **Relax at the Belton Chalet:** This chalet, as old as the park itself, is reminder of a bygone era of tourism. On chillier days, cuddle up at the stone fireplace; on warmer days, lounge at sunset on the deck with a local brew (page 44).

★ **Leap into Lake McDonald:** Take a refreshing swim in the park's largest lake, or catch the sunset over the water. The clear waters lure paddlers, boaters, anglers, scuba divers, photographers, and rock skippers (page 45).

★ **Climb to Apgar Lookout:** From this fire lookout, you can peer down at Lake McDonald, West Glacier, and the North Fork. You'll see a huge panorama of peaks from Canada to the park's southern tip (page 46).

★ **Take in the views from Huckleberry Lookout:** Walk along a top-of-the-world ridge where views stretch from Flathead Lake to Canada (page 47).

★ **Go Rafting on the Middle Fork of the Flathead River:** Ride on this Wild and Scenic River through rapids such as Screaming Right Turn, Bonecrusher, Jaws, and Could Be Trouble. The names say it all (page 51).

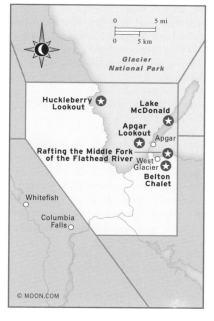

© MOON.COM

North Fork Valley and to Glacier's crowning highway, Going-to-the-Sun Road.

Today, many concessionaires are headquartered in West Glacier, just outside the national park boundaries. The small town has evolved into a seasonal mecca for rafting, guided hiking and backpacking, guided fishing trips, and horseback rides. Along with the train station, campgrounds, restaurants, motels, and shops, West Glacier is a place to gas up the car one last time before seeking the park's interior. On Lake McDonald's shores and inside the park, Apgar swarms in high season, too. Its restaurant, lodging, camping, shopping, boat ramp, and tiny west-side visitors center add to miles of lake sprawling with blue waters and enough shoreline to find a niche for solitude.

PLANNING YOUR TIME

This pair of bustling towns teem with visitors late May-September when motels, cabins, restaurants, and shops fling their doors open for business. By the end of September, Apgar and West Glacier look like ghost towns with only a select few establishments open year-round. Only 2 miles (3.2 km) apart, their atmosphere distinguishes them: Apgar sits on Lake McDonald inside the park, while West Glacier flanks the highway outside the park.

Make lodging reservations 13-16 months in advance for inside the park and 6-12 months in advance for outside the park. Verify the opening status of restaurants, lodgings, and services your before arrival. Use the park's **Recreational Access Display** (www.nps.gov/applications/glac/dashboard/) for real-time status of roads, parking lots, campgrounds, and weather.

Single-day visitors to the park generally bypass Apgar and West Glacier in favor of getting up to Logan Pass. But the two areas make excellent **base camps** for activities park-wide. For that reason, you can stay for

3-4 days, or a week or more. Plenty of **rental houses** and **cabins** surround West Glacier; these work well for stays of 4-7 days.

Summer temperatures usually average 70-85°F (21-29°C) during the day and 45-49°F (7-9°C) at night. Winter temperatures waffle between 0°F (-18°C) in Arctic cold fronts to 35°F (2°C).

HISTORY
Indigenous Peoples

For the **Ksanka people** (also known as the Salish and Kootenai Tribes, located on Flathead Lake), Lake McDonald held special significance. Ten thousand generations ago, legend says, the spirits first gave the Ksanka a ceremonial dance at their winter camp near Apgar. Called the Blacktail Deer Dance, the ceremony became an annual event, and the area became known as "the place where people dance." Today, the annual dance, now called the **Jump Dance,** takes place on the Flathead Reservation.

Homesteaders and Tourism

When the Great Northern Railway completed its westbound track in 1891, early tourists jumped off the train in Belton (now West Glacier). With no bridge across the Middle Fork of the Flathead, visitors rowed across the river and then saddled up for a horseback ride to Apgar. Finally, in 1895 a rough dirt road eased the journey, followed two years later by a bridge across the river.

Concurrently, Lake McDonald homesteaders leaped into the tourism business, offering cabins, meals, pack trips, boat rides, and guided tours. To coincide with Glacier's first summer as a national park, the Great Northern Railway opened Belton Chalet in 1910. After Glacier became a park, landowners along Lake McDonald retained their property as inholdings; they are still privately owned today.

Previous: Lake McDonald; floating down Middle Fork of the Flathead River; Huckleberry Lookout Trail.

West Glacier and Apgar

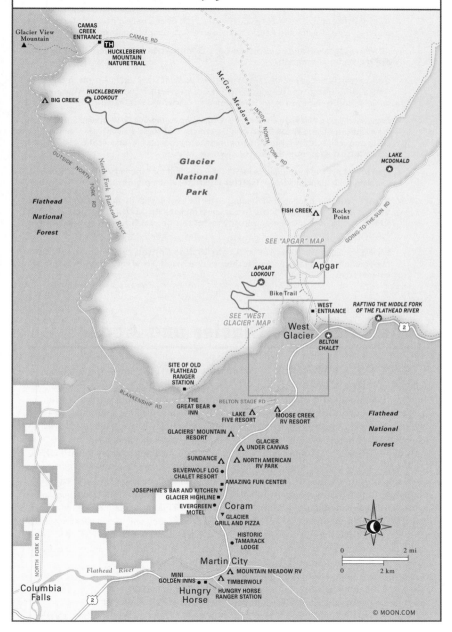

Glacier View Mountain

CAMAS CREEK ENTRANCE
CAMAS RD

TH HUCKLEBERRY MOUNTAIN NATURE TRAIL

McGee Meadows

HUCKLEBERRY LOOKOUT
BIG CREEK

INSIDE NORTH FORK RD

North Fork Flathead River

OUTSIDE NORTH FORK RD

Glacier National Park

LAKE MCDONALD

Flathead National Forest

FISH CREEK Rocky Point

GOING-TO-THE-SUN RD

SEE "APGAR" MAP

APGAR LOOKOUT

Apgar

Bike Trail

WEST ENTRANCE

RAFTING THE MIDDLE FORK OF THE FLATHEAD RIVER

2

SEE "WEST GLACIER" MAP

West Glacier

BELTON CHALET

SITE OF OLD FLATHEAD RANGER STATION

BLANKENSHIP RD

THE GREAT BEAR INN
BELTON STAGE RD

LAKE FIVE RESORT

MOOSE CREEK RV RESORT

Flathead National Forest

GLACIERS' MOUNTAIN RESORT

GLACIER UNDER CANVAS

SUNDANCE

NORTH AMERICAN RV PARK

SILVERWOLF LOG CHALET RESORT

AMAZING FUN CENTER

JOSEPHINE'S BAR AND KITCHEN
GLACIER HIGHLINE

EVERGREEN MOTEL

Coram

GLACIER GRILL AND PIZZA

HISTORIC TAMARACK LODGE

NORTH FORK RD

Martin City

Flathead River

MINI GOLDEN INNS

Hungry Horse

MOUNTAIN MEADOW RV

TIMBERWOLF

HUNGRY HORSE RANGER STATION

Columbia Falls

2

0   2 mi

0   2 km

© MOON.COM

Where Can I Find...?

- **Accessible campgrounds:** Inside the park, **Fish Creek** has eight accessible campsites plus showers and restrooms. **Apgar** has two accessible campsites and restrooms.

- **ATMs:** Find ATMs in Apgar at **Eddie's Cafe & Mercantile** and in West Glacier near the **West Glacier Mercantile.**

- **Cell reception:** Cell phones can get reception in **West Glacier.** In **Apgar,** reception is limited to the **village** and portions of **Apgar Campground.** Cell reception is not available on Going-to-the-Sun Road or U.S. 2 between West Glacier and East Glacier.

- **Gas:** Gas is **not available** inside the park, on Going-to-the-Sun Road, or on U.S. 2 between West and East Glacier. **West Glacier** is the last chance for gas, available year-round with a credit card at **Glacier Highland** across from the train depot or in summer at **West Glacier Gas Station** across from the West Glacier Mercantile.

- **Rental gear:** The headquarters for rental equipment for camping, hiking, backpacking, paddling, fishing, and bicycling is **Glacier Outfitters.** Some items may be reserved online.

- **Restrooms:** Flush toilets and running water for washing hands are available at **Apgar Visitor Center, Apgar Picnic Area,** across from the **Apgar boat launch,** and **Fish Creek Picnic Area.** Off-season, **vault toilets** are open at Fish Creek and Apgar Picnic Areas.

- **Wi-Fi:** You can connect to Wi-Fi at **Apgar Visitor Center.** Only a few hotels, private campgrounds, restaurants, and coffee shops between West Glacier and Hungry Horse provide internet access.

Exploring West Glacier and Apgar

VISITORS CENTERS
Apgar Visitor Center

Tucked in the woods at the four-way intersection just north of Glacier's west entrance station, the small **Apgar Visitor Center** (Going-to-the-Sun Rd., 406/888-7800, daily mid-May-early Oct., 8am-6pm daily mid-June-Aug., spring and fall hours shorten, weekends only in winter) is the place to find maps, Junior Ranger Program activity guides, trail and road conditions, fishing and boating information, and ranger program schedules for guided walks, astronomy programs, and evening amphitheater presentations. A few shelves also serve as the **Glacier National Park Conservancy bookstore** (406/892-3250, http://glacier.org). Outdoor interpretive signage highlights information for all major park regions. Paved biking and walking trails lead from the visitors center to Apgar Village, Lake McDonald, and Apgar Campground. The parking lot accommodates big RVs, and you can leave your car all day to hop shuttles or meet up for concession-operated tours.

The **Apgar Backcountry Permit Office** (406/888-7859 May-Oct., 406/888-7800 Nov.-Apr., 7am-4:30pm daily May-Sept., 8am-4pm daily Oct.) is opposite the old red schoolhouse in Apgar. This is the main office for acquiring permits for overnight backpacking or paddling trips. Rush hour is the first 2-3 hours of each morning in July and August; lines begin forming at 6am.

Alberta Visitor Information Center

Located in West Glacier, the **Alberta Visitor**

Information Center (125 Going-to-the-Sun Rd., 406/888-5743, www.travelalberta.com, 8am-7pm daily late May-early Sept., 8am-5pm daily early-late Sept.) is a building-size advertisement for Alberta, complete with dinosaur bones. For those heading on to Canada, the center is worth a stop to help with travel planning and pick up brochures and maps.

West Glacier Information Centers

Two visitors centers offer information on things to do surrounding Glacier. Located in Belton Train Depot, the **West Glacier Visitor Information Center** (junction of Going-to-the-Sun Rd. and U.S. 2, 406/892-3250, http://glacier.org, 9am-5pm daily summer) has the main Glacier Conservancy bookstore and information for Flathead Valley. The **Crown of the Continent Discovery Center** (12000 U.S. 2 E., 406/387-4405, www.crowndiscoverycenter.com, 10am-7pm daily early May-mid-Oct.) has regional planning information, hands-on displays, and brochures on geotourism activities that include national parks, national forests, World Heritage Sites, and wilderness areas in Montana and Canada.

ENTRANCE STATIONS

Crossing the West Glacier Bridge over the Middle Fork of the Flathead River officially is the entry to Glacier National Park. After the bridge, a parking pullout allows for photo-documenting your travel with the park sign. With 60 percent of Glacier's visitors entering here, be prepared for long lines on weekends and in summer.

West Glacier entrance station is usually staffed during daylight hours in summer and on weekends off-season. When unstaffed, use the self-pay cash-only kiosk to purchase a pass. If you don't have an annual pass, seven-day passes cost $35 per vehicle, $30 per motorcycle, and $20 for hikers and bikers. Winter rates drop to $25, $20, and $15, respectively. The entrance station hands out a map and the summer or winter edition of the park's newspaper.

From the rough, dirt Outside North Fork Road, the Camas Road connects with Apgar. The **Camas entrance** has a self-pay cash-only kiosk.

SHUTTLES AND TOURS
Shuttles

Glacier offers free **shuttle buses** (406/888-7800, www.nps.gov/glac, 9am-5pm daily

Get permits for backpacking at the Apgar Backcountry Permit Office.

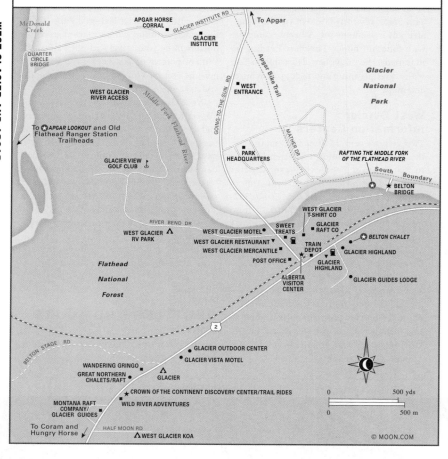

West Glacier

July-late Sept., every 15-30 min.) in summer around Apgar. The shuttles do not come with interpretive guides. The Apgar Visitor Center has the main shuttle stop, but stops (identified with signs) are also opposite the Apgar Campground Amphitheater and across from the Apgar Backcountry Permit Office in Apgar Village.

Shuttles go to most **trailheads** and all **lodges** on Going-to-the-Sun Road. From Apgar, shuttles run to **Avalanche,** where you can transfer to a shuttle to **Logan Pass;** a few

shuttles go directly to Logan Pass. It usually takes at least 90 minutes to ride the shuttle to Logan Pass. Transfer at Logan Pass to another shuttle to reach eastside destinations on the Sun Road.

During summer, lines form at shuttle stops, and you may have to wait for a bus or two. Some buses are equipped to carry **bikes,** and most are **wheelchair-accessible.** For Logan Pass, be sure to take a day pack with water, snacks, and extra clothing for fast-changing weather.

The shuttle system is slated for **expansion,** adding longer hours and more stops at Fish Creek Campground, the West Glacier entrance, and possibly other locations in West Glacier. Check online (www.nps.gov/glac) for the current status.

Bus Tours

Bus tours offer the easiest way to tour Going-to-the-Sun Road, and you'll learn about the park during the tour, thanks to interpretive guides onboard. Tours go to Logan Pass when it is open. For visitors in RVs, which are not permitted on the road, these are the way to go. Two companies have pickups in West Glacier or Apgar. Rates do not include park entrance fees, meals, taxes, or driver tips. Make reservations at least a day in advance, especially in midsummer.

Glacier Park's fleet of **red buses** (855/733-4522, www.glaciernationalparklodges.com, daily mid-June-mid-Sept., adults $44-100, kids half price) are the best way to tour in historic style, with roll-back tops allowing for unobstructed peak views and au naturel air-conditioning. Half-day, full-day, and evening tours have pickups at Apgar Visitor Center; some tours pick up at West Glacier KOA. Before Logan Pass opens, the red buses tour late May-mid-June around Huckleberry Mountain.

From the Apgar Visitor Center, the Blackfeet-owned **Sun Tours** (406/732-9220 or 800/786-9220, www.glaciersuntours.com, 9am-1pm daily June-Sept., adults $60, kids 6-12 $30) goes to Logan Pass and back. The air-conditioned 25-passenger coaches are comfortable, with extra-big windows enhancing the views. Blackfeet guides give insight into the park's rich Indigenous heritage from the days of the buffalo to modern spirituality.

Driving Tour
CAMAS ROAD

From Apgar, the 11.3-mile (18.2-km) **Camas Road** (open May-Oct.) links Lower McDonald Creek with the North Fork of the Flathead River. The road climbs along the base of the Apgar Range, traversing through the areas affected by the **2003 Robert Fire** and the **2001 Moose Fire,** which offer a contrast in post-burn forest succession.

Several signed **pullouts** are worth a stop if you can stand the mosquitoes. The **McDonald Valley Overlook** (first pullover after Fish Creek Rd.) gives a view of Lake McDonald and surrounding mountains through burned tree trunks.

Grab binoculars to peruse **McGee Meadows** (at 5.5 mi/8.9 km) for moose and birds. At 11.1 miles (17.9 km), a turnoff leads to **Huckleberry Mountain Nature Trail,** a 0.9-mile (1.4-km) self-guided loop in a thick lodgepole forest regrowth.

After the North Fork River, the Camas Road terminates at the **North Fork Road.** Bears frequent the Camas Road in spring; rangers haze them away from the roadway to prevent them from becoming conditioned to people and cars.

Sights

WEST GLACIER

The town of **West Glacier,** originally called Belton, was historically centered around the Belton Train Depot and Belton Chalet. Today, U.S. 2 divides the two, and West Glacier now has recreational concessions such as rafting, backpacking, hiking, and fishing.

From the highway, drive through the railroad tunnel to enter a village of vintage, brown 1938 buildings that house a bar, restaurant, ice cream store, gift shops, grocery store, and a motel. Fall finds yellow birch leaves covering the pavement as shops board their windows, leaving only the 230 year-round residents.

★ BELTON CHALET

In 1910, Glacier became a national park, and the **Belton Chalet** opened its doors to guests arriving via the Great Northern Railway. The first in a series of Swiss-themed railroad-company chalets built in the park, the Belton featured milkmaid-attired hostesses and flower-trellised walkways to greet guests. Over the years, the chalet changed hands, serving as housing for Civilian Conservation

Corps crews building Going-to-the-Sun Road as well as a pizza parlor and a bakery. After heavy snows destroyed roofs and floors in the late 1990s, owners restored the lodge and cabins. The chalet is on the National Register of Historic Places.

BELTON BRIDGE

Belton Bridge opened in 1920, allowing park visitors to drive across the Middle Fork of the Flathead River instead of rowing a boat. Ironically, this wood and cement bridge remained standing during the 1964 flood while torrents of water destroyed the newer bridge downstream. For a time, this bridge was used again while the new bridge was being repaired. The "old bridge," as locals call it, is now open for foot traffic only. It accesses the Boundary Trail, Middle Fork fishing spots, and calm but deep, chilly pools for swimming. To reach the bridge from West Glacier, ride a bike, walk, or drive east onto Old River Bridge Road; the road ends at a small turnaround with minimal parking (no RVs).

Belton Chalet

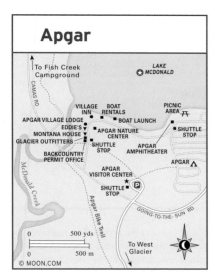

Apgar

To Fish Creek
Campground

CAMAS RD

LAKE
MCDONALD

VILLAGE
INN

BOAT
RENTALS

PICNIC
AREA

APGAR VILLAGE LODGE

BOAT LAUNCH

EDDIE'S
MONTANA HOUSE

GLACIER OUTFITTERS

APGAR NATURE
CENTER

SHUTTLE
STOP

SHUTTLE
STOP

APGAR
AMPHITHEATER

BACKCOUNTRY
PERMIT OFFICE

APGAR
VISITOR CENTER

APGAR

SHUTTLE
STOP

P

McDonald Creek

Apgar Bike Trail

GOING-TO-THE-SUN RD

0   500 yds

0   500 m

To West
Glacier

© MOON.COM

MIDDLE FORK OF THE FLATHEAD RIVER

The **Middle Fork of the Flathead River** collects water from deep within the Bob Marshall Wilderness Complex and Glacier National Park. Its north-shore high-water mark denotes the national park boundary. Designated a Wild and Scenic River, the Middle Fork (the shortened moniker favored by locals) vacillates between raging rapids and mesmerizing meanders. Anglers and swimmers gravitate to its blue-green pools. Rafters and kayakers splash through rapids known as Bonecrusher and Jaws. Hikers tootle along its Boundary Trail.

APGAR

Two miles (3.2 km) from West Glacier, **Apgar** is on the shore of the park's largest body of water, Lake McDonald. With Apgar Campground within walking distance and Fish Creek Campground a couple of miles away, Apgar crowds in summer but is still less harried than the West Glacier highway hubbub. It's a quintessential national park community. A restaurant, camp store, two inns, a boat ramp, swimming beaches, visitors center, campground, and picnic area cluster here at Lake McDonald's foot. Apgar's historic red schoolhouse now houses a gift shop. Most of Apgar opens May-September only.

Apgar Nature Center

For some free, fun, hands-on activities for kids, drop in the **Apgar Nature Center** (no phone, 10am-4pm daily mid-June-Aug.). Find the cabin in the woods across the street from Eddie's Cafe & Mercantile. With the help of interpretive rangers, learning stations offer lessons about wildlife, geology, and natural history. Rangers also lead talks and walks geared for Junior Ranger kids.

★ LAKE MCDONALD

Catching water from Glacier's longest river, **Lake McDonald** is 10 miles (16.1 km) long, 1.5 miles (2.4 km) wide, and 472 feet (144 m) deep. It is the park's largest and deepest lake. Squeezed between Howe and Snyder Ridges, both lateral moraines, the 6,823-acre (2,761-hectare) lake sits where an ancient glacier gouged out a trough. Larch forests that turn gold in fall rim the shores. On the lake, visitors fish, boat, paddle, and swim in its cold blue waters. Access the lakeshore via Fish Creek or Apgar Picnic Areas, the Apgar boat ramp, or the many pullouts along Going-to-the-Sun Road.

West Glacier and Apgar Hikes

Trail	Effort	Distance	Duration
Rocky Point	easy	1.4-1.6 mi (2.3-2.6 km) rt	1 hr
Apgar Lookout	moderate	7 mi (11.3 km) rt	4 hr
Huckleberry Lookout	strenuous	12 mi (19.3 km) rt	6 hr
Lake McDonald	easy	7 mi (11.3 km) one-way	3.5 hr
South Boundary Trail	easy	11.6 mi (18.7 km) rt	5 hr

Recreation

If Glacier has a recreation center, it's West Glacier and Apgar. The communities offer hiking, biking, rafting, horseback riding, paddling, boating, fishing, swimming, and golfing. West Glacier is the headquarters for white-water rafting, with two Wild and Scenic Rivers (nationally designated rivers protected for their wilderness and beauty) marking park boundaries.

DAY HIKES

Apgar has the only park trail that permits dogs. The 2-mile (3.2-km) paved Apgar Bike Trail connecting West Glacier and Apgar is open to walkers, leashed dogs, and bicyclists.

Most of the Apgar trails are accessible year-round, except for Huckleberry Lookout. In winter, you will need snowshoes or skis, and for a few trails, expect to add on 1-2 miles (1.6-3.2 km) across snow-buried roads to reach trailheads.

Rocky Point

Distance: 1.4-1.6 miles (2.3-2.6 km) round-trip
Duration: 1 hour
Elevation gain: none
Effort: easy
Trail surface: dirt with roots and rocks
Trailhead: Fish Creek Campground Loop D or the start of the Inside North Fork Road (see map p. 47)
Rocky Point is a short interpretive romp along Lake McDonald's north shore through the 2003 Robert Fire and up a rock promontory.

Places of heavy burn with slow regrowth alternate with lighter burn now clogged with lush greenery. Don't forget your camera: The view from Rocky Point looks up the lake toward the Continental Divide and grabs grand shots of Mount Jackson and Mount Edwards to the south. If the lake is calm, photos can capture stunning reflections. Snow leaves early and comes late to this trail, making it good for spring and fall hiking. From the promontory, make a loop back on the Lake McDonald Trail.

★ Apgar Lookout

Distance: 7 miles (11.3 km) round-trip
Duration: 4 hours
Elevation gain: 1,868 feet (569 m)
Effort: moderate
Trail surface: narrow, dirt with roots and rocks
Trailhead: end of Glacier Institute Road, 1.9 miles (3.1 km) from Going-to-the-Sun Road
Directions: Take the first left after the west entrance station at the Glacier Institute sign. At the first fork, follow the sign to the horse barn and veer left, crossing over Quarter Circle Bridge. Drive to the road's terminus at the trailhead (see map p. 49).

Beginning with a gentle walk, the trail soon climbs steeply uphill toward the first of three long switchbacks (hike in the morning on hot days). As the trail ascends, some large burned sentinels stand as relics from the 2003 Robert Fire amid the thick growth of new lodgepoles pressing in on the trail that used to be a road.

West Glacier and Apgar Hikes

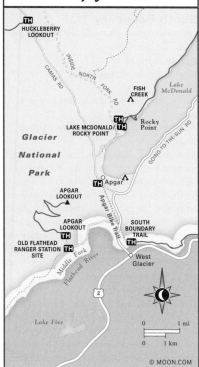

HUCKLEBERRY LOOKOUT TH

INSIDE NORTH FORK RD

CAMAS RD

FISH CREEK ⛺

Lake McDonald

Glacier

National

Park

LAKE McDONALD/ TH
ROCKY POINT TH

Rocky Point

GOING-TO-THE-SUN RD

Apgar ⛺

APGAR LOOKOUT ▲

APGAR LOOKOUT TH

Apgar Bike Trail

OLD FLATHEAD RANGER STATION SITE TH

SOUTH BOUNDARY TRAIL TH

West Glacier ○

Middle Fork
Flathead River

2

Lake Five

0   1 mi
0   1 km

© MOON.COM

Snippets of views look down on the Middle Fork, Rubideau Basin, the railroad tracks, and West Glacier. Following the third switchback, the trail traverses the ridge, which has snow in June, to the rebuilt lookout. From this 5,236-foot (1,596-m) aerie, tall trees allow only partial views of the park's southern sector, Lake McDonald, and peaks of the Livingston Range. Park communication radio antennas clutter the summit, but at least they are clustered in one location.

★ Huckleberry Lookout

Distance: 12 miles (19.3 km) round-trip
Duration: 6 hours
Elevation gain: 2,725 feet (831 m)

Effort: strenuous
Trail surface: narrow, dirt with roots and rocks
Trailhead: 6 miles (9.7 km) up Camas Road from Apgar, just past McGee Meadows (see map p. 48)

Huckleberry Lookout Trail is aptly named, for huckleberries do abound in this area. Due to a heavy concentration of huckleberries attracting a significant bruin population in fall, check with the park service for closure information. Snow often packs the upper trail until early July.

The trail begins with a gentle walk through lodgepole forest. Soon the path climbs, steadily gaining elevation among larches until it emerges on steep-sloped meadows and reaches a saddle at 4.5 miles (7.2 km). In a reprieve from the climb, the trail traverses two bowls until it crests the Apgar Range for the final scenery-laden ascent to the lookout at 6,593 feet (2,010 m). A spectacular view of the North Fork Valley and the park's Livingston Range unfolds. Glacier's six highest peaks are visible, as is Flathead Lake, Swan Peak, and Great Northern. During summer, the lookout is staffed. Evidence of the 2001 Moose Fire clings to Huckleberry Mountain as well as Demers Ridge below and the North Fork Valley.

Lake McDonald

Distance: 7 miles (11.3 km) one-way
Duration: 3.5 hours
Elevation gain: none
Effort: easy
Trail surface: narrow, dirt with roots and rocks
Trailhead: Fish Creek Campground Loop D or Inside North Fork Road southern entrance (see map p. 50)

While this year-round trail (use skis or snowshoes in winter) wanders mostly back in the trees paralleling the north shore of Lake McDonald, you can garner views of the peak-flanked lake when it pops out to the shoreline. The brushy trail also shows postfire forest succession. Burned by the 2003 Robert Fire and 2018 Howe Ridge Fire, the trail passes through lush new growth and stands of black or gray trunks. Most hikers opt to saunter out for a few miles to the backcountry campsite,

Huckleberry Lookout

perhaps drop a fishing line into the lake, and turn around again. Set up a car shuttle to hike the full length.

South Boundary Trail

Distance: 11.6 miles (18.7 km) round-trip to Lincoln Creek
Duration: 5 hours
Elevation gain: 400 feet (122 m)
Effort: easy
Trail surface: dirt with roots and rocks, narrow in places
Trailhead: behind park headquarters on Mather Drive's south end

After parking at headquarters, walk through the housing area to the trailhead. (Starting at Belton Bridge cuts off 1 mi/1.6 km, but offers minimal parking.) Follow the original entry point into the park, Old River Bridge Road, to the historic Belton Bridge, where the trail continues upstream. With gentle ascents and descents, the path hugs the north-shore hillside above the Wild and Scenic Middle Fork of the Flathead River.

This year-round trail won't feel like wilderness: Noise from the railroad and highway competes with the river's roaring white water. But it's a great place to watch rafters shoot rapids, swim in deep pools, or fish. The trail descends to a fine rocky beach at Lincoln Creek, a stopping point for rafters before they hit the white water. Backpackers can continue another 15 miles (24 km) upriver to Coal Creek or turn 10.5 miles (16.9 km) up Lincoln Creek to Lincoln Lake.

Guided Hikes

National Park Service naturalists guide hikes and walks around Apgar mid-June-mid-September. Days and times vary, and the hikes range from easy to strenuous. In winter, naturalists lead snowshoe trips to look for animal tracks. Consult the park newspaper or go online (www.nps.gov/glac) for schedules. These guided hikes are the best price of all: free.

Glacier Guides (11970 U.S. 2 E., West Glacier, 406/387-5555, http://glacierguides. com, mid-May-Sept.) leads day hikes,

Apgar Lookout

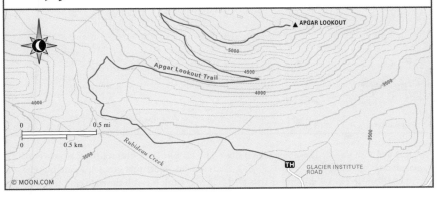

© MOON.COM

backpacking, and overnight chalet trips, but most destinations are outside the West Glacier-Apgar area. For day hiking, reservations are required, and rates include the guide service, a deli lunch, and transportation to the trailhead. Solo travelers can hook up with the daily group day hikes (July-early Sept., $105 pp), scheduled to a different destination each day. Custom day hikes cost $560 for 1-5 people. Backpacking trips depart every week for 3-6-day adventures; rates run around $220 per day and include the guide service, transportation to and from the trailhead, meals, and snacks. The company also guides overnight trips to backcountry chalets. Plan to tip your guide at least 15 percent for day hikes and 20 percent for overnights.

Rentals

From a yurt next door to the Backcountry Permit Office in Apgar, **Glacier Outfitters** (196 Apgar Loop Rd., 406/219-7466, www.goglacieroutfitters.com, 9am-5pm daily mid-May-late Sept) rents the biggest inventory of gear for hikers and backpackers. Find pepper spray, ice axes, crampons, backpacks and backpack baby carriers, trekking poles, tents, sleeping bags and pads, mess kits, water filters, and stoves for $6-30 per item per day. Pack rafts run $45 per day. Two backpacking

bundles ($52-90 pp) combine items into packages for a lower overall cost. Hikers and backpackers can also rent a limited selection of gear from **Glacier Outdoor Center** (12400 U.S. 2 E., West Glacier, 406/888-5454 or 800/235-6781, http://glacierraftco.com) and **Glacier Guides** (11970 U.S. 2 E., West Glacier, 406/387-5555, http://glacierguides.com).

BIKING

Bicycling Glacier National Park is not for everyone. Narrow, shoulderless roads are packed with curves, and most trails prohibit bikes. However, the West Glacier-Apgar area does provide off-road options that work better for families and casual riders.

Bicycle Trails

Especially good for families, a level, paved bicycle trail connects West Glacier with Apgar. Approximately 2 miles (3.2 km) long, the **Apgar Bike Trail** begins on the north side of the West Glacier Bridge. After dropping through the woods, it crosses through the National Park Service employee housing area before entering the forest again, where it continues on to Apgar, connecting the village, visitors center, and campground. Be cautious at two road crossings en route. The dirt **Fish Creek Bike Trail** provides a shortcut between

Lake McDonald

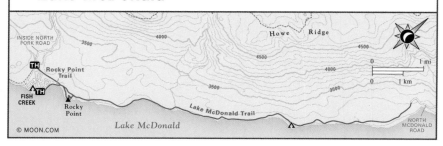

Apgar and Fish Creek. These two bike trails permit dogs on leashes.

The 10-mile (16.1-km) round-trip **Old Flathead Ranger Station** ride tours a combination of dirt road and trail that was once a road. It terminates at the confluence of the Flathead River's North and Middle Forks. Access the route from midway between West Glacier and Apgar on the Apgar Bike Trail, turning west onto the dirt Glacier Institute Road. At the first junction, follow the sign to the horse barn; at the second, hang a left toward Quarter Circle Bridge. About 0.5 mile (0.8 km) past the bridge, the Old Flathead Ranger Station Trail begins. Turn left, biking 3.4 miles (5.5 km) to the confluence and the site of the old ranger station.

The most challenging ride is the gravel, potholed **Inside North Fork Road** north of Fish Creek. The 6.5-mile (10.5-km) portion from Camas Creek to Anaconda Creek climbs and drops through regrowing fire zones until reaching the steep drop down Anaconda Hill. From Camas Creek, a total of 11 miles (17.7 km) of road is closed to vehicles due to flood damage. Flooding has eroded the roadbed at Anaconda Creek; only bikers capable of carrying their bikes while fording multiple creek cuts should cross the area to continue on. Early summer rides may need to contend with downed trees. Check with the park for current conditions (406/888-7800).

Cycling Road Tours

Inside the park, bicyclists have two options.

The 12-mile (19.3-km) rolling **Camas Road** is a scenic route that often opens to bicycles in May while it is still closed to cars; it usually stays snow-free until early November. From Apgar, it starts with a challenging climb before leveling out near McGee Meadows and then descending to the North Fork of Flathead River. Bicyclists on **Going-to-the-Sun Road** need to be ready to ride the curves along Lake McDonald (closed to bikes 11am-4pm July-Aug.) with cars at their elbows and no shoulders. It is *not* a family-friendly adventure.

Outside the park, the 10-mile (16.1-km) paved **Gateway to Glacier Trail,** built in 2016, parallels U.S. 2 from Hungry Horse to West Glacier.

Rentals, Guides, and Shuttles

In Apgar, **Glacier Outfitters** (196 Apgar Loop Rd., 406/219-7466, www.goglacieroutfitters.com, 9am-5pm daily mid-May-late Sept., $10-62) rents roadies, cruisers, hybrids, tandems, mountain bikes, kids bikes, and car carriers for two hours, four hours, or all day. Helmets are included. For tots, you can add on a tagalong or tow trailer. Also, **Eddie's** (236 Apgar Loop Rd., 406/888-5361, www.eddiescafegifts.com, 9am-5pm daily mid-May-late Sept., $10-45) rents bikes.

In spring, for cycling Going-to-the-Sun Road when it is closed to vehicles, **Glacier Guides** (11970 U.S. 2 E., West Glacier, 406/387-5555, http://glacierguides.com, May-road opening to vehicles, $110 pp, 2-person min.) leads bicycle tours. A **shuttle with a bike trailer** (mid-May-road opening to vehicles, 9am-5pm weekends only, free) runs from Apgar Visitor Center to Lake McDonald Lodge or Avalanche to add more parking options for cycling the closed portion of the Sun Road.

HORSEBACK RIDING

Swan Mountain Outfitters (406/387-4405 or 877/888-5557, www.swanmountainglacier. com, daily late May-early Sept.) operates two corral locations: one in Apgar and one in West Glacier. Reservations are strongly advised. For trail riding, be sure to wear long pants; you'll be a lot less sore afterward. For safety, wear sturdy shoes or hiking boots, not sandals. The outfitters do not take children under age seven or riders weighing over 250 pounds (113 kg).

Located on Glacier Institute Road northeast of the park entrance station, the **Apgar Corral** (summer 406/888-5010, $50-120) leads daily trail rides to three destinations in Glacier. An easy one-hour saunter to McDonald Meadows and a popular two-hour ride along the C. M. Russell Trail depart several times each day. The half-day ride to Apgar Lookout, which requires a minimum of four people, departs at 7:45am.

At the Crown of the Continent Discovery Center, the **West Glacier Corral** (12000 U.S. 2 E., 406/387-5005, $45-300) offers horseback tours through the lodgepole foothills of Flathead National Forest. One- and two-hour tours amble through the forest while the half-day and full-day rides climb to viewpoints. It also offers combination saddle-paddles, ride-and-dine, and cowboy cookout trips plus overnight trips for more time in the saddle.

WATER SPORTS
Rafting

Rafting may be the biggest activity in West Glacier. Near town, two Wild and Scenic-designated rivers converge after running along the boundaries of Glacier. With 219 combined miles (355 km) of recreation, the rivers offer scenery, wilderness, flat-water float sections, and white water. Rafting season runs **May-September,** with high water usually peaking in late May. By late August, both rivers run at their lowest levels with plenty of exposed, dry gravel bars.

★ MIDDLE FORK OF THE FLATHEAD RIVER

Bordering Glacier's southern boundary, the **Middle Fork of the Flathead** has scenic float sections interrupted by raging white water. The river's headwaters are deep within Glacier's immense southern valleys and the Bob Marshall Wilderness Complex, but a long segment parallels U.S. 2 with easy access points.

While the white water cannot compete with the Grand Canyon's monster rapids, the Middle Fork is a splashy place where rapids named **Screaming Right Turn, Jaws,** and **Pinball** provide the fun. Several **river accesses** offer places to launch and take out: Moccasin Creek, West Glacier, and Blankenship are the most crowded. Different sections are appropriate for overnights, day trips, fishing, and whitewater. While a few rapids at certain water levels are rated **Class IV,** the river along Glacier's boundary is primarily **Class II-III.** It's a good introductory paddle for a first-time river trip and kids. **Mountain Photography** (www. mountainphotography.net) shoots photos of commercial and private rafts in Bonecrusher Rapid.

NORTH FORK OF THE FLATHEAD RIVER

From Canada, the **North Fork of the Flathead** flows 59 miles (95 km) through the remote North Fork Valley. As the river enters the United States, it forms the western boundary of Glacier. Accessed via the bumpy, dirt Outside North Fork Road, the **Class II-III** river provides multiday float trips, day rafting, and fishing, although it does require river savvy with braided channels and logjams. Those looking for tamer water can take out at **Big Creek** before the Upper Fool Hen rapids.

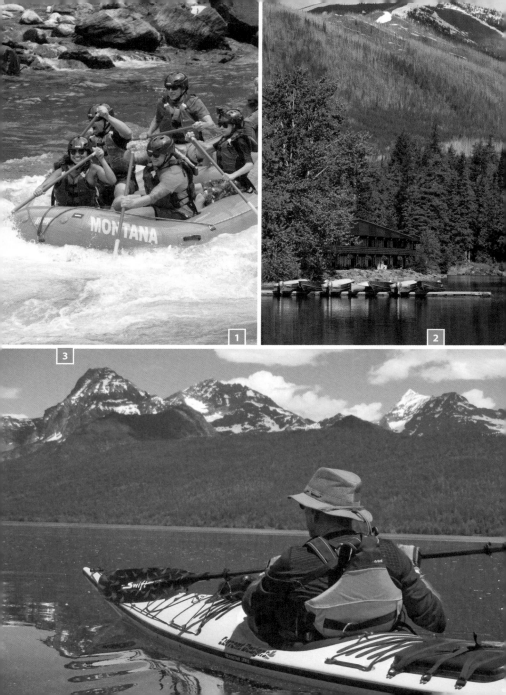

River accesses flank the North Fork Road. The river ends at the confluence with the Middle Fork at the Blankenship River Access, a 10-minute drive west of West Glacier.

GUIDES

The commercial rafting season runs **May-September,** with the biggest water in early summer. Four West Glacier rafting companies lead **half-day** and **full-day** trips on the Middle Fork as well as scenic, dinner, barbecue, and evening floats. They also do **saddle-paddle combinations** that put you on a horse and a boat the same day. Each company launches 4-6 half-day raft trips daily through the white-water section and guides overnight and multiday trips. Children should be at least six years old for white water, but younger ones can enjoy scenic float trips.

To compare companies (they're all very similar in cost), ask three questions: Is the 7 percent service fee included in the rate or added on, what size are the rafts and how many people do they carry (smaller rafts and fewer paddlers have a more exciting ride), and are wetsuits and booties included.

Per adult, expect to pay about $55-65 for half-day trips or $100-110 for full day; kids run about $10-25 cheaper. For more fun, tackle the white water in a small sport raft with more kick or on an inflatable kayak, otherwise known as a rubber ducky (add on $10-30 pp). Paddles, life jackets, and helmets are included in all rates, but some companies charge additional fees for wetsuits and booties. Plan on tipping the guide about 15 percent. **Mountain Photography** (406/862-6905, https://mountainphotography.net) captures the thrill of riding through Bonecrusher and has the photos available for you at your raft company following your trip.

Overnight rafting trips range 2-5 days; longer trips are usually paired with hiking, horseback riding, or backpacking. Expect to pay around $210-270 per adult per day for overnight rafting trips; rates for children run less. Specialty trips with cabin stays, horseback riding, or flights will cost more. Plan to tip guides 20 percent. When making reservations, clarify what you'll need to bring for your overnight. The companies can provide tents, sleeping bags, sleeping pads, and dry bags for your gear.

Glacier Raft Company (106 Going-to-the-Sun Rd., West Glacier, 406/888-5454 or 800/235-6781, http://glacierraftco.com) is right in West Glacier village adjacent to the river. White-water rafters debark at Middle Fork Bridge to walk two blocks back to the office. In addition to standard rafting options, Glacier Raft has combo packages pairing up half-day white-water rafting with half-day horseback riding or fly-fishing. Overnights go out for 2-4 days. This is the only local company permitted to guide trips on the Class III-IV upper Middle Fork of the Flathead River in the Great Bear Wilderness. Access requires a flight to a remote put-in near the headwaters for the four-day trip ($1,800).

Great Northern Whitewater (12127 U.S. 2 E., 406/387-5340 or 800/735-7897, http://greatnorthernresort.com) has the standard trips, plus it is the one company that offers river instruction through Glacier River School courses. Find them 1mile (1.6 km) west of downtown West Glacier.

Montana Raft Company (11970 U.S. 2 E., 406/387-5555, http://glacierguides.com) is the only company that can combine guided hiking in Glacier National Park with raft trips. In addition to standard raft trips, an extensive menu of hike-raft or backpack-raft combos can fill a day or a week. Overnight river trips float the Middle Fork or the North Fork of the Flathead River. Find MRC/Glacier Guides off the north side of the highway 1.5 miles (2.4 km) west of West Glacier.

Wild River Adventures (11900 U.S. 2 E., 406/387-9453 or 800/700-7056, http://www.riverwild.com), the smallest company, runs all the standard trips plus adds several paddle-saddle combos. One is a four-day campout

---

1: whitewater rafting on Middle Fork of the Flathead River **2:** rental boats in Apgar on Lake McDonald **3:** kayaker on Lake McDonald

adventure. Find Wild River on the south side of the highway 1.5 miles (2.4 km) west of West Glacier.

DIY FLOAT TRIPS

Got the river savvy and the gear to guide yourself? For locations of rapids and public lands for camping on overnight trips, purchase the waterproof *Three Forks of the Flathead Float Guide* ($13) from **Hungry Horse Ranger Station** (10 Hungry Horse Dr., Hungry Horse, 406/387-3800, www.fs.usda.gov/flathead). It can also be downloaded online (free, but not in waterproof flip-book format).

Flathead National Forest manages both rivers; the Forest Service is considering a permit system starting in 2021. Stop in the Hungry Horse Ranger Station, located 9 miles (14.5 km) west of West Glacier, for assistance in planning a self-guided overnight trip. Depending on where you camp, toilet systems and fire pans are required or recommended. However, all camping must be done on the national forest shore; no camping is allowed on Glacier's side, with the exception of Round Meadows (permit required) on the North Fork. Since private property abuts some river miles, you'll need to be knowledgeable about where you can camp.

RENTALS AND SHUTTLES

Glacier Raft Company (106 Going-to-the-Sun Rd., West Glacier, 406/888-5454 or 800/235-6781, http://glacierraftco.com) and **Montana Raft Company** (Glacier Guides, 11970 U.S. 2 E., West Glacier, 406/387-5555, http://glacierguides.com) cater to self-guided floaters from West Glacier down 11 miles (17.7 km) of Class I-II river to Blankenship. The package ($70-240) includes rafts or inflatable kayaks, paddles, helmets, life jackets, and shuttle setup. With a bit of instruction from an experienced guide, you can then float at your own pace.

The companies also offer equipment rentals and shuttle services. Per day rates for rafts, inflatable kayaks, paddleboards, oars, paddles, and frames run $50-150; dry bags,

toilet systems, camping equipment, wetsuits, throw bags, pumps, and repair kits cost $3-12 per item. Make advance reservations for gear. Montana Raft Company also runs shuttles to river access points on the North Fork or Middle Fork. Rates vary, depending on distances and whether you use your vehicle or theirs.

White-Water Kayaking

White-water kayakers drop into the **Middle Fork of the Flathead River,** which churns up Class II-III rapids. Kayakers play in the froth between Moccasin Creek and West Glacier, surfing Tunnel Rapids. Bring your own kayak; no rentals are available. Consult **Hungry Horse Ranger Station** (10 Hungry Horse Dr., Hungry Horse, 406/387-3800, www.fs.fed.us/r1/flathead) for current river conditions and requirements. **Glacier Kayak School** (12127 U.S. 2 E., West Glacier, 406/387-5340 or 800/735-7897, https://greatnorthernresort.com) teaches white-water kayaking to introduce beginners to paddling fundamentals and rolling.

Boating

With its vast water acreage, Lake McDonald attracts boaters, but it's never crowded, except around Apgar where boat rentals and the lake's only boat ramp are located. Due to threats from aquatic invasive species, the National Park Service has instituted rigorous requirements for boating in order to preserve the pristine condition of the water. The lake **opens for boating mid-May through October,** and all boaters must have **permits** issued by the inspection station (7am-9pm daily, shorter hours in May and late Sept.-Oct.) located across from the boat ramp in Apgar.

For most short-term visitors, the procedure alone for getting a permit prohibits trailering a powerboat from home, as all gas-powered boats and their trailers must be inspected,

1: swimming in Lake McDonald **2:** scenic float down Middle Fork of the Flathead River

Fishing in Glacier

With copious lakes, rivers, and streams, plus 22 species of fish, no angler should sit with a slack line in Glacier. Visitors typically can enjoy calm vistas and a few native trout.

FISHING TIPS

· Avoid a long hike to a remote lake to fish. In Glacier, remoteness does not necessarily mean good fishing. Some lakes have no fish due to waterfalls preventing fish migration.

· Since arrival at a high mountain lake will most likely be midday, when fishing is lackluster, stay overnight in the backcountry or at a nearby lodge. Then fish in the morning or evening, for best results.

· During early summer runoff, when river waters cloud with sediments, fish hang out on the bottom to feed; try lures that mimic insect larvae. Alternatively, fish in lakes instead.

· When streams run clear, fly-fishing is the most productive. Try to match a prominent hatch, or ask at fishing shops for advice on what draws current action.

· At lakes, look for inlets and outlets to fish, but be considerate of heavily trafficked areas.

· Trolling from a motorboat (where allowed) or canoe is the most effective way to fish for lake trout.

FISHING IN BEAR COUNTRY

· Bears pose special considerations. Since smells attract bears that travel waterways, lessen your bear encounter chances by keeping fishy scents away from clothing. Catch-and-release fishing minimizes attracting bears.

· For cleaning fish in the front country, dispose of the entrails in bear-resistant garbage cans. In the backcountry, go at least 200 feet (61 m) away from a campsite or trail, puncture the air

sealed, and quarantined for 30 days to completely dry out before a permit is issued. Electric-powered and nonmotorized boats can get a **same-day permit** and launch immediately upon inspection without quarantining, but only if they can be **hand-carried** to launch rather than trailered. Jet Skis, watercooled electric motors, and boats with water holding tanks and wash systems are not permitted. Due to unpredictable swirling winds on Lake McDonald, most sailboats go to other lakes outside the park.

RENTALS

For boating and fishing on Lake McDonald, **Glacier Park Boat Company** (406/257-2426, www.glacierparkboats.com, daily late May-Labor Day) rents rowboats and small motorboats for $18-25 per hour from the

Apgar boat dock next to Apgar Village Inn. Paddles, life jackets, and fishing regulations are included in the rates.

Paddling

With its monstrous shoreline, **Lake McDonald** is a treat for canoeing, kayaking, and paddleboarding, but watch for winds whipping up large whitecaps. When glassy calm waters prevail, you'd be hard-pressed to beat it at sunrise or sunset. The lake **opens to paddling mid-May through October.** Free **permits** are required for kayaks, canoes, paddleboards, rowboats, and inflatable kayaks or rafts. They are available following an inspection at the station (7am-9pm daily, shorter hours May and late Sept.-Oct.) across from the Apgar boat ramp. For launching, boats must be hand-carried.

bladder, and throw the entrails into deep water. Keep only what you can eat, and eat it as soon as you can.

NATIVE SPECIES

Until 1972 when fish stocking halted, an estimated 45-55 million fish and eggs were planted in Glacier's waters, introducing non-native arctic grayling, rainbow trout, kokanee salmon, brook trout, and Yellowstone cutthroat trout. Lake trout and lake whitefish also invaded the park waters through stocking in Flathead Lake.

The **bull trout** is listed as a **threatened species** under the Endangered Species Act. In Montana, this predatory fish, which can grow to 2 feet (0.6 m) long, now inhabits less than half of its original streams due to a number of factors, including habitat degradation. No fishing for bull trout is allowed; immediately **release** any that are caught incidentally. Look on the dorsal fin: no black, put it back.

fly-fishing

Glacier is also one of the few remaining strongholds for **westslope cutthroat trout,** which now inhabit only 2.5 percent of their original range. **Threatened** by interbreeding with rainbow trout, genetically pure populations of cutthroat remain in 15-19 park lakes. Conscientious anglers **release** them after catching them.

Learn to identify native and nonnative species. Follow park guidelines for harvesting or releasing fish. Best practices are to **release native fish** and keep only your limit of nonnative species.

For the best fishing recommendations, grab a copy of Russ Schneider's *Fishing Glacier National Park.*

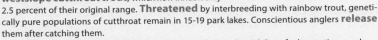

For paddling moving water, the scenic **Lower McDonald Creek** starts north of the Apgar boat launch on Lake McDonald and floats past beaver dams to Quarter Circle Bridge, a one-hour paddle. The **Middle Fork of the Flathead River** is gentle enough for canoeing and kayaking from West Glacier downriver to Blankenship, but the section includes one challenging rapid that can be portaged.

For paddlers, Lake McDonald has one prime tiny backcountry **campground** on the north shore, about 5 miles (8 km) from the Apgar boat ramp. It perches on a point with huge views up and down the lake, plus outstanding night sky watching. Pick up required overnight permits in person 24 hours in advance at the **Apgar Backcountry Permit Office** (406/888-7859 May-Oct., 406/888-7800 Nov.-Apr., adults $7 pp/night). You can also apply online for advance reservations (www.nps.gov/glac, $40) starting in mid-March. The campground was burned in the 2018 Howe Ridge Fire, so check on its status ahead of time.

RENTALS

Find gear rentals in Apgar daily late May-mid-September. All rentals come with life jackets and paddles. From the dock on the lake, **Glacier Park Boat Company** (406/257-2426, www.glacierparkboats.com, 9am-7pm, $18-25) rents paddleboards, canoes, single and double kayaks, and rowboats. **Glacier Outfitters** (196 Apgar Loop Rd., 406/219-7466, www.goglacieroutfitters.com, 9am-5pm, $24-36/2 hrs) rents paddleboards, kayaks, and canoes. They also have a 24-hour rental option, so you can take the boats elsewhere in Glacier. **Eddie's** (236 Apgar Loop Rd., 406/888-5361, www.eddiescafegifts.com, 9am-5pm, $20-30/2 hrs) rents paddleboards and kayaks.

Fishing

Lake McDonald, the park's biggest lake, has a reputation for mediocre fishing. Boats work best to troll for lake trout. For catch-and-release fly-fishing, **Lower McDonald Creek** from the lake to Quarter Circle Bridge works, but it's also heavily fished because of its easy access. For several miles in both directions from West Glacier, the **Middle Fork of the Flathead** presents good fishing, but be ready to contend with rafters and fishing outfitters. Because of the concentration of visitors in the West Glacier-Apgar area during high season, you may not feel like you're off in the wilderness when you toss in a line, but you just might pull in native trout. Good fishing usually starts by early July when the water clears.

REGULATIONS
Fishing inside Glacier National Park **does not require a license,** but waters here have some restrictions, including **bans on lead lures.** Pick up complete fishing rules at Apgar Visitor Center. Lake McDonald has no limit on lake trout or whitefish. Westslope cutthroat are catch-and-release only, and endangered bull trout must be released. Despite its name, Fish Creek is closed to fishing. Lake McDonald is open to fishing all year, but stream fishing in and outside the park runs from the third Saturday in May through November 30.

LICENSES AND RENTALS
Fishing outside Glacier on Flathead River drainages requires **Montana fishing licenses** (Montana residents: $21-31 season, $15 for 2 days; nonresidents: $50 for 2 days, $81 for 10 days, $111 season) for ages 12 through adults. Pick up licenses at **Glacier Outdoor Center** (12400 U.S. 2 E., West Glacier, 406/888-5454 or 800/235-6781, http://

glacierraftco.com). Glacier Outdoor Center also sells fishing gear and rents rods ($12-15/day), waders, and float tubes. In Apgar, **Glacier Outfitters** (196 Apgar Loop Rd., 406/219-7466, www.goglacieroutfitters.com, 9am-5pm daily mid-May-late Sept., $9-20) rents spin-casting and fly rods, including smaller models for kids. They also rent fishing kayaks ($28-102).

GUIDES
Four fly-fishing companies in West Glacier guide trips daily in drift boats on Glacier's boundary waters on the Middle Fork and the North Fork of the Flathead River, but none guide fishing adventures inside Glacier National Park. Guided fishing starts in late June when the waters clear and goes through mid-September. Reservations are mandatory.

Half-day ($400), full-day ($500), and overnight ($425-1,000/day) guided fishing trips for 1-2 people are available. Plan on tipping the guides about 15 percent. Tip higher if you catch lots of fish or for overnight trips. It's pricey, but the guides usually get you to the good fishing holes. Fly-fishing schools ($500 for 2 people) teach the basics of casting, mending, and catch-and-release for beginners. Rates include all equipment, such as life jackets, rods, and flies. A 7 percent service fee is added to all fishing trips, but some companies include it in the price. You'll also need to buy your own fishing license.

All West Glacier fishing companies are licensed with the state: **Glacier Guides** (11970 U.S. 2 E., 406/387-5555, http://glacierguides.com), **Montana Fly-Fishing Guides** (Great Northern Resort, 12127 U.S. 2 E., 406/387-5340 or 800/735-7897, http://greatnorthernresort.com), **Wild River Fishing Guides** (11900 U.S. 2 E., 406/387-9453 or 800/700-7056, www.riverwild.com), and **Glacier Anglers** (Glacier Outdoor Center, 12400 U.S. 2 E., 406/888-5454 or 800/235-6781, http://glacierraftco.com), which adds on its specialty four- or five-day Great Bear Wilderness fishing trips and one-hour casting school.

GOLF

Glacier View Golf Club (640 River Bend Dr., West Glacier, 406/888-5471, www. glacierviewgolf.com, daily Apr.-Oct., snow permitting, 18 holes $33) may tax your concentration as you tee off. Moose, elk, bears, and deer wander across the fairways, and the mountain views are hard to ignore. The 18-hole course has a pro shop, restaurant, practice green, driving range, lessons, cart rentals ($28), and club rentals ($20). To locate the golf course in West Glacier, turn west onto River Bend Drive and follow signs to the clubhouse. The club has RV hookups ($40).

THRILL SPORTS AND FAMILY FUN

The **Glacier Highline** (10167 U.S. 2 E., Coram, 406/387-5007, www.glacierhighline. com, 10am-5pm Mon.-Sat. mid-June-mid-Sept., adults $50, kids 12 and under $40) packs its aerial park full of ziplines, ropes courses, and treetop challenges. The climbing wall and giant swing cost extra. The **Amazing Fun Center** (10265 U.S. 2 E., Coram, 406/387-5902, http://amazingfuncenter.com, 9:30am-9pm daily late May-early Sept., $3-8 pp/activity, combo passes $16-32) has a two-level maze, go-carts, bumper boats, bank-shot basketball, and mini golf.

WINTER SPORTS

Winter converts the roads and trails around Apgar into easy **cross-country ski and snowshoe paths** late November-early April. Quiet and scenic, road skiing makes for easy route-finding with little avalanche danger at lower elevations. Roads are plowed into Apgar and up Lake McDonald's south shore. Beyond plowing, popular ski tours follow roads and trails to **Fish Creek Campground, Rocky Point, McGee Meadows,** and the **Old Flathead Ranger Station** near the Middle Fork and North Fork confluence. Those with stamina and skiing expertise climb to **Apgar Lookout.** For route descriptions, pick up *Skiing and Snowshoeing* in the visitors centers or online (www.nps.gov/glac). Skiers and snowshoers should be well equipped and versed in winter travel safety before venturing out.

Guides and Rentals

The National Park Service guides free weekend snowshoe tours from **Apgar Visitor Center** (406/888-7800) January-mid-March. Call for departure times for the two-hour

A skier tours West Glacier.

walks to look for animal tracks. Interpretive rangers point out how flora and fauna adapt to harsh winters. Hikers should wear winter footwear, dress in layers, and bring water. Rent snowshoes from the park service or at Flathead Valley shops.

Glacier Outdoor Center (12400 U.S. 2 E., 406/888-5454 or 800/235-6781, https:// glacierraftco.com, 7am-9pm daily summer, 9am-4pm Mon.-Fri. winter) rents snowshoes ($20). Guided snowshoe, cross-country ski,

and backcountry ski tours are available by reservation through Glacier Adventure Guides (406/892-2173 or 877/735-9514, www. glacieradventureguides.com, Dec.-Mar.). For solo travelers, it's the best way to get connected with avalanche-certified guides who know the routes and where to find pristine powder stashes. Lunch, snacks, park entrance fees, and equipment are included. Multiday trips are also available. Check online for rates; plan on tipping the guide 15-20 percent.

Entertainment and Shopping

Most park visitors take advantage of the long daylight hours (dark doesn't descend until almost 11pm in June) to explore everything they can instead of seeking nightlife. If you're looking to party, you can shoot pool in the West Glacier Bar, a classic dive bar nicknamed Freda's (200 Going-to-the-Sun Rd., 406/888-5359, www.glacierparkcollection. com, noon-1:30am daily late May-mid Sept.). It's attached to the West Glacier Restaurant. For music on select nights, head to the Stonefly Lounge (10154 US 2, Coram, 406/387-5440, www.stoneflylounge.com, 2pm-2am daily).

RANGER PROGRAMS

Every night in summer, Fish Creek Campground Amphitheater (9pm) and Apgar Campground Amphitheater (7:30pm) host free 45-minute park naturalist evening programs on wildlife, fires, and natural phenomena. Schedules are posted in campgrounds and at the visitors centers. In the Apgar Visitor Center parking lot (10pm-midnight), visitors can view stars and planets through telescopes when weather and dark skies permit. In July and August on clear days, rangers set up a special solar viewing telescope in the afternoon at Apgar Village Green. Consult the park newspaper or go online (www.nps.gov/glac) for scheduled dates and times.

SHOPPING
West Glacier and Apgar each have several small gift shops with souvenirs, T-shirts, and books. In Apgar, stop by Montana House of Gifts (198 Apgar Loop Rd., 406/888-5393, http://montanahouse.info, 9am-7:30pm daily June-Sept., 10am-5pm daily Oct.-May) for its locally made pottery, weaving, jewelry, crafts, and arts. Some is by Indigenous people.

For outdoor gear, three stores in West Glacier open during the summer season with limited inventories. Glacier Outdoor Center (12400 U.S. 2 E., 406/888-5454 or 800/235-6781, http://glacierraftco.com, 7am-9pm daily summer, 9am-4pm Mon.-Fri. winter) specializes in fishing, camping, and rafting gear. The Crown of the Continent Discovery Center (12000 U.S. 2 E., 406/387-4405, www. crowndiscoverycenter.com, 7:30am-9pm daily summer, shorter hours May and Oct.) carries gear for hiking, camping, and backpacking. Montana Raft Company/Glacier Guides (11970 U.S. 2 E., 406/387-5555 or 800/521-7238, http://glacierguides.com, 8am-8pm daily summer, hours and days vary in winter) sells hiking and rafting gear.

Located in the historic Belton Train Depot in West Glacier, the Glacier National Park Conservancy (406/888-5756, http://glacier. org, 9am-4:30pm daily summer, 9am-4:30pm Mon.-Fri. winter) sells books, posters, and maps of Glacier. This is the place to go for all reference, natural history, hiking, and picture books on the park. It also runs a tiny bookstore in the Apgar Visitor Center. You can also order products online.

While you can find huckleberry products in any gift shop, the **Huckleberry Patch** (8868 U.S. 2 E., Hungry Horse, 406/387-5000 or 800/527-7340, www.huckleberrypatch.com, 7am-10pm daily May-Oct., 11am-6pm daily Nov.-Apr.) cannery specializes in local jams, jellies, syrups, pie fillings, and preserves. It sells fresh-baked huckleberry pies, too.

Food

Glacier is a place for good home-style cooking, where tasty fresh-baked fruit pies are still the rage, rather than upscale or international fare. Seasonal restaurants cater to summer visitors; hours can shorten in spring or fall, and only a few remain open in winter.

INSIDE THE PARK
Apgar

As the only diner in Apgar, **Eddie's Café & Mercantile** (236 Apgar Loop Rd., 406/888-5361, www.eddiescafegifts.com, 8am-10pm daily May-mid-Sept.) has lines in midsummer. It serves breakfasts and lunches ($9-16), including hiker lunches to go. Dinner ($13-26) has burgers, sandwiches, trout, buffalo meatloaf, and steak. Montana microbrews or wine can accompany dinner. Dine inside or outside on the streetside deck. An outdoor stand serves ice cream cones and basic espresso drinks, and you can also buy convenience foods, drinks, camping supplies, ice, and firewood at Eddie's.

Picnic Areas

Two popular picnic areas, both with beach access, rim Lake McDonald's western shores. **Apgar Picnic Area** is just off Going-to-the-Sun Road on the lake's southwest corner, with a beautiful up-lake view to the Continental Divide. **Fish Creek Picnic Area** is next to Fish Creek Campground, where a 0.7-mile (1.1 km) hike leads out to Rocky Point for more views. Both have picnic tables, flush toilets, and fire rings with grills, but firewood is not provided, and gathering it is prohibited; purchase firewood in Apgar or West Glacier. On weekends and holidays, plan to nab a table early.

OUTSIDE THE PARK
West Glacier
CASUAL UPSCALE DINING

At the historic ★ **Belton Chalet** (12575 U.S. 2 E., 844/868-7474, www.glacierparkcollection.com, mid-May-early Oct., $8-38), you can dine in the intimate **Belton Grill** (5pm-10pm daily), by the fireplace in the **Taproom** (3pm-midnight daily), or on the **deck** watching trains and the sunset over Apgar Mountain. It serves shared plates, salads with local ingredients, and entrées that include bison meatloaf, Montana Wagyu beef, and fish.

FAMILY DINING

Two restaurants serve family café fare with breakfasts and lunches running $8-16 and dinners $10-33. Menus can pacify a variety of tastes, and adults can sip beer and wine. The **West Glacier Restaurant** (200 Going-to-the-Sun Rd., 406/888-5359, www.glacierparkcollection.com, 7am-9pm daily mid-May-late Sept.) caters to hungry hikers with sandwiches and burgers of all kinds: beef, elk, and lentil. The beer crowd heads to the adjacent bar, locally known as Freda's, to order saloon food. With a large menu, the family-owned **Glacier Highland** (12555 U.S. 2 E., 406/888-5427, http://glacierhighland.com, 7:30am-10pm daily mid-Apr.-mid-Oct.) bakes huckleberry pancakes for breakfast and serves fresh huckleberry pie for dessert. Dinner specialties include buffalo meatloaf, steak, and rainbow trout.

MEXICAN

From an orange food truck surrounded by festive picnic tables, the **Wandering Gringo** (12135 U.S. 2 E., 11:30am-7:30pm Wed.-Mon. late May-early Sept., $3-12) wraps up fresh tacos and burritos. Prepare for outside dining only and mosquitoes in early summer at this locals' hangout. In the Crown of the Continent Discovery Center, **La Casita** (12000 U.S. 2 E., 406/471-2570, noon-7:30pm Mon.-Sat. May-Sept., $5-20) dishes up authentic chimichangas, quesadillas, tacos, and mole with ample portions from family recipes. The salsas, guacamole, and tortillas are made fresh daily.

COFFEE AND ICE CREAM

Summer-only espresso and ice cream outlets are ubiquitous in this bustling corner of the park. In West Glacier, the **West Glacier Restaurant** (200 Going-to-the-Sun Rd., 406/888-5662, www.glacierparkcollection. com, 7am-9pm daily mid-May-late Sept.) has ice cream and espresso with outside seating in the parking lot. The **Crown of the Continent Discovery Center** (12000 U.S. 2 E., West Glacier, 406/387-4405, www. crowndiscoverycenter.com, 7:30am-9pm daily summer, shorter hours May and Oct.) sells espresso drinks, beer, wine, craft cocktails, and Montana-made ice cream.

GROCERIES

Open daily May-September, two stores carry convenience foods, beer, wine, camping items, ice, and firewood. Both stores shorten their hours in the shoulder seasons. In West Glacier, the **West Glacier Mercantile** (0.1 mi/0.2 km

west of U.S. 2-Going-to-the-Sun Rd. junction, 7am-9pm daily summer) adds a small selection of meats, fresh veggies, and fruits. Hikers can make lunches with premade sandwiches, fruit, energy bars, jerky, and snacks. Across from the Belton Train Depot, the **Glacier Highland** (12555 U.S. 2 E., 406/888-9982, 7:30am-10pm daily summer) has a reputation for cheaper beer and wine prices.

In summer, the **farmers market** comes to West Glacier 3:30pm-6:30pm on Friday afternoons adjacent to the West Glacier Mercantile. The nearest year-round grocery store is in Hungry Horse, 9 miles (14.5 km) west of the park entrance on U.S. 2. Look for the "Supermarket" sign. To hit the megastores that carry huge brand selections, you'll have to drive 30 minutes into Flathead Valley.

Coram

Located 5 miles (8 km) west of West Glacier, Coram has additional dining. Behind Glacier Distillery in an old cabin decorated with historical park photos, ★ **Josephine's Bar and Kitchen** (10245 U.S. 2 E., 406/300-4755, www.josephinesbar.com, 4pm-10pm daily late May-mid-Sept., $8-16) carries the name of an early Glacier Park bootlegger who sold hooch along the Middle Fork River. The bar serves fresh inventive cocktails, which you can sip in the cocktail room, the indoor dining room, or outdoors. The kitchen serves up a short menu of tasty small plates and yummy sandwiches, especially the prime rib with red onion marmalade.

With new owners in 2019, **Glacier Grill and Pizza** (10126 U.S. 2 E., 406/387-4223, 7am-10pm daily year-round, $7-25) has been a longtime family staple for any meal of the day due to its large menu, inexpensive beer, generous portions, and pizza.

Accommodations

On Lake McDonald's shore, the limited inside-park lodging at Apgar is extremely popular, so West Glacier options often serve as backup. But given that the communities are only 2 miles (3.2 km) apart and are connected by a bike and walking path, they are equally convenient to each other and their outdoor activities. Additional lodging is found in Coram and Hungry Horse. Montana tacks on a 7 percent **bed tax,** so your bill will be higher than the quoted room rate. You can also find private cabins and vacation homes to rent at **VRBO** (www.vrbo.com). Make reservations a year in advance to guarantee the lodging you want.

INSIDE THE PARK
Apgar

Reservations are a must at the two adjacent **lodges** in Apgar tucked at Lake McDonald's foot. They are located 0.3 mile (0.5 km) from Camas Road, and 0.8 mile (1.3 km) from Going-to-the-Sun Road. To preserve their get-away-from-it-all ambience, neither have air-conditioning, internet access, in-room phones, or TVs. Pay phones can be found outside the lobbies. Both share a block with a restaurant, mercantile, ice cream shop, boat rentals, several gift shops, a shuttle stop, and the Apgar Bike Trail. Although the area is a busy hive during the day, it quiets at night.

On Lake McDonald's beach, every one of the 36 guest rooms in the ★ **Apgar Village Inn** (62 Apgar Loop Rd., 855/733-4522, www.glaciernationalparklodges.com, late May-mid-Sept., $185-320, reservations available 13 months ahead) wakes up to an unobstructed million-dollar lake view. Although the nondescript guest rooms were redecorated in 2015, not much else has changed since it was built in 1956. Some guest rooms include kitchenettes, and family units can sleep up to six. Stairs access the 2nd floor.

Set back in huge old-growth cedars along McDonald Creek, **Apgar Village Lodge and Cabins** (33 Apgar Loop Rd., 844/868-7474, www.glacierparkcollection.com, late May-late Sept., $120-335, reservations available 13-16 months ahead) clusters 20 small motel rooms and 28 rustic cabins within a few steps of Lake McDonald. The creek cabins (6, 7, and 8) are particularly serene, mixed with a wonderful ambience of wildlife and the sound of the stream. Although older, the cabins have all been upgraded since the mid-1990s, and some come with kitchens. All baths contain shower stalls.

OUTSIDE THE PARK
West Glacier

Lodging in West Glacier is convenient for hopping on the train, going river rafting or fishing, and heading off on guided backpacking trips. Only 2 miles (3.2 km) from Lake McDonald, West Glacier lodging works as an easy backup to booked-out in-park locations. Be prepared, however, for nightly noise. It's not from people, who are tired from packing in so much activity during the long days, but from trains on the railway line. Bring earplugs if you're a light sleeper. During midsummer, most West Glacier lodging fills nightly; reservations are advised. Lower rates are available in spring and fall.

PURSUIT ACCOMMODATIONS

Pursuit operates several properties in West Glacier under the **Glacier Park Collection** (844/868-7474, www.glacierparkcollection.com). Usually rates are lower in spring and fall. All of their properties except the Belton Chalet are between the Middle Fork River, the railroad tracks, and West Glacier Village, and they are linked to the village by walking and biking trails.

The Glacier Collection has multiple **cabins** (late May-early Oct., $220-370). Some of the **West Glacier Cabins** (sleeping 2-6 people,

$160-250) sit on a bluff above the river. Other cabins, built in 2019, at the **West Glacier RV Park** ($200-300) have one queen bed and a double futon, plus a small kitchen and gas grill outside. The small, older, no-frills guest rooms at **West Glacier Village Motel** (200 Going-to-the-Sun Rd., late May-mid-Sept., $120-250) have 32 motel units without TVs and air-conditioning.

Located across from Belton Train Depot, the historic ★ **Belton Chalet** (12575 U.S. 2 E., mid-May-early Oct.) has a cozy lobby with a large fireplace. Stay in the main **lodge rooms** (late May-Sept., $145-225) or **cottages** ($350). Simple guest rooms are a slice of history: original wainscoting and wood floors, push-button lights, twig tables, and historical photos, but no phones, TVs, air-conditioning, or alarm clocks. Original closets were converted into in-room baths with showers. Nine balcony rooms take in the sunsets over the Apgar Range. Wireless internet and a restaurant are on-site.

LODGES

★ **Glacier Guides Lodge** (120 Highline Blvd., 406/387-5555 or 800/521-7238, http://glacierguides.com, May-mid-Oct., $170-235), owned by Glacier Guides/Montana Raft Company, is an ecofriendly lodge. It has 12 guest rooms for two people each with wireless internet access, TVs, mini-fridges, and air-conditioning. Continental breakfast is included with stays, and two lounge areas provide places to relax outside the guest rooms. Its location tucked back in the woods under mossy cliffs makes it one of the quietest places.

Ten minutes outside the town center, ★ **The Great Bear Inn** (5672 Blankenship Rd., 406/250-4220 or 406/212-3501, www.thegreatbearinn.com, late May-Sept, $235-340) offers seclusion in the woods and the most upscale lodging in West Glacier. Large lodge rooms come in several styles, with the high-end guest rooms including king beds, rock fireplaces, and balconies. All rooms have mini-fridges, televisions, and wine glasses.

Two cabins with lofts and kitchens offer more privacy.

CABINS

Two cabin complexes operated by raft companies sit less than a mile west of West Glacier's shops and restaurants. Both come with fully equipped kitchens, wireless internet access, TVs, and gas grills. ★ **Glacier Outdoor Center** (12400 U.S. 2 E., 406/888-5454 or 800/235-6781, http://glacierraftco.com, mid-Apr.-Oct., $160-1,100) has one-, two-, three-, and four-bedroom log cabins and homes that sleep 6-14 people. Set back from the highway amid birch trees surrounding a trout pond, the cabins include log furniture, decks, and gas fireplaces. Some have a washer and dryer. Part of the Great Northern Resort, **Great Northern Chalets** (12127 U.S. 2 E., 406/387-5340 or 800/735-7897, http://greatnorthernresort.com, May-mid-Oct., $155-425) rents one-, two-, and three-bedroom log chalets that can sleep 2-10 people. Set around a landscaped garden pond but in view of the highway, the cozy two-story chalets with kitchens are decorated in Glacier outdoor themes, and several have sweeping views of Glacier's peaks.

Set in forest back from the highway, the **West Glacier KOA** (355 Half Moon Flats Rd., 406/387-5341 or 800/562-3313, www.koa.com, May-Sept., $100-350) in 2016 added 19 new deluxe cabins that each sleep 2-8 people. They come with kitchens or kitchenettes, linens, and in-cabin bathrooms. Some have lofts, balconies or decks, gas grills, outdoor fire pits, or mountain views. One cabin is a log home ($600). For those on a budget, 28 bare-bones cabins have no kitchens, no bed linens (bring sleeping bags), and share communal campground bathrooms. Guests staying in cabins have access to campground amenities including a heated swimming pool, hot tubs, evening programs, an ice cream shop, Wi-Fi, and summertime breakfasts and dinners.

1: Apgar Village Inn 2: Glacier Outfitters 3: Glacier Guides Lodge

MOTELS

To have a TV and Wi-Fi, go to one of the 33 rooms in the **Glacier Highland** (12555 U.S. 2 E., 406/888-5427, http:// glacierhighland.com, May-Oct.), located across from the train depot. About 0.5 mile (0.8 km) west of the Belton Train Depot, **Glacier Vista Motel** (12340 U.S. 2 E., 406/888-5433, www.glaciervistamotel. com, mid-May-Sept.) perches on a hill with Glacier views and has an outdoor heated swimming pool.

Along U.S. 2

When lodging facilities in Apgar and near West Glacier's town center book up in summer, you can find alternatives lining the 9 miles (14.5 km) of U.S. 2 from West Glacier to Hungry Horse. In some locations, be prepared for trains rumbling by at night.

The **Silverwolf Log Chalet Resort** (160 Gladys Glenn Rd. and U.S. 2 E., 406/387-4448, www.silverwolfchalets.com, May-Oct.,

$135-240) has 10 two-person log chalets on a landscaped lawn under lodgepole pines enclosed in a privacy fence. Chalets include gas fireplaces, microwaves, coffeemakers, and mini-fridges. Rates include a continental breakfast basket.

In Coram, **Evergreen Motel** (10159 U.S. 2, 406/387-5365, http://evergreenmotelglacier. com, May-Oct., $110-180) has small cabins and motel rooms, some with kitchenettes.

Historic Tamarack Lodge (9549 U.S. 2 E., 877/387-4420, www.historictamaracklodge. com, year-round) has lodge rooms ($90-200), older motel rooms ($70-170), and 14 cabins ($115-345) set in the woods up on the hill. The cabins sleep 2-6 people, and most have kitchens.

In the town of Hungry Horse, **Mini Golden Inns** (8955 U.S. 2, 406/387-4313 or 800/891-6464, www.hungryhorselodging. com, May-Sept., $130-165) has 38 motel units with satellite television and wireless internet. Some have kitchenettes and are pet friendly.

Camping

Lake McDonald is the big attraction for camping, but if you require RV hookups and showers, you'll need to stay in commercial campgrounds outside the park near West Glacier. **Glacier Outfitters** (196 Apgar Loop Rd., 406/219-7466, www.goglacieroutfitters. com, 9am-5pm daily mid-May-late Sept.) rents car camping gear by the item ($6-34) or bundled in a package for 2-4 people ($161-280). The bundles may be reserved online.

INSIDE THE PARK

Two National Park Service-operated **campgrounds** (406/888-7800, www.nps.gov/ glac) flank Lake McDonald with sites under a forest canopy. Rustic and without hookups, they have flush toilets, fire rings with grills, disposal stations, shared hiker-biker sites ($5-8), amphitheaters for evening naturalist talks, firewood for sale, and sites that accommodate

large RVs. Due to the lakeside locations, away from highway and railroad noise, they are popular. Midsummer, they fill up by 8am-9am. Check online to find fill times for previous days (and past years) to plan your arrival for the best chance of snagging a campsite.

Find up-to-date information on Glacier's campgrounds on the **official park website** (www.nps.gov/glac, under "campground status") and the **Recreational Access Display** (www.nps.gov/applications/glac/dashboard/).

Fish Creek

Fish Creek Campground (end of Fish Creek Rd., June-early Sept., $23) is one of three campgrounds in the park that can be reserved starting six months in advance (877/444-6777, www.recreation.gov). It is also one of the larger park campgrounds, with 178 sites tucked under cedars, lodgepole pines, and larches. Loops C

Wildfires

In an average summer, 13 wildfires burn in Glacier, altering 5,000 acres (2,023 hectares) of forest landscape. Most are caused by lightning; about 80 percent of strikes hit the park's heavily timbered west side. Some are small and unseen while others send huge smoke plumes thousands of feet in the air.

In recent decades, as the climate heats up, fires are becoming larger, more severe, and scarier. In 2003 an onslaught of lightning strikes burned nearly 150,000 acres (60,703 hectares) in several separate fires, creating one of the largest fire seasons in the park's history. Raging winds shoved the Robert Fire over Apgar Mountain, burning 7,000 acres (2,833 hectares) in four hours. Campers, motel guests, and park personnel evacuated from West Glacier and Apgar while helicopters doused the fire with water scooped from Lake McDonald. More recently, 2017 and 2018 saw large fires close much of the Lake McDonald area for the summer. But even in these recent fire zones, plants and trees are already regenerating.

As flames eat up wood, ash falls to the ground, releasing nutrients. Similar to putting good fertilizer on a garden, the ash fosters energetic plant growth, especially with the open tree canopy permitting more sunlight to reach the ground. As a natural succession of greenery takes over, wildlife dependent on plant foraging finds improved habitat. In short, fires help maintain a natural balance. They also remove deadfall and insect infestations that can kill trees. Fires reduce the power of future fires and create forests that are more resistant to drought and nonnative plant invasions. Fire isn't the end of a forest, but an ongoing process of succession in an ever-changing landscape. See postfire forest regeneration for yourself on the **Camas Road, Inside Road** (north of Fish Creek Campground), **Lake McDonald Trail** (starting at Fish Creek Campground), and from **Apgar Lookout.**

Larch and ponderosa, with thick resin-less bark and minimal low branches, survive fires. Some species even rely on fires for reproduction: The lodgepole pine's serotinous cones require high heat to release their fast-growing seeds from the sticky resin. Ceanothus, hollyhock, and morel mushrooms flourish after fires.

Until 1968, federal policy suppressed all fires, which resulted in excessive fuel buildup, bug infestations, and elimination of some floral species. Today, the National Park Service manages each fire individually based on location, threats to structures, and firefighter safety. Though satellites and airplanes survey fires, lookouts are still staffed in summer at **Huckleberry** (page 47), **Scalplock** (page 222), **Numa** (page 83), and **Swiftcurrent** (page 125).

and D have the best sites, adjacent to the lake, although Loop B has some larger, more level sites. A few lukewarm token-operated showers are available. Eighteen campsites accommodate RVs up to 35 feet (10.7 m) long; 62 sites fit RVs up to 27 feet (8.2 m). To find Fish Creek, drive 1.25 miles (2 km) north from Apgar on Camas Road and turn right, dropping 1 mile (1.6 km) down to the campground. Lake McDonald Trail departs from the campground.

Apgar

Apgar Campground (Apgar Loop Rd., 0.4 mi/0.6 km from Going-to-the-Sun Rd., Apr.-Nov., $20) is within a short walking distance of Apgar Village, Lake McDonald,

and the shuttles. The campground has 194 sites, making it the park's largest, with group campsites too. For RVs, 25 sites fit up rigs to 40 feet (12.2 m). A paved trail connects with the main shuttle stop, the visitors center, and the Apgar Bike Trail. A separate walking path leads to Apgar Village's restaurant, gift shops, and boat dock. Primitive camping (Apr. and mid-Oct.-Nov., $10) has pit toilets available but no running water. In winter, you can camp free at the plowed Apgar Picnic Area. A vault toilet is there.

OUTSIDE THE PARK

Commercial campgrounds in the West Glacier vicinity are convenient for rafting, fishing, biking, and trail rides, but they are located outside the park. RVers can find full hookups and camping for big rigs. Standard amenities in these campgrounds include flush toilets, laundries, hot showers, camp stores, picnic tables, fire rings with grills, firewood, propane, disposal stations, playgrounds, and wired or wireless internet access. If you're a light sleeper, bring earplugs; many of the campgrounds hear the rumble and screech of passing trains. Rates are for two people with additional campers costing $5-12 per person.

Although most commercial campgrounds lean toward serving RVers and car campers, bikers and backpackers should ask about special rates in shared sites, which run around $10-15 per person. Many of the campgrounds offer rustic camping cabins or yurts, which have no kitchens or baths; bring your own sleeping bags or pay extra for clean linens, blankets, and towels. Commercial campgrounds tack on a 7 percent Montana bed tax to their rates. When you make your reservations, check for deals; many give discounts for internet registration, seniors, staying early or late in the season, and Good Sam, AAA, or military members. For July-August, make reservations in advance.

West Glacier

Opened in 2019, **West Glacier RV Park and Cabins** (River Bend Dr., 844/868-7474, www.glacierparkcollection.com, late May-late Sept., $75-100, no tents) is the newest campground. Campsites accommodate up to 80-foot (24-m) lengths in pull-through and back-in sites that have grass but no shade trees. Amenities include shower, coin-op laundry, and Wi-Fi. The campground is located between the Middle Fork River and railroad tracks and connects to West Glacier Village by walking and biking paths.

On 40 timbered acres (16 hectares) 0.5 mile (0.8 km) from West Glacier, **Glacier Campground** (12070 U.S. 2 E., 406/387-5689 or 888/387-5689, www.glaciercampground.com, May-Sept., $30-50) sits in lush

undergrowth that surrounds private sites separated by birch and fir trees. RV hookups are for water and electricity only, but the campground has a mobile pump-out service ($25). Several cabins ($45-70) share a covered outdoor cooking area with gas burners and a barbecue. Leashed pets are welcome. With the campground set back from the road, trees reduce highway and railroad noise. An open-air pavilion serves sandwiches.

Removed 1 mile (1.6 km) from U.S. 2 and 2.5 miles (4 km) west of the park entrance, **West Glacier KOA** (355 Half Moon Flats Rd., 406/387-5341 or 800/562-3313, www.koa.com, May-Sept., $40-105) is the only campground with a heated swimming pool (June-mid-Sept.) and a few hot tubs (all season). It also has patio campsites, full RV hookups, evening programs, horseshoes, an ice cream shop, summer barbecue dinners, and pancake breakfasts. Tucked in the forest away from the highway and railroad, this is one of the quieter campgrounds.

Coram and Hungry Horse

Commercial campgrounds (tents $30-40, hookups $40-85, May-Oct.) sprawl along U.S. 2 in the span between West Glacier and Hungry Horse. RV campsites at **Lake Five Resort** (540 Belton Stage Rd., 406/387-5601, www.lakefiveresort.com) enjoy lakefront access. **North American RV Park and Campground** (10640 U.S. 2 E., 800/704-4266, www.northamericanrvpark.com) spreads RV campsites and rental yurts in a big grassy area with shorter trees for satellite reception. **Moose Creek RV Resort** (11505 U.S. 2 E., 406/387-5280, winter phone 406/890-1886, https://moosevreekrv.com, mid-May-Sept.) has full hookups for RVs and tent campsites. One of the quietest RV campgrounds, **Mountain Meadows RV Park** (9125 U.S. 2 E., 406/387-9125, http://mountainmeadowsrv.com) spans 77 acres (31 hectares) of forested hillside with a stocked catch-and-release rainbow trout pond.

For upscale camping, **Under Canvas**

Glacier (101 Under Canvas Rd., 406/552-4195, www.glacierundercanvas.com, mid-June-mid-Sept., $80-400) provides luxury tenting. Canvas tents (some with en suite hot running water and bathrooms), tepees, a treehouse, and a cabin offer the poshy experience of cots, beds, wood and carpeted floors, private bathrooms, and other amenities.

Transportation and Services

TRANSPORTATION
Driving and Parking

Two-lane highways and roads dominate the West Glacier and Apgar area. Most roads are paved, although dirt and gravel byways reach river accesses.

Find public parking lots in West Glacier at the Alberta Visitor Information Center, streetside, on commercial properties north of the railroad underpass, and at the train depot. A large dirt parking lot sits on Old River Bridge Road behind several West Glacier businesses.

In Apgar, three small parking lots are in the village, and you can also park at the picnic area, and boat dock. The largest parking lot, where RVs will find room, is at Apgar Visitor Center; a paved path connects to the village.

Shuttles and Taxis

Meeting all train arrivals and departures, **Xanterra** (855/733-4522, www.glaciernationalparklodges.com, daily late May-late Sept., $5-10) shuttles rail passengers between West Glacier's Belton Depot and Apgar Village Inn or Lake McDonald Lodge. Reservations are mandatory.

Eagle Transit (406/758-5728, https://flathead.mt.gov/eagle) offers summer service from Flathead Valley stops in Kalispell, Columbia Falls, and Whitefish to connect with Apgar Visitor Center. Find the current schedule and rates online. **Glacier Taxi** (406-250-3603, http://glaciertaxi.com) takes travelers from the airport to West Glacier.

SERVICES

The West Glacier KOA and Glacier Campground have **laundries.** You can also get a **hot shower** ($5-8) at Glacier Campground and Glacier Outdoor Center.

A **year-round post office** is in West Glacier opposite the Alberta Visitor Information Center. **ATMs** are located in Apgar at Eddie's Cafe & Mercantile and in West Glacier near the gas station.

The headquarters for **rental equipment** for camping, hiking, backpacking, paddling, fishing, and bicycling is **Glacier Outfitters** (196 Apgar Loop Rd., 406/219-7466, www.goglacieroutfitters.com, 9am-5pm daily mid-May-late Sept.). Some items may be reserved online.

Daily newspapers are Kalispell's *Daily* and the *Great Falls Tribune*. Weeklies include *Hungry Horse News* and the free *Flathead Beacon* (www.flatheadbeacon.com).

Gas and Repairs

Gasoline is not available inside the park, on Going-to-the-Sun Road, or on U.S. 2 between West and East Glacier. West Glacier is the last chance for gas, available year-round with a credit card at **Glacier Highland** across from the train depot or in summer at **West Glacier Gas Station** across from the West Glacier Mercantile.

Cell Phone and Internet Access

Cell phones can get reception in West Glacier and Apgar, but it is intermittent in adjacent canyons and portions of Apgar Campground. Only a few hotels, private campgrounds, and businesses between West Glacier and Hungry Horse provide internet access. Wi-Fi is also at the coffee and spirits bar in the **Crown of the Continent Discovery Center** (12400

U.S. 2 E., West Glacier, 406/871-0754, www.crowndiscoverycenter.com, May-Sept.).

Emergencies

Call 911 for emergencies. To reach a ranger or the park service, call 406/888-7800. A seasonal **urgent-care clinic** operates in West Glacier (100 Rea Rd., 406/888-9224, 9am-4pm daily Memorial Day-Labor Day). The nearest hospitals are in the Flathead Valley: **Kalispell Regional Medical Center** (310 Sunny View Ln., 406/752-5111) and **North Valley Hospital** (1600 Hospital Way, 406/863-3500 or 866/223-9190) in Whitefish.

The nearest ranger station inside the park is **Glacier National Park headquarters** (406/888-7800), on Going-to-the-Sun Road west of the park entrance station. Turn onto the signed side road and take the first right into the parking lot for the headquarters building. You can also get assistance at the Apgar Visitor Center.

For concerns with the Flathead River system or in Flathead National Forest, stop in **Hungry Horse Ranger Station** (10 Hungry Horse Dr., Hungry Horse, 406/387-3800, www.fs.usda.gov/flathead). Find it south off U.S. 2 on the east end of town.

North Fork

The North Fork Valley defines rustic—and not

rustic as in cute and comfortable, but really backwoods. Remote and wild, it's the place to go for those who want to decompress.

A visit to the North Fork transports you back in time. Only a few flush toilets, no electricity unless solar powered, and no cell-phone service. The pace of life slows with the ambience of the Polebridge Mercantile and Northern Lights Saloon.

For the average traveler, the North Fork's nasty dirt roads alone deter interest. Brutal potholes, jarring washboards, and clouds of dust launch vehement debates about paving the North Fork Road, but pavement into this remote enclave would alter its nature forever.

The North Fork Valley spans diverse habitats from grassland prairies

Highlights

Look for ★ to find recommended sights, activities, dining, and lodging.

★ **Drive or bike the Inside Road:** Along this remote dirt road, keep an eye out for wildlife (page 78).

★ **Visit the off-the-grid town of Polebridge:** Drool over baked goods from Polebridge Mercantile and dine at Northern Lights Saloon (page 79).

★ **Paddle or hike at Bowman Lake:** At this remote lake, Rainbow Peak juts straight up from the lakeshore, while Thunderbird Mountain scrapes the sky behind nesting bald eagles (page 79).

★ **Backpack or paddle Kintla Lake:** Launch into some of the park's most isolated backpacking terrain or enjoy paddling these quiet waters (page 79).

★ **Climb to Numa Lookout:** Ascend the steep route almost 3,000 vertical feet (914 m) to a perch with views of Bowman Lake and the Rainbow-Carter massif (page 83).

★ **Hike to Glacier View:** This short but steep trail may tax your lungs, but you'll smell wild roses and relish the panorama at the top (page 86).

★ **Trek to Boulder Pass:** Hike through alpine meadows and glacier-carved scenery over this high pass to soak up the solitude (page 88).

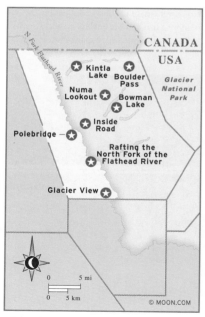

★ **Go River Rafting:** Let river time take over as you navigate the scenic North Fork of the Flathead River, which courses through prime wildlife habitat (page 89).

Avoid the Crowds

From June through August, even the remote North Fork clogs with vehicles in certain locations. When midsummer and weekend crowds fill the parking spots at Bowman and Kintla Lakes, the park service restricts access. One car must depart to admit one car in. Here are a few tips to avoid the queues:

- Go early in the **morning** to trailheads and boat launches.

- For **camping,** check the fill times for the previous day(s) online. Use that as your guideline for arrival to claim a spot at one of the four campgrounds inside Glacier Park, especially at the lakes.

- Check with the visitors center in Apgar or online with the Recreational Access Display for **traffic restriction status** before driving up the North Fork. You can also find congestion updates on Twitter @GlacierNPS. If you are already up the North Fork with no cell service, you can get updates at the Polebridge entrance station.

- If you just want to drive to the lakes for a "look see" and road trip, go in the **evening.** Your chances of seeing wildlife are better, and crowds thin out.

to alpine glaciers. It's home to an immense range of wildlife from huge grizzly bears to tiny pygmy shrews. Spruce trees 300 years old root the valley in deep history. Surrounded by thick subalpine fir forests, Bowman and Kintla Lakes have miles of empty shoreline dotted with only the boats of anglers or a few kayaks. Trails from the North Fork see only a few people, even in high season. Wildlife watchers can find animals and birds. Nothing chills the soul quite like the wild call of wolves in the dead of night.

PLANNING YOUR TIME

Visitors take several types of trips into the North Fork year-round. Summertime offers hiking, paddling, and backpacking, while winter has cross-country skiing and snowshoeing. In **one day,** sightseers can drive its dusty roads to go to the Polebridge Mercantile, tour to Bowman or Kintla Lakes, and finish by dining at Northern Lights Saloon. Avid hikers can also take one-day trips to admire big scenery and go huckleberry picking. But on day trips, you won't truly unwind. Before leaving West Glacier or Flathead Valley destined for North Fork lakes, check the park's **Recreational Access Display** (www.nps. gov/applications/glac/dashboard/) for real-time status for the access roads, weather, parking lots, and campgrounds; crowds sometimes force closures.

Those with a minimum of **three days** can soak up the backwoods atmosphere at rustic cabins, on a guided river rafting trip, fishing, or camping. Backpackers can get even farther away from civilization with **3-5 days.**

You must have a **car** to reach Logging Ranger Station, Bowman Lake, and Kintla Lake, as North Fork roads inside Glacier do not allow vehicles or RVs over 21 feet (6.4 m), nor trailers. **No public transportation** goes inside the park.

Make reservations for cabin stays six months in advance. For camping, plan to arrive in the morning to claim a spot.

Summer temperatures usually average 70-85°F (21-29°C) during the day and 45-49°F (7-9°C) at night. Hiking and backpacking into higher elevations will encounter temperatures about 10-15°F (6-8°C) cooler. Winter temperatures waffle between 0°F (-18°C) in Arctic cold fronts to 35°F (2°C).

HISTORY

In the late 1800s, handfuls of homesteaders, loggers, hunters, and trappers eked out

---

Previous: Bowman Lake in fall; fishing the North Fork of the Flathead River; monkeyflower near Boulder Pass.

North Fork

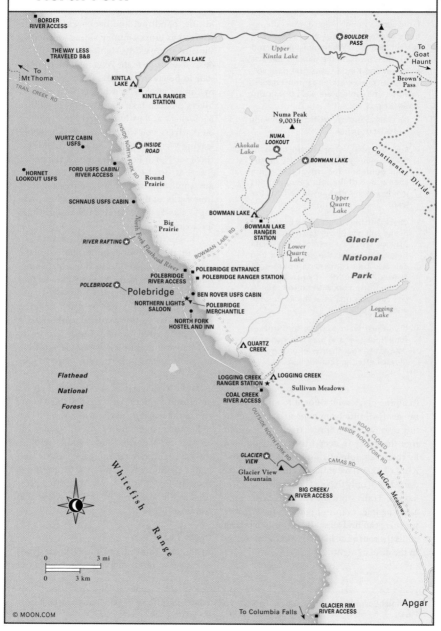

BORDER
RIVER ACCESS

THE WAY LESS
TRAVELED B&B

To
Mt Thoma

TRAIL CREEK RD

KINTLA LAKE

Upper
Kintla Lake

BOULDER
PASS

To
Goat
Haunt

Brown's
Pass

KINTLA
LAKE

KINTLA RANGER
STATION

Numa Peak
9,003ft

WURTZ CABIN
USFS

INSIDE
ROAD

NUMA
LOOKOUT

Akokala
Lake

HORNET
LOOKOUT USFS

FORD USFS CABIN/
RIVER ACCESS

Round
Prairie

BOWMAN LAKE

Continental Divide

SCHNAUS USFS CABIN

INSIDE NORTH FORK RD

Big
Prairie

Upper
Quartz
Lake

North Fork Flathead River

BOWMAN LAKE

RIVER RAFTING

BOWMAN LAKE RD

BOWMAN LAKE
RANGER
STATION

Glacier

POLEBRIDGE

POLEBRIDGE
RIVER ACCESS

POLEBRIDGE ENTRANCE

POLEBRIDGE RANGER STATION

Lower
Quartz
Lake

National

Park

Polebridge

BEN ROVER USFS CABIN

NORTHERN LIGHTS
SALOON

POLEBRIDGE
MERCHANTILE

Logging
Lake

NORTH FORK
HOSTEL AND INN

QUARTZ
CREEK

Flathead

National

Forest

LOGGING CREEK
RANGER STATION

COAL CREEK
RIVER ACCESS

LOGGING CREEK

Sullivan Meadows

ROAD CLOSED

INSIDE NORTH FORK RD

OUTSIDE NORTH FORK RD

GLACIER
VIEW

Glacier View
Mountain

CAMAS RD

McGee Meadows

BIG CREEK/
RIVER ACCESS

Whitefish Range

0   3 mi
0   3 km

GLACIER RIM
RIVER ACCESS

Apgar

To Columbia Falls

© MOON.COM

North Fork Wonders

TINY FAUNA

The North Fork Valley is home to the rare northern bog lemming, a small, brown-backed, gray-bellied rodent that seeks habitat in mats of thick, wet sphagnum moss. Weighing only 1 ounce (28 g)—the same as one heaping tablespoon of sugar—but growing up to 6 inches (15.2 cm) long, the tiny cousin of the Arctic lemming is a relic of the Pleistocene ice age. Although it's rarely seen, look for the small, neat piles of clipped grass it leaves along the mossy thoroughfares en route to underground nests. One study found that bog lemmings make up 2 percent of the pine marten's diet.

Glacier's smallest predator, the pygmy shrew, inhabits floodplains in the North Fork Valley. This tiny carnivore is one of North America's rarest mammals. Less than 2.5 inches (6.4 cm) in length and weighing 0.25 ounce (7.1 g), this shrew's voracious appetite for insects, slugs, snails, and carrion puts larger shrews to shame. One study watched a female eat three times her own body weight daily for 10 days. Their high metabolism echoes their respiration rate at 25 times more frequent than humans, and their hearts beat up to 1,320 times per minute when excited. To feed their high metabolic rates, pygmy shrews eat every couple of hours all day, year-round.

PLANTS

Carnivorous plants inhabit North Fork fens. The sundew attracts insects to its sparkling drop-lets, which look like morning dew. Sitting atop hairs lining its leaves, the sticky droplets, like wet cement, trap unsuspecting visitors. Slowly, the leaves curl around the victim as digestive juices work their magic. The bladderwort has also refined trapping. Buoyant bladders trap anything that swims, from mosquito larvae to fish fry. As prey passes, it brushes hairs that open a trapdoor that sucks water in along with the naive prey. Digestive enzymes make short work of the meal, with the trap reset in 15-120 minutes.

BIRDS

Birders find a feast for the eyes and ears in the North Fork. The valley teems with avian activity from 196 species and 112 nesters. Migratory birds stop on their flight highways to wintering ranges or summer nesting. To help with identification of Glacier's birds, pick up a bird list from visitors centers or on the park's website.

Raptors: Birds of prey find abundant food in the North Fork Valley. Numerous rodents, ground squirrels, songbirds, and carrion feed their appetites. The valley's forests attract sharp-shinned and Cooper's hawks. Bald eagles nest on Kintla and Bowman Lakes. Northern harriers, red-tailed hawks, goshawks, and American kestrels prowl above the prairies. At night, the hoots of large great-horned and pygmy owls haunt the air.

Waterfowl: With the Flathead River, many large lakes, swamps, and wetlands, waterfowl have no shortage of suitable habitat. Herons, ducks, grebes, geese, loons, and swans migrate through or nest in the plentiful waters.

Songbirds: The North Fork could be considered downright noisy at times. It's not from auto traffic, but from the scads of songbirds flitting among its trees and cattails. American redstarts, warbling vireos, kinglets, nuthatches, crossbills, sparrows, and warblers are just a few of the neotropical songbirds that migrate annually into the valley. In winter, you'll spot tree sparrows and redpolls.

Woodpeckers: After fires, dead standing timber attracts the three-toed woodpecker, pick-ing away for bugs. Watch for the large red-headed pileated woodpecker seeking carpenter ants.

a living in the North Fork Valley, connected to each other by a network of trails. In 1900, a Butte businessman, on a quest for oil at Kintla Lake, built the Inside North Fork Road, a 65-mile (105-km) wagon track riddled with ruts, bogs, and stumps. It was sufficient for hauling drilling equipment from Belton (now West Glacier) to Kintla Lake, where sleds skidded supplies across the frozen lake to drill Montana's first oil well in 1901. The road attracted more homesteaders, but Glacier becoming a national park threatened their hunting and timber livelihoods.

When Glacier achieved national park status in 1910, construction of the rough Outside North Fork Road two years later prompted many of the 35 homesteading families within the park boundaries to move across the North Fork of the Flathead River, outside the park boundary. In 1914 near Hay Creek, resident Bill Adair built a new two-story plank building to be the mercantile. The "Merc," as locals call it, is listed on the National Register of Historic Places. The area today is known as Polebridge, named for the funky, one-lane lodgepole North Fork River bridge that burned in the 1988 Red Bench Fire.

CULTURE

The North Fork is unique. It's a small, intimate community that prides itself on its rustic nature. Not L.L. Bean squeaky-clean cookie-cutter rustic, but real bucolic earthiness with no electricity and few phone lines. Generators and propane tanks provide lights and power, along with some solar energy. Year-round residents living off the grid and summer cabins are sprinkled around the floodplain. Most residents roll their eyes at visitors who complain about the North Fork Road; talk of paving raises the hackles of many, who don't want to see the North Fork changed.

The hub of valley life is **Polebridge,** where residents catch up on news, sometimes not much differentiated from gossip. Dogs run amok and lounge on the front porch. However, visiting canines must be leashed. Hand-painted signs will tell you so: "Local dogs at large." One of the warning signs at the Northern Lights Saloon claims, "Unleashed dogs will be eaten."

ECOLOGICAL SIGNIFICANCE

The North Fork area contains all five of Glacier's ecosystems: grassland prairies, aspen parklands, montane forests, subalpine, and alpine tundra. Rich floodplains teem with wildflowers, berries, shrubs, and trees. Fens abound with orchids, bladderworts, sundews, mosses, sedges, ferns, and bulrushes; McGee Meadows houses at least 50 species of flora. The rich flora provides a base for smaller mammals that in turn support large populations of grizzly and black bears, coyotes, mountain lions, and wolves. The sensitivity of the ecosystem prompted the North Fork Watershed Protection Act, which prohibits mining and natural resource extraction.

With the natural migration of wolves from Canada in the 1980s, Glacier saw its first wolf pack in 50 years and its first litter of pups in 1986. Numbers have since rebounded. Now wolf packs range across Montana, which has prompted the removal of the wolf as an endangered species. But don't expect to see a wolf around every tree; their numbers vary year to year, they roam up to 300 square miles (777 sq km), and they are elusive. But you may hear them at night. High concentrations of deer and elk make the North Fork Valley prime wolf habitat; to maintain its health, a wolf must eat 10 percent of its body weight in meat every day.

FIRES

Years of fire suppression policies led to thick lodgepole stands and bug infestations. The 38,000-acre (15,378-hectare) Red Bench Fire in 1988 saw policy change when the fire was allowed to run its natural course. Silver sentinels stand as a reminder that Polebridge was nearly wiped off the map. In 2001, the Moose Fire shot over Demers Ridge, burning 71,000 acres (28,733 hectares), over one-third inside Glacier. In 2003, the Wedge Canyon Fire

Where Can I Find...?

- **Cell reception:** There's **no cell service** here. Yes, really. Locals head up the North Fork specifically to cut the cord. It's a place to get away from social media and phone calls. Note: You also won't find any **power outlets** to recharge your phone. The North Fork is off the grid.

- **Garbage cans:** There aren't any. **Pack out everything** you bring up the North Fork.

- **Gas:** Gas up before going up the North Fork. There's gas at the **Polebridge Mercantile,** but it's pricey.

- **Rental gear:** Near the Polebridge Mercantile, **Polebridge Outfitters** rents paddle-boards, inflatable kayaks, and bikes.

- **Restrooms:** There are **vault toilets** at Bowman Picnic Area, Bowman Campground, Kintla Campground, Quartz Creek Campground, Logging Creek Campground, and river access sites on the North Fork of the Flathead (Canadian border, Ford, Polebridge, Big Creek, and Glacier Rim). **Polebridge Mercantile** has the only **flush toilet.**

- **Wi-Fi:** The North Fork has **no Wi-Fi.** Internet access is only via a computer at **Polebridge Mercantile** or for guests at select lodging properties.

burned 53,315 acres (21,576 hectares), jumping the North Fork River into the park and traveling up the side of Parke Peak, while the Robert Fire burned the valley's south end.

Evidence of each of these fires is obvious, but new lodgepole forests are overtaking the burns.

Exploring the North Fork

ENTRANCE STATIONS

The North Fork River is the boundary between national forest and national park. From the North Fork Valley, two roads cross the river into the park. On the south end, the paved **Camas Road** has a self-pay kiosk for entry fees. One mile (1.6 km) northeast of Polebridge, the **Polebridge Ranger Station** serves as an entrance and is staffed during summer only, but a self-pay kiosk is also available. Fees are $35 per vehicle, $30 per motorcycle, and $20 for hikers or bikers for seven days.

DRIVING TOURS
Outside North Fork Road

Open year-round, the Outside North Fork Road is the easier drive of the two dirt and gravel access roads. The two-lane road runs from Columbia Falls to the Canadian border. Be prepared for washboards, potholes, ruts, dust in summer, slush or mud in fall and spring, and ice in winter. The section between Camas Road and Home Ranch Bottoms gets periodic grading and dust inhibitors, and a short section south of Polebridge is paved.

Locals refer to this road as simply the "North Fork." Every few years, clamor arises about paving it, which many locals oppose because pavement would change the valley's nature. The North Fork Road is intermittently plowed in winter as far as the Canadian border, but do not attempt it without good snow tires. Carry chains and emergency supplies in the car.

From Columbia Falls, the North Fork Road leaves pavement just past Blankenship Road and follows the North Fork River for 13 miles

(20.9 km). After a junction with the paved Camas Road, an alternate access from Apgar, the road passes a few small, bucolic ranches whose pastures house cows and wild elk herds. Six miles (9.7 km) of pavement reappears at Home Ranch Bottoms, where cattle walk the road; drive with caution. At 32 miles (52 km) and about a one-hour drive, the road meets Polebridge Loop and the cutoff to the Merc, Inside North Fork Road, the Polebridge entrance to Glacier National Park, and **Bowman** and **Kintla Lakes.** Hand-painted signs warn drivers entering town: "Slow Down, People Breathing." Respect Polebridge's residents; speed kicks up a tremendous amount of dust in summer.

From the Polebridge junction, the road continues 22 more miles (35 km) north and another 45-minute drive toward Canada. It accesses the upper Whitefish Range trailheads, North Fork River, and Forest Service cabins. Although drivers used to cross into Canada here, the Canadian government closed the Trail Creek port of entry.

★ Inside Road

Not for everyone, the primitive gravel **Inside North Fork Road** (mid-May-Oct., no RVs over 21 ft/6.4 m; no trailers) throws precipitous narrow drops, curves, and climbs at drivers. Monster potholes, ruts, and washboards are commonplace; spaces wide enough for two vehicles to pass are rare. You're definitely off the beaten path on this bumpy trek, where speeds top out at 20 mph (32 kph), and two hours can be required to drive nearly 30 miles (48 km). High-clearance vehicles are best. On maps, it is marked as Glacier Route 7 or the Inside Road. Check with the park website, Apgar Visitor Center, or Polebridge Ranger Station for current conditions before embarking.

Since 2014, flood damage has closed an 11-mile (17.7-km) portion between Logging Creek and Camas Creek. Due to the closure, vehicles can no longer complete the whole road in one shot and must enter via two accesses. From the south, one access point goes from Fish Creek; the other access is midway at Polebridge.

From **Fish Creek,** just north of Fish Creek Campground, the road climbs through the 2003 Robert Fire. Atop the ridge, look for peekaboo views of **McGee Meadows,** a good wildlife-watching spot if you can squeeze your vehicle off the road and tolerate swarms of mosquitoes. Then compare fire regrowth as you drive through the 2001 Moose Fire and see the 2018 Howe Ridge Fire results to the east. The road terminates at the Camas Creek closure at 6.5 miles (10.5 km).

From the **Polebridge entrance station,** vehicles can go north or south on the Inside Road. Travel south to reach the Logging Ranger Station, Logging Creek trailhead, and two small, remote campgrounds: Quartz Creek in 8 miles (12.9 km) and Logging Creek in 10.5 miles (16.9 km). A few minutes north of the Polebridge Ranger Station, the curvy **Bowman Lake** road turns off Inside Road for 6 miles (9.7 km; 25 minutes) of snakelike driving eastward. Continuing northward, the Inside Road crosses **Big Prairie,** the largest of the North Fork's unique grasslands. **Round Prairie** follows at one-third the size. The road reenters the forest and passes through the 2003 Wedge Canyon Fire zone before dead-ending at Kintla Lake, 14 miles (22.5 km) north of the Polebridge entrance station. In summer, when cars pack out parking lots and campgrounds at Bowman and Kintla Lakes, the park restricts uphill traffic to the lakes. Cars are held back until space opens from departing vehicles. To avoid the lineup, plan to enter the park and head up to the lakes before 9am.

Sights

★ POLEBRIDGE

Polebridge, a tiny collection of cabins, a restaurant, and a store, is the hub of the North Fork. The red-planked **Polebridge Mercantile** (265 Polebridge Loop, 406/888-5105, https://polebridgemerc.com), or "Merc," listed on the National Register of Historic Places, was built in 1914. It sells not-to-be-missed bakery goods fresh from the propane oven: huckleberry bear claws, cinnamon rolls, cookies, and breads. Owner Will Hammerquist has kept the Merc's historic flavor intact despite swapping out the antique cash register for computerized sales powered by solar energy.

Next door to the Merc, the tiny **Northern Lights Saloon** (255 Polebridge Loop, 406/888-9963) looks like a ramshackle log cabin but packs in diners, with extras spilling outside onto picnic tables. Hikers celebrate their adventures here with Montana microbrews and lounge outside, staring at Rainbow Peak, while music livens the fun.

NORTH FORK OF THE FLATHEAD RIVER

Forming the western boundary of Glacier National Park, the **North Fork of the Flathead River** starts in Canada and ends near West Glacier at its confluence with the Middle Fork. Descending the North Fork Valley's diverse habitats, the 59 miles (95 km) of river flow through private, state, and federal lands. Designated as a Wild and Scenic River, the Class II river with six accesses is great for multiday float trips, day rafting, fishing, and scenic floating.

★ BOWMAN LAKE

Seven miles (11.3 km) northeast of Polebridge, **Bowman Lake** sits in a narrow, glacier-scoured trough at the terminus of a dirt road with a bouncing ride. The lake sprawls toward nesting bald eagles and Thunderbird Peak; its 0.5-mile (0.8-km) width squeezes in between the hulks of Numa and Rainbow Peaks, the latter rising 4,500 feet (1,372 m) straight up from the south shore. Lake waters offer paddling and fishing, and you can soak up evening quiet in the campground. In winter, the icy expanse and snow-laden crags call to cross-country skiers, who ski on the road pockmarked with wolf and elk tracks. Bowman Road limits vehicle length (21 ft/6.4 m maximum; no trailers).

BIG PRAIRIE

Located 30 miles (48 km) up the Inside North Fork Road, just 2 miles (3.2 km) past the Bowman Lake turnoff and 3 miles (4.8 km) from Polebridge, **Big Prairie** is the largest of four Palouse prairies in the North Fork. At 1 mile (1.6 km) wide and 4 miles (6.4 km) long, the prairie is a grassland with wheatgrass, fescues, oat-grass, and sagebrush. Because the Whitefish Range causes a rain shadow, the North Fork receives only 20 inches (51 cm) of precipitation per year, which fosters this drier flora.

★ KINTLA LAKE

Kintla Lake is a place to go only on purpose. Fifteen miles (24 km) of potholed road links Polebridge with the remote lake. Its tiny campground tucked deep in the trees offers quiet, a place to decompress. Cowering between Starvation and Parke Ridges, the 0.5-mile-wide (0.8-km) lake curves a little over 5 miles (8 km) up-valley, a prelude to **Upper Kintla Lake.** One trail starts along the north shore and runs toward the isolated Kintla-Kinnerly peak complex and Boulder Pass. Haul a canoe or kayak to Kintla Lake for secluded, serene (motors are banned) paddling. Kintla Road limits vehicle length (21 ft/6.4 m maximum; no trailers).

LOGGING CREEK RANGER STATION

The historic **Logging Creek Ranger Station,** built in 1907, is the oldest ranger station in Glacier National Park. With the current road closure on the Inside North Fork Road between Logging Creek and Camas Creek, the idyllic ranger station makes a good destination for a driving tour south from Polebridge.

MCGEE MEADOWS

Between Camas Road and the Inside Road, **McGee Meadows** is a wildlife-watching spot. During spring and early summer, the mosquito-infested fen is too wet to walk due to its soggy nature. As a fen, its low-oxygen waters build up dead plant matter, but nutrients feed it via precipitation and groundwater, making it fertile ground for diverse vegetation. The meadow is home to rare plants and over 50 species of flora: bulrushes, bladderworts, sphagnum moss, sundews, and orchids. Wildlife sightings can include bears, moose, deer, and a host of birds. Cross-country skiers tour the meadows in winter.

Recreation

DAY HIKES

Hiking in the North Fork leads to stunning vistas, but be prepared to earn your views by tromping through long, mosquito-ridden, thick-forested valleys. In this undeveloped area, you're on your own to get to trailheads; no shuttle service runs up the North Fork. On opposite sides of the valley, hikes depart east into Glacier or west into the Whitefish Range in Flathead National Forest. To take the pooch, go to the national forest.

While trails in Glacier National Park are well signed and maintained, Flathead National Forest trails are less so. Signs may only show a number with no distances, destinations, or directions. For that reason, hike with a topographic map in the national forest, and know how to read it. Expect to encounter deadfall and downed trees as well as brushy routes.

For hiking maps of Flathead National Forest, contact the **Glacier View Ranger District** (406/387-3800) in Hungry Horse. Topographic quad maps of the Whitefish Range can be purchased at outdoor sporting-goods stores in Flathead Valley. For hiking Glacier's trails, take along a topographic map from **Glacier National Park Conservancy** (406/892-3250, http://glacier.org).

Access to most North Fork Trails is based on snowpack. Some low-elevation trailheads become accessible by June; however, snow lingers on high passes through July. Hikers can climb Glacier View year-round, although winter requires snowshoes.

Kintla Lake

Distance: 13 miles (20.9 km) round-trip
Duration: 6 hours
Elevation gain: 267 feet (81 m) each way
Effort: easy but long
Trail surface: narrow dirt path with roots and rocks
Trailhead: Kintla Lake in Glacier National Park (see map p. 84)

The gentle trail cruises along Kintla Lake's north shore with an expanding view up the lake before its midsection tours back deep in the trees. Look for woodland flowers: trilliums, twisted stalk, queen's cup, fairybells, bunchberry, and bog orchids. Toward the head of the lake, the trail returns to a shoreline tour.

At 6.5 miles (10.5 km), the trail reaches the Kintla Lake backcountry campground. Pull out the binoculars, as you might see moose, bears, or bald eagles. Eat lunch near

---

1: Polebridge Mercantile and road signs **2:** one access point for the Inside North Fork Road **3:** Numa Lookout

North Fork Hikes

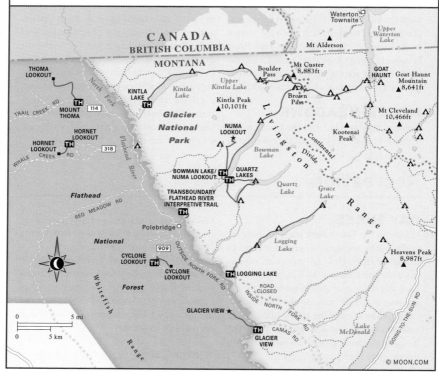

the community cooking site or on the beach rather than in or near backcountry sleeping sites. For a longer exploration, the trail continues through the 2003 Wedge Fire, growing with prolific pink fireweed, and past the dramatic Long Knife Waterfall to Upper Kintla Lake, 2.7 miles (4.3 km) farther. The road to Kintla Lake limits vehicle length (21 ft/6.4 m maximum; no trailers).

Bowman Lake

Distance: 13 miles (20.9 km) round-trip
Duration: 6 hours
Elevation gain: minimal
Effort: easy but long
Trail surface: narrow dirt path with roots and rocks
Trailhead: Bowman Lake in Glacier National Park (see map p. 85)

This easy-walking trail wanders the forested northwest shoreline of Bowman Lake to the backcountry campground at its head. For a stroll, walk it as far as you want and then turn around. The brushy trail nears the shore only a few times, where rocky beaches make for good break spots after June high water recedes. Intermittent views of the Square, Rainbow, and Carter massif poke out from the trees.

At the head of the lake, a backcountry campground with a marvelous pebble beach is a great place to have lunch, but eat near the community cooking site rather than near sleeping sites. Bring binoculars, because bald eagles nest at the lake's head. The road to Kintla Lake limits vehicle length (21 ft/6.4 m maximum; no trailers).

North Fork Hikes

Trail	Effort	Distance	Duration
Kintla Lake	easy	13 mi (20.9 km) rt	6 hr
Bowman Lake	easy	13 mi (20.9 km) rt	6 hr
Quartz Lakes	moderate	13.1-mi (21.1-km) loop	6.5 hr
Numa Lookout	moderately strenuous	10.2 mi (16.4 km) rt	5.5 hr
Logging Lake	easy	10.4-10.8 mi (16.7-17.4 km) rt	5.5 hr
Mount Thoma	strenuous	10 mi (16.1 km) rt	5 hr
Hornet Lookout	easy	2 mi (3.2 km) rt	1 hr
Transboundary Flathead River Interpretive Trail	easy	0.3-mi (0.5-km) loop	20 min
Cyclone Lookout	moderate	5.6 mi (9 km) rt	3 hr
Glacier View	strenuous	4.5 mi (7.2 km) rt	4.5 hr

Quartz Lakes

Distance: 13.1-mile (21.1-km) loop
Duration: 6.5 hours
Elevation gain: 1,410 feet (430 m) to Upper Quartz, 910 feet (277 m) on return from Lower Quartz
Effort: moderate
Trail surface: narrow dirt path with roots and rocks
Trailhead: Bowman Lake in Glacier National Park
(see map p. 85)

In June, early parts of the trail burst with calypso orchids while the path crossing Cerulean Ridge is still buried under snow. Less than 0.6 mile (1 km) up the trail, the path splits. You'll return to this junction at the end of the loop. Take the left fork, heading to Quartz Lake. The trail climbs through thick spruce and fir forests until it crests Cerulean Ridge. As the trail drops 1,000 feet (305 m) to Quartz Lake, it enters the 1988 Red Bench burn, where lodgepole regrowth affords peekaboo views of Vulture Peak and the lakes. At Quartz Lake, lunch with a view at the patrol cabin beach located on an unmarked spur trail at the trail junction after the backcountry campsites. Anglers can fish for native trout.

From Quartz Lake, the trail cuts through mosquito bogs and rainforest, passing Middle Quartz Lake, and drops to a backcountry campsite at Lower Quartz Lake's outlet. From here, it climbs 1.5 miles (2.4 km) through thick young lodgepoles to the top of Cerulean Ridge before dropping back to the junction. For families with kids, an out-and-back excursion just to Lower Quartz Lake may be easier, at 7.4 miles (11.9 km) round-trip. The road to Bowman Lake limits vehicle length (21 ft/6.4 m maximum; no trailers).

★ Numa Lookout

Distance: 10.2 miles (16.4 km) round-trip
Duration: 5.5 hours
Elevation gain: 2,927 feet (892 m)
Effort: moderately strenuous
Trail surface: narrow dirt path with roots, rocky
Trailhead: Bowman Lake in Glacier National Park
(see map p. 85)

Although the bulk of the trail crawls through deep forest, the view from Numa Lookout is well worth the climb. Following the northwest shore of Bowman Lake, the trail winds 0.6 mile (1 km) through damp cedars to a junction. Take the left fork. The trail climbs steadily uphill past a small, boggy mosquito pond.

Kintla Lake

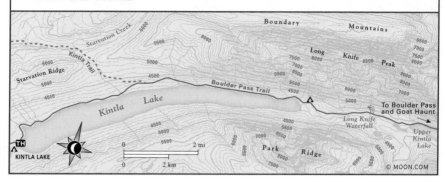

After the trail switchbacks up the final climb within eyesight of the lookout, the treed slope breaks into dry, open meadows. At 6,970 feet (2,124 m), the lookout, which is staffed during fire season, has views across Bowman Lake at the steep massif of Square, Rainbow, and Carter Peaks. The road to Bowman Lake limits vehicle length (21 ft/6.4 m maximum; no trailers).

Logging Lake

Distance: 10.4-10.8 miles (16.7-17.4 km) round-trip
Duration: 5.5 hours
Elevation gain: 469 feet (143 m)
Effort: easy
Trail surface: narrow dirt path with roots and rocks
Trailhead: Logging Creek on the Inside North Fork Road in Glacier National Park (see map p. 86)

The trail attracts anglers fishing for cutthroat. Above Logging Creek, the trail climbs quickly at the start but then levels out across a timbered ridgeline opened up by fire. Views span the creek canyon, aspen-flanked hillsides, and the Vulture Peak complex. At the lake, drop at the first junction to the ranger cabin beach for lunch or head to the second junction to the backcountry campsite (eat your lunch in the community cooking site rather than near the tent sites). Beaches look up-lake to Mount Geduhn and Anaconda Mountain. The road to the trailhead limits vehicle length (21 ft/6.4 m maximum; no trailers).

Mount Thoma

Distance: 10 miles (16.1 km) round-trip
Duration: 5 hours
Elevation gain: 2,880 feet (878 m)
Effort: strenuous
Trail surface: narrow dirt path with roots; rocky
Trailhead: on Trail Creek Road in Flathead National Forest
Directions: Drive north of Polebridge on the Outside North Fork Road approximately 13 miles (20.9 km) to Trail Creek, 6 miles (9.7 km) from the Canadian border. Turn left and drive 3 miles (4.8 km) to the trailhead on the right.

The forested trail starts off gently but soon pitches into an uphill grunt. The brushy trail sometimes has downed trees barring the path, requiring climbing and worming through branches. But soon it breaks out into a high ridgeline meadow with bluebells. At the end of the ridge, the trail climbs a series of switchbacks to the summit.

The summit is well worth the hike for its two-nation view. Glacier's peaks sprawl to the southeast. Below, the border swath between Canada and the United States slices an unnaturally straight line across the valley. In Canada, a mosaic of clear-cuts leads up to Akamina-Kishinena Provincial Park bordering Waterton National Park. To the south, the Whitefish Range layers off peak after peak as far as the eye can see.

Bowman Lake Trails

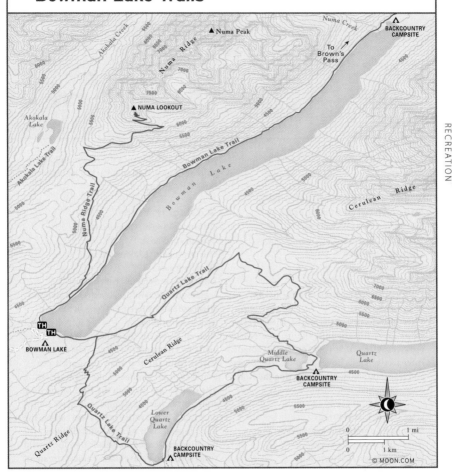

Hornet Lookout

Distance: 2 miles (3.2 km) round-trip

Duration: 1 hour

Elevation gain: 747 feet (228 m)

Effort: easy

Trailhead: Hornet Road's terminus in Flathead National Forest

Trail surface: narrow dirt path with rocks

Directions: Ten miles (16.1 km) north of Polebridge, turn west onto Whale Creek Road (Forest Rd. 318) for 4 miles (6.4 km), then turn north,

climbing on narrow Hornet Road (Forest Rd. 9805) for 5.2 miles (8.4 km).

A short climb uphill through huckleberry, fireweed, and bear grass leads to a small lookout with great views of Glacier's skyline and the North Fork Valley. Silvered trees remain from the 2003 Wedge Fire; you'll get a good look at the full scope of the burn. While the drive may take longer than the hike, the lookout makes a great kid destination with rewarding views for adults. To spend the night,

Logging Lake

© MOON.COM

rent the U.S. Forest Service lookout (for 1-2 people).

Transboundary Flathead River Interpretive Trail

Distance: 0.3-mile (0.5-km) loop
Duration: 20 minutes
Elevation gain: flat
Effort: easy
Trail surface: narrow dirt path
Trailhead: on the north side of Northern Lights Saloon in Polebridge

This short trail with eight interpretive stops gives insight into the unique North Fork ecosystem that is shared with Canada. Interpretive signs cover history, fire, bears, and transboundary issues affecting the North Fork watershed.

Cyclone Lookout

Distance: 5.6 miles (9 km) round-trip
Duration: 3 hours
Elevation gain: 1,034 feet (315 m)
Effort: moderate
Trail surface: narrow dirt path with roots and rocks
Trailhead: On the North Fork Road south of Polebridge, turn west into Flathead National Forest onto Forest Road 376 for 1.25 miles (2 km). Turn south onto Forest Road 909 for 4.2 miles (6.8 km).

The trail begins on an old road but soon narrows into a path that switchbacks up through a lodgepole forest. During huckleberry season, you may find a good crop of berries. At the summit, the lookout provides views of the Whitefish Range and straight across the

North Fork Valley into the Bowman Lake region of Glacier National Park. The lookout is staffed in summer.

★ Glacier View

Distance: 4.5 miles (7.2 km) round-trip
Duration: 4.5 hours
Elevation gain: 2,725 feet (831 m)
Effort: strenuous
Trail surface: narrow dirt path; rocky
Trailhead: junction of Camas and North Fork Roads in Flathead National Forest; trail sign says "Demers Ridge" (see map p. 88)

A steep climb up the side of Demers Ridge leads to Glacier View. Its name says it all: Views from the top span the park's peaks. You'll even see Flathead Lake in the distance. The trail passes through the 2001 Moose Fire zone, with charred stumps and silver toothpick trees. In the valley below, you can see the fire's mosaic as it burned with different intensities and leaped tree glades. In June, wild roses scent the air amid a botanical dream of wildflower species.

Right from the start, the trail makes no bones about going uphill: There are no flats to warm up the legs. But with a decent pair of lungs, the steep ascent is not bad. Just adopt a slow, steady pace and you'll reach the top, where meadows afford a scenic top-of-the-world place to lunch with Glacier's peaks from Canada to its southern border spread across the skyline. The fire removed shade from the

1: Boulder Pass Trail 2: Glacier View

Glacier View

slopes, so the trail bakes in the August heat. In winter, snowshoers trek up.

Guides and Rentals

Glacier Guides (406/387-5555 or 800/521-7238, http://glacierguides.com) has the sole guiding concession for Glacier National Park. While most day-hiking trips head elsewhere, many multiday backpacking trips begin or finish at the Bowman and Kintla trailheads. **Glacier Adventure Guides** (406/892-2173, www.glacieradventureguides.com) leads day hikes up Glacier View in Flathead National Forest.

If you need to rent hiking or backpacking gear, including pepper spray, pick it up in Apgar from **Glacier Outfitters** (196 Apgar Loop Rd., 406/219-7466, www.goglacieroutfitters.com, 9am-5pm daily mid-May-late Sept.) before coming up the North Fork.

BACKPACKING

The North Fork launches some of the most remote backpacking trips in Glacier. Two trails converge to cross the Continental Divide to reach Goat Haunt on Waterton Lake. The two most popular routes depart from Kintla and Bowman Lakes. A lack of shuttles adds a degree of difficulty to logistics.

Backpackers going overnight in Glacier need permits (adults $7 pp/night). Pick them up 24 hours in advance in person at the **Apgar Backcountry Permit Office** (406/888-7859 May-Oct., 406/888-7800 Nov.-Apr.) before

coming up the North Fork. You can apply for advance reservations online starting in mid-March (www.nps.gov/glac, $40). No permits are needed in Flathead National Forest for overnight trips.

TOP EXPERIENCE

★ Boulder Pass
33 MILES (53 KM)

Starting at the foot of Kintla Lake, the 4-6-day route takes in Upper Kintla Lake, Boulder Pass, Hole-in-the-Wall Cirque, and Brown Pass and finishes at Goat Haunt at the foot of Waterton Lake. A 2,800-foot (853-m) climb packs in the 5.6 miles (9 km) between Upper Kintla Lake and Boulder Pass, but otherwise the elevation gains are gentler. The highest camp, at Boulder Pass, boasts a wall-less pit toilet with expansive views of Agassiz Glacier and Kintla Peak, and the Hole-in-the-Wall camp is prized for meadows of rampant wildflowers. Of the nine campsites along the route, the most scenic are Upper Kintla Lake head (UPK), Boulder Pass (BOU), Hole-in-the-Wall (HOL) and Lake Frances (FRA). Due to snow clogging Boulder Pass and Hole-in-the-Wall in early summer, advance reservations are only available starting August 1. But often the route can open up by mid-July for walk-in permits 24 hours in advance. Hiking in reverse by starting at Goat Haunt spreads the elevation gain out over more miles.

Setting up shuttles is the biggest logistical challenge. You need a car to reach Kintla

Lake and for some portions of the route back. Some backpackers rely on hitchhiking, which is legal in Montana, but it is unreliable, especially in the North Fork.

Brown Pass
28 MILES (45 KM)

From the trailhead at the foot of Bowman Lake, the three-day out-and-back trip goes to a lower-elevation pass, a good backpacking option earlier in summer. The brushy trail parallels the northwest shore to a large backcountry campground (BOW) at the head of Bowman Lake. Camp here for one night. With an early departure to ascend Brown Pass (BRO), you should have time to hike into the Hole-in-the-Wall cirque. Return to the trailhead in one day.

Due to the lower elevation of Brown Pass, this route is usually snow-free by mid-July. Advance reservations start for Brown Pass on July 15, but walk-in permits are available earlier if the campground melts out. Backpackers can also use this route for a point-to-point hike to Goat Haunt (24 mi/39 km total) or over Boulder Pass to Kintla Lake (38 mi/61 km total). The junction at Brown Pass links with both destinations.

BIKING

With the North Fork's rough gravel roads, mountain biking is the only way to go. A portion of the Outside North Fork Road is on the Great Divide Mountain Bike Route between Banff and Mexico.

In June, when moisture still clings to gravel and dirt, riding roads is less dusty, but you'll eat your share of mosquitoes. During dry spells, plan on drowning in clouds of dust. To dodge vehicles, ride the closed section of the **Inside Road** between Camas Creek and Logging Creek. Littered with wolf scat, the 4.5 miles (7.2 km) from Logging Creek Ranger Station to Anaconda Creek tours along Sullivan Meadows, ponderosas, and aspens. The 6.5-mile (10.5-km) segment from Camas Creek to Anaconda Creek climbs and drops through regrowing fire zones until reaching the steep drop down Anaconda Hill. Flooding has eroded the roadbed at Anaconda Creek; only bikers capable of carrying bikes while fording multiple creeks should cross the area. Due to flooding and downed trees, the route is best to ride starting midsummer after water levels drop and crews saw downed trees. Check with the park for current conditions (406/888-7800).

For mountain bikers who like challenges, including fording creeks while carrying your bike, a 53-mile (85-km) loop from Apgar links together the Inside North Fork Road, Outside North Fork Road, and paved Camas Road. The Inside Road adds serious elevation gain as it climbs and drops through five creek drainages. Due to the remoteness, be ready to self-rescue in case of emergency. The rugged ride requires carrying only minimal supplies as a two-day overnight. Stay at the North Fork Hostel, dine at the Northern Lights Saloon, and breakfast on baked goodies at the Merc.

Rentals, Shuttles, and Guides

Make reservations for rentals, shuttles, and guided trips. You can rent mountain bikes and e-bikes in Polebridge from **Polebridge Outfitters** (265 Polebridge Loop, 406/888-5229, www.polebridgemerc.com, $25-110). The **Whitefish Shuttle** (406/212-0080, https://whitefishshuttle.com) run shuttles for bikers from Whitefish and guided bike trips. Rates vary by numbers of participants and activity.

WATER SPORTS
★ Rafting

Floating the Wild and Scenic **North Fork of the Flathead River** decompresses life to river pace on Class II waters. Despite the lazy ambience, the North Fork throws challenges at rafters, kayakers, and canoers. Log jams pose hazards, and braided channels can dead-end; this is not a river for a first-time paddler. Between Big Creek and Glacier Rim, the Class III Upper Fool Hen rapids can flip the unwary. Paddlers can avoid this stretch by taking out at Big Creek. Seven river put-ins stagger down

Tips for Wildlife-Watching

- **Safety for you and safety for the wildlife is important.** For spying wildlife up close, use a good pair of binoculars.

- **Do not approach wildlife.** Although our inclinations tell us to scoot in for a closer look, crowding wildlife puts you at risk and endangers the animal, often scaring it off. Sometimes simply the presence of people can habituate an animal to hanging around people; with bears, this can lead to more aggressive behavior.

- **Let the animal's behavior guide your behavior.** If the animal appears twitchy, nervous, or points eyes and ears directly at you, back off: You're too close. The goal is to watch wild animals go about their normal business, rather than to see how they react to disruption. If you behave like a predator stalking an animal, the creature will assume you are one. Use binoculars and telephoto lenses for moving in close rather than approaching an animal.

- **Most animals tend to be more active in morning and evening.** These are also optimum times for photographing animals in better lighting.

- **Blend in with your surroundings.** Rather than wearing loud colors, wear muted clothing that matches the environment.

- **Relax.** Animals sense excitement. Move slowly around them because abrupt, jerky movements can startle them. Look down, rather than staring animals directly in the eye.

- **Don't get carried away.** If you're only watching for big, showy megafauna like bears and moose, you could miss a small carnivore like a short-tailed weasel.

- **Use field guides.** They'll help with identification and understanding the animal's behavior.

- **Animals use the North Fork roads for travel paths.** But don't expect to see them around every corner, due to the thick forests. If you see wildlife along a road, use pullouts or broad shoulders to drive completely off the road. Do not block the middle of the road. Use the car as a blind to watch wildlife, but keep pets inside. If you see a bear, you're better off just driving by slowly. Bear jams tend to condition the bruin to become accustomed to vehicles, one step toward getting into more trouble.

- Several **Glacier Institute** (406/755-1211, www.glacierinstitute.org) courses visit the North Fork for wildlife-watching.

the river's 59 miles (95 km) from the Canadian border to its confluence with the Middle Fork: the border, Ford, Polebridge, Coal Creek, Big Creek, Glacier Rim, and Blankenship. Flows peak in late May, with low water in August. In July, the average float time from the border to Blankenship is 16 hours, which most floaters tend to break into three days.

Flathead National Forest's **Glacier View Ranger District** (Hungry Horse Ranger Station, 406/387-3800, www.fs.usda.gov) can answer questions on floating the river and rules regarding permits, costs, camping, day use, waste containment, and fire scar prevention. It sells the *Three Forks of the Flathead Float Guide* ($13), which provides details on camping, rapids, and navigation; you can also download the maps from the website. This will help you respect the rights of private-property owners along the river.

OVERNIGHTS

All camps must be set up on the western shore rather than Glacier National Park's eastern shoreline. Camping is first-come, first-served only and is free in Flathead National Forest and on state lands. Round Prairie, on

1: mountain bikers on the Inside Road **2:** river rafter on the North Fork of the Flathead River

Glacier's bank, is the one exception; this back-country campground requires a permit, which you can pick up at the **Apgar Backcountry Permit Office** (406/888-7859 May-Oct., 406/888-7800 Nov.-Apr., www.nps.gov/glac, $7 pp/night, $40 advance reservation available mid-Mar.).

GUIDES

Several river rafting companies lead overnight trips down the North Fork; however, none base their operations in the North Fork Valley. All commercial outfitters begin their trips in West Glacier. Due to the Class II nature of the river, the float trips are great for families and kids.

RENTALS AND SHUTTLES

In Polebridge, **Polebridge Outfitters** (265 Polebridge Loop, 406/888-5229, www. polebridgemerc.com, $60-250) rents a paddle raft for six people and inflatable kayaks for one or two people. Rates include paddles and life jackets. The gear is in demand, so make reservations in advance.

Rubber rafts, inflatable kayaks, and overnight gear are available to rent in West Glacier from **Glacier Guides** (406/387-5555, https:// glacierguides.com). The company also runs shuttles for rafters on the North Fork of the Flathead River.

Boating and Paddling

The remote **Kintla Lake** and **Bowman Lake** (open June-Sept.) have prime paddling for kayaks, canoes, and paddleboards. Kintla allows only hand-propelled watercraft, while Bowman allows non-trailered electric motors of 10 horsepower or less. No gas-powered boats or Jet Skis are allowed on either lake, which makes their quiet waters appeal to paddlers. While both lakes have stellar paddling on calm days, their waters can kick up with lusty winds in minutes. For sailing or sailboarding, constrictive mountains create challenging conditions. Wildlife closures are marked with orange buoys at the head of each lake, where bald eagles nest.

All boaters and paddlers must pick up **permits** after an inspection at the station across from the Apgar boat ramp (7am-9pm daily June-Sept.) **before driving up the North Fork.** With a backcountry permit, paddlers can camp overnight in campgrounds at the heads of Kintla and Bowman Lakes. Be aware: The roads to Kintla and Bowman Lakes limit vehicle length (21 ft/6.4 m maximum; no trailers).

In Polebridge, **Polebridge Outfitters** (265 Polebridge Loop, 406/888-5229, www. polebridgemerc.com, $60-80) rents paddleboards and inflatable kayaks (single or double). Make reservations online.

Fishing

Anglers are attracted to the North Fork for its native fish: westslope cutthroat and bull trout. Be able to identify each, as they are catch-and-release only. Bull trout have pink or orange spots on their sides, and they lack black on their backs; cutthroats have a red slash under their jaw.

Kintla and **Bowman Lakes** are the main lakes accessible by car for fishing. Shorelines near their campgrounds rim with trails. For hikers, the three **Quartz Lakes** hop with native trout and whitefish. Along the Inside North Fork Road, most of the western creek drainages provide some fishing, with various degrees of accessibility. Fishing closures in the area include Upper Kintla Lake and Kintla Creek between the two Kintla Lakes, Bowman Creek above the lake, and Logging Creek between Logging and Grace Lakes.

The most popular North Fork Valley fishing is on the **North Fork of the Flathead River,** where seven river accesses (Canadian border, Ford, Polebridge, Coal Creek, Big Creek, Glacier Rim, and Blankenship) allow for fishing and raft launching. Anglers also fish around the Camas Bridge.

Several commercial outfitters guide overnight fishing trips on the North Fork River. All fishing outfitters base their operations out of West Glacier. Find rental gear in West Glacier, too.

LICENSES AND REGULATIONS

The North Fork River's high-water line on the eastern shore is Glacier National Park's western boundary. When fishing the North Fork River from the east bank, park regulations apply; when fishing from the west bank, state regulations apply. Inside the park, fishing licenses are not required, but outside the park, **Montana fishing licenses** (Montana residents: $21-31 season, $15 for 2 days; nonresidents: $50 for 2 days, $81 for 10 days, $111 season) are required for ages 12 through adults.

Purchase licenses at **Glacier Outdoor Center** (12400 U.S. 2 E., West Glacier, 406/888-5454 or 800/235-6781, https://glacierraftco.com) or Flathead Valley sporting shops **before driving up the North Fork.** Find fishing-license information and how to order licenses in advance online (www.fwp.mt.gov).

HUNTING

Hunting is illegal in Glacier National Park. But in the North Fork, Flathead National Forest holds popular deer, elk, and bird hunting grounds. Get regulations, seasons, and license info from **Montana Fish, Wildlife, and Parks** (www.fwp.mt.gov).

WINTER SPORTS

Cross-Country Skiing and Snowshoeing

Roads in the North Fork Valley convert to easy, avalanche-free **cross-country ski and snowshoe trails** in winter. But don't expect pristine smooth snow: The North Fork thrives as a winter habitat for moose, wolves, deer, elk, snowshoe hares, coyotes, and bobcats, whose tracks pockmark the roads. Grab a track identification book to help in deciphering the prints. The nearest ski and snowshoe rentals are in Flathead Valley.

Park at the Polebridge entrance station to ski to **Bowman Lake,** touring 0.5 mile (0.8 km) north on the Inside Road before climbing 6 miles (9.7 km) up to Bowman Lake's frozen shores. **Big Prairie, Inside Road,** and **Hidden Meadows** all provide other routes starting from the same point. For route descriptions, pick up a free brochure on skiing and snowshoeing from Apgar Visitor Center or online (www.nps.gov/glac).

For an overnight in Flathead National Forest, skiers traverse 12 miles (19.3 km) up Whale Creek Road to stay in Ninko Cabin on the flanks of Thompson-Seton Mountain. For information on this trip, call **Glacier View Ranger Station** (406/387-3800).

Snowmobiling

While snowmobiles are not permitted in Glacier, they are allowed in Flathead National Forest in the Whitefish Range, where snowfall piles up 6-12 feet (1.8-3.7 m) deep. December-April, snowmobilers ride unplowed roads heading west off the North Fork Road. The **Flathead Snowmobile Association** (www.flatheadsnowmobiler.com) grooms a few routes. **Glacier View Ranger Station** (406/387-3800) regulates snowmobile use, seasons, and closures, and it has maps; check for current conditions and restrictions. The nearest rentals are in Flathead Valley.

ENTERTAINMENT AND EVENTS

Instead of red, white, and blue marching bands, Polebridge's annual **Fourth of July Parade** has cross-dressers, beer-can draggers, bicycles, the 1956 Polebridge fire truck, and rafts. The more slightly off-kilter, better. Hundreds of people line the dirt main street for the noon parade that's really not a parade. Parking is a nightmare, and it's a two-for-one show as the parade goes up the street and then back down the same street. Enter for free; watch for free. Who's in charge? No one knows.

Live music happens outdoors at the **Northern Lights Saloon** (255 Polebridge Loop, Polebridge, 406/888-9963) in summer. Artists include solo musicians and bands.

Food

OUTSIDE THE PARK
Polebridge

A rustic solar-powered restaurant in a tiny, funky old log cabin built in 1912, the ★ **Northern Lights Saloon** (255 Polebridge Loop, 406/888-9963, www.thenorthernlightssaloon.com, 11am-9pm daily late May-mid-Sept., $10-30) is where hikers stop to celebrate with a beer, a glass of wine, or a cocktail, and then linger over a meal. Expect to relax over your meal rather than gobble and go; this is not a fast-food joint. The limited menu has vegetarian options, plus elk burgers and rainbow trout. Saturday night usually serves prime rib. The unique backwoods ambience is the draw. Some people even drive up the North Fork just to go to here. Outdoor seating makes for great people-watching, and live music happens frequently in summer.

For limited groceries, camping stove fuel, propane, fishing tackle, and beer, stop at the ★ **Polebridge Mercantile** (265 Polebridge Loop, 406/888-5105, https://polebridgemerc.com, daily Apr.-Oct., 7am-9pm summer, shorter hours in other seasons). You can pick up forgotten camping items and groceries, but don't expect a broad selection of choices. Hundreds of fresh-from-the-oven pastries, cookies, lunch breads, and cinnamon rolls based on recipes passed down through successive owners march out the door daily. Other treats include espresso and ice cream. Get deli sandwiches to-go for the road or trail.

Accommodations

OUTSIDE THE PARK

North Fork lodging is off the grid. With no electricity, power comes from generators or solar panels. Lights are propane, woodstoves provide heat, and phone lines only reach Polebridge. However, despite the rusticity, the State of Montana still charges a 7 percent bed tax. **Private cabins** sprinkle around the North Fork. Find options such as rustic one-roomers and log homes online at **VRBO** (www.vrbo.com) under "Polebridge."

Polebridge

Located 0.25 mile (0.4 km) south of the Merc and Northern Lights Saloon, the ★ **North Fork Hostel** (80 Beaver Dr., 406/888-5241, https://nfhostel.com, late May-early Sept., $30-80) offers a mix of hostel bunks, cabins, and unique accommodations. Reservations are strongly advised. The hostel may be off the electric grid, but far from "roughing it." A huge storage battery powers phone, fax, and Wi-Fi. Propane powers the lights, cooking stove, and refrigerator, with a few kerosene lights added in. Wood heats up the cedar hot tub. The hostel has a shared living room, fully equipped kitchen, outhouses, and baths with hot showers. Lodging options include mixed dorm bunks, private guest rooms, and an assortment of tepees, cabins, and a 1950s trailer called the Green Zucchini. Bring food, towels, and sleeping bags, or rent linens ($5).

The hostel also rents out the nearby wood-heated **Square Peg Ranch Cabin** ($100-160), which can sleep six people. The kitchen is equipped with propane lights, a fridge, and cooking range. Cold running water, solar-heated showers, and outhouses complete the rustic stay. Bring sleeping bags or sheets, food, towels, and containers to haul fresh drinking

---

1: Northern Lights Saloon in Polebridge **2:** Wurtz Cabin

water from the hostel. Minimum stay is three nights.

Located 4 miles (6.4 km) south of Polebridge, ★ **North Fork Cabins** (8954 North Fork Rd., 406/871-7717, polebridgecabins.com, May-Aug., $95-185) have propane heat, generator electricity, private baths with flush toilets and showers, and private fire pits. Named for Bowman and Kintla Lakes, the larger cabins sleep five and have kitchenettes. The porches have outstanding views. Numa Peak and Kootenay Cabins sleep three and lack kitchens. Rates are higher on weekends and holidays.

Polebridge Mercantile Cabins (265 Polebridge Loop, 406/888-5105, https:// polebridgemerc.com, $90-125) has four tiny, bare-bones cabins that have stoves, coolers, and outhouses, but no running water. You can get water at the Merc, and the stay comes with a breakfast voucher for the bakery.

North of Polebridge

For those looking to get away from it all, ★ **The Way Less Traveled Bed and Breakfast** (16485 North Fork Rd., 406/261-5880, www. thewaylesstraveled.com, year-round, $75-145) is about as remote as you can get and still have the comforts of civilization. Proprietors Paul and Nancy Winkler encourage guests to unplug in favor of soaking up nature. Located 17 miles (27 km) north of Polebridge and 3 miles (4.8 km) south of the Canadian border, the bed-and-breakfast has three themed guest rooms. Two queen rooms share a bath, but the king room has a private bath and deck. The B&B also has a cozy cabin with a deluxe outhouse and solar shower. Breakfast is served in the dining room surrounded by wildlife-watching windows or on the deck accompanied by loons singing on a nearby lake. A generator powers lights, hot water, satellite TV, and Wi-Fi.

Flathead National Forest

The **U.S. Forest Service** maintains six rental cabins scattered across the North Fork in **Flathead National Forest** (Glacier View Ranger District, Hungry Horse, 406/387-3800, www.fs.usda.gov/flathead, $40-75). With a three-night maximum stay, the cabins have beds, outdoor vault toilets, kitchens equipped with propane cookstoves, outdoor fire pits, and firewood. Bring water (no running water), bedding, and food. The cabins do not permit pets, tents, or RVs. Reservations are mandatory (877/444-6777, www.recreation.gov). After confirmation, you'll get the cabin combination. You must clean up at the end of your stay and pack garbage out with you.

Three cabins are available year-round. The deck at **Schnaus** yields sweeping views of Glacier's Livingston Range, making it a local favorite for its sunrises and sunset alpenglow. The cabin, which sleeps 12, has vehicle access right up to the front door and is less than 1 mile (1.6 km) from the North Fork River. Located on the North Fork River, **Ben Rover,** which sleeps eight and has drive-up access, is popular for skiing to Bowman Lake in winter, walking to the Merc in summer, and fishing right out the front door. The farthest north, **Wurtz Cabin,** which sleeps 12, is an old 1913 homestead with a large yard on the west side of the North Fork Road. The river is within a 15-minute walk.

Three small cabins offer seasonal lodging. In a drafty, tiny 1922 building perched atop a mountain, **Hornet Lookout** (mid-June-Oct.), which sleeps two, requires a 1-mile (1.6-km) hike from your vehicle. The lookout has a small cupola with spectacular views of Glacier. **Ford** (late May-Mar.), which was built in 1922 as part of the ranger station, sleeps eight. It has drive-up access and is adjacent to a river access site. **Ninko** (Dec.-Mar.), which sleeps seven, requires a 12-mile (19.3-km) ski or snowmobile trek to reach its remote forested setting.

Camping

National park campgrounds are rustic first-come, first-served camps. Small, private campgrounds lack hookups. If you require hookups and disposal stations, go to West Glacier or Columbia Falls.

INSIDE THE PARK

Glacier's seasonal **North Fork campgrounds** (406/888-7800, www.nps.gov/glac) are only accessible via rough dirt roads. **Vehicle lengths are limited** (21 ft/6.4 m maximum, no trailers) due to the narrow lane. The attraction is the quiet and smaller campgrounds, which have pit toilets, fire rings, and picnic tables. While the park prohibits firewood collecting in the campgrounds, you can collect dry, downed firewood on the North Fork roads once inside the park. Early September-October, Bowman and Kintla Campgrounds permit **primitive camping** ($10). Bring water or haul it from lakes and streams to boil or purify. These campgrounds are mosquito-filled in summer, serene in September, and closed in winter when the roads are buried in snow. Midsummer, Kintla and Bowman can fill up by 11am Friday-Saturday and midafternoon Sunday-Thursday. Check online for fill times for the previous several days and for past years' fill times to gauge your arrival to claim a spot.

Find up-to-date information on Glacier's campgrounds on the **official park website** (www.nps.gov/glac, under "campground status") and the **Recreational Access Display** (www.nps.gov/applications/glac/dashboard/).

Kintla Lake

At the foot of Kintla Lake, ★ **Kintla Lake Campground** (June-mid-Sept., $15) is 15 miles (24 km) north of Polebridge. The tiny 13-site campground is tucked under large trees, with hand-pumped water and small sites that are close together. One hiking trail leads up-lake and beyond to Upper Kintla Lake and Boulder Pass.

Bowman Lake

At the foot of Bowman Lake, ★ **Bowman Lake Campground** (late May-early Sept., $15) is 7 miles (11.3 km) from Polebridge. Its 48 sites, the largest of the North Fork's campgrounds, spread out under a mixed conifer forest. It has running water, and a five-minute walk leads to the lakeshore and the boat ramp. Trails connect to Quartz Lakes, Numa Lookout, Akokala Lake, and up Bowman Lake to Brown Pass.

Quartz Creek and Logging Creek

Two tiny campgrounds flank the Inside Road in the woods south of Polebridge. They are best for tent campers who can drive the rugged road. No running water is available, so bring your own or plan to purify stream water. Arrive by midafternoon to allow plenty of time to go elsewhere if either campground is full.

With seven campsites, **Quartz Creek Campground** (July-Nov., $10) sits 6 miles (9.7 km) southeast of Polebridge adjacent to Quartz Creek. From the campground, a 6.8-mile (10.9-km) rough trail with infrequent maintenance follows the creek up to Lower Quartz Lake. Located 8.3 miles (13.4 km) southeast of Polebridge, **Logging Creek Campground** (July-Sept., $10), adjacent to Logging Creek Ranger Station, has only seven sites. This is a popular site for anglers heading to Logging Lake.

OUTSIDE THE PARK
Polebridge

One small private campground around Polebridge has camping in summer. Add 7 percent tax to the rates. The **North Fork Hostel** (80 Beaver Dr., 406/888-5241, https://nfhostel.com, $25) accommodates tenters.

Flathead National Forest

Located 20 miles (32 km) north of Columbia Falls and 13 miles (20.9 km) from Apgar on North Fork Road, **Big Creek Campground** (Glacier View Ranger District, 406/387-3800, mid-May-late Sept., $16-24) is in Flathead National Forest. It can be accessed via a five-minute drive on a gravel road from the Camas Road park entrance. Several of the campground's 22 sites can accommodate 40-foot (12-m) RVs and trailers among large cottonwoods and dog-hair firs. Drinking water is available, along with vault toilets. Prime campsites line the North Fork of the Flathead River, with easy fishing access. You can collect firewood here, but by August the surrounding woods are scoured. Make reservations (877/444-6777, www.recreation.gov) six months in advance.

Transportation and Services

TRANSPORTATION
Driving and Parking

Plan on being friendly with ubiquitous dirt roads with potholes, washboards, and dust. Only a 6-mile (9.7-km) section of the Outside North Fork Road is paved around Home Ranch Bottoms. Forget public parking lots. Find parking at businesses and roadside in Polebridge. Be aware that the roads inside the national park limit vehicle length (21 ft/6.4 m maximum; no trailers).

SERVICES

You won't find strip malls or services up the North Fork. Forget the ATMs, post office, television, visitors centers, and shopping. Phone lines run only as far as Polebridge. The **Polebridge Mercantile** (265 Polebridge Loop) has a **pay phone** on its front porch, but it works intermittently. In most locations, **outhouses** and **vault toilets** take the place of flush toilets.

Gas and Repairs

Gas up before going up the North Fork. The gas sold at the **Polebridge Mercantile** (265 Polebridge Loop) is expensive. Vehicle repairs are not available; call Flathead Valley mobile vehicle services, which will charge by the mile to come to you.

Cell Phone and Internet Access

Locals head up the North Fork delighted to cut the technological umbilical cord. It's a place to get away from social media and phone calls with mostly nonexistent cell service. Internet access is only available on the **Polebridge Mercantile** computer or for guests at select lodging properties.

Emergencies

For emergencies, get to Polebridge to call 911 or contact a Glacier National Park ranger at the park entrance. The nearest hospitals are in the Flathead Valley: **Kalispell Regional Medical Center** (310 Sunny View Ln., Kalispell, 406/752-5111) and **North Valley Hospital** (1600 Hospital Way, Whitefish, 406/863-3500).

The **Polebridge Ranger Station** (406/888-7800, year-round) sits 1 mile (1.6 km) from Polebridge across the North Fork River at the park entrance. During summer, **Logging Creek Ranger Station** on the Inside North Fork Road is staffed, as are stations at **Bowman and Kintla Lakes;** however, these seasonal rangers may be out patrolling miles of backcountry.

Going-to-the-Sun Road

Historic Going-to-the-Sun Road is a testament to human ingenuity and nature's wonders. In the road's 50 miles (81 km), an incomparable diversity unfolds, with surprises around each corner.

Tunnels, switchbacks, arches, and a narrow two-lane highway cutting across precipitous slopes reveal feats of engineering. Cedar rainforests give way to windblown subalpine firs, broad lake valleys lead into glacial corridors, monstrous vertical cliff walls abut wildflower gardens, and waterfalls spew from every pore. Defying gravity, ragged peaks rake the sky, crowning all.

This National Historic Landmark and Historic Civil Engineering Landmark is a place to savor every nook and cranny. Oohs and aahs

Highlights

Look for ★ to find recommended sights, activities, dining, and lodging.

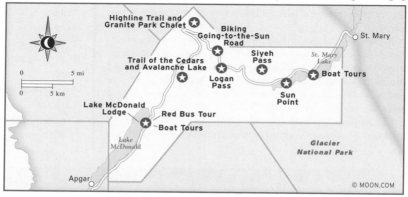

★ **Take a Red Bus Tour:** Ride over Logan Pass in style in 1937 vintage touring buses for superb views and perhaps a dousing from the Weeping Wall (page 107).

★ **See the park's two largest lakes by boat:** Hop aboard *Little Chief* to tour **St. Mary Lake** or the *DeSmet* to visit **Lake McDonald** (page 107).

★ **Visit Lake McDonald Lodge:** Sit on the back porch of this historic lodge. The rustic hunting motif harks back to an earlier park era (page 112).

★ **Touch the Continental Divide at Logan Pass:** At the apex of Going-to-the-Sun Road, waters stream from either side toward the Pacific and Atlantic Oceans (page 116).

★ **Take in the views from Sun Point:** This windy promontory is surrounded by dramatic peaks rising on both sides of St. Mary Lake (page 118).

★ **Follow the Trail of the Cedars and hike to Avalanche Lake:** Walk through the easternmost Pacific rainforest in the United States and then venture to a scenic subalpine lake (page 123).

★ **Hike the Highline Trail to Granite Park Chalet:** Follow a wildflower-packed trail clinging high on cliffs along the Garden Wall to a historic backcountry chalet where bear-watching is a worthy pastime (page 125).

★ **Climb to Siyeh Pass:** This is one of the most scenic and diverse trails in Glacier, loaded with colorful wildflowers and sedimentary strata (page 128).

★ **Bike Going-to-the-Sun Road:** Bicycle in spring before the road opens to cars or in summer, with the slow pace of your climb yielding intimate views (page 133).

punctuate every sweep in the road as stunning scenery unfolds. Stopping at myriad pullouts along the road, sightseers burn through scads of digital pixels. The sheer immensity of the glacier-chewed landscape leaves visitors gasping, "I can't fit it all in my photo."

To stretch your legs, well-signed short paths guide hikers through a dripping rainforest, along a glacial moraine, amid mountain goats, and beside a roaring waterfall. Those ready to put miles on their boots should tackle at least one of the longer high alpine trails, where you'll feel you've reached the apex of the world, sending your spirit soaring.

The Sun Road, as locals call it, is one place you won't want to miss. Its rugged beauty leaves a lasting impression.

PLANNING YOUR TIME

Snow, avalanches, and weather make Going-to-the-Sun Road unpredictable, although its western tail is plowed all winter to Lake McDonald Lodge. In the **lower elevations** of the road, campgrounds, lodging, and restaurants are generally open **June through September.** The alpine road segment from Avalanche to Rising Sun, including Logan Pass, opens when plows clear the road, repair winter damage, and reinstall log guardrails, sometime from mid-June to mid-July. Before driving, check the park's **Recreational Access Display** (www.nps.gov/applications/glac/dashboard/) for real-time status of the Sun Road, including weather, campground availability, and major parking lot availability. RVers and bicyclists need to be aware of road restrictions that apply to their mode of travel; find this information on the park website (www.nps.gov/glac).

You can sightsee the entire Sun Road over and back in **one day.** But you'll only have time for a short hike or two—if you can find parking. Without stopping for sightseeing, you'll need **two hours** to drive Going-to-the-Sun Road **one way** from Apgar to St. Mary. Packing a lunch alleviates waiting in restaurant lines; there are no food services in the alpine section. The Logan Pass parking lot fills to capacity from 8am to 5pm in summer. Consider taking a **tour bus** rather than driving yourself; that way you can absorb the scenery better, and your bus is guaranteed parking at Logan Pass and other stops. Be aware: On busy summer days, Going-to-the-Sun Road draws far more than double the amount of cars than parking spaces. Bring your patience and plan accordingly for sightseeing or hiking. Avid hikers and backpackers will want to spend **three days** in this area, although you can still reach trailheads here if you're staying elsewhere.

Coveted lodging locations on the Sun Road demand **reservations 13 months in advance.** For campgrounds, which are first-come, first served, plan to arrive at 8am or earlier to cruise for a spot or wait in line until a spot becomes available.

At low elevations around Lake McDonald and St. Mary Lake, summer temperatures usually average 70-85°F (21-29°C) during days and 45-49°F (7-9°C) at night. Logan Pass and higher elevation trails will encounter temperatures that are often 10-15°F (6-8°C) cooler. St. Mary is often windier than Lake McDonald, and on some days, the lakes may have beach weather while Logan Pass sits under a cloud. At the lakes, winter temperatures can waffle from just above freezing to -10°F (-23°C) during Arctic cold fronts with wind chills much lower. Snow falls usually November-April, but Logan Pass and higher elevation trails can have snow storms any month of the year.

HISTORY
Early Development

In 1895, Lake McDonald boomed with tourism brought by the railroad's arrival in West Glacier. Hauling a steamboat up from Flathead Lake, George Snyder shuttled guests from Apgar to his 12-room hotel, where Lake

Previous: Hidden Lake; Avalanche Gorge on Trail of the Cedars; Siyeh Pass Trail.

Going-to-the-Sun Road

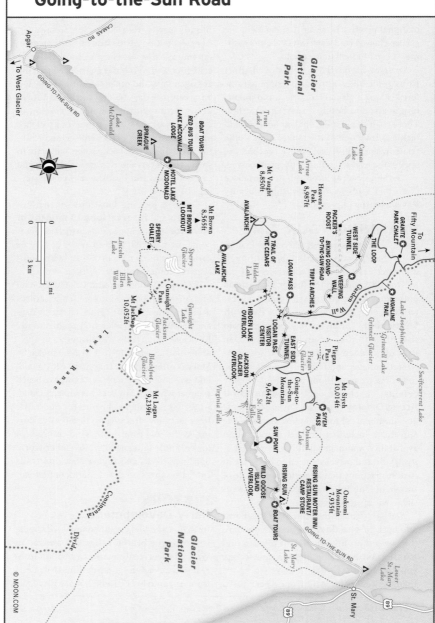

Apgar

To West Glacier

CAMAS RD

GOING-TO-THE-SUN RD

Glacier National Park

Lake McDonald

SPRAGUE CREEK

BOAT TOURS
RED BUS TOUR
LAKE MCDONALD LODGE

HOTEL LAKE MCDONALD

Trout Lake

Camas Lake

Arrow Lake

Heaven's Peak 8,987ft

Mt Vaught 8,850ft

MT BROWN LOOKOUT

Mt Brown 8,565ft

SPERRY CHALET

Sperry Glacier

Lincoln Lake

Lake Ellen Wilson

AVALANCHE

AVALANCHE LAKE

TRAIL OF THE CEDARS

Hidden Lake

HIDDEN LAKE OVERLOOK

Gunsight Pass

Gunsight Lake

Jackson Glacier

Mt Jackson 10,052ft

Blackfoot Glacier

Mt Logan 9,239ft

Lewis Range

Continental Divide

PACKER'S ROOST

WEST SIDE TUNNEL

BIKING GOING-TO-THE-SUN ROAD

WEEPING WALL

TRIPLE ARCHES

THE LOOP

Fifty Mountain

GRANITE PARK CHALET

To

Lake Josephine

HIGHLINE TRAIL

Grinnell Lake

Grinnell Glacier

Swiftcurrent Lake

LOGAN PASS

Mt Siyeh 10,014ft

Piegan Pass

SIYEH PASS

LOGAN PASS VISITOR CENTER

EAST SIDE TUNNEL

JACKSON GLACIER OVERLOOK

Going-to-the-Sun Mountain 9,642ft

Piegan Glacier

St. Mary Falls

Virginia Falls

SUN POINT

Otokomi Lake

Otokomi Mountain 7,935ft

WILD GOOSE ISLAND OVERLOOK

RISING SUN

BOAT TOURS

RISING SUN MOTER INN/ RESTAURANT/ CAMP STORE

St. Mary Lake

GOING-TO-THE-SUN RD

Glacier National Park

St. Mary

Lower St. Mary Lake

89

0   3 km

0   3 mi

© MOON.COM

Avoid the Crowds

Be aware that a busy midsummer day can draw 7,000 cars to Going-to-the-Sun Road, but parking spots are limited to far less than half that. Bring patience, and always have an alternate plan if you can't find parking where you want to go, including Logan Pass.

- During high season (mid-June-Aug.), the **Logan Pass parking lot** fills up by 8am. After that, cars must vacate before you can claim a space. There's no trolling for parking spots or even dropping people off to use the restrooms while you circle. If your goal is Logan Pass, get an early start and go straight there. For an evening alternative, arrive around 5pm when the parking lot clears out; with long lingering daylight and a sack dinner in your pack, you can hike to Hidden Lake Overlook with minimal people on the trail.

- If you need **restrooms** and can't get into the Logan Pass parking lot, the closest toilets are at Jackson Overlook or Sun Point on the east side or The Loop and near Logan Creek on the west side. Plan ahead to use facilities at Lake McDonald Lodge, all picnic areas, or Rising Sun before heading to Logan Pass in case you can't get in the parking lot.

- **Take a tour** instead of driving yourself. The red buses or Sun Tours are guaranteed parking at Logan Pass.

- If you are riding the shuttles to trailheads or Logan Pass, catch the earliest **morning shuttles** for shorter lines.

- **Parking spots** fill by 8:30am for trailheads for Trail of the Cedars, Avalanche Lake, and St. Mary and Virginia Falls. If you can't reach the trailhead early, then your alternative is to hop the free shuttle or go after crowds abate, usually beginning around 4:30pm. For evening hiking on these trails, make loads of noise for safety in bear country.

- To dodge heavy **traffic** and congested overlooks, drive the road to see the sunrise or sunset. As a bonus, you'll get better lighting for photos. Stop at sights such as Wild Goose Island for early morning light or Oberlin Bend for evening alpenglow. Depart your lodging at 6am for a morning drive, or go up to Logan Pass after 4:30pm to enjoy the lengthy evenings in July and August.

- Going-to-the-Sun Road is **open 24/7.** For exceptional dark star-filled skies, take a dusk drive to Logan Pass for stargazing on a moonless night.

McDonald Lodge currently sits. With Sperry Glacier's discovery a year later and funding from the railroad, Dr. Lyman Sperry and 15 of his students built the Gunsight Pass and Sperry spur trail to accommodate horse travel between St. Mary and Lake McDonald. While the west side surged with turn-of-the-20th-century tourism, on the east side, Roes Creek (Rose Creek at Rising Sun) boomed as a short-lived mining town that was vacated with the Alaska gold rush.

Lodges and Chalets

Under dubious circumstances, perhaps a poker game, John and Olive Lewis gained ownership of George Snyder's hotel in 1906.

Moving the old hotel, they built a cedar and stone lodge facing Lake McDonald. Opening in 1914, this Glacier Hotel imitated the Swiss theme of Great Northern Railway hostelries that were springing up park-wide. John Lewis spent his own money to cut part of the road from West Glacier along Lake McDonald, including grading and bridge-building. In 1922, the road reached Glacier Hotel, ballooning hotel visitation due to burgeoning automobile travel. In 1930, Great Northern Railway purchased Glacier Hotel and changed the name to Lake McDonald Lodge. Two years later, the railroad company sold the lodge to the National Park Service.

Meanwhile, Great Northern Railway

frenetically erected chalets between 1912-1914 at Sun Point, Gunsight Lake, and Sperry—all linked by trail over Gunsight Pass. A year later, Granite Park Chalet was added as a trail destination from Many Glacier Hotel and Sun Point. With packed bunk-bed dorms and canvas tents outside, Granite and Sperry Chalets housed nearly four times the number that each sleep today. Their popularity increased in the 1920s as wealthy visitors averaged 21 days touring on horseback with Park Saddle Horse Company. However, Gunsight Chalet lasted only five years, wiped out by an avalanche.

The 1932 opening of Going-to-the-Sun Road collided with the Great Depression and a love for auto travel, which hastened the demise of the chalets. Visitors traveling by horseback plunged; instead, auto drivers sought more affordable places to stay. In 1940, the railroad company built East Glacier Auto Cabins (now Rising Sun Motor Inn), where two people could rent a cabin without a shower for $1.75. Finally, World War II park closures, deteriorating buildings, and increased costs of supplying the chalets taxed the railroad company to the point where it razed Going-to-the-Sun Chalets and sold Sperry and Granite Park Chalets to the National Park Service for $1.

Building the Road

Nearly 20 years of planning and construction went into building Going-to-the-Sun Road, fueled by infatuation with the automobile. Various passes were proposed for the "Transmountain Highway," its original name, but the National Park Service selected Logan Pass. The plan called for 15 switchbacks up the west side, later replaced with one long switchback, and Congress appropriated $2 million for its construction.

Surveying the route required the tenacity to hang by ropes over cliffs and tiptoe along skinny ledges, perhaps causing the 300 percent crew turnover in three months. Over six seasons, three companies excavated rock using only small blast explosives and minimal power tools to create tunnels, bridges, the Triple Arches, and guard walls. With power equipment unable to reach the East Side Tunnel, crews cleared its 408-foot (124-m) length by hand-boring about 5 feet (1.5 m) per day.

In fall of 1932, the first automobile chugged over Logan Pass. The following July, over 4,000 people attended dedication ceremonies at Logan Pass to celebrate. The event ended with a peace ceremony for the Blackfeet, Kootenai, and Flathead people.

Although guardrails, surfacing, and grading were not completed until 1935, nearly 40,000 visitors flocked to the road in its first year despite its rough tread and the Great Depression. Until the late 1930s, crushed rock covered its surface. Finally, in 1938, the National Park Service embarked on a 14-year project to pave the scenic highway, which was completed at last in 1952.

Exploring Going-to-the-Sun Road

Going-to-the-Sun Road connects West Glacier and St. Mary with 50 miles (81 km) of one of the most scenic highways in the United States. Crossing Logan Pass at 6,646 feet (2,026 m) on the Continental Divide, the road links the two immense glacier-carved valleys of McDonald and St. Mary. From Lake McDonald, the road ascends 3,400 feet (1,036 m) to the pass; from St. Mary, it rises about 2,200 feet (671 m).

VISITORS CENTERS

The one place everyone wants to go is Logan Pass, but its visitors center is small, and the parking lot crowds by 8am. We all put up with the crowds because no one wants more pavement and a larger building impinging on the meadows. Unprepared visitors arrive expecting a resort atmosphere at **Logan Pass Visitor Center** (406/888-7800, 9am-7pm daily

Where Can I Find...?

- **Cell reception:** Most of the Sun Road does not get cell service due to surrounding peaks. **Granite Park Chalet** has cell service, but be aware that many visitors go there to get away from technology, so be discreet in your phone use. **Public pay phones** are at **Lake McDonald Lodge** and **Rising Sun Motor Inn.** You can purchase cards for the pay phones at the camp stores.

- **Drinking water:** There are **water bottle refill stations** at Lake McDonald Lodge, Logan Pass, and Rising Sun. You can also get water in the **campgrounds:** Sprague Creek, Avalanche, and Rising Sun.

- **Food:** Restaurants and camp stores that sell food are located only at **Lake McDonald Lodge** and **Rising Sun Motor Inn** on Going-to-the-Sun Road. No food or drinks are sold at Logan Pass.

- **Gas:** No gas is available on Going-to-the-Sun Road. Gas up in **West Glacier** or **St. Mary** before driving up the road.

- **Restrooms:** Toilets are few and far between on this historic highway, and popular areas have big lines. **Flush toilets** are available at Sprague Creek Picnic Area, Lake McDonald Lodge, Logan Pass Visitor Center, and Rising Sun. **Vault toilets** are available at Avalanche Picnic Area, Logan Creek, The Loop, Logan Pass, Jackson Glacier Overlook, and Sun Point. Only the campgrounds and lodges have **running water** for washing hands.

- **Shuttle stops:** Shuttle stops are located at all **lodges, campgrounds, Logan Pass,** and most **trailheads** on Going-to-the-Sun Road. They are also at Apgar Village, Apgar Visitor Center, and St. Mary Visitor Center.

- **Wi-Fi:** Wi-Fi is available in **lodges,** but for guest use only. The closest public Wi-Fi is at **Apgar Visitor Center** and **St. Mary Visitor Center.**

mid-June-Aug., hours shorten Labor Day-mid-Sept.), but it's a seasonal outpost with an information desk, a few displays, and a tiny **Glacier National Park Conservancy bookstore** (406/888-5756, https://glacier.org).

While a fireplace crackles upstairs on cold days, one bench allows only a few to snuggle up to its heat. Flush toilets are available downstairs and vault toilets at the parking lot. The center has a water bottle refill station, but no food or beverage sales. Due to the elevation, expect harsher weather including wind, rain, and snow even in August. Don't be surprised if you left the lowlands in sunny summer only to arrive at Logan Pass in winter.

ENTRANCE STATIONS

Both ends of Going-to-the-Sun Road have entrance stations, at **West Glacier** and **St. Mary.** Staffed during daylight hours in summer and on weekends only fall-spring, the stations hand out national park maps and the *Waterton-Glacier Guide*, the park's newspaper, updated twice annually. If you miss working hours, you can use the self-pay cash-only kiosks, on the right just beyond the booths. If you don't have an annual pass, get a seven-day pass ($35 per vehicle, $30 per motorcycle, $20 per biker, hiker, or pedestrian in summer; winter rates drop to $25, $20, and $15).

SHUTTLES AND TOURS

Taking shuttles and tours to Logan Pass are the way to go. Even when parking lots are full, tour buses are **guaranteed parking** at the pass, and shuttles have designated stops.

Shuttles

Going-to-the-Sun Road shuttles (406/888-7800, www.nps.gov/glac, 9am-5pm daily July-late Sept., free) enable point-to-point hiking on some of Glacier's most

spectacular trails. Due to their popularity, boarding lines of an hour or more often form. But going car-free to trailheads outweighs disappointments of full parking lots. The shuttles do not come with interpretive guides like the bus tours. The shuttles stop at designated locations: trailheads, campgrounds, picnic areas, lodges, and Logan Pass. Get on or off at any of the stops denoted by signs, each one featuring a different animal print. For Logan Pass, be sure to take a day pack with water, snacks, and extra clothing for fast-changing weather. Some shuttles also have bike racks, and most are wheelchair-accessible.

On the west side, shuttles depart every 15-30 minutes. Heading east, Avalanche serves as a transfer stop, where you can then board a shuttle to Logan Pass. From Apgar Visitor Center to Logan Pass takes 90 minutes or more; from Avalanche takes 45 minutes or longer. From locations on the Sun Road, you can also take shuttles to Apgar and back.

On the east side, shuttles depart every 30-40 minutes to run between St. Mary Visitor Center and Logan Pass. The ride to Logan Pass takes about one hour with stops.

The shuttle system is slated for **expansion,** adding longer hours and more stops. Check online (www.nps.gov/glac) for the current status.

For point-to-point hikers on the Highline and Piegan Pass Trails, Xanterra runs a **shuttle** (855/733-4522, www.glaciernationalparklodges.com, 4 times each way daily early June-mid-Sept., one-way $7-14, first-come, first-served). This service links Many Glacier Hotel and Swiftcurrent Motor Inn with St. Mary Visitor Center.

★ Red Bus Tour

In historic style, red jammer buses tour visitors over Going-to-the-Sun Road in vintage 1930s White Motor Company sedans operated by **Xanterra** (855/733-4522, www.glaciernationalparklodges.com, daily mid-June-mid-Oct., adults $46-106, children half price). On good-weather days, the jammers (tour bus drivers known for their storytelling) roll the canvas tops back for spectacular views of the Continental Divide. Without a roof, it's one of the most scenic ways to feel the expanse of the glacier-carved terrain. From Lake McDonald Lodge, Rising Sun Motor Inn, Apgar Visitor Center, and St. Mary Visitor Center, tours depart daily to explore Going-to-the-Sun Road and Logan Pass: The Crown of the Continent tour takes a full day, but half-day Logan Pass tours depart multiple times daily. Evening tours are available in July-August. Fees do not include meals, taxes, park entrance fees, and gratuities. Reservations are required.

Blackfeet Bus Tour

A Blackfeet-led tour provides a different perspective, with emphasis on the Blackfeet people's cultural and natural history. **Sun Tours** (406/732-9220 or 800/786-9220, www.glaciersuntours.com, June-Sept., adults $60-70, kids 6-12 $35) drives air-conditioned 25-passenger coaches with extra-big windows for taking in the massive mountains on Going-to-the-Sun Road. Four-hour Logan Pass tours depart daily from St. Mary (9:30am) with a Rising Sun pickup shortly after. The tour goes up the east side of Going-to-the-Sun Road, explores Logan Pass, and drives down the west side to Big Bend to see the Weeping Wall before returning. Make reservations at least one day in advance. Westside tours depart Apgar Visitor Center at 9am. Meals, park entrance fees, and gratuities are not included.

★ Boat Tours

Lake McDonald and St. Mary, the park's largest lakes, dominate the lowlands along the Sun Road. **Glacier Park Boat Company** (406/257-2426, https://glacierparkboats.

1: the *DeSmet* on Lake McDonald 2: shuttle stop along Going-to-the-Sun Road 3: Logan Pass Visitor Center

Red Buses

Historic jammer buses tour Going-to-the-Sun Road.

Red buses are Glacier icons. Built by Ohio's White Motor Company specifically for national park touring, the red buses became a symbol of the nation's western parks. Red bus fleets disappeared from parks like Yosemite, Yellowstone, and Grand Canyon by the 1950s. Today, Glacier is the only park that has steadfastly held on to its 33 scarlet prizes.

The canvas tops of the buses roll back to create an open-air touring car, so guests ride in historic style over Going-to-the-Sun Road, covering up with blankets if temperatures cool down. Nicknamed "jammers" or "gear jammers" for the tremendous noise their gears made while shifting, the vintage 25-foot-long (7.6-m), 17-passenger vehicles first drove Glacier's curvy roads in 1936 as the park's second generation of touring sedans. Decades later, as automatic transmissions replaced the manual transmissions and power steering eased driving Going-to-the-Sun Road's curves, jammers continued to tour folks through Glacier until 1999, when safety concerns sidelined the red rigs.

The fleet was donated to the National Park Foundation, which contracted with Ford Motor Company to rehabilitate the vehicles. One was kept intact for historical purposes. For the others, Ford kept the historical appearance, but converted them to run on gasoline or propane. Check out a jammer grill up close to see both White and Ford logos.

Owned now by Glacier National Park and maintained by the park's concessionaire, Xanterra, the red buses each log about 10,000 miles (16,093 km) per summer. The buses are currently rotating through another rehabilitation to add replicas of historic dashboard gauges and an electrical hybrid system to reduce fuel use. Wood frames and specialized components must be crafted by hand. In winter, the buses are housed in a climate-controlled facility in Columbia Falls.

com) runs boat tours on both. Make advance reservations by phone with a credit card or buy tickets at the boat docks up to three days in advance. Some have ranger naturalists aboard.

At the boat dock behind Lake McDonald Lodge, hop on the historic *DeSmet* (adults $23, kids $11) for a one-hour tour. Tours depart at 11am, 1:30pm, 3pm, 5:30pm, and 7pm daily mid-May-late September, although early and late cruises end on Labor Day. With a 90-passenger capacity, the 1930s-vintage wooden boat motors to the lake's core, where surrounding snow-clad peaks pop into sight.

Go for a prime seat on the top deck; bring a jacket for marginal weather.

At the Rising Sun boat dock on St. Mary Lake, catch a ride on *Joy II* or *Little Chief* (adults $34, kids $17) as it braves the lake's choppy waters. Views of Sexton Glacier and Wild Goose Island can't be beat, but be ready for some healthy wind. Daily departures launch for 90-minute cruises at 10am, noon, 2pm, 4pm, and 6:30pm daily mid-June-early September. See Baring Falls at a stop, or take a guided two-hour hike to St. Mary Falls.

TOP EXPERIENCE

Driving Tour

Of all the driving tours in Glacier National Park, **Going-to-the-Sun Road,** the 50-mile (81-km) historic transmountain highway bisecting Glacier's heart, stands in a class by itself. For some, scary tight curves that hug cliff walls produce white-knuckle driving. But for most, its beauty, diversity, color, flora, fauna, and raw wildness will leave an impression like no other. For that reason, many park visitors drive it more than once during their stay. For big waterfall shows and snow left from winter, drive it in late June or early July. For alpine wildflowers, go in late July or early August. For fewer crowds, go mid-September-mid-October.

From July through August, expect crowds around Avalanche, The Loop, Oberlin Bend, Logan Pass, Lunch Creek, Siyeh Bend, St. Mary Falls, and Sun Point. To avoid the hordes, drive in early morning or early evening, when lighting is better for photography and wildlife is more active. In midsummer, the Logan Pass parking lot fills by 8am. The park service controls the entrance, admitting a car only when one departs. If the parking lot is full, forgo Logan Pass for the time being and return later in the day. While pullouts are 0.5 mile (0.8 km) east and west of the pass, the shoulderless road does not afford safe walking to the pass, and tromping across the fragile meadows is taboo.

Although you can drive its 50 miles (81 km) in two hours with no stops, most visitors take all day. Construction, sightseeing, and traffic slow travel. Don't be anxious with it; just sit back and enjoy the view. Pack drinking water, snacks, and lunch to avoid frustration. Most restaurants around Glacier sell box or sack lunches. The road passes through a wonderland whose development has been kept in check; no one wants to see more buildings.

SEASON AND HOURS

Going-to-the-Sun Road is open 24 hours daily mid-June through mid-October...usually. Weather, construction, fires, and snow can affect its status. Weather, plowing, and sometimes construction will dictate the spring opening, which has no set date. The earliest opening of the Sun Road was May 16 while its latest opening was July 13 due to snowpack. In years with heavy snow and stormy springs, Logan Pass tends to open mid-June or later. During summer the road may close temporarily for snowstorms, washouts, accidents, or fires. The park regularly updates **road status reports** (406/888-7800, www.nps.gov/glac).

In fall, the road usually closes in mid-October, baring construction requiring an earlier closure. Heavy snowfall can also close the road earlier.

In spring or fall, when parts of the Sun Road are closed to vehicles for construction, plowing, or snow, bicyclists and hikers can tour the road, especially on weekends when crews may not be working. Before biking the road, check by phone or online for status, as schedules and conditions change daily.

Snow buries the Sun Road in winter. The usual vehicle closure runs from Lake McDonald Lodge to St. Mary late October-spring, but cross-country skiers and snowshoers trek the lowland corridors where avalanche danger is minimal.

VEHICLE RESTRICTIONS

Large vehicles are restricted on Going-to-the-Sun Road **between Avalanche**

Driving Going-to-the-Sun Road and Logan Pass

DRIVING TIPS

- Follow posted **speed limits,** and turn on your **headlights.**

- Take **lunch, snacks,** and **drinks.** Between Lake McDonald Lodge and Rising Sun, no food or drinks are sold.

- Watch for **bicyclists.** Although bicycle restrictions are in effect during July and August on the road's west side, the narrow roadway, lack of shoulders, and curves squeeze cyclists. Show them courtesy by slowing down to ease around them.

- Expect **construction delays.** Seasonal repair work can reduce traffic to a single lane.

- Check for **closures.** Heavy rain, snowstorms, fires, and accidents may close portions of the road. Entrance and ranger stations as well as lodges have current updates on the road status. You can also call 406/888-7800 or check the **Recreational Access Display** (www.nps.gov/applications/glac/dashboard/) for real-time status of the road, including weather and parking lot availability.

- Be prepared for all types of **weather.** Sunny skies may prevail in the valleys while visitors at Logan Pass creep along slowly in a dense fog on icy pavement.

- Passengers with a **fear of heights** should sit on the driver's side of the car for ascending the west side and descending the east. This will put you farthest from the cliff edges.

- **Cell phones** get little or no service on the Sun Road. Turn them off and enjoy the views.

- Bring **patience,** and prepare for delays.

SIGNS OF A ROOKIE SUN ROAD DRIVER

- **Burning brake smell.** Use second gear to slow your speed on descents rather than riding the brakes down the mountain.

- **Dangling extension mirror.** Retract or remove those extension mirrors for fifth-wheels or trailers before driving the narrow west side below Logan Pass.

- **Center-line hugger.** Stay in your own lane. You're more apt to scrape another vehicle on the skinny road than drive off the cliff. Acrophobes should let someone else drive.

- **Traffic slug.** Rather than holding up traffic by stopping in the road to take pictures, use pullouts.

Campground and Rising Sun. Because the road is narrow and has overhangs, **vehicles must be less than 21 feet (6.4 m) in length, 10 feet (3 m) high, and 8 feet (2.4 m) wide.** These dimensions include side mirrors, bumpers, and bike racks. Remember to retract side extension mirrors; you'll see broken ones in the gutter claimed by cliff walls. Even though smaller truck-camper units may be allowed, drivers will feel pinched on the skinny road.

ROAD CONSTRUCTION

Maintenance is interminable on Going-to-the-Sun Road. Avalanches, torrential downpours, and snows constantly wreak havoc. Summer snowstorms and heavy rains cause washouts that require annual repairs. A warming climate has turned loose snow avalanches into wet slabs that tear off rock guard walls. Because snowy winters constrict repairs to 4-6 months, summer means construction, which may reduce driving to one skinny lane in places. Road construction is a fact of life, but it's amazing to see repair action in this cliff-ridden environment far different from a normal highway. Expect them and enjoy the scenery while you wait.

Going-to-the-Sun Road's recent $270 million rehabilitation project, completed in 2019, addressed critical repairs for weather damage plus wear and tear from over a half-million vehicles that travel the road annually. The work has improved road safety, pavement, parking, guardrails, drainage, cracks, and deteriorating roadbeds, all while maintaining the historic character, fabric, and width of the road.

PLOWING

Every April, snowplows take to Going-to-the-Sun Road to heave more than 100,000 cubic yards of snow off the pavement. It's a big deal. Avalanche piles range 30-50 feet (9-15 m) thick from The Loop to Logan Pass. Just east of the pass, a 50- to 80-foot-deep (15- to 24-m) snowdrift, called the Big Drift, clings to a 40-degree slope. Plowing takes several months. Up to 30 equipment operators, mechanics, and snow specialists dig in with more than 20 machines: excavators, bulldozers, sweepers, loaders, and rotary blowers.

More than 60 avalanche swaths between The Loop and Siyeh Bend smash snow onto the road. Sometimes crews replow the same pavement over and over, or plow themselves out at night to go home. Heavy rains, fog, and whiteouts also hamper progress. Debris cleanup and installation of more than 463 removable steel-backed log rails add to the challenge.

Unfortunately, the changing climate in Glacier is affecting the annual spring plowing of the Sun Road. With warmer nighttime temperatures failing to drop below freezing, the snowpack does not solidify in its daily cycle. The softer snow results in heavy, wet slab avalanches that crash onto the Sun Road, endangering plow crews and damaging the already cleared roadway. These conditions make plowing dangerous. So why not just plow it open before the nighttime temps heat up? If the road is plowed too early and those avalanches come down as huge slabs rather than loose snow, they tear up the road, which adds monstrous repair costs.

If the road doesn't open by mid-June, everyone gets nervous, from local businesses to the governor of Montana; local economies are directly tied to the road's opening. Glacier National Park's website tracks plow progress with daily reports (www.nps.gov/glac) and photos (www.flickr.com/photos/glaciernps).

Sights

The following Going-to-the-Sun Road sights are listed as visitors see them driving from the West Entrance Station to St. Mary Entrance Station; those driving from St. Mary should work backwards. Use signs and your park map to locate sights. *Going-to-the-Sun Road Driving Guide* (Glacier National Park Conservancy, 406/892-3250, https://glacier.org, $10) adds more stops and detail, plus has a large map.

LAKE MCDONALD

The largest lake in the park, **Lake McDonald** is hard to miss since it is 10 miles (16.1 km) long. It fills a valley hollowed out by a monstrous, several-thousand-foot-deep glacier. Lining the trough, **Howe** and **Snyder Ridges** are lateral moraines left from that ice-age bulldozer. Today, the lake's water plummets to a frigid depth of 472 feet (144 m). Hugging the southeastern shore, the road has frequent **pullouts** for photos, rock-skipping, or relaxation; the best pullouts are midway between Apgar and Sprague Campground. If glassy waters reflect Stanton Peak, snag a photo.

★ LAKE MCDONALD LODGE

At Lake McDonald's east end, the historic **Lake McDonald Lodge** was designed to resemble a hunting lodge. The tall, stately cedar-log lobby cluttered with stuffed goats and mounted heads of bighorn sheep, deer, elk, and moose is a taxidermist's delight or an animal-rights activist's nightmare. Look for the woodland caribou still represented among the furry creatures here, even though it no longer exists in the park. Because this National Historic Landmark was built prior to the road, the front door actually opens lakeside, facing the original boat approach.

LOWER MCDONALD FALLS

Shortly after Lake McDonald Lodge, a left turn goes on North Lake McDonald Road. After crossing McDonald Creek, park at the trailhead on the right to meander on a **hard-surface accessible trail** (0.6 mi/1 km rt, 30 min, easy) on a path through the mossy forest to roaring **Lower McDonald Falls.**

MCDONALD CREEK

Originating near the Continental Divide, **McDonald Creek** is the longest river in the park at 25.8 miles (41.5 km) and definitely more than a creek, but let's not quibble about nomenclature. The Sun Road follows the river for 7 miles (11.3 km) along tumbling rapids and waterfalls. When stopping for a look, be extremely cautious of hazardous slippery rocks. Unseen algae, mosses, and swift cold waters have been lethal for the unwary. At **Upper McDonald Creek Falls,** wooden stairs descend to observation platforms where you can watch water roiling through scoured rock. At **Red Rocks,** an **accessible graded path** goes to a wooden overlook above the large rock slabs that constrict the river.

TRAIL OF THE CEDARS

At Avalanche, **Trail of the Cedars** runs through a rainforest, the easternmost in the country. A **wheelchair-accessible boardwalk** and **hard-surface trail** (0.9 mi/1.4-km, 30-45 min, easy) passes water-carved Avalanche Gorge. Grandfather 500-year-old western red cedars, hemlocks, and towering black cottonwoods form a dense canopy that cools the forest floor, where mosses, lichens, Pacific yew, and devil's club grow in the rich duff. Some topple over from heavy rain, snow, and wind.

AVALANCHE PATHS

Between Avalanche and Logan Creek, the road sneaks through a slim corridor below the **Glacier Wall** and **Mount Cannon,** which are loaded with **avalanche paths.** Snow, set in motion thousands of feet above, roars down gullies, uprooting trees and snapping them like toothpicks. In early summer, scour the slope for remnants of avalanches: ice, snow, and rock rubble piled up. Grizzly and black bears forage for carcasses along these avalanche paths in hopes of stumbling across some unfortunate mountain goat. Bring binoculars or spotting scopes to aid in bear-watching from a safe distance.

WEST SIDE TUNNEL

An engineering marvel, the **West Side Tunnel** is 192 feet (58.5 m) long, with two stunning alcoves framing Heavens Peak. Early in the season, the alcoves drip with thin-sheeted waterfalls; hop through the spray to reach the dry, rock-hewn guardrails. Photographers especially enjoy working the alcoves into framing pictures of Heavens Peak. To walk to the alcoves, park in pullouts below the tunnel. Convertible drivers should beware of splatters from the early summer waterfall on the tunnel's uphill side.

1: bighorn sheep at Big Drift **2:** Lake McDonald Lodge **3:** McDonald Creek **4:** view of Bird Woman Falls from Going-to-the-Sun Road

The Continental Divide

At Logan Pass, you can take your photo next to a sign that says you're atop the Continental Divide. But what is it?

The Continental Divide runs the length of North America from Alaska and the Yukon to Mexico. Along the Rocky Mountains, it is the highest point in the land, dividing stream runoff in two directions: westward to the Pacific and eastward to Hudson Bay and the Gulf of Mexico. In Glacier National Park, the Continental Divide runs along the top of the Livingston Range from Canada south to Trapper Ridge and West Flattop, where it leaps to the Lewis Range.

To cross the Continental Divide, drive over Logan Pass or Marias Pass. You can hike across the divide on several passes: Brown, Swiftcurrent, Hidden Lake, Gunsight, Cut Bank, Dawson, Two Medicine, and Firebrand. Beginning in New Mexico, the 3,100-mile (4,989-km) Continental Divide Trail ends here, with its last 110 miles (177 km) in Glacier National Park.

Glacier's Continental Divide also stands in a class by itself, for it houses a tri-oceanic divide. It's the only one in the United States. (Western Canada's Mount Columbia is the continent's other significant three-way oceanic divide.) Not particularly high by Glacier's standards, Triple Divide Peak stands at only 7,397 feet (2,255 m) above sea level. But its placement on the Continental Divide with connecting ridge spurs splits waters in three directions: Hudson Bay Creek, Atlantic Creek, and Pacific Creek. Their names cite their eventual destinations via the Saskatchewan, Missouri, and Columbia Rivers.

THE LOOP

Going-to-the-Sun Road has one massive hairpin turn known as **The Loop.** With parking lots both below and above the switchback, it's a popular stop for views and a trailhead to Granite Park Chalet. Across the valley, the 8,987-foot (2,739-m) **Heavens Peak** makes a stunning backdrop for a family photo. Early in the season, the peak will be snow-covered; by late August, only a few snowfields remain. In 2003 the **Trapper Fire** blew through The Loop; evidence of the burn lingers in skeletal trees.

GLACIATION

Between Alder Creek and Haystack Falls, stop at one of the **pullouts** to peek down McDonald Valley. Once filled with several-thousand-foot-thick ice, the valley's U shape shows the gouging, scouring, and carving of the behemoth glacier, known as **glaciation,** as it chugged around the Glacier Wall approximately two million years ago. Through the trough, McDonald Creek courses 26 miles (42 km) and ends at Lake McDonald. Test your vertigo by gazing 2,500 feet (762 m) below; you'll see Going-to-the-Sun Road, with cars looking tiny like ants as they drive the narrow corridor.

BIRD WOMAN AND HAYSTACK FALLS

About 2 miles (3.2 km) past The Loop, look for the sign marking **Bird Woman Falls.** Many assume the sign denotes the cascade crossing under the road. That stair-step waterfall is actually **Haystack Creek,** whose ledges evolved from eroding layers of Belt Sea sedimentary rock created 800 million to 1.6 billion years ago. To see Bird Woman Falls, look across the valley for waters tumbling nearly 500 feet (152 m) from a hanging valley, lounging like a hammock between Mount Oberlin and Mount Cannon. Early summer runoff pumps both falls full of water that dwindles to late August trickles.

1: Weeping Wall in early summer **2:** Sunrift Gorge at the base of the Siyeh Pass Trail **3:** Wild Goose Island on St. Mary Lake

WEEPING WALL AND BIG BEND

As its name implies, the **Weeping Wall** does weep, but it's a moody thing. In early summer the wall wails profusely, enough to douse cars driving the inside lane. Roll up windows unless you want a shower. In August, drips slow to a trickle. At the Weeping Wall, the road affords no room to pull over; instead, drive ahead into the bowl named **Big Bend** to find parking on both sides of the road. Avalanches careen from Mount Gould into Big Bend, often leaving snow until mid-July.

TRIPLE ARCHES

One of the most striking engineering marvels on Going-to-the-Sun Road, **Triple Arches** requires a slow drive to see, for no pullouts offer a view. You can see this feature only driving uphill, as it is behind downhill traffic. Approximately 1.5 miles (2.4 km) past Big Bend, you'll come upon the arches abruptly. Start watching for them as you enter some very narrow S-turns. As you drive over the arches, don't think about the stonework repairs that suspend them.

GARDEN WALL

In the 3 miles (4.8 km) from Big Bend to Logan Pass, the peaks above the road form an arête, a wall carved by glaciers on two sides. Below its top cliffs, wildflower meadows bloom with every color of the rainbow: white cow parsnip, pink spirea, yellow columbine, purple nodding onion, and blue gentian. You may pass more than 30 varieties of plants. For this reason, this wild botanical wonderland has been dubbed the **Garden Wall.** For a better look at the Garden Wall, hike the Highline Trail from Logan Pass.

OBERLIN BEND OVERLOOK

As Going-to-the-Sun Road climbs its final mile to Logan Pass, it sweeps around a large curve below Mount Oberlin. Park on the uphill lane side for the wheelchair-accessible path to **Oberlin Bend Overlook.** Mountain goats wander in the subalpine fir thickets; look for newborns with only nubbins for horns. The overlook provides the best spot for photographing the road's west-side climb plus the Continental Divide and peaks marching toward Canada. Look far north for **Mount Cleveland,** the park's highest peak.

TOP EXPERIENCE

★ LOGAN PASS

Logan Pass sits atop the **Continental Divide** at 6,646 feet (2,026 m). With its altitude and location between mountainous hulks, weather can be chilly even in midsummer. For evidence, look at the gnarled trees, growing low in krummholz or thick mats for protection against the elements. Explore the visitors center and scan surrounding slopes for goats, bighorn sheep, and bears. In June skiers and snowboarders hike the flanks of Mount Clements for turns. In late July, the pink alpine laurel, paintbrush, and monkeyflower reach their prime. Logan Pass contains more than 30 rare plants and mosses. Meadows at this elevation are fragile, with short-lived flora, so stick to the paths. On the paved trails around the visitors center, special interpretive signs with hand-cranked speakers appeal to kids. Two must-do trails depart from Logan Pass: Hidden Lake and the Highline Trail. You may also see the National Park Service "Bark Ranger" in action; for wildlife safety, the trained border collie herds bighorn sheep and mountain goats away from high traffic areas and confrontations with humans.

BIG DRIFT

Those driving when the road first opens get a treat just east of Logan Pass: **Big Drift** towers on both sides of the road, making a thin corridor bounded by immense snow walls. Winds deposit heavy snows in this zone just east of Logan Pass. At a record 98 feet (30 m) thick, Big Drift remains the last obstacle for

1: waterfall and Triple Arches on Going-to-the-Sun Road **2:** Logan Pass

1

2

spring road clearing. By August, snow piles disappear.

LUNCH CREEK

Spilling from a cirque between Piegan and Pollock Mountains, **Lunch Creek** makes for a scenic stop at the first bend east of Logan Pass. Sans picnic tables, the pullout's rock guard wall serves as a good impromptu lunch counter. Drag out your binoculars; often bighorn sheep cruise the slopes above, but they're hard to see with their camouflage tan matching the rocks. Fed by a glacier melting into an underground stream, waterfalls spew from the side of Piegan Mountain.

EAST SIDE TUNNEL

Crews excavated entirely by hand the 408 feet (124 m) of the **East Side Tunnel**, the larger of the road's two tunnels. For safety, flip on your headlights. To stop for photos, drive to the downhill side to find pullouts, which are also good stops for spotting bighorn sheep and shooting **Going-to-the-Sun Mountain,** from which the road acquired its name.

SIYEH BEND

Below Going-to-the-Sun Mountain, the road swoops through **Siyeh Bend** with parking above and below the giant curve. A trailhead leads to Piegan and Siyeh Passes via Preston Park, a meadowland of fuchsia paintbrush and purple fleabane. For a short stroll, walk up the creek crossing under the road to the junction of two creeks. The short walk passes gorgeous wildflower blooms in late July. Siyeh Bend (*Siyeh* means "mad wolf") is named for the 10,014-foot (3,052-m) barren peak towering above. From the uphill side of the bend, you can also see Blackfoot Glacier to the south.

JACKSON GLACIER OVERLOOK

This is the best view of a glacier from Going-to-the-Sun Road, but binoculars are handy to aid vision. Although trees creep higher around **Jackson Glacier Overlook,** you can still spot Jackson Glacier 6 miles (9.7 km) away. Jackson Glacier joined its neighboring Blackfoot Glacier in the early 1900s, but the two glaciers melted into separate ice fields by 1939. A trail departs here for Gunsight Lake and Pass. More views are available in the next several pullouts east.

REYNOLDS CREEK FIRE

In summer 2015, the **Reynolds Creek Fire** burned from Jackson Overlook to Rising Sun along 7 miles (11.3 km) of Going-to-the-Sun Road, opening up views of mountains and St. Mary Lake. The road cuts through patches of heavy burn and lighter flares from the 4,850-acre (1,963-hectare) fire. By the following summer, shooting stars, paintbrush, and false hellebore appeared across the burn, while woodpeckers, wind, and snow started peeling blackened bark from trees.

SUNRIFT GORGE

Stroll 75 feet (23 m) uphill to see the narrow canyon called **Sunrift Gorge.** Baring Creek cascades through the dark gorge like a knife slicing cake. The 2015 Reynolds Creek Fire jumped the gorge, leaving the dank rock walls as a grotto for ferns and mosses. Parking on both sides of the road is cramped, and it is a trailhead for Siyeh Pass, although most hikers opt to start at Siyeh Bend instead. Below the road, a trail also drops to **Baring Falls** (0.6 mi/1 km, 20 min, moderate) but requires a stiff climb back up.

★ SUN POINT

The often windy **Sun Point** on St. Mary Lake marks the site of the park's most popular early chalet colony: Going-to-the-Sun Chalets. Accessed via boat from St. Mary, the chalets launched visitors into Glacier's interior. For the best views of the site, walk five minutes on the trail from the parking lot to the top of the rock promontory jutting into St. Mary Lake. Spectacular views from there take in Going-to-the-Sun Mountain, Fusillade Mountain, and the Continental Divide. The area also has restrooms, a picnic loop, interpretive signage, and a trail leads to **Baring Falls** (1.2 mi/2 km rt, 45 min, easy).

WILD GOOSE ISLAND OVERLOOK

One of the most photographed spots in Glacier National Park, tiny **Wild Goose Island** is dwarfed in St. Mary Lake's blue waters. Locate parking on both sides of the road. From the overlook, the Continental Divide serves as the backdrop for the tiny island, with Fusillade Mountain as the prominent central pyramid. For the best lighting, visit this spot in early morning or at sunset. Take a photo, and then check the nearest gift shop for the same photo; you'll find it on postcards, on calendars, and in books.

RISING SUN

Rising Sun offers one of the best short walks on St. Mary Lake. A 10-minute walk along the beach goes from the picnic area to the boat launch, but hold on to your hat, as winds often rage. From the boat dock, boat tours on the *Little Chief* cruise on St. Mary Lake. Rising Sun also has a campground, camp store, restaurant, and cabins. It's also a jumping-off spot for hiking to Otokomi Lake.

TWO DOG FLATS

A series of grassland meadows interspersed by aspen groves lines the road from Rising Sun to St. Mary. Known as **Two Dog Flats,** the meadows can be good areas for watching elk, coyotes, bears, and birds in early morning or late evening. From here you can see two hydrological wonders to the south: Triple Divide Peak and Divide Mountain. Triple Divide Peak sits atop the Continental Divide, and its waters head toward the Pacific Ocean, Hudson Bay, and the Gulf of Mexico. Divide Mountain, along with the sweeping moraine heading east, marks the division between the huge Saskatchewan and Missouri watersheds.

ST. MARY LAKE

The second-largest lake in the park, **St. Mary Lake** fills a much narrower valley than its larger counterpart, Lake McDonald. At 9 miles (14.5 km) long and 292 feet (89 m) deep, it forms a blue platform out of which several stunning red argillite peaks rise. Its width shrinks in The Narrows to less than 0.5 mile (0.8 km), where buff-colored Altyn limestone resisted erosion. This strata contains the most ancient exposed rock in the park.

Recreation

DAY HIKES

Hikes off Going-to-the-Sun Road are top-notch. Around Lake McDonald, trails all begin in the forest, but climb to incredible heights. At Logan Pass and eastward, most trails provide quicker access to alpine meadows and spectacular scenery. Shorter trails are ultra-crowded in midsummer; you may feel like you're walking in a parade to Avalanche Lake, St. Mary Fall, or Hidden Lake Overlook. Longer hikes such as Siyeh Pass or Gunsight Lake get away from the masses.

The season for Going-to-the-Sun Road hiking is limited by snow and the road's opening and closing. Even though the Sun Road may open to reach trailheads, snow buries high-elevation trails such as Mount Brown, Sperry Chalet, Sperry Glacier, Granite Park Chalet, Highline, Hidden Lake Overlook, Piegan Pass, and Siyeh Pass sometimes until mid-July. Do not attempt to cross steep snowfields without ice axes and crampons; falling can be deadly. Snow often returns to these high-elevation trails in September. Lower-elevation trails such as Snyder Lake, Trail of the Cedars and Avalanche Lake, St. Mary and Virginia Falls, and Gunsight Lake retain snow until early May, but can be hiked snow-free through October. Even after the Sun Road closes for winter, vehicles can still

Going-to-the-Sun Road Hikes

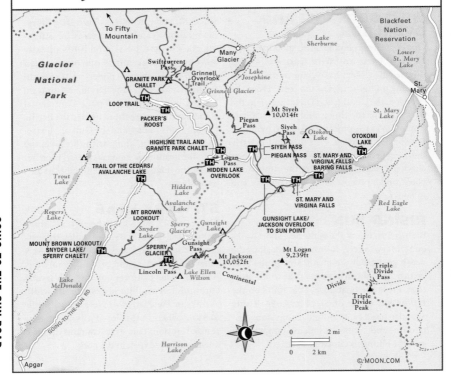

reach the Sperry trailhead at Lake McDonald Lodge; take snowshoes or skis, and for upper-elevation destinations, avalanche gear (beacon, shovel, and probe).

Mount Brown Lookout

Distance: 9.9 miles (15.9 km) round-trip
Duration: 6 hours
Elevation gain: 4,258 feet (1,298 m)
Effort: strenuous
Trail surface: narrow dirt path with roots and rocks
Trailhead: Sperry Trailhead, across Sun Road from Lake McDonald Lodge parking lot and shuttle stop (see map p. 122)

One word describes this hike: *steep.* It'll feel much longer than it is, and the signs may read longer until they catch up with the new GIS measurements. The trail starts out climbing through moderate switchbacks, but at 1.6 miles (2.6 km), turning off the Sperry Trail, the next five switchbacks are lung-busters. After these, the remaining 20 switchbacks level out into a more reasonable ascent. Since the Sprague Fire of 2017 burned trees on Mount Brown, sun bakes the climb on hot days. Get an early start and take plenty of water.

Toward the top, alpine meadows bloom with bear grass and huckleberry patches as the trail works its way along the ridge to the renovated lookout. From this false summit (Mount Brown is higher to the east), you'll get dizzy peering down to Lake McDonald and the lodge. While you zoom binoculars

Going-to-the-Sun Road Hikes

Trail	Effort	Distance	Duration
Mount Brown Lookout	strenuous	9.9 mi (15.9 km) rt	6 hr
Snyder Lake	moderate	8.4 mi (13.5 km) rt	4 hr
Sperry Chalet	strenuous	12.4 mi (20 km) rt	6.5 hr
Sperry Glacier	strenuous	6.9 mi (11.1 km) rt	4 hr
Trail of the Cedars and Avalanche Lake	easy-moderate	0.9-mi (1.4-km) loop-6.1 mi (9.8 km) rt	0.5-3 hr
Granite Park Chalet via The Loop Trail	moderate-strenuous	8 mi (12.9 km) rt	4 hr
Highline Trail and Granite Park Chalet	strenuous	7.4 mi (11.9 km) or 11.4 mi (18.3 km) one-way	5-6 hr
Hidden Lake Overlook	moderate	2.6-5 mi (4.2-8 km) rt	2-4 hr
Piegan Pass	moderate	8.8 mi (14.2 km) rt	4-6 hr
Siyeh Pass	strenuous	10 mi (16.1 km) one-way	6 hr
Gunsight Lake	moderate	13 mi (20.9 km) rt	6.5 hr
Jackson Overlook to Sun Point via St. Mary and Virginia Falls	easy	6.7 mi (10.8 km) one-way	3.5 hr
St. Mary and Virginia Falls	easy	2-3.4 mi (3.2-5.5 km) rt	1-2 hr
Baring Falls	easy	0.6 mi (1 km) or 1.2 mi (1.9 km) rt	1 hr
Otokomi Lake	moderate	10.5 mi (16.9 km) rt	5.5 hr

GOING-TO-THE-SUN ROAD
RECREATION

in on Granite Park Chalet, Swiftcurrent Lookout, and the Continental Divide, protect your lunch from the overly curious mountain goats.

Snyder Lake

Distance: 8.4 miles (13.5 km) round-trip
Duration: 4 hours
Elevation gain: 1,996 feet (608 m)
Effort: moderate
Trail surface: narrow dirt path with roots and rocks
Trailhead: Sperry Trailhead, across Sun Road from Lake McDonald Lodge parking lot and shuttle stop (see map p. 122)
Follow the Sperry Trail up its early steep pitches

until 0.1 mile (0.2 km) beyond the Mount Brown turnoff. Turn east onto the Snyder Lake Trail, which parallels the north hillside above Snyder Creek through portions of the 2017 Sprague Fire. After crossing the base of a talus slope and a brushy avalanche zone, the trail reaches the lake, a favorite for anglers.

Sperry Chalet

Distance: 12.4 miles (20 km) round-trip
Duration: 6.5 hours
Elevation gain: 3,312 feet (1,009 m)
Effort: strenuous
Trail surface: narrow dirt path with roots and rocks
Trailhead: Sperry Trailhead, across Sun Road from

Mount Brown and Sperry Chalet Trails

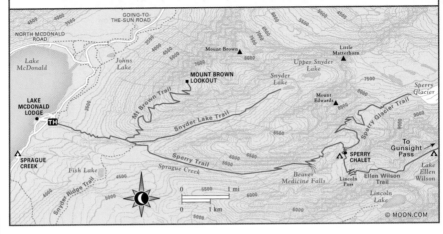

Lake McDonald Lodge parking lot and shuttle stop (see map p. 122)

The historic chalet is an attraction in itself; however, the 2017 Sprague Fire burned the dorm, requiring closure and rebuilding. Now that's it re-opened, you can once again hike to the chalet for lunch and pie. The climb begins with moderate switchbacks through a hemlock forest, where the fire's burned patches take over and wildflowers go crazy. After crossing Snyder Creek at 2 miles (3.2 km), the trail takes a long traverse around Mount Edwards, easing up in elevation before switchbacking again up avalanche slopes. Because of the mules and horses using this same route when Sperry Chalet is open, the trail sometimes smells like a barnyard and can require dexterity for dodging equine droppings buzzing with blackflies. The upper elevations also retain snow into early July.

With more than 1 mile (1.6 km) to go, you'll spot the chalet clinging to a cliff overhead. The trail crosses Sperry Creek before ascending its final switchbacks, passing the turnoff to Sperry Glacier en route. If mountain goats don't stand in your way, you'll arrive at the dining hall's door. Snowshoes or skis and avalanche gear are required in winter.

Sperry Glacier

Distance: 6.9 miles (11.1 km) round-trip from Sperry Chalet or 19.3 miles (31.1 km) round-trip from Lake McDonald Lodge

Duration: 4 hours or 10 hours

Elevation gain: 1,598 or 4,900 feet (487 or 1,494 m)

Effort: strenuous to ultra-strenuous

Trail surface: narrow dirt and rocky path

Trailhead: Sperry Chalet (see map p. 122)

In one day, the colossal grunt up is grueling and the knee-pounding descent brutal. Those staying at Sperry Chalet or Sperry Campground can hike the shorter route to the glacier. The upper part of the trail through the stairway is usually snow-free July through early October.

Start on the Sperry Chalet Trail, hiking through the 2017 Sprague Fire, until reaching the switchbacks above the Sperry Creek bridge. If starting from Sperry Chalet or backcountry campsites, descend the few switchbacks to the signed junction. From the Sperry Glacier trail sign, the trail wraps upward around a glacial cirque below waterfalls and immense cliffs. It switchbacks up past alpine tarns, flower gardens, snowfields lingering into August, and glacially carved rock ledges before it seemingly disappears into a

Trail of the Cedars and Avalanche Lake

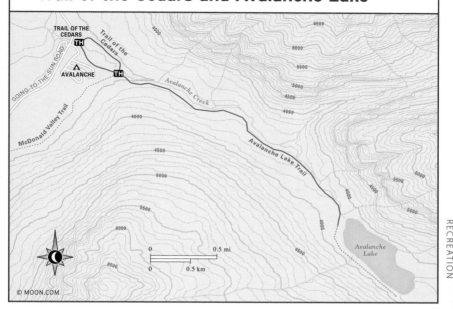

TRAIL OF THE CEDARS

Trail of the Cedars

AVALANCHE

GOING-TO-THE-SUN ROAD

TH

TH

Avalanche Creek

Avalanche Lake Trail

McDonald Valley Trail

Avalanche Lake

0   0.5 mi

0   0.5 km

© MOON.COM

GOING-TO-THE-SUN ROAD

RECREATION

cliff. But voilá: A steep stairway leads through the cliff to Comeau Pass and the basin above. In the Sperry Glacier basin, a different world awaits. Snowfields, moraines, and ice mark this environment, with very sparse trees and flowers. From here, follow vertical markers across the snow-covered trail or glacial rubble to the overlook. Do not walk out on the glacier, which has hidden crevasses and waterways.

★ Trail of the Cedars and Avalanche Lake

Distance: 0.9-mile (1.4-km) loop to 6.1 miles (9.8 km) round-trip

Duration: 0.5-3 hours

Elevation gain: none-477 feet (none-145 m)

Effort: easy-moderate

Trail surface: accessible boardwalk and hard surface on Trail of the Cedars; dirt, roots, rocks for Avalanche Lake

Trailhead: across the Sun Road from Avalanche Picnic Area and shuttle stop (see map p. 123)

With interpretive signs, the Trail of the Cedars boardwalk, reconstructed in 2018, guides walkers and wheelchairs on a loop that crosses two footbridges over Avalanche Creek. The route tours the lush rainforest, where fallen trees become nurse logs, fertile habitat for hemlocks and tiny foamflowers. Immense black cottonwoods furrowed with deep-cut bark and huge 500-year-old western red cedars dominate the forest. At Avalanche Gorge, the creek slices through red rocks. To finish the 0.9-mile (1.4-km) loop, continue on the hard-surface walkway past large burled cedars to return to the trailhead.

The trailhead to Avalanche Lake departs from the southeast end of Trail of the Cedars. Turn uphill for the short grunt to the top of the water-carved Avalanche Gorge. Be extremely careful: Too many fatal accidents have occurred from slipping. From the gorge, the trail climbs steadily through woods littered with glacial erratics. Some of these large boulders strewn when the glacier receded still

Granite Park Chalet Trails

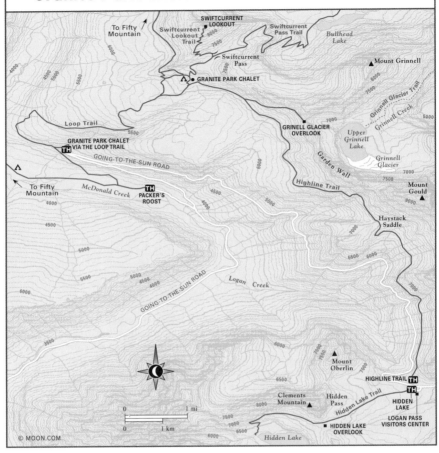

retain scratch marks left from the ice. At the top, 1.9 miles (3.1 km) from the trailhead, a cirque with steep cliffs and tumbling waterfalls cradles the lake. An additional 0.7-mile (1.1-km) path goes to the lake's less-crowded head, where anglers find better fishing.

High season sees streams of people, some incredibly ill prepared, with no drinking water and inappropriate footwear like flip-flops or heels. Avoid midday crowds by hiking this trail earlier or later in the day, but make noise for bears.

Granite Park Chalet via The Loop Trail

Distance: 8 miles (12.9 km) round-trip

Duration: 4 hours

Elevation gain: 2,402 feet (732 m)

Effort: moderate-strenuous

Trail surface: narrow dirt path with roots and rocks

Trailhead: The Loop Trailhead and shuttle stop (see map p. 124)

The Loop Trail is mostly used by hikers exiting the Highline Trail, but when the Highline Trail has too much snow, this trail makes a worthy hike with Granite Park Chalet as a scenic destination. Since the 2003 Trapper Fire, views have improved, but the lack of shade means there is little relief from the sun's blazing heat.

The trail crosses a tumbling creek before joining up with the Packer's Roost trail at 0.6 mile (1 km). Note this junction: You do not want to miss it when hiking back down. From here, the trail climbs two long switchbacks before it crests into the upper basin to the chalet. In June or by late September, snow can cover the last mile or so. The chalet (July-early Sept.) has no running water but does sell candy bars. Bring cash to purchase bottled water, carry your own, or filter water from the campground stream just below the chalet.

★ Highline Trail and Granite Park Chalet

Distance: 7.4 miles (11.9 km) to Granite Park Chalet, 11.4 miles (18.3 km) to The Loop

Duration: 5-6 hours

Elevation gain: 975 feet (297 m) up; 3,395 feet (1,035 m) down

Effort: strenuous

Trail surface: narrow, dirt and rocky

Trailhead: across Going-to-the-Sun Road from Logan Pass parking lot and shuttle stop (see map p. 124)

Many first-time hikers stop every 10 feet to take photos on this hike, which scares severe acrophobes with its exposed thousand-foot drop-offs. The trail drops from Logan Pass through a cliff walk above the Sun Road before crossing a flower land that gave the Garden Wall arête its name. At 3 miles (4.8 km), nearly all the elevation gain is packed into one climb: Haystack Saddle appears to be the top, but it is only halfway. After the high point, the trail drops and swings through several large bowls before passing Bear Valley to reach Granite Park Chalet atop a knoll at 6,680 feet (2,036 m). Due to steep, snow-filled avalanche paths, the park service keeps the trailhead at Logan Pass closed usually into early July. New regulations are under

consideration regarding the first section of the Highline: these may include making the trail one-way only from Logan Pass, adding an exit trail to Big Bend, and using a timed permit entry.

Stronger Highline hikers can add on side trails to Grinnell Glacier Overlook (a steep 1.6 mi/2.6 km rt) and **Swiftcurrent Lookout** (4.2 mi/6.8 km rt). To exit the area, some hikers opt to hike out over Swiftcurrent Pass to Many Glacier (7.6 mi/12.2 km) and catch shuttles; backpackers continue on to Fifty Mountain (11.9 mi/19.2 km farther) and Goat Haunt (22.5 mi/36.2 km farther). Most day hikers head down The Loop Trail (4 mi/6.4 km) to catch the shuttle.

The chalet (July-early Sept.) does not have running water. Carry your own, filter water from the stream below the chalet, or purchase bottled water. Day hikers may also use the outdoor picnic tables or chalet dining room but do not have access to the kitchen. On a rainy day, a warm fire offers respite from the bluster and a chance to dry out. Sodas and candy bars are also sold.

Hidden Lake Overlook

Distance: 2.6 miles (4.2 km) round-trip to overlook, 5 miles (8 km) round-trip to lake

Duration: 2-4 hours

Elevation gain: 482 feet (147 m)

Effort: moderate

Trail surface: wide boardwalk with stairs and rocky dirt

Trailhead: behind Logan Pass Visitor Center and shuttle stop (see map p. 124)

Regardless of crowds, Hidden Lake Overlook is a spectacular hike. Avoid long lines of hikers by going shortly after sunrise or in the evening. The trail is often buried under feet of snow until mid-July or later, but tall poles mark the route. Once the trail melts out, a boardwalk climbs the first half through alpine meadows where fragile shooting stars and alpine laurel dot the landscape with pink. The trail ascends through argillite: Look for evidence of mud-cracked and ripple-marked rocks from the ancient Belt Sea. Above, Mount

Piegan and Siyeh Passes

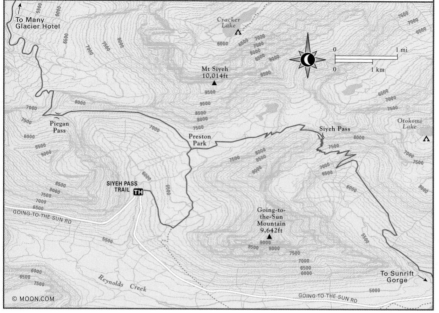

Clements reveals various sea sediments in colorful layers.

The upper trail climbs past moraines, waterfalls, mountain goats, and bighorn sheep. At Hidden Pass on the Continental Divide, the trail reaches the platform overlooking the lake's blue waters. For ambitious hikers or anglers, the trail continues 1.2 miles (1.9 km) down to the lake. Just remember: What drops 776 feet (237 m) must come back up. After late September, bring ice cleats for walking the trail.

Piegan Pass

Distance: 8.8 miles (14.2 km) round-trip, 11.5 miles (18.5 km) to Many Glacier
Duration: 4-6 hours
Elevation gain: 1,739 feet (530 m)
Effort: moderate

1: Trail of the Cedars **2:** Gunsight Pass **3:** Highline Trail

Trail surface: dirt path with roots and rocks
Trailhead: Piegan Pass Trailhead at Siyeh Bend and Siyeh Bend shuttle stop (see map p. 127)

Piegan Pass, named for the Pikuni or Piegan people of the Blackfeet Nation, sneaks a close look at the Continental Divide. After climbing 2 miles (3.2 km) through subalpine forest and turning north at the first trail junction, the trail breaks out into Preston Park, bursting with purple fleabane, blue gentians, white valerian, and fuchsia paintbrush. During the climb, spy four glaciers: Piegan, Jackson, Blackfoot, and Sperry, the latter seen through trees. A signed trail junction in Preston Park, loaded with flower meadows, splits the Piegan Pass Trail from the Siyeh Pass Trail. The trail is often snowbound until early July.

Shortly after the junction, the Piegan Pass Trail heads into the seemingly barren alpine zone as it crosses the base of Siyeh Peak. But miniature flowers bloom and serve as food for pikas. The trail sweeps around a large bowl where two steep snowfields often linger into July to Piegan Pass. Rather than returning to Siyeh Bend, some hikers opt for continuing on to Many Glacier Hotel to link in with shuttles to return.

★ Siyeh Pass

Distance: 10 miles (16.1 km) point to point
Duration: 6 hours
Elevation gain: 2,278 feet (694 m)
Effort: strenuous
Trail surface: dirt path with roots and rocks
Trailhead: Piegan Pass Trailhead at Siyeh Bend and Siyeh Bend shuttle stop (see map p. 127)

Siyeh Pass Trail crosses through such different ecosystems that the entire trail nearly captures the park's diversity in one 10-mile (16.1-km) segment. It usually holds big deep snowfields until at least early July. The trail begins with a 2-mile (3.2-km) climb through subalpine forest broken by meadows, where it passes two well-signed junctions; go left at the first, right at the second. As the trail leads through **Preston Park,** one of the best flower meadows, with purple fleabane and fuchsia paintbrush, Piegan Glacier comes into view. When switchbacks ascend above the tree line, the elevation gain provides a further look at the hanging valley in which it sits.

The switchbacks appear to lead to a saddle, which is Siyeh Pass. But eight more turns climb above the pass before swinging through a cliff to the divide between Boulder and Baring Creeks. Be wary of your lunch; there are aggressive golden-mantled ground squirrels here. Due to the elevation, snow can bury the steep switchbacks south of the divide until mid-July. Sexton Glacier hunkers protected from the afternoon sun by Going-to-the-Sun Mountain (accessible via a 1-mi/1.6-km spur trail). The trail descends in 3,446 feet (1,050 m) of elevation past goats, bighorn sheep, and a multicolored cliff band before traversing the flanks of Goat Mountain and dropping a couple hot miles through the 2015 Reynolds Creek Fire to end at the Sunrift Gorge on Going-to-the-Sun Road.

Gunsight Lake

Distance: 13 miles (20.9 km) round-trip
Duration: 6.5 hours
Elevation gain: 710 feet (216 m)
Effort: moderate
Trail surface: narrow dirt path with roots and rocks
Trailhead: Gunsight Trailhead at Jackson Glacier Overlook shuttle stop

Gunsight Lake is a tantalizer. For those who hike in for the day, more high country beckons

Piegan Pass

beyond it. The trail begins with a 1-mile (1.6-km) drop down to Reynolds Creek, where the 2015 fire started, before gently climbing through a forest of boggy moose ponds that breed mosquitoes. After passing a spur trail leading to Florence Falls, the trail breaks out into flower meadows, climbing along the flanks of Fusillade Mountain. Incomparable views of the wild Blackfoot and Jackson Glaciers sprawl across the scoured basin.

Surrounded by avalanche corridors, the lake sits at the base of Jackson Peak (10,064 ft/3,068 m), one of the six highest peaks in the park. From here, a 1-mile (1.6-km) spur trail wanders back into the Jackson Glacier basin before disappearing in meadow seeps. Another trail climbs to Gunsight Pass (2.8 mi/4.5 km farther) and on to Sperry Chalet (7 mi/11.3 km farther) before descending to Lake McDonald Lodge (20 mi/32 km total), a feat seasoned hikers do in one day. Be ready on the return hike from Gunsight Lake to Jackson Glacier Overlook to climb 543 feet (166 m) in the last mile.

Jackson Overlook to Sun Point via St. Mary and Virginia Falls

Distance: 6.7 miles (10.8 km) one-way
Duration: 3.5 hours
Elevation gain: 216 feet (66 m)
Effort: easy
Trail surface: narrow dirt path with roots and rocks
Trailhead: Gunsight Trailhead at Jackson Glacier Overlook shuttle stop or Sun Point shuttle stop

With shuttles, this point-to-point hike between Jackson Overlook and Sun Point is an easy adventure. You can go either direction, although starting at Jackson Overlook yields a descending route. En route, a side spur tacks on scenic St. Mary and Virginia Falls. The 2015 Reynolds Creek Fire opened up views of mountains, river cascades, and the stunning blue of St. Mary Lake.

From Jackson Overlook, drop to Reynolds Creek. When the trail forks, continue eastward following the descending river. At the falls junction, turn right to explore

mesmerizing blue-green St. Mary Falls (0.4 mi/0.6 km) and climb several switchbacks to misty Virginia Falls (0.7 mi/1.1 km farther). Return to the junction to continue east over bluffs blooming with stonecrop overlooking St. Mary Lake. (Ignore signs for Going-to-the-Sun Road parking lot spurs.) Tally up your third waterfall, Baring Falls, just before the trail climbs to Sun Point for the outstanding views west of St. Mary Lake and the Continental Divide.

St. Mary and Virginia Falls

Distance: 2-3.4 miles (3.2-5.5 km) round-trip
Duration: 1-2 hours
Elevation gain: 216 feet (66 m)
Effort: easy
Trail surface: dirt path with roots and rocks
Trailhead: St. Mary Falls Trailhead or shuttle stop (see map p. 130)

In midsummer, the trail sees a constant stream of people. Two trailheads depart from Going-to-the-Sun Road. The west trailhead descends from the shuttle stop. The east trailhead launches from the vehicle parking lot. Both trails connect with the St. Mary Lake Trail leading to the falls. Between the trailheads and St. Mary Falls, the 2015 Reynolds Creek Fire burned the forest, opening up views of surrounding mountains and the St. Mary River. On hot days, hike it in the morning.

The trail drops 1 mile (1.6 km) through several well-signed junctions en route to St. Mary Falls, a multi-drop falls through a mini-gorge into blue-green pools. After crossing the wooden bridge at St. Mary Fall, the trail switchbacks up 0.7 mile (1.1 km) to Virginia Falls, a broad veil-type waterfall spewing mist. A short spur climbs to the base of Virginia Fall. Be wary of slippery rocks and strong, cold currents at both falls. Nesting near both waterfalls, water ouzels (American dippers) are dark gray birds easily recognized by their dipping action, up to 40 bends per minute.

Baring Falls

Distance: 0.6 mile (1 km) or 1.2 miles (1.9 km) round-trip

St. Mary Lake Trails

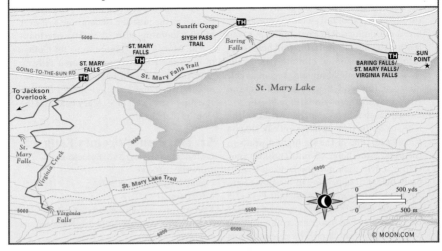

Duration: 1 hour

Elevation gain: minimal, but 120 feet (37 m) back up to Sunrift Gorge trailhead

Effort: easy

Trail surface: narrow dirt path with roots and rocks

Trailhead: Sunrift Gorge or Sun Point parking lot or shuttle stop (see map p. 130)

From Sunrift Gorge, start by dropping south of the road bridge over Baring Creek. The 0.3-mile (0.5-km) trail follows the creek down to the trail from Sun Point. Turn right to reach Baring Falls (originally named Weasel Eyes by the Blackfeet, meaning "huckleberries").

From Sun Point, the 0.6-mile (1-km) trail gradually descends to lake level where it crosses the creek below Baring Falls. The 2015 Reynolds Creek Fire burned the forest, but it opened up views of surrounding mountains and St. Mary Lake. On hot days, hike it in the morning. For an extended option with three waterfalls, the trail continues to St. Mary and Virginia Falls (4.6 mi/7.4 km rt).

Otokomi Lake

Distance: 10.5 miles (16.9 km) round-trip

Duration: 5.5 hours

Elevation gain: 2,008 feet (612 m)

Effort: moderate

Trail surface: narrow dirt path with roots and rocks

Trailhead: behind Rising Sun Motor Inn, Rising Sun shuttle stop

Otokomi Lake makes a good early or late season hike, due to its lower elevation. The 2015 Reynolds Creek Fire burned the first half of the trail on the flanks of Otokomi Mountain, reducing shade and increasing the heat factor on hot days, but opening up views. Climbing immediately uphill, the trail soon levels out into a gentle ascent above Rose Creek. Pause for breaks near the creek, where fragile shooting stars grow next to rock slabs. As the trail leads uphill, it swings southwest for the last mile of open bear-grass meadows and red argillite talus slopes. At the lake, scan the cliffs above for mountain goats, and wade the outlet to get to open lunch spots on the west shore.

Guides

Mid-June–mid-September, park naturalists (406/888-7800, www.nps.gov/glac) guide free hikes at Avalanche, Sun Point, and Logan Pass. Both the Avalanche Lake and Hidden Lake Overlook hikes are extremely popular, so expect to walk in a long train of people. They

Almost Backpacking: Hiking Overnight

Between backcountry chalets and front-country cabins, hikers can sleep in a bed rather than on the ground in tents. Just load up day packs with a few essentials (water, lunch, snacks, extra clothes, and a toothbrush) to relish backpacker advantages without lugging heavy packs. Trails for these adventures usually open by mid-July. With shuttles, you can hike in one trail and out another. Advance reservations are imperative.

GRANITE PARK CHALET

- **Overnighting:** Order bed linens and freeze-dried meals to avoid carrying a sleeping bag and heavy food to this hostel-type chalet. Bring a water filter. Make reservations in mid-January: 888/345-2649, www.graniteparkchalet.com.

- **Hiking:** From Logan Pass, the 7.4-mile (11.9-km) **Highline Trail** goes north along the Garden Wall to the chalet on a knoll with a 360-degree view of surrounding peaks and glaciers. On the second day, leave the crowds behind by hiking 10 miles (16.1 km) round-trip on the Northern Highline to **Ahern Pass.** On the third day, climb 4.2 miles (6.8 km) round-trip to **Swiftcurrent Lookout** for views of the park from end to end, and after lunch, drop 4 miles (6.4 km) downhill to **The Loop.**

- **Logistics:** Leave the car at Apgar Visitor Center or Lake McDonald Lodge. Use Going-to-the-Sun Road shuttles to connect with trailheads at Logan Pass and The Loop.

SPERRY CHALET

- **Overnighting:** The full-service chalet provides meals (dinner, breakfast, and sack lunch) and guest rooms with fresh linens and bedding. Make reservations in mid-January: 888/345-2649, www.sperrychalet.com.

- **Hiking:** From Lake McDonald Lodge, slog up 6.2 miles (10 km) on a trail that climbs 3,500 feet (1,067 m) in elevation to **Sperry Chalet.** On your second day, grab your lunch and head for the 6.9-mile (11.1-km) round-trip trail to **Sperry Glacier.** To exit Sperry on the third day, hike the strenuous 14-mile (22.5-km) route over **Lincoln and Gunsight Passes** to **Jackson Glacier Overlook.**

- **Logistics:** Leave the car at Lake McDonald Lodge. Use Going-to-the-Sun Road shuttles to connect with trailheads at Lake McDonald Lodge and Jackson Glacier Overlook.

SWIFTCURRENT

- **Overnighting:** Stay in **Swiftcurrent Motor Inn** cabins or motel rooms; dine for breakfast and dinner in its restaurant. Make reservations 13 months in advance: 855/733-4522, www.glaciernationalparklodges.com.

- **Hiking:** From Logan Pass, launch for 15.2 miles (24.5 km) along the **Highline Trail** to **Granite Park Chalet** and then over **Swiftcurrent Pass** to descend past several lakes in **Swiftcurrent Valley** to **Swiftcurrent Motor Inn.** On the second day, climb the 11.5-mile (18.5-km) trail under the Continental Divide over **Piegan Pass** to **Siyeh Bend.**

- **Logistics:** Leave the car at St. Mary Visitor Center. Use Going-to-the-Sun Road shuttles to connect with trailheads at Logan Pass and Siyeh Bend.

also guide longer hikes, like Siyeh Pass, and hikes with boat tours on St. Mary Lake. Pick up the park newspaper or go online (www. nps.gov/glac) for current destinations and schedules.

Glacier Guides (11970 U.S. 2 E., West Glacier, 406/387-5555, https://glacierguides. com, mid-May-Sept.) runs the trail-guiding concession in the park. Solo travelers can hook up with its weekly trips on trails to Avalanche Lake, Highline, Virginia Falls, and Piegan Pass (start dates vary pending snowpack, $120 pp), which meet at its West Glacier office. Families and small groups can arrange to meet their own guide elsewhere ($650 for up to five people). Both include guide service, deli lunch, and transportation to the trailhead. The guides also lead popular three-day trips to Granite Park Chalet or Sperry Chalet and one trip that goes to both chalets. These trips (starting at $1,290 pp) include all meals, transportation to the trailhead, guide services, linens, and lodging. The company also has three- to six-day backpacking trips that depart weekly (June-mid-Sept., $675-1,290 pp), some via Sun Road trailheads. Reservations are required. Plan to tip your guides at least 15 percent for day trips and 20 percent for overnights.

BACKPACKING

Going-to-the-Sun Road launches onto spectacular backpacking trails. With shuttles running in summer on the road, point-to-point trips are logistically easy. Leave your vehicle in St. Mary, Apgar, or at Lake McDonald Lodge; avoid taking up prime parking spaces at Logan Pass.

Permits (adults $7 pp/night) for these trips are in high demand. Pick them up 24 hours in advance in person at the **Apgar Backcountry Permit Office** (406/888-7859 May-Oct., 406/888-7800 Nov.-Apr.) or **St. Mary Visitor Center** (406/888-7800, late May-early Oct.), but plan to be in line at 6am. Better yet, apply online in mid-March for advance reservations (www.nps.gov/glac, $40). Pick up walk-in permits for these trips as soon

as the campsites are snow-free, which can be in mid-July. But advance reservations for camps at Fifty Mountain, Lake Ellen Wilson, and Sperry are only available after August 1.

Gunsight Pass
28 MILES (45 KM)

This four-day trek is best hiked from Jackson Glacier Overlook west over Gunsight Pass to finish at Lake McDonald Lodge, but you can do it in reverse or shorten it to three days by skipping one overnight. Spend the first night at Gunsight Lake (GUN). Then, climbing over Gunsight Pass, often crossing a steep snowfield or two in July and encountering mountain goats, descend to the boulder camp at Lake Ellen Wilson (ELL) for the second night. For the third night, a short ascent pops over Lincoln Pass to Sperry Chalet campground (SPE), which was burned in the 2017 Sprague Fire. Set up camp, hang your food, and day hike up through Comeau Pass to Sperry Glacier. On the final day, descend to Lake McDonald Lodge.

Fifty Mountain
32 MILES (52 KM)

Permits for this four-day trek are coveted due to the miles of high-elevation trekking along the Continental Divide. While you can do the loop either direction, most people choose to start at Logan Pass to gain the elevation by vehicle rather than on foot. Traipse along the Garden Wall to reach the backcountry campsites below Granite Park Chalet (GRN). Get an early start for the second day for 12 miles (19.3 km) of climbs and descents through Ahern Pass, Cattle Queen basin, Mineral Creek basin, and Kootenai Pass. Snowfields can be tricky in July: A steep one bars the trail in the cliffs before Ahern, and the Cattle Queen melts into a dangerous snow bridge. Climb around to be safe. The day finishes with a long climb to the high point before dropping through gorgeous flower meadows to camp at Fifty Mountain (FIF). In the morning, take a side trip to Sue Lake Overlook (2.7 mi/4.3

km round-trip) before packing up to cross West Flattop to the Flattop Camp (FLA). On the last day, finish with a downhill hike to Packer's Roost. To catch the shuttle, hike 1.4 miles (2.3 km) uphill to reach The Loop on the Sun Road.

TOP EXPERIENCE

★ BIKING GOING-TO-THE-SUN-ROAD

Going-to-the-Sun Road is an unforgettable bicycle trip. While the 3,500-foot (1,067 m) climb up the west side seems intimidating, it's not steep, just a constant uphill grind amid stunning scenery. During construction in the 1920s, the road grade stayed at 6 percent because cars of the era required rigorous shifting at a steeper grade; that helps maintain a minimal incline for cyclists.

Locals relish **spring riding** when the Sun Road is closed to cars. Cycling begins in early April as soon as snowplows free the pavement while the west-side road remains closed to vehicles from Lake McDonald Lodge or Avalanche, and the east side remains closed from Rising Sun. Riders climb up as far as plowing operations permit. By May, it is such a popular activity that free bicycle-carrying **shuttles** (mid-May–road opening to vehicles, 9am-5pm weekends only) run from Apgar and Lake McDonald Lodge to the Avalanche road closure to expand parking options. Mother's Day often brings out wee ones on tricycles, training wheels, tagalongs, and trailers. Call or consult the park website (406/888-7800, www.nps.gov/glac) to check on access, as construction or spring plowing limits cycling some days. **Glacier Guides** (800/521-7238, https://glacierguides.com) leads bicycling trips on the west side as long as the road is closed. In Apgar, **Glacier Outfitters** (406/219-7466, www.goglacieroutfitters.com) rents bikes, tagalongs, trailers, and car racks. In **fall,** as portions of the road close again to vehicles, cycling sans cars resumes until snow arrives.

In **summer,** when the road opens to vehicles, strong riders who are comfortable being pinched between cliffs and cars head for Logan Pass. Some riders return the way they came; others continue on to the other side. Local racers make a 142-mile (229-km) loop (Going-to-the-Sun Road, U.S. 89, MT 49, and U.S. 2) in one day; tourers take two days.

Locals also celebrate the full moon with a bone-chilling night ride. It's dangerous (injuries and one fatality have occurred), but an otherworldly experience. At dusk or at night, biking requires tail reflectors and a front light.

Restrictions and Safety

Cyclists must be prepared to ride the narrow, shoulderless road with a constant stream of cars. Due to heavy midday traffic, **bicycles are restricted on the Sun Road during summer.** Biking is not permitted 11am-4pm daily June 15-Labor Day in two sections on the west side: along Lake McDonald between the Apgar Road junction and Sprague Creek, and climbing uphill between Avalanche Campground and Logan Pass. If starting from the west side, head out from Lake McDonald by 6:30am for adequate time to pedal to Logan Pass. In early summer, long daylight hours allow for riding after 4pm, when traffic lessens. The east side has no restrictions, but is still easier to ride early or late in the day with fewer cars on the road. Some free shuttle buses are equipped with bicycle racks in case you need a lift. Catch the shuttles only at official stops.

Because the Sun Road is so narrow, **it is not the place for a family ride, except when the road is closed to cars.** While laws do not mandate helmets, wear one anyway, considering most drivers are gaping at the views rather than paying attention to the road. Wear bright colors for visibility, and consider tacking reflectors or flags on your bike. Be sure to carry plenty of water: exertion, wind, and altitude can lead to a fast case of dehydration. Before heading out, check your brake pads, as the screaming downhill off the Continental Divide can wear them down to nubbins. Both mountain bikes and road bikes are appropriate here, but with skinny tires, be wary of obstacles: debris, grates, rockfall, and ice.

HORSEBACK RIDING

Located across Going-to-the-Sun Road from the Lake McDonald Lodge complex, **Swan Mountain Outfitters** (406/387-4405 or 877/888-5557, corral 406/888-5121, www. swanmountainglacier.com, early June-Sept., $55-200) leads trail rides through the forest. Valley bottom rides include a one-hour forest and two-hour McDonald Creek ride that depart several times daily. They tour on a trail through lichen-laden cedars and firs with peekaboo views of peaks. Full-day rides go to Trout Lake and Sperry Chalet. Wear long pants and hiking boots or sturdy shoes. Kids need to be at least seven years old.

WATER SPORTS
Boating and Paddling

Glacier has instituted strict boating and paddling guidelines in order to protect its pristine waters from aquatic invasive species. The lakes are only open in summer and only available by **permit** to boaters and paddlers who have passed an inspection. Jet Skis are banned on all lakes. For most short-term visitors, the procedure alone for getting a permit prohibits its trailering a powerboat from home, as all gas-powered boats and their trailers must be inspected, sealed, and quarantined for 30 days to completely dry out before a permit is issued. Electric-powered and hand-propelled watercraft can get a same-day inspection and permit to launch immediately without quarantining. Get inspections daily at **St. Mary Visitor Center** (7am-4:30pm daily June-Sept.) or in Apgar for **Lake McDonald** (7am-9pm daily mid-May-Oct., shorter hours May and late Sept.-Oct.).

Due to vehicle length (21 ft/6.4 m) and height (10 ft/3 m) restrictions, towed boats and some rooftop-carried boats may not cross Going-to-the-Sun Road between Avalanche and Sun Point. Although river kayakers drool at the rapids on McDonald Creek, the creek is closed to all boating due to nesting harlequin ducks.

LAKE MCDONALD

Lake McDonald (open mid-May-Oct.) has only one boat ramp in Apgar, but hand-carried craft can launch from Sprague Creek Picnic Area or several pullouts along the lake. When the lake is placid, these locations make for prime morning and evening paddling. Motorized boats are permitted after inspections.

At the Lake McDonald Lodge boat dock, **Glacier Park Boat Company** (dock 406/888-5727 or 406/257-2426, https:// glacierparkboats.com, $15-28/hour) rents paddleboards, rowboats, double kayaks, and small motorboats. Paddles, life jackets, and fishing regulations are included.

ST. MARY LAKE

St. Mary Lake (open June-Sept.) allows only hand-propelled watercraft and electric non-water-cooled engines on motorized boats. All watercraft must be launched by hand-carrying down the boat ramp at Rising Sun; no trailers are allowed to enter the water. No boats are available to rent. From the Rising Sun boat ramp, you can go across and up-lake to Silver Dollar Beach below Red Eagle Mountain. Notorious wild winds whip up quickly on St. Mary Lake; keep alert to conditions.

Fishing

Glacier provides a stunning backdrop for fishing. No fishing licenses are required, but use barbless hooks for catch-and-release to protect westslope cutthroat and bull trout. Pick up current fishing regulations at visitors centers or online (www.nps.goc/glac). No fishing guide service operates inside the park.

Need tackle? The camp stores at Lake McDonald Lodge and Rising Sun sell a few items, like line and flies. The nearest rental location for fishing gear is in Apgar at **Glacier**

1: spring biking on Going-to-the-Sun Road 2: trail ride along McDonald Creek

Outfitters (196 Apgar Loop Rd., 406/219-7466, www.goglacieroutfitters.com, 9am-5pm daily mid-May-late Sept., shorter hours in shoulder seasons).

MCDONALD VALLEY

Heavily fished, Lake McDonald is a haven for kokanee, lake trout, whitefish, and cutthroat. It has no limit on lake trout or lake whitefish. Boats tend to produce better results than shore fishing, but you'll see plenty of beach casting. Beyond the largest lake, fishing is sporadic at best. Although scads of anglers rim McDonald Creek, the river has a reputation for leaving hooks bare. As for Fish Lake: A 3-mile (4.8-km) climb from Lake McDonald Lodge accesses the tiny, lily-padded shallow lake, where a few westslope cutthroat reside. Snyder Lake, a 4.2-mile (6.8-km) climb from Lake McDonald Lodge, also has small cutthroat and is a little more open than Fish Lake's brushy shore. Ignore Avalanche Creek and head instead for Avalanche Lake, where endemic westslope cutthroat have been kept genetically pure by the gorge's falls. This lake is heavily fished; for better action, wade one of the chilly inlet streams on its south end.

LOGAN PASS

Via a 2.5-mile (4-km) trail from Logan Pass, Hidden Lake holds good-size Yellowstone cutthroat trout in spite of its elevation and its reputation as the highest lake in the park with fish. The outlet and nearby lakeshore are closed until July 31 due to bears feeding on spawning trout.

ST. MARY VALLEY

St. Mary Lake has beautiful scenery, but not spectacular fishing. It's best fished from boats rather than the shoreline. Upper St. Mary River isn't much better: You often see anglers below St. Mary Falls, but few catching fish. Gunsight Lake, the best fishing lake, requires a 6.5-mile (10.5-km) hike from Jackson Glacier Overlook; expect wind, late snowpack, and brush along the shore.

Windsurfing

Of all the park's lakes, St. Mary Lake is the one windsurfers occasionally use. Easterlies rage down the valley; however, high mountains and erratic valley confluences create swirly winds on its west end. The lake is not a beginner sailboarding area; experience in self-rescue is paramount. Those who sail these frigid waters usually launch from Rising Sun Picnic Area and wear a wetsuit.

WINTER SPORTS

Since winter buries Going-to-the-Sun Road with snow from Lake McDonald Lodge to St. Mary, the road attracts **cross-country skiers and snowshoers** November-early April. Touring up the gated road's lower elevations goes through relatively avalanche-free zones. The gentle grade makes for good gliding suitable for beginners. For snowshoers, etiquette requires blazing a separate snowshoe trail rather than squishing the parallel ski tracks flat. Some park ski trails are mapped online (www.nps.gov/glac).

In McDonald Valley, ski tours lead past McDonald Creek and Upper McDonald Creek Falls to Avalanche Campground (6 mi/9.7 km one-way). Some skiers cross the bridge at Sacred Dancing Cascade to loop back on the river's north side, but snow coverage is more variable in the trees. A gentle forest ski leads to John's Lake, but as a destination, it's not much. Some skiers head up to Snyder Lakes, but be ready for the narrow trail descending through tight trees on the way back down. Blue-sky days attract hearty snowshoers to Mount Brown Lookout.

On the east side, a good, flat 6-mile (9.7-km) ski heads to Rising Sun along Two Dog Flats; however, high winds often strip sections of the roadway bare.

Between Rising Sun and Avalanche Creek, Going-to-the-Sun Road sees significant avalanche activity. Do not attempt to ski any of this section without experience, know-how, and safety gear (avalanche transceivers, shovels, and probes). Check current conditions at www.flatheadavalanche.org. When Logan

Pass opens in June, skiers and snowboarders can hike up the Hidden Lake Overlook trail for turns on the lingering snowpack.

Guides and Rentals

Glacier Adventure Guides (406/892-2173, www.glacieradventureguides.com) leads full-day and overnight trips for cross-country touring, backcountry skiing, and snowshoeing. If you're a solo traveler, it's the best way to get accompanied into the backcountry with avalanche-certified guides to find pristine powder stashes. Lunch, snacks, and some equipment are included, although ski rentals need to be picked up in Flathead Valley. For deep backcountry, ski in to an igloo to spend the night. Call for rates; plan on tipping the guide 15-20 percent.

Entertainment and Shopping

RANGER PROGRAMS

Lake McDonald Lodge (8:30pm) and Rising Sun Amphitheater (8pm) host 45-minute nightly park naturalist programs. Check for schedules at campground information boards and hotel activity desks, or pick up the park newspaper. Topics range from fires to birds. Best of all, they're free. Some of the programs feature the **Native America Speaks** program, one of the best ways to learn about the park's rich culture and history. At Lake McDonald Lodge, Blackfeet musician and poet **Jack Gladstone** periodically presents a unique mix of music and Indigenous legends.

International Dark Sky Events

With minimal light pollution, Logan Pass is one of the best places to view the night sky. The Big Sky Astronomy Club collaborates with the park service to host **Logan Pass Star Parties** with constellation tours and telescope viewing of planets, star clusters, and nebulae. Several events (9:30pm-midnight, late July-early Sept.) take place with limited admission. For admittance, each vehicle must have a ticket; they are free from Apgar or St. Mary Visitor Centers. Tickets go fast, so plan to be at the visitors center by 8am on the day before the event to get them. For dates, consult the park newspaper or check online (www.nps.gov/glac).

SHOPPING

Find gift shops in Lake McDonald Lodge, Two Dog Flats Grill at Rising Sun, and camp stores in both locations. They carry a selection of books, maps, T-shirts, postcards, and jewelry. The Logan Pass Visitor Center has a small bookstore.

Food

INSIDE THE PARK

Logan Pass has no food services or vending machines. The nearest restaurants on the west side are at Lake McDonald Lodge, 21 miles (34 km) below the pass. On the east side, Rising Sun has the only restaurant, 12 miles (19.3 km) from Logan Pass.

Restaurants

Xanterra (855/733-4522, www.glaciernationalparklodges.com) operates these park restaurants. Local sourcing, sustainability, farm-to-table, and organic products form the backbone for their menus. Options include vegan, gluten-free, and child selections, plus

GOING-TO-THE-SUN ROAD

FOOD

flexibility with add-on toppings for salads and pastas. For hikers and sightseers on Going-to-the-Sun Road, sack lunches ($12-15) are sold at Lake McDonald Lodge and Rising Sun; order them a day in advance. No reservations are taken for any of these restaurants.

LAKE MCDONALD

At **Lake McDonald Lodge** (288 Lake McDonald Lodge Loop, 855/733-4522, daily mid-May-late Sept.), the headliner dining room is ★ **Russell's Fireside Dining Room,** decorated with chandeliers painted in Indigenous patterns and full of historical ambience. The north windows have a peeka-boo lake view, but during dinner the blinds usually need to be pulled down as the hot sun blazes in. Breakfast (6:30am-10am, $9-18) is a choice of continental buffet, full buffet, or menu entrées. Lunch (11:30am-2pm, $10-18) serves small plates, burgers, sandwiches, salads, and pasta. Dinner (5pm-9:30pm, $17-30) can go casual with burgers, salads, and pasta or full-on dining with charcuterie, shared appetizers, and plated entrées of fish or meats.

Also in the lodge, the cozy **Lucke's Lounge** (11:30am-10pm, $10-19), adjacent to the lodge's dining room, serves a more limited menu of appetizers, sandwiches, burgers, salads, and pasta. The bar also stocks plenty of local microbrews along with wine and craft cocktails. The best option for families is the cafeteria-style **Jammer Joe's Grill and Pizzeria** (11am-9pm, closes early Sept., $11-22), due to broad menu choices and foods with kid appeal. Located across from the lodge, the restaurant serves pizza, pasta, wraps, burgers, and salads. Its lunch buffet helps with quicker eating to get back on the road.

RISING SUN

Located at Rising Sun across from the motor inn, **Two Dog Flats Grill** (406/732-5523, daily mid-June-mid-Sept.) is the only restaurant on the east flank of Going-to-the-Sun Road. It serves breakfast 6:30am-10am ($6-11). Lunch and dinner are served 11am-10pm ($10-26), with full plated dinners starting at 5pm. The casual American fare includes sandwiches, burgers, pasta, salads, and home-style grill dinners. Beer and wine are available, too. Ask for a south window table to see Red Eagle Peak, although pines are stretching higher into the views. When crowded with bus tours midsummer, you may have to wait for a table. If the line is really long, go 6 miles (9.7 km) east to St. Mary for more dining options;

the camp store at Lake McDonald

the evening return drive offers good wildlife-watching along Two Dog Flats.

Groceries

You're best off stocking up on groceries before settling in for several days along the Sun Road. But for last-minute supplies, **camp stores** (7am-9pm daily mid-June-mid-Sept.) are located at the Lake McDonald Lodge complex and Rising Sun. Both camp stores carry limited items, but you can pick up ice, firewood, stove gas, and other camping supplies, as well as convenience-store groceries, beer, wine, gifts, and newspapers. Hikers can buy trail food for lunches.

Picnic Areas

Only four areas accommodate the picnic basket on Going-to-the-Sun Road. All except Sun Point permit fires in the fire rings with grills, but bring your own firewood, as gathering is prohibited. Picnic tables are available, but due to bears, do not leave your picnic gear unattended. Adjacent to the campground, **Sprague Creek Picnic Area** tucks tightly in the trees between Going-to-the-Sun Road and Lake McDonald, with more road view than scenery; however, short paths access the shoreline. Flush toilets are available. **Avalanche Creek Picnic Area** is across the street from the campground and has larger rebuilt vault-toilet restrooms. Picnic sites are under cedar shade adjacent to McDonald Creek. Trailheads for Trail of the Cedars and Avalanche Lake are across the street. **Sun Point Picnic Area** has great views up St. Mary Valley to the Continental Divide, but watch the paper plates, as the wind can howl. Trails lead to Sun Point and Baring Falls. It has vault toilets. **Rising Sun Picnic Area** is adjacent to St. Mary Lake, with open sites slightly buffered from wind by aspen trees. If winds rage, however, hold everything down. Short paths through the trees access the shoreline. It has flush toilets.

Logan Pass has no picnic area, and the National Park Service does not allow coolers outside of vehicles except in picnic areas. If you want to "picnic" with the views, the best method is to pack a sack lunch to eat on a trail or at one of the many pullouts along the road. Most restaurants in and around the park sell takeout lunches ($10-15) that you can order a day in advance of your trip. Many of the pullouts on the Sun Road offer places to eat a sack lunch with an outstanding view: You can sit on the historic rock wall at **Lunch Creek pullout** (1.4 mi/2.3 km east of Logan Pass) or on the boulders at **Big Bend** (2.3 mi/3.7 km below Logan Pass).

Accommodations

INSIDE THE PARK
Going-to-the-Sun Road

Accommodations on Going-to-the-Sun Road are scarce with none at Logan Pass. Lodges generally do not have TVs or air-conditioning. Add the 7 percent state bed tax to rates. Rooms go fast for these prime locations; make **reservations 13 months in advance** for Lake McDonald Lodge and Rising Sun Motor Inn.

LAKE MCDONALD

On the west side of Going-to-the-Sun Road 21 miles (34 km) from Logan Pass, two lodging options sit near the head of Lake McDonald in a complex that has boat tours, boat rentals, red bus tours, horseback riding, trailheads, restaurants, and a camp store. Trailheads depart to Snyder Lake, Mount Brown, Sperry Chalet, Sperry Glacier, and Lincoln Pass. Limited internet is available.

A National Historic Landmark, ★ **Lake McDonald Lodge** (288 Lake McDonald Lodge Loop, 855/733-4522, front desk 406/888-5431, www.glaciernationalparklodges.com, mid-May-late Sept., $118-515) graces the southeast lake shore. Centered around a massive stone fireplace and hunting lodge-themed lobby full of trophy specimens hung by John Lewis, the original owner, the complex has four types of accommodations: main lodge rooms, cabin rooms, Cobb House suites, and Snyder Hall. A $3 million renovation in 2016-17 revamped some cabins and lodge rooms. Dial back your expectations to the mid-1900s with telephones as the only in-room amenities, and you'll be delighted with the location and historical ambience. Some lakeside rooms have views. Most rooms are small with bathrooms converted from original closets. Upstairs rooms lack elevator access. Snyder Hall has shared bathrooms. Cobb House has two-room suites with televisions. Wireless internet is available in the lobby and reading room.

An old 1950s-style two-story motel sits behind the camp store. **Motel Lake McDonald** (3 Lake McDonald Lodge Loop, 844/868-7474 or 403/888-5100, www.glacierparkcollection.com, mid-June-mid-Sept., $180-200) sits in deep cedars with no lake views. Spartan rooms have no elevator access to the 2nd floor and no phones; a pay phone is at the office.

RISING SUN

It's hard to beat Rising Sun's location 12 miles (19.3 km) from Logan Pass on the east side of Going-to-the-Sun Road. Listed on the National Register of Historic Places, **Rising Sun Motor Inn** (2 Going-to-the-Sun Rd., 855/733-4522, www.glaciernationalparklodges.com, mid-June-mid-Sept., $182-200) became the answer for motorists traveling to Glacier during World War II; it was the only facility that stayed open. Not much has changed at this funky 1940s motor inn with its board-and-batten construction, except that rooms were revamped in 2016. Expect no in-room phones,

TVs, or air-conditioning, but an outdoor pay phone and portable fans are available. Rooms have diminutive private baths. The complex has a restaurant, store, limited wireless internet, and a hiker shuttle stop. The trail to Otokomi Lake begins near the store, and access to St. Mary Lake is across the street, along with the boat tour dock.

Backcountry

Glacier has two backcountry chalets built by the Great Northern Railway. Accessed only by trails, these National Historic Landmarks are rustic stone and log edifices owned by the National Park Service and operated by **Belton Chalets** (888/345-2649, early July-early Sept.). Set in scenic alpine mountain goat and grizzly bear terrain, solitude and beauty are chalet amenities. Watching wildlife and sunsets provides quiet evening entertainment, and stargazing is spectacular. The chalets have no electricity. Reservations are required. Online bookings for the upcoming summer go fast, starting in early January. Hiker shuttles stop at all the Sun Road trailheads for the chalets.

TOP EXPERIENCE

GRANITE PARK CHALET

Set at the same elevation as Logan Pass, ★ **Granite Park Chalet** (www.granite-parkchalet.com) sits atop a knoll with a 360-degree view. The main chalet contains the kitchen, dining room, and guest rooms. More rooms are in another building. Twelve guest rooms sleep 2-6 people each ($120 first person in room, $82 per added person). This chalet functions somewhat like a hostel for its 35 guests per night: Bring your own sleeping bag. Meals are not supplied; haul your own food to cook in the kitchen. Pots and pans are available for cooking on the 12-burner propane stove with an oven, but you'll need to bring your own mugs, plates, bowls, eating utensils, and water filter. With **no running water,** guests haul water for cooking and washing from 0.2 mile (0.3 km) away. For hikers looking to lighten their load, purchase linen service ($25 for sheets, a pillow, and blankets), preorder freeze-dried food ($2-15/item), and purchase environmentally friendly disposable plates and utensils. Take a flashlight to find the composting vault toilets at night (no flush toilets). Pack along earplugs, as snores resound through thin walls. No alcohol is sold or allowed in the dining hall, but you can pack along beverages for sipping in guest rooms and haul the containers out with you along with all of your garbage. Most hikers reach the chalet from Logan Pass (7.4 mi/11.9 km), The Loop (4 mi/6.4 km), or Swiftcurrent (7.6 mi/12.2 km).

SPERRY CHALET

The Sprague Fire burned ★ **Sperry Chalet** (www.sperrychalet.com) in 2017, but it has fortunately been rebuilt. It offers hikers and horseback riders three meals and a warm bed, which means hauling only a day pack with some extra clothing. Set in a timbered cirque, the chalet has a dining hall, lodge, and several National Park Service buildings. Private lodge rooms sleep 2-6 people each ($240 for first person in room, $160 per additional person in room) in bunks or beds with bedding included. Faucets put out cold water only. Country roasts rotate for nightly dinners, but the menu has maintained culinary sensibilities from the 1950s, with canned fruits and vegetables. Trail lunches packed for you are plain, with a meat sandwich (no lettuce or tomato), candy bars, and fruit leather. However, outstanding bakery goods use traditional decades-old recipes for cookies, freshly baked breads, and pies. To reach Sperry, hike 6.2 miles (10 km) up from Lake McDonald or 14 miles (22.5 km) over two passes from Jackson Glacier Overlook.

Camping

INSIDE THE PARK

In the interior of Going-to-the-Sun Road, three campgrounds (406/888-7800, www.nps.gov/glac, $20) offer coveted locations, but none are at Logan Pass. These are rustic campgrounds with no hookups. Amenities include shuttle stops, flush toilets, cold running water, picnic tables, and fire rings with grills; buy firewood locally. Shared sites ($5-8 pp) for hikers and bikers have bear-resistant food storage.

These campgrounds can fill up by early morning with all sites first-come, first-served. Use the park's **Recreational Access Display** (www.nps.gov/applications/glac/dashboard/) to check fill times from the previous several days and historically from the previous year to gauge when to arrive to claim a first-come, first-served campsite.

If campgrounds are full, go to Apgar, West Glacier, or St. Mary. Remember that RVs or vehicle-trailer combos over 21 feet (6.4 m) cannot travel the Sun Road between Avalanche Campground and Sun Point. For hookups, hit commercial campgrounds outside the park in St. Mary or West Glacier. For RVs seeking a dump station, go to Apgar or Rising Sun Campgrounds.

Lake McDonald

The small **Sprague Creek Campground** (0.9 mi/1.4 km southwest of Lake McDonald Lodge, mid-May-mid-Sept.) is a prize right on Lake McDonald's shore in a timbered setting with shaded sites. A few have prime waterfront. Unfortunately, several sites also abut Going-to-the-Sun Road, with a nice view of cars driving by. After dark, the road noise plummets, so it's not like tenting next to a major highway. A skinny, paved road accesses 25 short and narrow sites (no towed units, RVs must be smaller than 21 ft/6.4 m). Kayakers and canoers have lakefront access, and beach sunsets rank as spectacular. At 22 miles (35 km) from Logan Pass, it has quick access to the high country, and it's 5 minutes from Lake McDonald Lodge and the camp store. Midsummer, Sprague often fills by 8am.

Set in a cedar-hemlock and fern rainforest, ★ **Avalanche Campground** (6 mi/9.7 km northwest of Lake McDonald Lodge, mid-June-early Sept.) makes the closest west-side base for exploring Logan Pass, 16 miles (26 km) away. Its 87 campsites are convenient for hiking to Avalanche Lake, since the trail departs from the campground's rear. The rainforest, with its dark, overgrown forest canopy, allows little sunlight to hit picnic tables. The moist area sprouts thick patches of thimbleberries and sometimes a good collection of mosquitoes. RVs are limited to 26 feet (7.9 m). Midsummer, Avalanche can fill by 10am.

St. Mary Lake

Located only 12 miles (19.3 km) east of Logan Pass and 6 miles (9.7 km) west of St. Mary, ★ **Rising Sun Campground** (6 mi/9.7 km west of St. Mary, late May-mid-Sept.) tucks on the lower hillside of Otokomi Mountain by St. Mary Lake. The sun drops down early behind Goat Mountain, creating a long twilight at the campground. While the 2015 Reynolds Creek Fire bypassed the larger trees in the lower campground, it left burnt trees on the hillside above the upper campsites. The 83-site campground is a few minutes' walk to a restaurant, a camp store, and hot showers. Beach access is across Going-to-the-Sun Road, with a picnic area, boat ramp, and boat tours. The Otokomi Lake trailhead is behind the adjacent inn. RVs can only be 25 feet (7.6 m). Midsummer, the campground can fill by 9am.

Transportation and Services

TRANSPORTATION
Driving and Parking

Be prepared for driving the narrow, two-lane Going-to-the-Sun Road. Between Avalanche and Sun Point, **RVs** are not allowed: **Rigs** must be smaller than 21 feet (6.4 m) long, 8 feet (2.4 m) wide, and 10 feet (3 m) high. Drivers who have extended side mirrors should pull them in to avoid losing them on cliffs.

Limited parking is at Logan Pass, with the lot filling up 8am-5pm. Other parking lots often fill early morning at Avalanche, The Loop, and St. Mary Falls trailheads.

Shuttles

The park shuttle service (July-Sept., free) operates on the Sun Road, stopping at all lodges, trailheads, and Logan Pass. For arriving Amtrak travelers, **Xanterra** (855/733-4522, www.glaciernationalparklodges.com, daily late May-late Sept., one-way $5-10, by reservation only) picks up visitors at the Belton Depot in West Glacier to go to Lake McDonald Lodge.

SERVICES

Restrooms are few and far between on this historic highway. **Flush toilets** are available at Sprague Creek Picnic Area, Lake McDonald Lodge, Logan Pass Visitor Center, and Rising Sun. **Vault toilets** are available at Avalanche Picnic Area, Logan Creek, The Loop, Logan Pass, Jackson Glacier Overlook, and Sun Point. Only the campgrounds and lodges have **running water** for washing hands.

Showers (one token for eight minutes $3) are available at Rising Sun. For **laundry,** you'll have to go to West Glacier or St. Mary. Find **ATM machines** at Lake McDonald Lodge and Rising Sun Motor Inn. The Lake McDonald Lodge complex has a small seasonal **post office** (10am-2pm Mon.-Fri. summer) across from the **camp store.** Local newspapers, the *Great Falls Tribune* and Flathead Valley's *Daily Interlake,* are sold in camp stores at Lake McDonald Lodge and Rising Sun.

Gas and Repairs

Gas is not available on Going-to-the-Sun Road. Gas up in West Glacier or St. Mary. Rangers can sometimes assist with minor repairs, such as jumping dead car batteries, but call mobile services from Flathead Valley for major repairs.

Cell Phone and Internet Access

While some cell phones pick up service at high elevations on the Sun Road, most do not get service in the valleys due to the surrounding peaks. Granite Park Chalet has **cell service,** but be aware that many visitors go there to get away from that, so be discreet in your phone use. **Public pay phones** are at Lake McDonald Lodge, Rising Sun, and Avalanche Campground. You can purchase calling cards for them at the Rising Sun and Lake McDonald camp stores. The Sun Road is a place to break the technological umbilical cord. Public internet access is not available.

Emergencies

If you have an emergency on Going-to-the-Sun Road, call 911. If you cannot leave the scene to make a phone call, flag down a vehicle heading up or down the pass to notify the nearest ranger (usually at Logan Pass, St. Mary Visitor Center, or by phone from Lake McDonald Lodge). For other assistance, call the **National Park Service** (406/888-7800).

On the west side of the Sun Road, a seasonal **urgent-care clinic** (100 Rea Rd., West Glacier, 406/888-9224, 9am-4pm daily Memorial Day-Labor Day) operates, but the nearest hospitals are in Flathead Valley: **North Valley Hospital** (1600 Hospital Way, Whitefish, 406/863-3500) and **Kalispell Regional Medical Center** (310 Sunny View Ln., Kalispell, 406/752-5111). On the east side, the Blackfeet Reservation houses the **Blackfeet Community Hospital** (760 Blackweasel Rd., Browning, 406/338-6154).

St. Mary and Many Glacier

On Glacier's east side, mountains graze the sky

and drop abruptly to wide-open grassland prairies. Below sheer cliffs, elk browse. Aspen leaves chatter in only a hint of breeze.

From valley floors, a wild panorama of Glacier's peaks runs across the western skyline, dominated by red sediments and milky sapphire lakes. Ice fields cling for dear life to cliffs as the summer sun shrinks them each year. It's a place of extravagant color, where tumbling waterfalls and pink, purple, white, and yellow wildflowers intoxicate the eyes.

Due to the Continental Divide, wind is a constant companion. It shapes trees into gnarled, bent wonders and whips up whitecaps on lakes in seconds. But every minute yields another view to fill pixels

Highlights

Look for ★ to find recommended sights, activities, dining, and lodging.

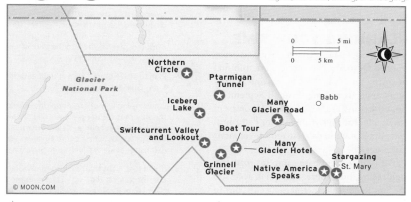

Northern Circle ★

Glacier National Park

Ptarmigan Tunnel ★

Iceberg Lake ★

Many Glacier Road ★

Babb

Swiftcurrent Valley and Lookout ★

Boat Tour ★

Many Glacier Hotel ★

Grinnell Glacier ★

Native America Speaks ★

Stargazing ★
St. Mary

© MOON.COM

★ **Take a Boat Tour:** Hop on a Many Glacier boat tour for two scenic rides with unbeatable views. Launch on Swiftcurrent Lake and stroll to Lake Josephine for the second boat (page 152).

★ **Drive Many Glacier Road:** Take this scenic drive, which features wildflowers, landscapes, wildlife, and sunsets that turn the peaks rosy with alpenglow (page 154).

★ **See Grinnell Glacier:** Check out the park's most-visited glacier, either from afar or by hiking up close, before it melts completely (pages 155 and 161).

★ **Stay at Many Glacier Hotel:** The park's grandest lodge has an enormous four-story log lobby and two-story floor-to-ceiling dining room windows (page 157).

★ **Climb to Swiftcurrent Valley and Lookout:** Atop the Continental Divide, you'll survey glaciers and peaks for as far as you can see (page 161).

★ **Plunge into Iceberg Lake:** Swim with icebergs! Tucked below goat-studded cliffs, the lake gleams with ice floating in blue waters (page 162).

★ **Walk through Ptarmigan Tunnel:** This hiker's tunnel was built in the 1930s. The dark corridor ends with a burst of red rocks and blue skies on the north side (page 163).

★ **Backpack the Northern Circle:** This historic 52-mile (84-km) route goes through Ptarmigan Tunnel, the Belly River, fishing lakes, two passes, and countless wildflower meadows (page 166).

★ **Go Stargazing:** Peer at stars, planets, and nebulae at night at the St. Mary Observatory via telescopic images on large screens (page 169).

★ **Learn about Indigenous traditions:** Gain a better understanding of Blackfeet culture through storytelling, song, and dance at **Native America Speaks** (page 170).

with rugged scenery. No wonder the Blackfeet called Glacier the "Backbone of the World."

While St. Mary is the eastern portal to Glacier's famed Going-to-the-Sun Road, Many Glacier is a setting of dreams: chiseled peaks, idyllic lakes, pastoral meadows. The morning sunrise gleams gold across the rampart of peaks. Loons call across glassy lakes. Grizzly bears forage on hillsides, clawing at the ground for glacier lily bulbs. By evening, when the trails vacate, the sunset paints royal hues above the Continental Divide. Dark descends, with a multitude of stars. And if you're lucky, the northern lights dance across the sky.

PLANNING YOUR TIME

St. Mary and Many Glacier are best from **May to October,** but services are minimal in spring and fall. Most hotels and restaurants open from June through September. **Reservations** are imperative: 13 months in advance for **lodging,** 6 months for **camping.** Sometimes you can nab last-minute rooms or campsites.

For a convenient base camp for road-trip sightseeing, boat tours, and quick access to the Sun Road and other park locales, stay in St. Mary for **3-4 days.** Those looking to hike without climbing back into the car should stay in Many Glacier for **3-5 days.**

Many Glacier Road will have a huge construction project happening during summer 2021 that will cause long delays. Due to construction, the road will only be open in 2021 from mid-May to mid-September. Use the park's **Recreational Access Display** (www.nps.gov/applications/glac/dashboard/) for real-time status of Many Glacier Road, parking lots, weather, and campground availability.

Summer temperatures usually average 70-85°F (21-29°C) during days and 40-49°F (4.5-9°C) at night. Hiking and backpacking into higher elevations will encounter temperatures

Avoid the Crowds

In summer, Many Glacier's popularity and St. Mary's location as the eastern gate to Going-to-the-Sun Road bring on crowds and congested traffic. Summer 2021 will see construction delays on the Many Glacier Road.

- On congested days when parking lots pack out, the National Park Service limits entrance to the Many Glacier Road or at St. Mary Visitor Center. You can find out when this happens on Twitter @GlacierNPS, by checking the park's **Recreational Access Display** (www.nps.gov/applications/glac/dashboard/), and at visitors centers. Unless you have reservations for lodging or camping, go elsewhere in the park when restrictions are in effect.

- Plan to arrive before 8am at trailheads in Many Glacier.

- For camping without reservations, check the fill times for the previous day(s) online. Use that as your guideline for arrival to claim a spot at first-come, first-served campsites at Many Glacier and St. Mary.

- If you just want to drive into Many Glacier for a "look-see," go in the evening. Your chances of seeing wildlife are better when crowds hunker in at lodges and camps.

- If you want to go to St. Mary Visitor Center, arrive before or after the 10am-4pm rush hours.

often 10-15°F (6-8°C) cooler. Winter temperatures waffle between -10°F (-23°C) in Arctic cold fronts accompanied by frigid wind chills to 35°F (2°C).

HISTORY
Grinnell's Glacier

George Bird Grinnell first saw his namesake glacier in 1887. The editor of *Forest and Stream* magazine, the precursor to *Field and*

Previous: Grinnell Lake from Grinnell Glacier Trail; Grinnell Lake and Glacier basin; Many Glacier tour boat on Swiftcurrent Lake.

St. Mary and Many Glacier

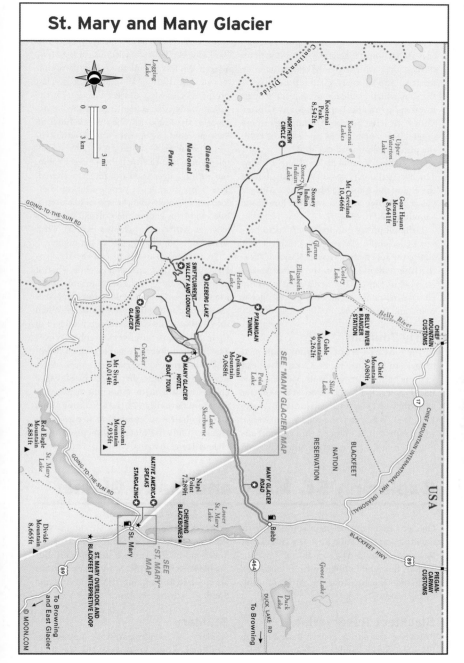

Continental Divide

Logging Lake

Kootenai Peak 8,542ft

NORTHERN CIRCLE

Kootenai Lakes

Upper Waterton Lake

Glacier National Park

Stoney Indian Pass

Stoney Indian Lake

Mt Cleveland 10,466ft

Goat Haunt Mountain 8,641ft

GOING-TO-THE-SUN RD

Glenns Lake

Cosley Lake

SWIFTCURRENT VALLEY AND LOOKOUT

Helen Lake

ICEBERG LAKE

Elizabeth Lake

Belly River

BELLY RIVER RANGER STATION

CHIEF MOUNTAIN CUSTOMS

GRINNELL GLACIER

PTARMIGAN TUNNEL

Gable Mountain 9,262ft

Chief Mountain 9,080ft

SEE "MANY GLACIER" MAP

Cracker Lake

Apikuni Mountain 9,068ft

MANY GLACIER HOTEL

Poia Lake

Slide Lake

17

Mt Siyeh 10,014ft

BOAT TOUR

Lake Sherburne

CHIEF MOUNTAIN INTERNATIONAL HWY (SEASONAL)

BLACKFEET NATION RESERVATION

Red Eagle Mountain 8,881ft

Okotoki Mountain 7,935ft

USA

GOING-TO-THE-SUN RD

St. Mary Lake

NATIVE AMERICA SPEAKS

STARGAZING

Napi Point 7,239ft

MANY GLACIER ROAD

CHEWING BLACKBONES

Divide Mountain 8,665ft

89

ST. MARY OVERLOOK AND BLACKFEET INTERPRETIVE LOOP

St. Mary

SEE "ST. MARY" MAP

Lower St. Mary Lake

Babb

464

BLACKFEET HWY

89

PIEGAN-CARWAY CUSTOMS

Goose Lake

DUCK LAKE RD

Duck Lake

To Browning and East Glacier

To Browning

© MOON.COM

0

0

3 km

3 mi

Stream, explored Glacier over two decades, during which he lobbied Congress for preservation. Congress agreed to purchase the eastern portion of lands for $1.5 million from the Blackfeet, who desperately needed money for food and supplies. Grinnell negotiated the sale, which created a forest reserve open to prospecting and hunting. Many Glacier Valley attracted hordes of would-be miners digging for copper, silver, and gold. In 1898, the mining boom gave rise to Altyn, a town located where Sherburne Reservoir is today. The burg ballooned to 800 residents, but by the end of 1902 it was a ghost town. Meager yields could not compete with the lure of the Klondike gold rush.

Grinnell pressed on in his efforts to preserve Glacier. Finally, in 1910, President Taft signed the act creating Glacier National Park, the 12th national park in the United States. In recognition of Grinnell's efforts, Many Glacier bears his name on a glacier, peak, point, and three lakes.

Early Tourism

In the hustle to create ways for train passengers to stay in Glacier, Great Northern Railway built a dirt road from Midvale (now East Glacier) to St. Mary and Many Glacier and threw up chalets in both locales between 1911-1913. When dry, the road was drivable; when rains fell, it mutated into treacherous muck. From the train station, guests arrived by car in 2.5 hours or by stagecoach in 4 hours. Other guests arrived via the Inside Trail on an overnight horseback trip, stopping at Cut Bank Chalets. Poor site selection for the Many Glacier chalets meant the loss of two chalets and the dining hall to avalanches. That prompted choosing another location for the grand Many Glacier Hotel, to be the "showplace of the Rockies." The upscale hotel on Swiftcurrent Lake opened in 1915 with luxuries of hot and cold running water, steam heat, telephones, and electric lights in every room. But within a decade, visitor interests altered. The Depression, fewer people who could afford pricey hotels, and the appeal of automobile road trips caused the railroad company to erect Swiftcurrent Cabins in 1933. They soared into popularity at $2.25 per night.

In 1936, high winds forced the Heavens Peak fire over the Continental Divide, where it promptly ate up 33 of the Swiftcurrent cabins. Many Glacier Hotel was next, but employees saved it by dousing the roof with water. When they apprised the railroad's vice president of their success, he uttered the reply: "Why?" The hotels and chalets had become a financial noose around the railroad's neck. After new highway routes bypassed the St. Mary chalets, causing them to fall into disuse, they were torn down in 1948; the remaining Many Glacier chalets succumbed to fire and avalanches. Only the historic showplace Many Glacier Hotel remains.

Exploring St. Mary and Many Glacier

Glacier's eastern ecosystem sprawls across national park lands and the Blackfeet Reservation, divided by an artificially straight border. Bears and elk know no boundaries, and sometimes neither do cattle, ranging astray inside Glacier.

across the summits of Chief Mountain, Napi Point, and Divide Mountain, crossing the lower end of Sherburne Reservoir and sliding between the two St. Mary Lakes. Permits are required for camping, fishing, hiking, and boating on the reservation.

Blackfeet Reservation

Bordering the park's eastern boundary are Blackfeet Nation lands. The boundary slices

St. Mary

St. Mary is the eastern portal to Going-to-the-Sun Road. At the junction of the Sun Road

Where Can I Find...?

- **ATMs:** The **supermarket** in St. Mary and the lodge at **St. Mary Village** have ATMs. In Many Glacier, find ATMs at **Swiftcurrent Motor Inn** and **Many Glacier Hotel.**

- **Cell reception:** There's **no cell service** in Many Glacier. Many Glacier and Swiftcurrent Motor Inn have **pay phones.** St. Mary has **limited service.**

- **Gas:** Two gas stations are in **St. Mary** on U.S. 89, one on either side of the junction with Going-to-the-Sun Road. **Babb** has a gas station across from Thronson's General Store. Many Glacier has no gas services.

- **Restrooms:** In **Many Glacier,** find public restrooms with **flush toilets** and **running water** at the campground, picnic area, Swiftcurrent Motor Inn lobby, and Many Glacier Hotel. In **St. Mary,** restrooms are at St. Mary Visitor Center, St. Mary Campground, and the lodge lobby at St. Mary Village.

- **Wi-Fi:** There's Wi-Fi at **St. Mary Visitor Center.** Limited wireless internet is available for guests in the lobbies of Many Glacier Hotel, Swiftcurrent Motor Inn, and the lodge at St. Mary Village. **Johnson's of St. Mary** and **St. Mary KOA** also have Wi-Fi.

- **Wildlife:** You can often spot **bighorn sheep, mountain goats,** and **grizzly bears** on the slope of **Mount Altyn** and **Mount Henkel** in Many Glacier. Binoculars will aid in viewing.

and the Blackfeet Highway (U.S. 89), the town clusters at the park boundary along the highway. Only the visitors center and St. Mary Campground are within the park; the town, restaurants, grocery stores, lodging, and commercial campgrounds are on the Blackfeet Reservation.

Many Glacier

Get used to the lingo: Locals refer to the Swiftcurrent Valley as Many Glacier, even though that is technically not its name; only the hotel and the campground actually use that name. Ultra-scenic Many Glacier derived its name from the string of small glaciers that populate its peaks: Grinnell, Salamander, Gem, North Swiftcurrent, and South Swiftcurrent.

Babb

Between St. Mary and Many Glacier is Babb, a blink-and-you'll-miss-it village on the Blackfeet Reservation. A few houses tuck behind a small seasonal grocery store and motel, along with two bars, and two restaurants. Its year-round post office and elementary school

serve families ranching between St. Mary and the Canadian border.

Belly River

North of Many Glacier in two valleys lined with good fishing lakes, the Belly River is home to tales of Joe Cosley, one of the park's most notorious rangers. The Belly, as locals call it, is undeveloped backcountry with no hotels or restaurants. While day hikers can reach a couple of the Belly's lakes in one long day, the area is a backpacking haven.

VISITORS CENTERS

Located at the St. Mary entrance to Glacier National Park, the **St. Mary Visitor Center** (406/888-7800, www.nps.gov/glac, 8am-5pm daily late May-early Oct., open until 6pm July-mid-Aug.) is the largest visitors center in the park. It houses a small Glacier National Park Conservancy **bookstore** (406/892-3250, http://glacier.org), theater, and displays on Native American cultural history. Astronomy programs that celebrate this International Dark Sky Park take place outdoors, where you can see night sky features from the **St.**

Mary Observatory telescope on two high-resolution screens. Walk to the visitors center via a trail and wooden bridge from the campground or on the paved pathway from St. Mary; drive through the park entrance to reach the parking lot.

Inside the center, find **backcountry permits** (7am-4:30pm daily late May-late Sept.), fishing regulations, Going-to-the-Sun Road updates, *Junior Ranger Activity Guides*, and information on free guided hikes and presentations with park naturalists. The theater hosts slide presentations, evening naturalist programs, and the popular Two Medicine Lake Singers and Dancers.

The visitors center is also a shuttle stop: To avoid parking hassles at Logan Pass, park your car here all day for free and catch the free shuttle up Going-to-the-Sun Road.

In Many Glacier, between the picnic area and Swiftcurrent parking lot adjacent to the campground, the small **Many Glacier Ranger Station** (milepost 12.4, Many Glacier Rd., 406/888-7800, 7am-4:30pm daily late May-late Sept.) has hiking info, maps, trail conditions, bear-sighting information, guidebooks, and backcountry permits.

ENTRANCE STATIONS

The park staffs entrance stations at **St. Mary** (year-round) at the eastern gateway of Going-to-the-Sun Road and in **Many Glacier** (May-Oct.). Both have self-pay cash-only kiosks for when the stations are unstaffed. If you don't have an annual pass, get a seven-day pass ($35 per vehicle, $30 per motorcycle, $20 per biker, hiker, and pedestrian in summer; $25, $20, and $15 in winter).

SHUTTLES AND TOURS
Shuttles

Shuttles enable point-to-point hiking on some of Glacier's most spectacular trails. Going car-free to trailheads outweighs the disappointment of full parking lots. The shuttles do not come with interpretive guides like the bus tours. Use shuttle combinations for two trails linking Going-to-the-Sun Road and Many Glacier: The Highline Trail and Piegan Pass Trail.

Going-to-the-Sun Road shuttles (406/888-7800, www.nps.gov/glac, 9am-5pm daily July-late Sept., free) depart every 30-40 minutes to run between St. Mary Visitor Center and Logan Pass, where you can transfer to west side shuttles for the Lake McDonald Valley. The ride to Logan Pass takes about one hour with stops at all trailheads, campgrounds, picnic areas, and lodges. Boarding lines of an hour or more often form for the shuttles. For Logan Pass, be sure to take a day pack with water, snacks, and extra clothing for fast-changing weather. Some shuttles have bike racks, and most are wheelchair-accessible. The shuttle system is slated for **expansion,** adding longer hours, more stops, and maybe a fee.

St. Mary

BLACKFEET
NATION
RESERVATION

Lower
St. Mary
Lake

WEST SHORE RD

ST. MARY
KOA

St. Mary River

To Babb

89

ST. MARY

NATIVE AMERICA SPEAKS
STARGAZING   JOHNSON'S OF ST. MARY/
JOHNSON'S WORLD FAMOUS
HISTORIC RESTAURANT

ST. MARY
VISITOR CENTER
PARK CAFE   RED EAGLE
MOTEL

ST. MARY
ENTRANCE

GOING-TO-THE-SUN RD

PARK GROCERY

COTTAGES
AT GLACIER

ST. MARY LODGE
AND RESORT

St. Mary
Lake

ST. MARY
SUPERMART

1913 RANGER
STATION

89

Glacier
National
Park

ST. MARY SCENIC OVERLOOK AND
BLACKFEET INTERPRETIVE LOOP

Red Eagle Trail

0   500 yds

0   500 m

© MOON.COM

Many Glacier

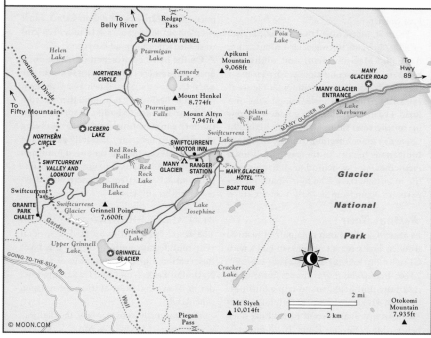

To Belly River

Redgap Pass

PTARMIGAN TUNNEL

Poia Lake

Helen Lake

Ptarmigan Lake

Apikuni Mountain 9,068ft

MANY GLACIER ROAD

To Hwy 89

Continental Divide

NORTHERN CIRCLE

Kennedy Lake

MANY GLACIER ENTRANCE

To Fifty Mountain

Mount Henkel 8,774ft

Ptarmigan Falls

Mount Altyn 7,947ft

Apikuni Falls

Lake Sherburne

NORTHERN CIRCLE

ICEBERG LAKE

Swiftcurrent Lake

SWIFTCURRENT MOTOR INN

SWIFTCURRENT VALLEY AND LOOKOUT

Red Rock Falls

MANY GLACIER

RANGER STATION

MANY GLACIER HOTEL

BOAT TOUR

Glacier

Swiftcurrent Pass

Red Rock Lake

Bullhead Lake

National

GRANITE PARK CHALET

Swiftcurrent Glacier

Grinnell Point 7,600ft

Lake Josephine

Park

Garden

Grinnell Lake

Upper Grinnell Lake

GOING-TO-THE-SUN RD

GRINNELL GLACIER

Cracker Lake

Wall

© MOON.COM

Piegan Pass

Mt Siyeh 10,014ft

0   2 mi

0   2 km

Otokomi Mountain 7,935ft

Two shuttle systems operate on the east side, linking with St. Mary. Find their respective schedules online. For point-to-point hikers on the Highline or Piegan Pass Trails, **Xanterra** (855/733-4522, www.glaciernationalparklodges.com, early June-mid-Sept., adults $14, kids $7) runs a shuttle between St. Mary Visitor Center and Many Glacier with stops at Many Glacier Hotel and Swiftcurrent Motor Inn. Best for connecting with the Going-to-the-Sun Road shuttles, these first come-first served shuttles have four departures each way per day. **Pursuit Glacier Park Collection** (844/868-7474, www.glacierparkcollection.com, June-Sept., $15-30 one-way) runs shuttles on the east side of the park between St. Mary, Two Medicine, and East Glacier. Make reservations at least 24 hours in advance or pay the driver in cash when you board.

Bus Tours

While tours can travel the east side of Glacier in early summer, they may not access Logan Pass and the entire Going-to-the-Sun Road until it is open. Rates for tours do not include meals, taxes, park entrance fees, and gratuities. Reservations are required.

Daily tours leave Many Glacier Hotel and St. Mary on **historic red buses** (855/733-4522, www.glaciernationalparklodges.com, early June-mid-Sept., 2.5-8 hrs, adults $44-102, kids half price). Departure times vary based on pickup locations: Many Glacier Hotel, Swiftcurrent Motor Inn, St. Mary Lodge, or Rising Sun Motor Inn. These scenic buses are charmers; on good-weather days, the jammers (tour bus drivers) roll back the canvas tops for unlimited skyward views. No air-conditioning needed! Full-day and several-hour tours head to Logan Pass,

152

hitting almost every scenic stop on Going-to-the-Sun Road. The Old North Trail tour goes to Two Medicine and Glacier Park Lodge in East Glacier.

From St. Mary, **Sun Tours** (406/732-9220 or 800/786-9220, www.glaciersuntours.com, daily mid-May-mid-Sept., $60 adults, $35 kids) drives air-conditioned 25-passenger buses with extra-large windows for big scenery, an asset on the historic Going-to-the-Sun Road. Led by local Blackfeet guides who grew up on the reservation, the tours highlight Glacier's rich connection with the Blackfeet, Indigenous history in the park, traditional medicines, stories behind peak names, and life in buffalo days. The four-hour tour departs at 9:30am from St. Mary Visitor Center.

★ Boat Tour

In Many Glacier, jump on a pair of historic wooden boats for a tour of two lakes with **Glacier Park Boat Company** (406/257-2426, http://glacierparkboats.com, daily mid-June-mid-Sept., round-trip adults $34, children $17). Catch the 1961-vintage *Chief Two Guns* at Swiftcurrent Lake's boat dock behind Many Glacier Hotel. In 75 minutes, you'll cruise across the lake, hike five minutes over a hill, hop aboard the 1945 *Morning Eagle* for a cruise on Lake Josephine, and return. Don't forget your camera, although you may have difficulty cramming the view into the lens. Tours depart at 9am, 11am, 2pm, and 4:30pm, with additional launches at 1pm and 3pm from July 1, and 8:30am from mid-July. Two of the launches offer guided round-trip walks to Grinnell Lake (2 mi/3.2 km), and the earliest boat has a ranger-led hike to Grinnell Glacier. Tours sell out, but you can make reservations by phone or in person at the dock at least one day in advance.

Hikers also use the boats as **shuttles** to cut down trail mileage. You can catch one-way return boats (half price) at the Lake Josephine upper dock; pay cash as you board. You may have to wait for a few launches to get on, but the captain runs the boat until all hikers are shuttled.

Driving Tours

Visitors to St. Mary have options for touring in all directions. Since St. Mary is the eastern portal for **Going-to-the-Sun Road,** most people head to Logan Pass 18 miles (29 km) westward when the road is open.

On the Blackfeet Reservation, roads cross open range where **cattle or horses wander onto the roads.** Slow down and give them room. Ol' Bessie may just stand there staring at you and refuse to budge. If so, a toot on the horn can sometimes help, but avoid being obnoxious. If necessary, carefully pass in the other lane. Even though the speed limit sign says 70 mph (113 kph), slow down at night due to livestock. Brakes frequently screech as drivers nearly hit animals.

BLACKFEET HIGHWAY

The **Blackfeet Highway** (U.S. 89, open year-round) runs entirely on the Blackfeet Reservation along the east side of Glacier National Park from the Canadian border to Browning. Most of it traverses aspen ranchland.

Driving north from St. Mary, the highway undulates past **Lower St. Mary Lake** and Thunderbird Island. This section is one of the few roads with shoulders, making driving easier. Rounding the lake's outlet, watch for waterfowl and views to the north of Chief Mountain and Old Sun Glacier on Mount Merritt. The road passes Duck Lake Road (7.3 mi/11.7 km north of St. Mary), Many Glacier Road and Babb (9 mi/14.5 km), and Chief Mountain Highway (14 mi/22.5 km) before reaching the Canadian border (24 mi/39 km). The highway becomes AB-2 in Canada.

Driving south from St. Mary, the Blackfeet Highway heads to **Two Medicine, Browning,** and **East Glacier.** Two miles (3.2 km) up the hill, stop at **St. Mary Scenic Overlook and Blackfeet Interpretive Loop** for panoramic views of the St. Mary

---

1: tour boat in Many Glacier. **2:** bighorn sheep **3:** wildflowers along Many Glacier Road

Valley. As the road climbs to St. Mary Ridge through the 2006 Red Eagle Fire, it crosses Hudson Bay Divide, which sends water to the Missouri and Saskatchewan Rivers. Several lanes allow for passing, but within a few miles the road pinches into a curvy, rolling, narrow, shoulderless trek through willow bogs and beaver ponds divided by aspen groves. Turns are blind; take them slowly to avoid cyclists or cows on the road. At 20 miles (32 km) from St. Mary, turn right onto MT 49 (closed in winter), a road with more curves than a snake, heading toward Two Medicine (38 mi/61 km) and East Glacier (33 mi/53 km), or stay left to reach Browning (32 mi/52 km).

★ MANY GLACIER ROAD

The 12-mile-long (19.3-km) **Many Glacier Road** (Glacier Rte. 3, open May-Oct.) is a stunning drive into **Swiftcurrent Valley.** Drive slowly to avoid wildlife. From Babb, the road follows Swiftcurrent Creek upstream across Blackfeet Nation lands. Watch for bears, particularly around dusk. If you spot a bear, drive by slowly to watch rather than stop and create a bear jam (which condition bears to be comfortable around cars). Above all, stay in the car for safety. In 2021, Many Glacier Road will have a huge construction project (to repair roadbed damage) that will cause long delays, and the road will only be open mid-May to mid-September.

After the road rises to reach Sherburne Dam (mile 4.8/km 7.7), it follows the reservoir's north shore, crossing into the park over the cattle grate, but you won't reach the park entrance station for another 3 miles (4.8 km). Check the shoreline for deer, bears, and sometimes errant cows. Wildflower meadows with early July's pink sticky geraniums and lupine line the road. Scenic stops have views of Sherburne Reservoir and up the valley to **Grinnell Glacier.**

At the end of the road, you'll reach **Many Glacier Hotel** (mile 11.5/km 18.5), the picnic area (mile 12.1/km 19.5), and ranger station and campground (mile 12.3/km 19.8).

It terminates at Swiftcurrent Motor Inn and trailheads.

DUCK LAKE ROAD

Montana 464, known locally as the **Duck Lake Road** (year-round), leaves U.S. 89 at the east end of Lower St. Mary Lake (7.3 mi/11.7 km north of St. Mary, 1.7 mi/2.7 km south of Babb). Locals use this road via Browning for faster access between the park's northeast sections and East Glacier. Although the mileage is longer (53 mi/85 km from St. Mary to East Glacier rather than 33 mi/53 km via U.S. 89), the straighter road affords easier driving, especially for RVs. It's also faster: Speed limits reach 70 mph (113 kph) on stretches. The road climbs over St. Mary Ridge, passing Duck Lake at 3 miles (4.8 km). From the top of the ridge above Duck Lake, which is the divide between the Missouri and Saskatchewan drainages, the road heads southward across the Blackfeet Reservation to Browning (34 mi/55 km from U.S. 89) through bison and cattle ranches with Glacier's peaks dominating the western skyline.

CHIEF MOUNTAIN INTERNATIONAL HIGHWAY

A seasonal road, **Chief Mountain International Highway** links Glacier and Waterton Lakes National Park. Its season and hours are those of the Canadian and U.S. immigration and customs stations at the border (9am-6pm daily mid-May-June and Sept., 7am-10pm daily June-Labor Day). With its start 4 miles (6.4 km) north of Babb, the 30-mile (48-km) road undulates over rolling aspen hills and beaver ponds on the Blackfeet Reservation as it curves around blocky Chief Mountain to the border. A few unmarked pullouts offer good photo ops.

As the road rounds Chief Mountain, it enters Glacier National Park. There is no entrance station here, and no payment is required. The road reaches the international border and Chief Mountain border crossing at 15 miles (24 km). Passports are required for crossing into Canada.

Sights

ST. MARY RIVER

Between St. Mary Visitor Center and St. Mary Campground, Going-to-the-Sun Road crosses the **St. Mary River,** a waterway connecting the two St. Mary Lakes. You can park near the stone bridge to take a look. Find larger parking at the visitors center and walk 0.3 mile (0.5 km) through prairie smoke flowers to a scenic wooden bridge that connects to the campground. Look for killdeer, among other birds. For anglers, this river offers some of the best local fishing. You can drop a line in from the wooden footbridge, but not from the Going-to-the-Sun Road bridge.

ST. MARY LAKES

In pockets left from 1,200-foot-deep (366-m) Pleistocene ice age glaciers, **St. Mary Lake** and **Lower St. Mary Lake** stand as testament to glacial forces. The lakes collect water from snowmelt and some of the largest glaciers left in the park: Blackfoot and Jackson Glaciers. Their waters meander toward the Canadian border and into the Saskatchewan River to Hudson Bay. With the valley sucking air down from the Continental Divide, frequent winds swirl up large whitecapped waves. See the lakes from Going-to-the-Sun Road and U.S. 89.

ST. MARY SCENIC OVERLOOK AND BLACKFEET INTERPRETIVE LOOP

Two miles (3.2 km) south of St. Mary on U.S. 89, the **St. Mary Scenic Overlook** has an impressive panoramic view of the upper St. Mary Valley, St. Mary Lake, and Glacier's peaks. The 0.2-mile (0.3-km) paved, wheelchair-accessible **Blackfeet Interpretive Loop** begins from the overlook's parking area at a sculpture of a woman and a travois. The route tours metal tepee sculptures at overlooks, while interpretive signage tells stories of the Blackfeet. On the highway, look for signs that say, "Turnout ½ mile."

DIVIDE MOUNTAIN

Divide Mountain rises 8,665 feet (2,641 m) in elevation, the last in a string of peaks guarding St. Mary Valley's south. Silvered remnants of the 2006 Red Eagle Fire flank its slopes. From the summit, the mountain drops east to St. Mary Ridge, running for miles onto the prairie. The ridge is a lateral moraine, deposited by a Pleistocene glacier that formed the valley. This ridge, along with Divide Mountain, separates the waters flowing into the Saskatchewan and Missouri Rivers.

1913 RANGER STATION

Follow the signs on a five-minute drive from Going-to-the-Sun Road (0.2 mi/0.32 km) from the junction with U.S. 89, just south of St. Mary Visitor Center) to the **1913 Ranger Station.** A small parking area leads uphill on a three-minute walk to the historic building. Adjacent to it is the Lubec Ranger Station Barn, which was moved here in 1977; its restored weather-split logs and chinking make it more photo-worthy than the ranger station.

★ GRINNELL GLACIER

Like all glaciers in northwest Montana, **Grinnell Glacier** is melting. Located in Many Glacier, the ice field reached its peak size around 1850, when it filled the entire hanging valley under Mount Gould and connected with Salamander Glacier. Lateral moraines mark its original size. By 1930, the glacier receded, separating from Salamander and forming a lake at its snout. Today, the ice has thinned and shrunk considerably. See a bit of the glacier with binoculars from the Many Glacier Road, or for a closer inspection, hike to the most-visited glacier in the park.

SWIFTCURRENT LAKE

Originally called McDermott Lake, **Swiftcurrent Lake** took its name from the Blackfeet term for swift-flowing water, a name that George Bird Grinnell promoted for the area. The lake, however, does not have fast-flowing waters. Located in Many Glacier, its bays attract loons and mergansers. Moose eat the shoreline willows. A beaver lodge sits at the inlet of Swiftcurrent Creek. Enjoy the lake by paddling, riding the tour boat, circling it by trail, or sitting on Many Glacier Hotel's deck.

TOP EXPERIENCE

★ MANY GLACIER HOTEL

Built in 1915, the National Historic Landmark **Many Glacier Hotel** (milepost 11.5, Many Glacier Rd., 855/733-4522, www. glaciernationalparklodges.com, mid-June-mid-Sept.) graces Swiftcurrent Lake's shore. The five-story, 211-room hotel is owned by the National Park Service and is operated by Xanterra. A $30 million restoration straightened the leaning structure, restored the dining room to its historic look, revamped the lobby, rebuilt the historic helical stairway to the lower level, and replaced windows, doors, the roof, siding, and decks. Warm up on a cold day around the huge fireplace in the massive lobby, or lounge on its large deck overlooking Swiftcurrent Lake and a mountainous panorama. Join park naturalists for a tour of the historic hotel: Check the park newspaper for the current schedule.

WILDLIFE-WATCHING

Bears congregate heavily in the Swiftcurrent Valley due to abundant food sources. One of the best places to see them is feeding on the slopes of Mount Altyn and Mount Henkel on the north side of the Many Glacier Road. With binoculars, you can see bears, along with **mountain goats** and **bighorn sheep,** from the Many Glacier Hotel deck and Many Glacier Picnic Area. Rangers often set up a spotting scope in the Swiftcurrent parking lot for wildlife-watching.

Recreation

DAY HIKES

Around **St. Mary,** hiking options are limited to mosquito-ridden beaver ponds, a lake, or a peak scramble. For hiking, most visitors go up Going-to-the-Sun Road or drive 21 miles (34 km) to Many Glacier where options are plentiful.

In **Many Glacier,** because routes lead quickly to stunning high country, trails are crowded. Most trailheads depart from Many Glacier Hotel, Swiftcurrent parking lot, or the picnic area. Although trail junctions are extremely well signed, maps are helpful to navigate the maze, especially trails crisscrossing Grinnell Valley. St. Mary Visitor Center and Many Glacier Ranger Station have free non-topographic maps of hiking trails in both areas. They are also online (www.nps.gov/glac).

Because of dense bear populations in Many Glacier, trails are closed from time to time to let an aggressive or feeding bear cool off. Check for current trail status with the ranger station, Many Glacier Hotel's activity desk, or online.

Trails are accessible depending on road openings to trailheads and snow. Snow usually blankets trails late October-late May. Most lower-elevation trails melt out by late May, and the park service starts installing seasonal bridges over rivers; most are removed in late September. Higher-elevation trails, such as Cracker Lake, Grinnell Glacier, Swiftcurrent

---

1: St. Mary Scenic Overlook and Blackfeet Interpretive Loop **2:** Grinnell Glacier

St. Mary and Many Glacier Hikes

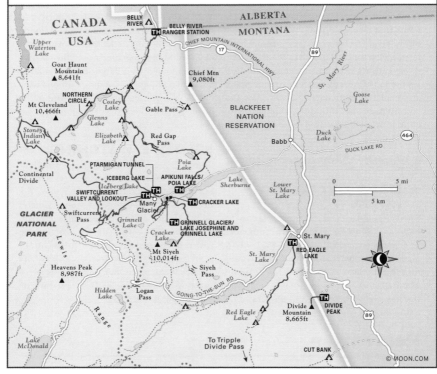

Pass, Ptarmigan Tunnel, and Iceberg Lake retain snow as late as mid-July and usually get snow-covered again by October. Check trail status reports at ranger stations and online (www.nps.gov/glac) for updates.

Hikes are listed in order from the south at St. Mary north to the Canadian border.

Red Eagle Lake

Distance: 16 miles (26 km) round-trip
Duration: 7.5 hours
Elevation gain: 480 feet (146 m)
Effort: easy but long
Trail surface: narrow dirt path with roots and rocks
Trailhead: at the 1913 Ranger Station parking lot in St. Mary

After following an old road for 1 mile (1.6 km), the trail climbs gently through the 2006 Red Eagle Fire, where wildflowers are madly growing back. The burn continues to the lake, where it started. Watch for bear diggings, where grizzlies rototill for glacier lily bulbs or go after ground squirrels. Red Eagle Mountain looms ahead, and grand views northwest to Going-to-the-Sun Mountain unfold. About halfway, the trail crosses Red Eagle Creek twice on swinging bridges before reaching the lake that was home to a large tent camp in the 1920s, famous for fishing.

Apikuni Falls

Distance: 1.6 miles (2.6 km) round-trip
Duration: 1 hour
Elevation gain: 570 feet (174 m)
Effort: moderate
Trail surface: narrow and rocky dirt path

St. Mary and Many Glacier Hikes

Trail	Effort	Distance	Duration
Red Eagle Lake	easy	16 mi (26 km) rt	7.5 hr
Apikuni Falls	moderate	1.6 mi (2.6 km) rt	1 hr
Poia Lake	moderate	13.2 mi (21.2 km) rt	6.5 hr
Cracker Lake	moderate	12.5 mi (20.1 km) rt	6 hr
Lake Josephine and Grinnell Lake	easy	2.2-7.8 mi (3.5-12.6 km) rt	1-4 hr
Grinnell Glacier	moderate-strenuous	11 mi (17.7 km) rt	6 hr
Swiftcurrent Valley and Lookout	easy-strenuous	3.6-16.2 mi (5.8-26 km) rt	2-8 hr
Iceberg Lake	moderate	10.4 mi (16.7 km) rt	5 hr
Ptarmigan Tunnel	moderate-strenuous	11.4 mi (18.3 km) rt	5 hr
Belly River Ranger Station	moderate	12 mi (19.3 km) rt	6 hr

Trailhead: Grinnell Glacier interpretive site, 10.4 miles (16.7 km) west on Many Glacier Road (see map p. 160)

Apikuni Falls springs from a hanging valley, which you can see from the trailhead. The short walk starts out across a flat meadow where wildflowers bloom thickly in July: geraniums, arrowleaf balsamroot, paintbrush, lupine, and stonecrop. But soon, the path steepens to climb to the cliffs between Mount Altyn and Apikuni Mountain, where the falls drop out of the basin above. Those with scrambling skills can climb a rough trail into the upper hanging valley.

Poia Lake

Distance: 13.2 miles (21.2 km) round-trip
Duration: 6.5 hours
Elevation gain: 1,511 feet (461 m)
Effort: moderate
Trail surface: narrow dirt path with roots and rocks
Trailhead: Grinnell Glacier interpretive site, 10.4 miles (16.7 km) west on Many Glacier Road (see map p. 160)

One of Many Glacier's less crowded routes, the trail to Poia Lake climbs through aspen groves and wildflower meadows blooming with pink sticky geraniums to crest the forested Swiftcurrent Ridge before dropping to the lake. Be prepared for manure and trail destruction from the daily horseback trail-ride concession. Pass through the campground and drop to the lake, where spur paths cut through the willows to the beach. The return trip requires a 600-foot (183-m) climb back over the ridge. Backpackers continue on from Poia over Red Gap Pass.

Cracker Lake

Distance: 12.5 miles (20.1 km) round-trip
Duration: 6 hours
Elevation gain: 1,182 feet (360 m)
Effort: moderate
Trail surface: narrow and muddy path, with roots and rocks
Trailhead: south end of Many Glacier Hotel parking lot (see map p. 161)

If you can stand the muddy, horse-rutted, manure-filled first 1.5 miles (2.4 km), where trail rides travel multiple times a day, the rest of the hike is extremely scenic and not nearly as crowded as other Many Glacier hikes. If you meet horses, step below, not above, the trail to let them pass. At the Cracker Flats junction,

Apikuni Falls and Poia Lake

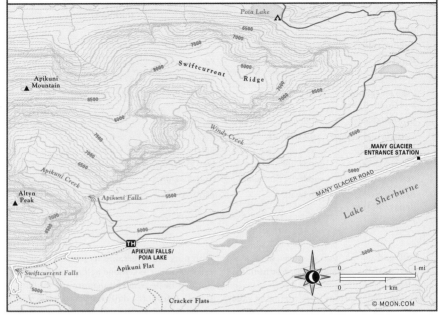

leave the messy trail behind and stomp the mud and manure from your boots. Climb up switchbacks into the Cracker Valley, where avalanche paths break up the forested trail and give way to bluebell and lupine meadows in the final stretch.

Once you reach Cracker Lake, bypass the backcountry campground and drop to the inlet for the best lunch spot on the shore. Glacial flour clouds the lake water, turning it a rich milky turquoise. The gutsy take a quick dive in the frigid water. Siyeh Peak, at 10,014 feet (3,052 m), rises abruptly up a gigantic cliff face, a skyscraping 4,000 feet (1,219 m) above the lake.

Lake Josephine and Grinnell Lake

Distance: 2.2-7.8 miles (3.5-12.6 km) round-trip
Duration: 1-4 hours
Elevation gain: minimal
Effort: easy

Trail surface: dirt and rocks
Trailheads: on the south side of Many Glacier Hotel, at Swiftcurrent Picnic Area, or via the tour boat (see map p. 162)

For a 2.2-mile (3.5-km) round-trip walk, catch the tour boat across Swiftcurrent Lake and Lake Josephine to hike to Grinnell Lake. For a longer hike, begin from Many Glacier Hotel, following the trail winding around Swiftcurrent Lake to the boat dock opposite the hotel. A third starting point begins at the picnic area, where it follows Swiftcurrent Lake to that same boat dock.

From the boat dock, pop over the hill to Josephine Lake, where the trail hugs the north shore until it splits off to Grinnell Glacier. Stay on the lower trail to wrap around Josephine's west end to the Grinnell Lake junction. Turn right and follow the trail over a swinging bridge. At the lakeshore, enjoy Grinnell's milky turquoise waters and the giant falls across the lake. Although you can return to the trailheads via the south lakeshore trail, it is not as scenic due to deep forest. Shorten the hike by catching the tour boat back.

★ Grinnell Glacier

Distance: 11 miles (17.7 km) round-trip
Duration: 6 hours
Elevation gain: 1,619 feet (493 m)
Effort: moderate-strenuous
Trail surface: narrow and rocky dirt path; rock steps
Trailheads: on the south side of Many Glacier Hotel, at Swiftcurrent Picnic Area, or via the tour boat (see map p. 162)

Cracker Lake

In early summer, a large steep snowdrift frequently bars the path into the upper basin until early July; check on status before hiking. The most accessible glacier in the park, Grinnell Glacier still requires stamina as most of its elevation gain packs within 2 miles (3.2 km). Many hikers take the boat shuttle, cutting the length to 7.8 miles (12.6 km) round-trip, or just trimming 2.5 miles (4 km) off the return. To hike the entire route from the picnic area, follow Swiftcurrent Lake's west shore to the boat dock. From Many Glacier Hotel, round the southern shore to meet up with the same dock. Bop over the short hill and hike around Lake Josephine's north shore.

Toward Josephine's west end, the Grinnell Glacier Trail diverges uphill. As the trail climbs through multicolored rock strata, Grinnell Lake's milky turquoise waters come into view below. Above, you'll spot Gem Glacier and Salamander Glacier, both shrunken to static snowfields, long before Grinnell Glacier appears. The trail ascends on a cliff stairway where a waterfall douses hikers before passing a rest stop with outhouses. A steep grunt up the moraine leads to a stunning view. Trot through the maze of paths crossing the bedrock to Upper Grinnell Lake's shore, but do not walk out on the glacier's ice, as it harbors deadly hidden crevasses.

★ Swiftcurrent Valley and Lookout

Distance: 3.6-16.2 miles (5.8-26 km) round-trip
Duration: 2-8 hours
Elevation gain: 100-3,496 feet (30.5-1,066 m)
Effort: easy-strenuous
Trail surface: narrow dirt path with roots and rocks
Trailhead: Swiftcurrent parking lot in Many Glacier (see map p. 163)

This popular trail leads to various destinations along a scenic path dotted with lakes, waterfalls, moose, glaciers, and wildflowers. The trail winds through pine trees and aspen groves as it rolls gently up to **Red Rock Lake and Falls** at 1.8 miles (2.9 km). At the top of the falls, a knoll provides a viewpoint to scan hillsides with binoculars for bears. The trail

Grinnell Glacier Trails

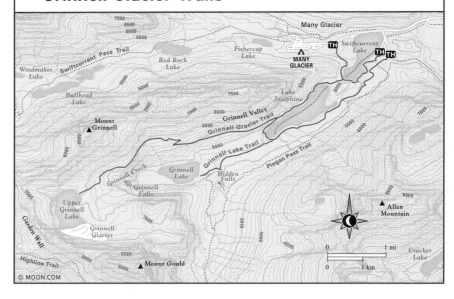

continues level through meadows rampant with Sitka valerian in July to Bullhead Lake at 3.9 miles (6.3 km). Scan scree slopes for bighorn sheep.

From the lake, the trail switchbacks uphill. It cuts around a cliff face before reaching **Swiftcurrent Pass** at 6.6 miles (10.6 km). From here, Granite Park Chalet is 0.9 mile (1.4 km) downhill. To reach the lookout, take the spur trail up 1.4 more miles (2.3 km) of switchbacks (you'll lose count of them). The lookout surveys almost the entire park: glaciers, peaks, wild panoramas, and the plains. Many Glacier Hotel looks minuscule. Enjoy the one-of-a-kind view from the outhouse. For a different descent, drop to The Loop to catch a shuttle.

★ Iceberg Lake

Distance: 10.4 miles (16.7 km) round-trip
Duration: 5 hours
Elevation gain: 1,193 feet (364 m)
Effort: moderate
Trail surface: narrow dirt path with roots and rocks

Trailhead: behind Swiftcurrent Motor Inn cabins in Many Glacier (see map p. 163)

One of the top hikes in Glacier, the trail to Iceberg Lake begins with a short, steep jaunt straight uphill, with no time to warm up your muscles gradually. Within 0.4 mile (0.64) you reach a junction. Take note of the directional sign here, and watch for it when you come down. On the return, some hikers zombie-walk right on past it.

From the junction, the trail maintains an easy railroad grade to the lake. Make noise on this trail, known for frequent bear sightings. Wildflowers line the trail in July: bear grass, bog orchids, penstemon, and thimbleberry. One mile (1.6 km) past the junction, the trail rounds a red argillite outcropping with views of the valley. As the trail swings north, it enters a pine and fir forest and crosses Ptarmigan Falls at 2.6 miles (4.2 km), a good break spot where aggressive ground squirrels will steal your snacks. Do not feed them; feeding only trains them to be more forceful. Just beyond the falls, the Ptarmigan

Swiftcurrent Valley, Iceberg Lake, and Ptarmigan Tunnel

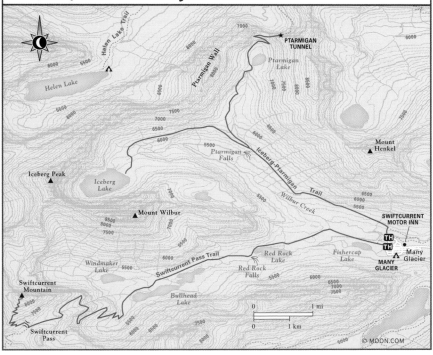

Tunnel Trail veers right. Stay straight to swing west through multiple avalanche paths. After crossing a creek, the trail climbs the final bluff, where a view of stark icebergs against blue water unfolds. Brave hikers dive into the lake, but be prepared to have the frigid water suck the air from your lungs.

★ Ptarmigan Tunnel

Distance: 11.4 miles (18.3 km) round-trip

Duration: 5 hours

Elevation gain: 2,304 feet (702 m)

Effort: moderate-strenuous

Trail surface: narrow dirt path with roots and rocks

Trailhead: behind Swiftcurrent Motor Inn cabins in Many Glacier (see map p. 163)

Depending on snowpack, the tunnel doors usually open mid-July-late September; check to confirm the status. Traversing the same trail as Iceberg Lake, the route begins with a steep uphill climb before leveling out into a gentle ascent around Mount Henkel. Just past Ptarmigan Falls, at 2.8 miles (4.5 km) the Ptarmigan Tunnel route veers right off the Iceberg Trail. The climb goes aggressively uphill for 1 mile (1.6 km) before assuming an easier uphill grade through meadows to Ptarmigan Lake.

From the lake, the route to the tunnel leads up another 800 feet (244 m) via two switchbacks on a scree slope. Tiny, fragile alpine plants struggle to survive on this barren slope: Protect them by staying on the trail rather than cutting the switchbacks. The 183-foot (56-m) tunnel, 6 feet (1.8 m) wide and 9 feet (2.7 m) tall, cuts through Ptarmigan

Wall. Walk through for the burst of red rock color on the other side. Admire the trail engineering along the north side's cliff wall and drop down 0.25 mile (0.4 km) to see Old Sun Glacier on Mount Merritt.

Belly River Ranger Station

Distance: 12 miles (19.3 km) round-trip
Duration: 6 hours
Elevation gain: 745 feet (227 m) on return
Effort: moderate
Trail surface: narrow dirt path with roots and rocks
Trailhead: Chief Mountain border crossing parking lot on Chief Mountain Highway

A trail used by backpackers to access Elizabeth, Helen, Cosley, Glenns, and Mokowanis Lakes, the Ptarmigan Tunnel, and Stoney Indian Pass, the Belly River Trail attracts day hikers for the views of Chief Mountain and Pyramid Peak in the distance. Anglers also drop lines into the Belly River. The trail begins with a descent down to the valley floor. Look for scratches in the aspen bark where elk have rubbed to remove the velvet from their antlers.

As the trail undulates gently across the valley floor, it traverses aspen groves and open meadows blooming with lupine and paintbrush. At the pastoral Belly River Ranger Station, listed on the National Register of Historic Places, you can envy the backcountry rangers who spend their summers staring at Gable Mountain's colorful strata, the spires of the Stoney Indian Peaks, and Mount Cleveland, the highest peak in the park.

Guides

In Many Glacier and St. Mary, options abound for guided hikes. The National Park Service leads hikes to various scenic destinations mid-June–mid-September, including full-day hikes to Grinnell Glacier and Iceberg Lake. Some trips combine with boat tours to cross Swiftcurrent Lake and Lake Josephine. Although the hikes are free, you'll need to pay for the boat ride. The park's guided hikes are great for solo hikers to be in the company of others in bear country and to glean tidbits of natural history, but be prepared for hiking in very large groups; some have more than 30 people in midsummer. For schedules, check the park newspaper or go online (www.nps. gov/glac). For full-day hikes, pack along water, snacks, lunch, and extra clothes.

Glacier Guides (406/387-5555 or 800/521-7238, http://glacierguides.com) leads day hikes and backpacking trips in the park's northeast region. While solo travelers can join the weekly Iceberg Lake hike (Fridays July-Aug., $120 pp), families and small groups can hire a guide (June-Sept., $650 for up to five people) for any trail. The guide will meet you at your lodge or campground in St. Mary or Many Glacier to hike. All hikes require reservations and include guide service, deli lunch, and transportation to the trailhead. The company also has three-, four-, and six-day backpacking trips that depart weekly (June-mid-Sept., $225/day), some that frequent the Belly River. Plan on a 15 percent gratuity for day trips and 20 percent for overnights.

BACKPACKING

Popular backpacking trails follow historic horse-packing routes from the 1920s in this region, and shuttles aid in reaching trailheads. In June, the Belly is outstanding for backpacking when snow still buries high passes.

Permits (adults $7 pp/night) for these trips are in high demand. Pick them up 24 hours in advance in person at the **Apgar Backcountry Permit Office** (406/888-7859 May-Oct., 406/888-7800 Nov.-Apr.), **St. Mary Visitor Center** (406/888-7800, late May-late Sept.), or **Many Glacier Ranger Station** (406/888-7800, late May-late Sept.). Lines begin forming an hour before the 7am opening. Permits are available until 4pm. For advance reservations, apply online starting in mid-March (www.nps.gov/glac, $40).

1: hikers descending from Swiftcurrent Pass
2: Iceberg Lake **3:** Ptarmigan Tunnel Trail from Belly River **4:** trail ride with Swan Mountain Outfitters

Belly River Country

North of Many Glacier, the Belly River is wild backcountry. With no roads accessing the valley, entry is on foot or horseback. From Many Glacier, two routes cross into the Belly: Ptarmigan Tunnel and Red Gap Pass via Poia Lake. Three other trails reach the Belly via other routes: The shortest is from the Chief Mountain border crossing; longer routes go from Goat Haunt over Stoney Indian Pass or from Lee Ridge. To locals, the area is simply known as the Belly.

The Belly is home to the headwaters of the Saskatchewan River, which flows to Hudson Bay. The **Belly River** may have been named for the Gros Ventre (French for "Big Belly") people, and the **Mokowanis River** for a Blackfeet term that refers to a buffalo's stomach. Thirty-three backcountry campsites are strung up and down the two valleys, as well as lakes: Elizabeth, Helen, Cosley, Glenns, and Mokowanis. At the confluence of the two valleys, the historic Belly River Ranger Station, which is staffed in summer, sits idyllic amid aspen groves and fields of wild sticky geraniums staring up at Stoney Indian Peaks and Mount Cleveland, the park's highest peak.

For **backpackers,** the Belly is the place to go in June. Backcountry campsites at the low-elevation lakes open weeks before higher-elevation trails. For **anglers,** the rivers and lakes hop with fish.

TOP EXPERIENCE

★ Northern Circle
52 MILES (84 KM)

Hike the five- to seven-day Northern Circle in either direction to take in prime fishing lakes and high passes. The loop makes logistics easy. Start and finish at one of five trailheads: Swiftcurrent, Iceberg-Ptarmigan Tunnel, Poia Lake, Chief Mountain Customs, or Goat Haunt.

The classic route is from Many Glacier. Launch up to Ptarmigan Tunnel to drop into the Belly River drainage. Then connect Elizabeth, Cosley, and Glenns Lakes (fording the outlet river at Cosley) to ascend the Mokowanis River drainage. The route pitches up to Stoney Indian Pass and quickly plunges to Stoney Indian Lake, where the campground's wall-less pit toilet takes in surrounding peaks. After descending into Waterton Valley, the trail climbs to the immense meadows at Fifty Mountain. A long day traipses up and down through multiple high-elevation basins along the Continental Divide to the Granite Park Chalet before crossing over Swiftcurrent Pass to return to Many Glacier, exiting at the Swiftcurrent trailhead.

Of the 12 backcountry campsites on or near the route, the best are at the foot of Elizabeth Lake (ELF), Cosley Lake (COS), Stoney Indian Lake (STO), Fifty Mountain (FIF), and Granite Park (GRN). Ptarmigan Tunnel usually opens mid-July, and the park service usually opens steep snowfields between Fifty Mountain and Granite Park by late July. Get walk-in permits for July, but advance reservations for Fifty Mountain and Stoney Indian Lake are only available starting August 1. Prepare for high-elevation snow in September.

Red Eagle Lake and Triple Divide Pass
30 MILES (48 KM)

Plan three days for an out-and-back trip to Red Eagle Lake and Triple Divide Pass. Camp at the head (REH) or foot (REF) of the lake for two nights. Anglers should take rods, as the lake has yielded record trout. From the trailhead near St. Mary, the rolling route crosses through aspen groves and wildflower meadows and over two swinging bridges to reach Red Eagle Lake. On the middle day, ford Red Eagle Creek and climb 15 miles (24 km) round-trip to Triple Divide Pass, a summering range for bighorn sheep.

To extend the trip to Two Medicine (32 mi/52 km total, 4-5 days), continue south from the pass on the Inside Trail to Morning Star

Lake (MOR). From there, go over Pitamakin Pass to Old Man Lake (OLD) or up Pitamakin and Dawson Passes to No Name Lake (NON). Both routes end at Two Medicine Lake.

The passes are usually snow-free by mid-July, although a few steep snowfields can linger on north slopes. Advance reservations start at Red Eagle Lake in mid-June, but not until July 15 for Morning Star, Old Man Lake, and No Name Lake.

BIKING

Bicycling the east side of Glacier National Park is all about big scenery road biking, as trails do not permit mountain bikes. No bike rentals are available, so bring your own. The National Park Service campgrounds at St. Mary and Many Glacier provide shared biker-hiker campsites ($5-8 pp) on a first-come, first-served basis. The sites have bear-resistant food storage containers.

East-side roads are generally narrow with no shoulders, a challenge for novice riders. Some vehicles nearly push riders off the road. Due to heavy traffic during July-August, riding earlier or later in the day is easier. Outside the park, roads cut through open range; cow herds and horses may be on the road, plus plentiful cow pies. Moose and bears are also common, especially early and late in the day. With bears capable of running up to 40 mph (64 kph), you won't be able to outride them. Carry bear spray; some cyclists whoop or holler to make noise to alert bears to their presence.

East-side roads are notorious for high winds. Expect strong easterlies. Heading in the right direction produces a nice tailwind; pushing against the bluster is tough.

Scenic Roads

Cyclists riding on **Going-to-the-Sun Road** the 18 miles (29 km) from St. Mary to Logan Pass have no restrictions. Bicycling the 12-mile (19.3-km) **Many Glacier Road** is extremely picturesque. Bicycling **Chief Mountain International Highway** 15 miles (24 km) to the customs station provides

sustained climbs and sailing descents while rounding the imposing Chief Mountain. Watch for a few rough gravel patches and cattle.

Blackfeet Highway

Cycling the Blackfeet Highway (U.S. 89) from the Canadian border to St. Mary is easier than pedaling other roads in the area. The undulating road is wider, straighter, and has small shoulders. Riding south on U.S. 89 from St. Mary to East Glacier starts on a wide thoroughfare with big shoulders for a climb atop St. Mary Ridge. But then the spacious road suddenly squeezes into a skinny, curvy ribbon with blind corners and little place to go when large vehicles hog the road. From a cycling perspective, it's a fun ride with the rolling terrain, but blind corners have a tendency to make riders brake for safety and then curse the loss of momentum.

HORSEBACK RIDING

Adjacent to the Many Glacier Hotel parking lot, **Swan Mountain Outfitters** (406/387-4405 or 877/888-5557, corral 406/732-4203, www.swanmountainglacier.com, June-mid-Sept., $55-200) guides one- and two-hour rides departing several times daily for Lake Josephine and Cracker Flats. Half-day rides leave twice daily for Grinnell Lake. All-day rides (lunch not included) go on varied trails. This is trail riding; the nose of one horse will be in the tail of another, sometimes in a long string of 15 horses. However, the scenery is well worth the ride. Wear long pants and hiking boots or tennis shoes for these rides. Kids must be at least eight years old. Reservations are recommended.

WATER SPORTS
Boating and Paddling

Glacier National Park and the Blackfeet Reservation have instituted strict boating and paddling guidelines in order to protect pristine waters from aquatic invasive species. All watercraft coming into the area must stop at inspection stations.

INSIDE THE PARK

Glacier's east-side lakes offer outstanding paddling, but the larger lakes are subject to big winds. Be aware of changing conditions for safety. The park's east-side lakes **open June-September** and are only available by **permit** to boaters and paddlers who have passed an inspection. Non-trailered electric-powered and hand-propelled watercraft can get a same-day inspection and permit to launch immediately. Jet Skis and gas-powered motorboats are banned.

Many Glacier has smaller lakes that are more protected from big winds, surrounded by stunning scenery and sometimes moose. Only nonmotorized boats are permitted: sailboats, kayaks, rowboats, paddleboards, and canoes. Kayakers can cross Swiftcurrent Lake and paddle the connecting slow-moving Cataract Creek upstream to Lake Josephine, where a shoreline loop makes a scenic tour. The public boat ramp on **Swiftcurrent Lake** sits east of the picnic area. Get inspections and permits at the **Many Glacier Ranger Station** (7am-4:30pm daily, free). Rent canoes, rowboats, and single or double kayaks from **Glacier Park Boat Company** (boat dock at Many Glacier Hotel, 406/257-2426, http://glacierparkboats.com, daily mid-June-mid-Sept., $18-22/hour) for use only on Swiftcurrent Lake. Paddles and life jackets are included.

St. Mary Lake has lustier winds that can challenge unskilled boaters, but that skilled windsurfers enjoy. The lake allows only non-trailered electric-powered motorboats and hand-propelled watercraft. Get inspections and permits at the **St. Mary Visitor Center** (7am-4:30pm daily, free) before driving west to the boat launch at Rising Sun.

OUTSIDE THE PARK

On the Blackfeet Reservation, motorized boats can launch after getting inspected. **Lower St. Mary Lake** has a public boat ramp at Chewing Blackbones Campground (milepost 37.3, U.S. 89, $20 launch fee plus $10 conservation permit). Motorboats are also allowed on **Duck Lake** (milepost 29 on Duck Lake Rd., MT 464) but not waterskiing.

Fishing

INSIDE THE PARK

Fishing inside Glacier National Park requires no license. However, pick up current fishing regulations at St. Mary Visitor Center or Many Glacier Ranger Station.

In **St. Mary,** go below St. Mary Lake to ply St. Mary River's deep channels for rainbow trout. But the best fishing requires a 7.5-mile (12.1-km) hike to **Red Eagle Lake,** the site of a 16-pound (7.3-kg) state record native westslope cutthroat. Those with serious commitment and willpower pack in float tubes.

With its numerous lakes, the **Many Glacier Valley** offers lots of fishing holes: Grinnell, Josephine, Swiftcurrent, Red Rock, Bullhead, and Ptarmigan Lakes. Don't be deceived into lugging gear to Iceberg, Upper Grinnell, or Poia Lakes, which have no fish. Cracker and Slide Lakes are closed to fishing. Cataract Creek between Lake Josephine and Swiftcurrent Lake contains brook trout.

Pools and riffles in the **Belly River Valley** offer endless angling along the Belly and Mokowanis Rivers. Lakes are also good fisheries, especially **Elizabeth Lake** for arctic grayling and rainbow trout.

OUTSIDE THE PARK

While trophy rainbow trout used to be the norm, anglers now pull 16-inch (40.6-cm) brown or cutthroat trout from **Duck Lake.** This stocked fishery is best from a boat or a float tube. In winter, ice fishing is permitted. Non-tribal members need a Blackfeet fishing permit, which is available online (http://blackfeetfishandwildlife.net, $20/1 day, $45/3 days, $75 season).

Wildlife in Many Glacier

Many Glacier is regaled as a wildlife-watching area. So where are the best places to spot wildlife? The park service often sets up a spotting scope in the Swiftcurrent parking lot for watching wildlife.

Bighorn Sheep: Open slopes, pruned of tall vegetation by winter avalanches, make good bighorn sheep habitat. They prefer broken cliffs for protection and meadows for feeding. Use binoculars to see them above tree line on the slopes of Mount Altyn and Mount Henkel. Look for them in the final mile around the moraine on the Grinnell Glacier Trail and in grassy meadows in the upper portion of the Iceberg Lake Trail.

Grizzly Bears: Due to plentiful food sources, Many Glacier has one of the thickest concentrations of grizzly bears in Glacier. They frequent the trails, so make noise to let them know you are there. From the Swiftcurrent Trail around Red Rock Lake, use binoculars to scan the lower slopes of Grinnell Point for bears. From Many Glacier Road near Swiftcurrent Lake, look on the lower slopes of Mount Altyn.

Moose: With abundant lakes, Many Glacier provides excellent moose habitat. Not only can you spot them while driving the road, but also when hiking trails or sitting on the Many Glacier Hotel deck in the early morning. The Swiftcurrent Trail passes three lakes where moose hang out: Fishercap, Red Rock, and Bullhead. They swim across Grinnell Lake and eat water plants in Swiftcurrent and Josephine Lakes.

Mountain Goats: These white denizens of Glacier's alpine find safety in cliffs and adjacent high meadows. In fact, the kids can navigate cliffs within 24 hours of birth. Binoculars are useful for watching them. Spot mountain goats in the upper red cliffs on Mount Altyn and Mount Henkel. They also scamper around the steep cliffs surrounding Iceberg Lake and Grinnell Point.

Pika: These non-hibernating members of the rabbit family collect flowers and greens all summer to dry for winter food. High-elevation talus slopes and large rockfalls with adjacent meadows yield the best habitat. You can find them around Apikuni Falls, and most likely will hear their telltale "eep" before you spot them.

Wolverines: These elusive weasels prefer high elevations near snowfields and glaciers. Hiking to lingering snowfields and ice around Swiftcurrent Pass, Grinnell Glacier, and the north side of Piegan Pass provides the best possibility of spotting them. You might even see pairs hunting together.

Entertainment and Shopping

RANGER PROGRAMS

The park service runs many free programs during summer about natural history, wildlife, and astronomy. Check the park newspaper or go online (www.nps.gov/glac) for schedules. The park service leads **tours** of the historic **Many Glacier Hotel.** In the Swiftcurrent parking lot, rangers usually set up a **spotting scope** to watch bighorn sheep, mountain goats, and bears on the hillsides.

Park naturalists present 45-minute **evening programs** in Many Glacier Hotel, Many Glacier Campground Amphitheater, St. Mary Campground Amphitheater, and St. Mary Visitor Center nightly at 7:30pm or 8pm, depending on location. Indoor programs include slide shows; outdoor programs feature speakers.

★ Stargazing

Astronomy programs take place at the St. Mary Visitor Center parking lot. The **St. Mary Observatory** has **stargazing events** (10pm-midnight) when weather and dark skies permit. The telescope transfers real-time images onto two high-definition outdoor screens for viewing. On sunny days, rangers set up a **solar telescope** for viewing solar activity (11am-2pm, July-Aug.).

The Legend of Joe Cosley

The Belly River backcountry is rife with legends of the park's favorite renegade ranger, Joe Cosley. A fur trapper long before Glacier became a national park, Cosley trapped animals to sell their hides and carved his name on thousands of trees.

When Glacier achieved parkhood in 1910, Cosley was hired as the Belly's first ranger. But for Cosley, ranger duties became a vehicle for poaching, even near West Glacier right under the superintendent's nose. He sold hides in Canada and furnished paying clients with big game.

Cosley's mountain man reputation grew due to self-generated legends. He told more than one woman he named Elizabeth Lake for her, said he buried a diamond ring in a Belly poplar, and claimed to have hiked 35 miles (56 km) between Polebridge and Waterton in 3.5 hours for a dance.

Finally, in 1914, after sending rangers to nab him poaching, the superintendent threw Joe off the payroll. After serving with Canadian forces in World War I, Joe weaseled his way back into the Belly to trap and hunt. Meanwhile, the new 24-year-old Belly ranger, Joe Heimes, discovered footprints leading to one of Cosley's caches. Heimes arrested Cosley, who was twice his age. After repeated attempts at escape, Cosley succumbed only when Heimes tied his feet. Heimes made Cosley carry a pack with the evidence of traps and beaver pieces for the long snowy hike over a pass, a drive, and a train ride to jail in Belton (now West Glacier).

In 1929, Glacier saw its most notorious trial. Cosley pleaded guilty but claimed Heimes framed him with the evidence. The commissioner pronounced him guilty with a $125 fine and 90 days in jail. Claiming a fatal disease, Cosley asked for clemency. To avoid a death in his jail, the commissioner suspended the sentence due to Joe's visibly fast-failing health. Friends paid his fine; Cosley walked free.

Two hours later, supplied with snowshoes and trail grub, the cured Cosley hiked over the Continental Divide to his cache in the Belly. Within two days after his trial, he sold 55 beaver, 21 marten, and 22 mink hides for $4,129 in Canada.

For more of Cosley's adventures, read *Belly River's Famous Joe Cosley* by Brian McClung.

★ NATIVE AMERICA SPEAKS

For more than three decades, Glacier's naturalist programs have included the acclaimed **Native America Speaks** program in summer. Look for shows in park lodges, St. Mary Visitor Center, and at campground amphitheaters, including Chewing Blackbones outside Babb. Free 45-minute evening campground amphitheater shows feature members of the Blackfeet, Salish, and Kootenai people who use storytelling, humor, and music to share their culture and heritage. Check the park newspaper for the current schedules and location of presentations.

Two specialty programs occur throughout the summer. **Jack Gladstone,** a Grammy-nominated Blackfeet musician, presents his **Triple Divide: Heritage and Legacy** (www.jackgladstone.com) which blends storytelling and music into a one-hour multimedia walk through Glacier's history from the Blackfeet perspective. At the St. Mary Visitor Center's auditorium, the **Two Medicine Lake Singers and Dancers** draw standing-room-only crowds for demonstrating Blackfeet dances in full traditional regalia. Traditional, jingle, fancy, and grass dances display different footwork and body movements. For the finale, visitors can join in the Round Dance. Tickets (adults $5, kids 12 and under free) go on sale the Monday before a performance for the 90-minute show, and they sell out quickly.

SHOPPING

St. Mary has a handful of gift shops. Expect to see merchandise heavily branded with popular moose and bear themes. Many Glacier Hotel has a gift shop below the lobby; access it via the helical stairway.

Food

Because Many Glacier has minimal choices, locals staying here for several days will drive to Babb (12 mi/19.3 km away) or St. Mary (21 mi/34 km) away) to hit other eateries. Nothing beats driving back into Many Glacier at sunset, with ample opportunities for wildlife-watching. Be aware that restaurants and grocery stores in Babb and St. Mary do not serve alcohol during North American Indian Days, a reservation-wide four-day celebration beginning the second Thursday in July. Alcohol sales are also prohibited on other selected days, such as graduation in June. Because of their location in the park rather than on the reservation, restaurants in Many Glacier can still serve alcohol on those days.

For hikers and travelers, sack lunches ($12-17) are sold at St. Mary Village, Many Glacier Hotel, and Swiftcurrent; order these a day in advance.

INSIDE THE PARK

Many Glacier eateries and camp stores are operated by **Xanterra** (855/733-4522, www.glaciernationalparklodges.com, daily mid-June-mid-Sept.), the park concessioaire. No reservations are accepted, so you may have to wait for a table in midsummer. Menus rely on local, fresh, and organic sourcing served with healthy, gluten-free, vegan, and child options plus choices for toppings and portions. The restaurants serve craft cocktails, beer, and wine.

Restaurants
MANY GLACIER HOTEL
In Many Glacier Hotel (milepost 11.5, Many Glacier Rd.), the ★ **Ptarmigan Dining Room** underwent a renovation that unmasked the original railroad beams and take the restaurant back to its historic look. Massive windows look out on Swiftcurrent Lake, Grinnell Point, and Mount Wilbur. For the best views to watch the bears, ask

to sit near the north windows facing Mount Altyn. For breakfast (6:30am-10am, $12-18), choose between a continental buffet or hot entrée buffet. Lunch (11:30am-2:30pm, $10-22) serves pasta, salads, sandwiches, and burgers. Dinner (5pm-9:30pm, $12-44) has prime rib, Wagyu steak, duck, fish, or more casual burgers, pasta, and salads. Grab small plates, sandwiches, salads, and pasta in the adjacent **Swiss Room bar** (11:30am-10pm, $8-21).

SWIFTCURRENT MOTOR INN
At the Swiftcurrent Motor Inn complex, **'Nell's** (2 Many Glacier Rd., front desk 406/732-5531, 6:30am-10pm, $6-16) has tables with maps for discussing trails. Named in honor of George Bird Grinnell, the café crowds at mealtimes due to its location adjacent to the campground, cabins, and motel. Breakfast can go light or traditional. Appetizers, sandwiches, pasta, pizza, and salads frame the diner-style lunch and dinner menu.

Groceries
In Many Glacier, you'll find two convenience stores with limited groceries. In the basement of Many Glacier Hotel, **Heidi's Snack Shop** (milepost 11.5, Many Glacier Rd., 6am-9:30pm daily mid-June-mid-Sept.) sells coffee, espresso, soda pop, snacks, sandwiches, newspapers, beer, and wine. Located across the parking lot from Many Glacier Campground in the Swiftcurrent Motor Inn, the **Swiftcurrent Campstore** (milepost 12.5, Many Glacier Rd., 7am-10pm daily mid-June-mid-Sept.) carries groceries, camping and hiking supplies, T-shirts, gift items, newspapers, beer, wine, firewood, and ice. Hikers can cobble together trail snacks and lunches from either store.

Picnic Areas
Many Glacier's small picnic area (milepost

12.2, Many Glacier Rd.) crams with picnickers toting binoculars to scan for bears on Mount Altyn. It's a popular picnic site and can be crowded in midsummer. If you want to roast marshmallows in one of the fire pits, buy firewood at the Swiftcurrent Campstore; gathering wood is prohibited. From the Swiftcurrent Picnic Area to the bridge over Swiftcurrent Creek, the **Swiftcurrent Nature Trail** (0.5 mi/0.8 km rt, 15 min, easy) is a packed surface **wheelchair-accessible** interpretive trail.

OUTSIDE THE PARK
St. Mary
RESTAURANTS

Located in the lodge at **St. Mary Village** (junction of Going-to-the-Sun Road and U.S. 89, 406/892-2525, front desk 406/732-4431, www.glacierparkcollection.com, daily early June-late Sept.), the **Snowgoose Grille** looks up at striking Singleshot Mountain. The dining room serves up breakfast (6:30am-10am, $9-15), lunch (11:30am-2:30pm, $12-16), and dinner (5pm-9:30pm, $14-31). No reservations are taken, which can sometimes mean waiting in line. For an alternative, you can order sandwiches and appetizers in the adjacent **Mountain Bar** (11:30am-10pm daily), or on warm days sit on the deck overlooking Divide

Creek to watch the sunset with a Montana microbrew. Across the lobby from the bar, find espresso at **Glacier Perk** (6am-7pm daily). **Curly Bear Café** (10am-8:30pm, $6-10), located in the mini shopping strip near the gas pumps, is the closest thing in St. Mary to fast food, with subs and ice cream.

St. Mary is home to two family-run cafés, where reservations are not taken and no alcohol is served. The Hilton family runs the **Park Café** (3147 U.S. 89, 406/732-9979, https://parkcafeandgrocery.com, 7am-9pm daily early June-mid-Sept., hours shorten early and late season, $10-22). Homemade berry pies are baked every morning, and they serve breakfast, lunch, and dinner with a few Tex-Mex options. For a throwback experience, ★ **Johnson's World Famous Historic Restaurant** (21 Red Eagle Rd., 406/732-5565, http://johnsonsofstmary.squarespace.com, 7am-9pm daily mid-May-late Sept., $9-27) serves up most of its daily large-portion specials family style with home-baked bread. Located at Johnson's Resort of St. Mary, the small, old-fashioned restaurant with red-checked tablecloths serves its eggs, bacon, and hash browns all on one big platter for the entire table. The family-style soup lunch shows up in a large tureen with fresh-baked bread.

the Snowgoose Grille at St. Mary Village

Dinner features country foods, served individually or family style.

Drop in to **Rising Sun Pizza** (3141 U.S. 89, 406/732-9995, 4:30pm-11pm daily May-Oct., $15-22) for wings, local craft beers, and pizza with homemade sauces and fresh dough. Or order to go for your campsite.

GROCERIES

In St. Mary, you can stock up on supplies at two summer-only (daily June-Sept.) grocery stores on U.S. 89. Hours shorten in early summer and fall. The largest grocery store, the **St. Mary Supermarket** (St. Mary Village, 406/732-4431, 8am-8pm), is a glorified convenience store with beer and wine, some fresh produce, meats, and camping, fishing, and automotive supplies. Shoulder seasons see skimpy fresh fare. The **Park Grocery and Gift Shop** (3147 U.S. 89, 406/732-4482, https://parkcafeandgrocery.com, 7am-9pm) carries Montana microbrews, along with convenience-store items, groceries, fishing tackle, and backpacking supplies. St. Mary stores do not sell alcohol during Blackfeet celebration days, including North American Indian Days (2nd Thurs.-Sun. in July). For big grocery stores, head to Browning.

Babb

RESTAURANTS

In Babb, the Thronson family runs ★ **Glacier's Edge Café** (4013 U.S. 89, 406/732-5530, 7:30am-8pm daily June-Sept., $9-18), serving up diner fare for breakfast, lunch, and dinner, including burritos, burgers, and barbecue pork. Plates have big portions, and the huckleberry milkshakes are huge. South of Babb, in a bright purple building, **Two Sisters Café** (3600 U.S. 89 N., 406/732-5535, www.twosistersofmontana.com, 11am-9pm daily June-Sept., $11-30) serves up homemade fare, with hand-cut fries and big portions for lunch and dinner. Rainbow trout topped with huckleberry aoli and the Red burger packed with bacon, cheese, grilled mushrooms, onions, and Creole sauce are the house specialties. You can also get vegetarian, gluten-free, and dairy-free meals. Montana microbrews, wine, cocktails, and margaritas are served.

Not for vegetarians, **Cattle Baron Supper Club** (3990 U.S. 89, 406/732-4033, 5pm-10pm daily mid-June-Sept., $25-66) is a meat palace owned by local Blackfeet. Up the log spiral staircase above the Babb Bar, once known as the roughest bar in Montana, the restaurant serves dinners where the baked potato isn't the biggest thing on the plate. Be ready to gorge, for steak cuts are humongous and rib eyes even larger. Sides include hot bread from a four-generation recipe. The log lodge pays tribute to Blackfeet history with painted wall stories and a sculpture of a buffalo jump. During midsummer, make reservations.

GROCERIES

Located in Babb, **Thronson's General Store** (4013 U.S. 89, 406/732-5530, 9am-5pm Mon.-Sat. May-Sept.) stocks convenience items, fishing and camping supplies, but no beer or wine.

Accommodations

St. Mary has access to Going-to-the-Sun Road, a modern hotel, and is within day-trip range for Many Glacier, Two Medicine, and Waterton. Many Glacier has a destination location smack in the heart of hiking country; you can park the car for a few days without using it. In both locations, bills will include a 7 percent Montana bed tax.

INSIDE THE PARK

In Many Glacier, **Xanterra** (855/733-4522, www.glaciernationalparklodges.com) runs two lodges. These are historic locales with no TVs or air-conditioning. Make **reservations 13 months in advance.**

Many Glacier Hotel

★ **Many Glacier Hotel** (milepost 11.5, Many Glacier Rd., front desk 406/732-4411, early June-mid-Sept., $220-590) is the largest of the park's historic lodges and the most popular due to its stunning location. Set on Swiftcurrent Lake, the immense hotel cowers below surrounding peaks. The lodge centers around its massive four-story lobby with a huge fireplace. Some guest rooms and suites (some with decks) face the lake, while east-side guest rooms get the sunrise, with a unique morning wake-up call as the horses jangle to the corral. A Swiss theme pervades the hotel, with bellhops dressed in lederhosen and gingerbread cutout deck railings. Activities include paddling, trail riding, red bus and boat tours, and hiking.

From being the "showplace of the Rockies," the hotel slipped into disrepair, prompting Congress to allocate $30 million to renovate the National Historic Landmark. An extensive rehabilitation completed in 2017 straightened the structure, repaired decks, replaced windows, and renovated guest rooms by re-enameling old-fashioned claw-foot tubs and adding insulation to the walls, making the guest rooms quieter. But the baths are small; many were created from the original closets. No elevators access the upper floors. Rooms have phones, and the lobby has limited wireless internet. A restaurant, lounge, convenience store, and gift shop are on-site. When the hotel opened in 1915, it was considered the epitome of luxury; today that is hardly the case, but what the hotel lacks in amenities it makes up for in historical ambience, dramatic scenery, bear-watching, and convenience to trailheads. Trails to Cracker Lake, Grinnell Lake, Piegan Pass, and Grinnell Glacier depart from the hotel. Other trails depart from Swiftcurrent, 1 mile (1.6 km) away.

Swiftcurrent Motor Inn

At Many Glacier Road's terminus, **Swiftcurrent Motor Inn** (2 Many Glacier Rd., front desk 406/732-5531, mid-June-mid-Sept., $120-200) has cabins and simple motel rooms. Heated cabins come with or without bathrooms. For austere units without baths, a central comfort station and shower house with lukewarm water awaits. Guest rooms have no in-room phones. Pay phones are outside the camp store, and wireless internet is in the lobby; the complex also has laundry and a restaurant. Historical charm isn't the lure but rather the price and utter convenience to trailheads such as Red Rock and Bullhead Lakes, Granite Park Chalet, Swiftcurrent Pass and Lookout, Iceberg Lake, and Ptarmigan Tunnel.

OUTSIDE THE PARK
St. Mary

St. Mary is located outside the park on the Blackfeet Reservation at the eastern portal of Going-to-the-Sun Road. Amenities are limited, especially internet access. In most

1: Many Glacier Hotel **2:** cabin at St. Mary Village

The Extinction of Glaciers

"Where's the best place to go to watch the glaciers go by?" Locals chuckle when someone who slept through 7th-grade earth science asks this question. Glaciers don't move like a herd of elk, but they are moving ice. Due to climate change, scientists from the U.S. Geological Survey (USGS) estimate that most of the park's glaciers will soon become static snowfields.

WHAT ARE GLACIERS?

Glaciers are moving ice. A glacier's upper end, called the accumulation zone, piles with snow, compressing into the ice's mass. With a at least 100 feet (30.5 m) of depth and 25 acres (10 hectares) of surface area, glaciers will move inches per day. That movement separates glaciers from static snowfields.

Glaciers may look similar to snowfields, but they aren't. They have crevasses, debris bands, and moraines. When ice inches over rocky humps, the rigid surface cracks into crevasses; some shoot hundreds of feet deep. Bands of rock debris pile atop the ice, carried along in lines that reveal the glacier's movement over years. When the ice melts, rock rubble is left in lateral or terminal piles, known as moraines. Snowfields lack these features.

HOW MANY GLACIERS REMAIN?

Once glamorous diamonds, the park's current glaciers are relics from a mini ice age that peaked around 1850 with more than 150 glaciers. Since then, the glaciers have thinned, shrunk, broken into pieces, or melted entirely. While early melt rates tended to be slow, the last century saw warmer summers and less snow trigger rapid melting that sped up each decade. A glacier shrinks when the math doesn't add up: when more ice melts annually than it makes. Around 25 glaciers remain; some are likely no longer true glaciers due to halting movement.

WHY ARE THE GLACIERS MELTING?

Glacier National Park is a laboratory for studying climate change because the park's higher elevations have warmed at three times the rate of the overall planet. Average temperatures in Glacier now run 2°F (1.1°C) hotter than they did in the mid-1900s, and the park now sees 30 fewer days with below-freezing temperatures. Warmer summers with more days above 90°F (32°C) and shorter snowpack seasons are the norm. The USGS monitors the park's glaciers as climate barometers, using surface measurements, aerial photography, and repeat photography for comparisons between years.

HOW ARE THE GLACIERS MELTING?

As glaciers retreat, some fracture into patches while others form lakes at their snouts—actions that both speed up melting. Jackson and Blackfoot Glaciers, seen from Going-to-the-Sun Road, used to be joined as one, but today they are two distinct glaciers. Grinnell and Salamander Glaciers,

locations, Wi-Fi is slow and usually only available in lobbies.

ST. MARY VILLAGE

A large complex of hotel rooms, cabins, and motel rooms at the entrance to Going-to-the-Sun Road, ★ **St. Mary Village** (junction of U.S. 89 and Going-to-the-Sun Rd., 844/868-7474, www.glacierparkcollection.com, early June-late Sept., $109-390) sprawls across a large junction. The resort surrounds itself mostly with parking lots rather than natural landscape, and the 82-acre (33-hectare) complex has shopping, restaurants, a bar, a coffee shop, and a grocery. You can walk five minutes to the park entrance and St. Mary Visitor Center.

St. Mary Village has several different options ranging from value rooms to upscale accommodations. At the high end, the

Grinnell Glacier is fast melting into a lake and pile of rock rubble.

once joined, split into two separate glaciers, and in the 1930s, a lake formed at the snout of Grinnell Glacier. Now the ice shrinks every year, while Upper Grinnell Lake grows larger.

WHAT WILL HAPPEN WHEN THE GLACIERS MELT?

Glacier National Park's ecosystem will change; the most obvious will be an increase in forest elevations. More trees aren't necessarily disastrous, but with more forests eventually come more fires. Animals and birds, especially those living on the fringes of their habitat, may seek a food base elsewhere. Heat-intolerant pikas, for instance, may not survive warmer temperatures. Water, now seemingly so abundant, may not shed from the mountains in the sustained runoff from glaciers or at temperatures kept cool by the ice, threatening the survival of cold-loving bull trout and affecting irrigation and salmon runs.

Follow the ongoing study of Glacier National Park's glaciers and see comparative photography at www.usgs.gov/centers/norock. Learn more about the park's glaciers online (www.nps.gov/glac/learn/nature/glaciersoverview.htm). Walk through Many Glacier Hotel's hallway from the lobby to the dining room to see repeat photography of glaciers: early and current.

three-story 48-room **Great Bear Lodge** contains modern hotel comforts in chic lodge style with satellite TV (limited channels), air-conditioning, wet bars, mini-fridges, and the only elevator in the immediate Glacier environs. Superior guest rooms include fireplaces and jetted tubs, and all rooms enjoy the sound of the creek and stunning views of Singleshot Mountain from private decks. Third-floor guest rooms have larger panoramic mountain views.

Less-pricey guest rooms cluster in older lodges and small cabins. Great for small families, the **Glacier Cabins** line up along Divide Creek. The cozy, modern one-bedroom cabins include kitchenettes and porch picnic tables for enjoying the creek ambience. The older **main lodge** has tiny cedar-walled guest rooms with small baths. Upgraded guest rooms in the **West Lodge** include satellite TV and air-conditioning. Older **East Motel** guest rooms do not have either, but they allow pets. Due to the proximity to the highway, some of the rooms have road noise. The newest options are **tiny homes** that sleep four people and have kitchenettes and detached nearby bathhouses.

CABINS AND MOTELS

High on a bluff with spectacular views of Glacier, the seven upscale ★ **Cottages at Glacier** (300 Going-to-the-Sun Road E., 406/309-4231, www.thecottagesatglacier.com, mid-May-mid-Oct., $275-725) offer big picture windows with the most dramatic scenery in St. Mary. The spacious two-bedroom cabins can sleep 6-9 and have large decks facing the mountains, gas barbecues, fully equipped kitchens, rock fireplaces, air-conditioning, satellite TV, DSL internet, and a sleeper sofa in the living room. A two-night minimum is required.

The ★ **St. Mary KOA** (106 West Shore Dr., 406/732-4122 or 800/562-1504, www.goglacier.com, mid-May-Sept., $90-400) has a variety of cabins. The cheapest have no baths or kitchens and require you to bring sleeping bags and use the communal building showers and toilets. The higher-end cabins are homes that come with baths, kitchens, and bedding. Amenities at the KOA include barbecues, outdoor pool, hot tub, splash park, and wireless internet.

Sitting above St. Mary and with views of Napi Point, **Johnson's of St. Mary** (21 Red Eagle Rd., 406/732-4207, http://johnsonsofstmary.squarespace.com, mid-May-late Sept., $75-187) rents a few cabins. Next door, the **Red Eagle Motel** (23 Red Eagle Rd., 406/732-4453, www.redeaglemotelrvpark.com, mid-Apr.-Oct., $110-140) has 23 plain guest rooms that have small bathrooms with showers. Some rooms were renovated in 2018.

Babb

Near Duck Lake, **Park Cabin Company** (75 West Shore Duck Lake Rd., 406/407-0809, www.parkcabinco.com, May-Sept., $215-315) has several one- and two-bedroom cabins with kitchens. A two-night stay is required. In Babb, the older **Thronson's Motel** (4013 U.S. 89, 406/732-5530, May-Sept., $135-155) has 14 rooms above the general store with a restaurant across the street. It is run by a fifth-generation Babb family.

Camping

While Many Glacier has only one campground with no hookups, St. Mary has commercial campgrounds with hookups for RVs. If the inside park campgrounds fill up, head to a commercial one in St. Mary rather than up Going-to-the-Sun Road to Rising Sun, which usually fills up first.

St. Mary is convenient for exploring Going-to-the-Sun Road, and it works as a home base for day trips to Waterton, Many Glacier, and Two Medicine. However, if you envision parking the car, setting up a tent for a couple of days, and hiking straight from the campground, then Many Glacier is where you need to be. Cell service is available at St. Mary, but not in Many Glacier.

INSIDE THE PARK

The inside-park campgrounds run by the National Park Service (406/888-7800, www.nps.gov/glac) have flush toilets, dump stations, picnic tables, fire rings with grills, and running water. Campground hosts usually sell firewood. Check the park's **Recreational Access Display** (www.nps.gov/applications/glac/dashboard/) for historic fill times and current status to know when to arrive for first-come, first-served campsites. You can make **reservations** (877/444-6777, www. recreation.gov, $10 reservation fee) for summer starting six months in advance.

St. Mary

St. Mary Campground (milepost 0.9, Going-to-the-Sun Rd., mid-May-mid-Sept., $23) has 183 sites sitting in open meadows or tucked among aspens. Sites fill midsummer by 8am. For the best views, the C loop sites stare at Divide and Red Eagle Mountains, but in August heat, they can be hot. Four token-operated showers with lukewarm water are available. A few campsites can fit RVs up to 35 feet (10.7 m), but most are shorter. A trail crosses the St. Mary River on a wooden bridge to connect with the visitors center, St. Mary's restaurants, shuttles, and shops, but it has no access to St. Mary Lake. This campground has shoulder-season primitive camping (late Apr.-mid-May and late Sept.-Nov., $10) and winter camping (free) with pit toilets and no water.

Many Glacier

★ **Many Glacier Campground** (end of Many Glacier Rd., late May-mid-Sept., $23) packs 110 treed sites at the base of Grinnell Point. As the most coveted campground in the park, **reservations** are essential. In 2021, all campsites will be in the reservation system. For 2022, half of the sites can be reserved in advance, but for first-come, first-served campsites, plan to arrive by 7am. A few sites can fit RVs up to 35 feet (10.7 m), but most fit RVs only up to 21 feet (6.4 m). Nearby trails depart for Red Rock, Bullhead, and Iceberg Lakes as well as Ptarmigan Tunnel and Swiftcurrent Pass. From the picnic area, a five-minute walk down the road, trails depart to Lake Josephine and Grinnell Lake, Grinnell Glacier, and Piegan Pass. Across the parking lot, Swiftcurrent Motor Inn has a restaurant, laundry, hot showers, and a camp store. If bears frequent the campground, tent camping may be restricted, with only hard-sided vehicles allowed. In fall (mid-Sept.-Oct.), after the campground water is turned off for the season, **primitive camping** ($10) is allowed here. There are pit toilets. Primitive camping will be suspended in 2021 due to road construction.

OUTSIDE THE PARK
St. Mary

In St. Mary, most commercial campgrounds have flush toilets, hot showers, picnic tables, laundries, camp stores, Wi-Fi, and hookups for electricity, water, and sewer (and will add

day use tepees at Chewing Blackbones Campground

a 7 percent state bed tax to your bill). One mile (1.6 km) away from the hubbub of St. Mary and on Lower St. Mary Lake, **St. Mary KOA** (106 West Shore Dr., 406/732-4122 or 800/562-1504, www.goglacier.com, mid-May-Sept., tents $48-62, RV hookups $62-120, $5-12 pp beyond two) is on the St. Mary River and Lower St. Mary Lake in a huge meadow where elk appear in spring and fall. Prime campsites flank the river. You can rent kayaks to paddle the lake. The outdoor pool and huge hot tub claim mountain views, and kids go for the splash park. Amenities include espresso, pet sitting, bike rentals, and an outdoor restaurant (late June-Aug.), which serves breakfasts and barbecue dinners.

Sitting atop a bluff with a panoramic view of Glacier from premium RV sites, the older **Johnson's Campground** (21 Red Eagle Rd., 406/732-4207, http://johnsonsofstmary.squarespace.com, mid-May-late Sept.) overlooks St. Mary. It sprawls in a grassy setting broken up by chattering aspens. With 75 tent sites ($34) plus 82 RV sites with hookups ($39-59), the campground can usually accommodate latecomers when inside-park campgrounds are full. The bathrooms are old. Amenities include a camp store, laundry, a dump station, a restaurant, and wireless internet in the lobby. Restaurants and shops in St. Mary are a five-minute walk down the hill.

Heart of Glacier RV Park (23 Red Eagle Rd., 406/450-0035, www.redeaglemotelrvpark.com, May-Oct., $45-50) has a 24-site RV park with full hookups, but no shower or bathroom facilities.

Babb

On Lower Two Medicine Lake, **Chewing Blackbones Campground** (3719 U.S. 89, 406/732-4046, June-Sept., tents $25-45, RV hookups $35-55) is owned by the Blackfeet Nation. The campground has showers, flush toilets, laundry, day use tepees, a camp store, and a boat launch ($20 plus $10 conservation fee). Grass surrounds most campsites. In June, **hard-sided camping** may be required here due to bears. Make reservations through **Reserve America** (www.reserveamerica.com).

Transportation and Services

TRANSPORTATION
Driving and Parking

Two-lane roads connect St. Mary with Many Glacier. Find public parking at the St. Mary Visitor Center, Swiftcurrent, Many Glacier Hotel, and trailheads.

SERVICES

In Many Glacier, **public showers** ($3), which are often cold to lukewarm, and **laundry facilities** are available behind Swiftcurrent Campstore; purchase tokens for both in the store.

Find **showers** ($5-10) at St. Mary KOA and Johnson's Campground in St. Mary, and at Chewing Blackbones Campground in Babb. St. Mary KOA and Chewing Blackbones have **coin-op laundries.** Find **ATMs** and **pay phones** at Many Glacier Hotel, Swiftcurrent Motor Inn, the supermarket in St. Mary, and St. Mary Village.

Babb has a **year-round post office** (4016 U.S. 89). St. Mary has a **seasonal post office** at Johnson's Campground. The local newspaper is the *Great Falls Tribune.*

Gas and Repairs

Two gas stations are in St. Mary on U.S. 89, one on either side of the junction with Going-to-the-Sun Road. Babb has a gas station across from Thronson's General Store. Many Glacier has no gas services. Repairs need to be made by mobile services.

Cell Phone and Internet Access

Planning to use your cell phone in Many

Glacier? Keep dreaming. There's **no coverage.** If you require **cell service,** stay in St. Mary. **Limited wireless internet** is available for guests in the lobbies of select motels and St. Mary's commercial campgrounds.

Emergencies

In an emergency, call 911. To contact a ranger, call 406/888-7800. The nearest hospital is **Blackfeet Community Hospital** (760 Government Sq., Browning, 406/338-6154).

Rangers like to keep apprised of all bear sightings and encounters, especially bears close to the trail. Report your sightings to the **St. Mary Visitor Center** or **Many Glacier Ranger Station.** Backpackers who need assistance in the Belly can find the **Belly River Ranger Station** in the backcountry at the junction of the Cosley Lake, Elizabeth Lake, Gable Pass, and Chief Mountain Trails.

Two Medicine and East Glacier

Quiet and removed, Glacier's southeast corner harbors a less-traveled wonderland. It's a favorite part of the park for many locals.

It's away from the harried corridor of Going-to-the-Sun Road with its endless line of cars. With no hotel in Two Medicine, you'll find trails far less clogged on day hikes than at Many Glacier. Just because it sees fewer people, however, does not make it less dramatic.

A string of three lakes curves through the Two Medicine Valley below Rising Wolf Mountain, a red hulking monolith. Its sheer mass is larger than any other peak in the park. Even though glaciers vacated this area within the past 150 years, their footprints are left in swooping valleys, cirques with blue lakes, and toothy spires. Two Medicine

Highlights

Look for ★ to find recommended sights, activities, dining, and lodging.

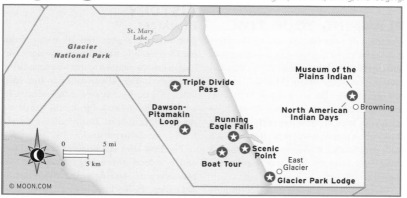

★ **Take a Boat Tour:** Board the historic *Sinopah* for the best way to see Two Medicine Lake. The wooden tour boat has plied these waters since 1927 (page 188).

★ **Watch Running Eagle Falls:** See water plunge from the top and from an underground chute in this waterfall named for Pitamakin, a Blackfeet woman warrior (page 191).

★ **Visit Glacier Park Lodge:** Wander through gardens up to the front door of this historic hotel, where three-story Douglas fir logs hold up its massive lobby (page 191).

★ **Learn about Indigeous traditions at Museum of the Plains Indian:** This tiny museum in Browning offers in-depth information about Blackfeet history and culture (page 192).

★ **Hike to Scenic Point:** High above Two Medicine Lake, you'll gain a top-of-the-world view. Stare across the plains on a clear day, and you may see Minneapolis (page 193).

★ **Traverse the Dawson-Pitamakin Loop:** Skitter on a narrow trail along the Continental Divide thousands of feet above blue lakes and forested valleys for broad views of peaks and glaciers (page 197).

★ **Climb to Triple Divide Pass:** This scenery-laden, less-traveled pass is also the summer terrain of bighorn sheep (page 198).

★ **Celebrate at North American Indian Days:** Join this colorful festival in Browning featuring Blackfeet regalia, traditional dancing, horse racing, and rodeos (page 203).

Lake, the park's highest road-accessible lake at 1 mile (1.6 km) high in elevation, shimmers in a valley strewn with hiking trails.

Around the corner, the tiny East Glacier burg on the Blackfeet Reservation struggles in winter with frigid temperatures accompanied by winds strong enough to blow trains off the tracks. But in summer, it buzzes with activity. The Great Northern Railway's historic headliner hotel, Glacier Park Lodge, dominates the town with its immense Douglas fir lobby. Train travelers taste the history as they step from the depot across a garden walkway to the hotel, framed by the mountains of Dancing Lady and Henry. Hiking, golf, Blackfeet-led and red bus tours, horseback riding, and swimming delight guests. At night, only the clatter of passing trains breaks the quiet.

PLANNING YOUR TIME

The town of **East Glacier** on the Blackfeet Reservation contains services and amenities outside the park. It has small, mostly seasonal motels, one of the original historic lodges, restaurants, and the train depot. Most visitors treat East Glacier as a **base camp,** leaving on day trips to elsewhere in the park. But the location means lots of drive time to reach some park locales. It's best to stay here for **2-3 days** before moving on to stay elsewhere in the park.

Twelve miles (19.3 km) and a 20-minute drive northwest, **Two Medicine** has trails galore and a scenery-loaded campground surrounded by mountains. Trails launch right from the campground, making a **three-day** stay worthwhile. Two Medicine can also be a **one-day** destination from East Glacier or most other park locales. Check the park's **Recreational Access Display** (www.nps. gov/applications/glac/dashboard/) for real-time status of Two Medicine Road, parking lots, weather, and the campground.

Twelve miles (19.3 km) and a 15-minute drive east is **Browning,** the center of the

Blackfeet Reservation. By population and size, it is a bigger town than East Glacier, but has limited lodging and restaurants. Take an hour to tour the Museum of the Plains Indian, and spend a day at North American Indian Days in early July.

Summer temperatures usually average 65-80°F (18-27°C) during days and 40-43°F (4.5-6°C) at night. Hiking and backpacking into higher elevations will encounter temperatures often 10-15°F (6-8°C) cooler. Strong winds are common and can sometimes be brutal on high-elevation trails, such as Dawson or Two Medicine Passes. Winter temperatures waffle between -10°F (-23°C) in Arctic cold fronts made even more frigid by wind chills to 35°F (2°C).

HISTORY
Blackfeet

Two Medicine acquired its name from Blackfeet legends. According to one story, two Piegan groups planned to meet for a medicine ceremony in the valley. Failing to find each other, they both celebrated independently. In another version, two lodges for the sun dance sat on either side of Two Medicine Creek. Either way, the name stuck.

The 1896 land sale between the Blackfeet and the federal government included the Two Medicine area. Starving and nearly decimated as a nation, the Blackfeet swapped part of their reservation land from the Continental Divide to the current reservation boundary for $1.5 million, a mere pittance considering the worth of the park lands.

Early Park Days

The Great Northern Railway began laying tracks in 1891 from Cut Bank to Midvale (East Glacier) and west over Marias Pass. As railroad developer James J. Hill sought means to increase ridership on his new line, he spawned a grand plan: a lodge to greet Eastern guests first arriving at Glacier and several chalets

---

Previous: Scenic Point Trail; Triple Divide Pass Trail; Blackfeet performer at North American Indian Days.

Two Medicine and East Glacier

To Red Eagle Lake

Triple Divide Peak 8,020ft

Mt. James 9,375ft

TRIPLE DIVIDE PASS

Lake Isabel

DAWSON-PITAMAKIN LOOP

Cut Bank Pass

Medicine Grizzly Lake

Morning Star Lake

Lone Walker Mountain 8,502ft

Old Man Lake

Medicine Grizzly Peak 8,315ft

CUT BANK RANGER STATION

Dawson Pass

Pitamakin Pass

Red Mountain 9,377ft

CUT BANK

Two Medicine Pass

Upper Two Medicine Lake

No Name Lake

Sinopah Mountain 8,271ft

Rising Wolf Mountain 9,513ft

Glacier

CUT BANK RD

Rockwell Falls

Boat Tour

National

Cut Bank Ridge

Continental Divide

Cobalt Lake

Aster Falls

Pray Lake

RUNNING EAGLE FALLS

Park

To St. Mary

Appistoki Falls

TWO MEDICINE RANGER STATION

TWO MEDICINE ENTRANCE

Appistoki Peak 8,164ft

SCENIC POINT

Lower Two Medicine Lake

TWO MEDICINE RD

49

KIOWA JUNCTION

89

To West Glacier

SEE "EAST GLACIER" MAP

GLACIER PARK LODGE

LOOKING GLASS HILL

East Glacier

2

BLACKFEET NATION RESERVATION

89

Two Medicine River

2

MUSEUM OF THE PLAINS INDIAN

NORTH AMERICAN INDIAN DAYS

Browning

89

464

To St. Mary

0   2 km
0   2 mi

© MOON.COM

East Glacier

To Two Medicine ↑

To Browning ↗

JACOBSON'S
● COTTAGES

EAST GLACIER
MOTEL AND CABINS ●

WHISTLE STOP RESTAURANT
▼

● BROWNIE'S HOSTEL/
BROWNIE'S BAKERY AND DELI

MOUNTAIN PINE MOTEL ●

■ RANGER STATION

TRAVELERS
REST LODGE
●

2

■ BEAR TRACK TRAVEL CENTER

■ POST OFFICE

BLACKFOOT AVE

49

GLACIER PARK LODGE
GOLF COURSE

WHISTLING
SWAN
MOTEL

GLACIER AVE

☆ GLACIER
PARK LODGE

TRAIN
DEPOT ■

● CIRCLE R
MOTEL

WASHINGTON ST
MEADE ST

THE
BROWN
HOUSE

SERRANO'S/
BACKPACKER'S INN

GLACIER PARK
TRADING CO ■

DAWSON AVE

ROCK 'N ROLL BAKERY:
GEAR AND GOODNESS

■ TWO MEDICINE
GRILL

0   100 yds

0   100 m

▼ BURGER
BOX

MONTANA AVE

● DANCING
BEARS
INN

LINDHE AVE

To Bison Creek Ranch B&B
and Marias Pass

⋀ Y LAZY R
RV PARK

© MOON.COM

sprinkled in the park's most scenic spots for places to tour. For early visitors getting off the train in 1911, a bumpy wagon ride led to a tent enclave with canvas walls and wooden floors at Two Medicine Lake with a dormitory and dining hall added later. By 1915, guests arrived on horseback via trail, the first leg on the Inside Trail connecting to Cut Bank and St. Mary Chalets; the three-day horseback tours cost $13.25. In the wake of the Depression, World War II closures, and increasing auto traffic, the Two Medicine Chalets met their demise. They were torn down; only the dining hall remained, now the Two Medicine store.

Where Can I Find...?

- **ATMs:** Find ATMs at **Glacier Park Trading Company** and **Glacier Park Lodge.**

- **Cell reception:** There's service in **East Glacier** and **Browning,** and oddly enough, sometimes you can get a signal at **Cut Bank Campground.** There's no reception in **Two Medicine.**

- **Gas:** Two Medicine has no gas station, but **East Glacier** has an **Exxon** at the Bear Track Travel Center at the east end of town on U.S. 2 and **Grizzly Gas** on MT 49 at the Sears Motel. **Browning** has several gas stations.

- **Restrooms:** In **Two Medicine,** restrooms with **flush toilets** and **running water** are located at the end of the road adjacent to the camp store. The **picnic area** and **campground** also have restrooms.

- **Shuttles:** Shuttles run between **Glacier Park Lodge** in East Glacier, **Two Medicine,** and the lodge at **St. Mary Village.** Reservations are recommended at least 24 hours in advance.

- **Wi-Fi:** Internet access is available at **Brownie's, Bear Track Travel Center,** and some accommodations such as the lobby of **Glacier Park Lodge.**

Exploring Two Medicine and East Glacier

RANGER STATIONS

On Two Medicine Road at the campground junction, **Two Medicine Ranger Station** (406/888-7800, 7am-5pm daily summer) has current trail information and issues backcountry permits. You can also find out about park naturalist programs, fishing, and trail conditions. The ranger station plots bear sightings on a large wall map, which is worth a look just for fun, and sells annual Blackfeet conservation permits ($10 pp) for hiking over Scenic Point to East Glacier.

ENTRANCE STATIONS

The **Two Medicine Entrance Station** is located approximately 4 miles (6.4 km) up **Two Medicine Road.** It is staffed during daylight hours daily in the summer. During shoulder seasons, staffing is reduced to weekends only or not at all, but you can use the self-pay cash-only kiosk. If you don't have an annual pass, get a seven-day pass ($35 per vehicle, $30 per motorcycle, $20 per hiker, biker, and pedestrian). Maps and the *Waterton-Glacier Guide* are available.

The Cut Bank Road has no entrance station nor a self-pay kiosk.

TOURS
Bus Tours

For those who have limited time to explore, two bus tours go from Glacier Park Lodge in East Glacier to Going-to-the-Sun Road and Logan Pass, daily mid-June through mid-September. Reservations are required. Rates ($102-105 adults, kids about half price) do not include meals, park entrance fees, taxes, and gratuities. Plan to tip guides about 15 percent.

Historic **red buses** (855/733-4522, www.glaciernationalparklodges.com, 9am-5pm) driven by storytelling jammer drivers are the vintage way to tour. The canvas tops roll back when the weather permits, which is especially good for whole-sky views on the **Big**

Sky Circle Tour, which loops over Marias Pass to Lake McDonald and then on Going-to-the-Sun Road over Logan Pass to St. Mary and back to East Glacier.

Departing Glacier Park Lodge or Browning, **Sun Tours** (406/732-9220 or 800/786-9220, www.glaciersuntours.com, 8am-3:30pm daily June-Sept.) runs 25-passenger air-conditioned buses with extra-large windows to catch the big views. Tours go through St. Mary to Logan Pass and back. Led by local Blackfeet guides who live on the reservation, the tour highlights Glacier's connection with the Blackfeet, including peak names, cultural history, plants, wildlife, and geology.

★ Boat Tour

The **Sinopah** (Glacier Park Boat Company, 406/257-2426, http://glacierparkboats.com, June-mid-Sept., adults $17 round-trip, kids half price) started service on Two Medicine Lake in 1927 and has never left its waters. The 45-foot (13.7-m), 49-passenger wooden boat cruises up-lake five times daily for 45-minute tours (9am, 10am, 11am, 1pm, 3pm, and 5pm) while the captain narrates history, trivia, and natural phenomena. Two trips daily also in-corporate a guided hike to Twin Falls (0.9 mi/1.4 km one-way). An 8am trip starts up

in July, geared as a shuttle for early hikers. Make reservations by phone at least a day in advance; you can also buy tickets at the dock three days in advance.

Hikers use the tour boat as a **shuttle** to shorten mileages on trails. You can pay half price in cash for one-way return rides upon boarding at the head of the lake. If too many people are waiting, the boat runs extra trips to retrieve all hikers waiting at the upper dock.

Blackfeet Reservation Tours

Darrell Norman, a Blackfeet member who runs the Lodgepole Gallery and Tipi Village in Browning, leads private **Blackfeet Cultural Historical Tours** (406/338-2787, www.blackfeetculturecamp.com, May-Sept., starting $150) to buffalo jumps and tepee ring sites on the Blackfeet Reservation. He accompanies you in your car.

Driving Tours
TWO MEDICINE ROAD

Four miles (6.4 km) north of East Glacier, **Two Medicine Road** (late May-Oct.) diverges off MT 49 for a 7.5-mile (12.1-km) scenic venture up Two Medicine Valley. Beginning on the Blackfeet Reservation, it winds through quaking aspen above Lower

The *Sinopah* provides boat tours and shuttles hikers across Two Medicine Lake.

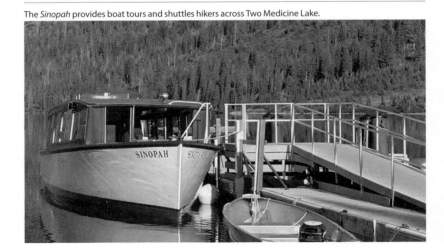

Blackfeet Nation

Located on the east side of Glacier, the Blackfeet Reservation extends across rolling plains from the Canadian border to south of East Glacier, covering 1.5 million acres (0.6 million hectares). Smaller than it originally was, it is home to nearly two-thirds of the 17,000-plus members of Blackfeet Nation.

HISTORY

Originally from north of the Great Lakes, the Blackfeet are related by language to the Algonquin peoples. As Europeans landed in North America in the 1600s, the Blackfeet were one of the first nations to move westward, adopting a nomadic lifestyle hunting buffalo in what is now Saskatchewan, Alberta, and Montana. Small bands, each led by a chief, met for summer medicine-lodge or sun-dance rituals before separating for winter. The loose Blackfeet Confederacy contained several independent nations: the Blackfeet, Kainai (Blood), Piikani (Piegan), and Siksika. Today, the latter three are primarily in Alberta, Canada.

tepee on display for North American Indian Days

The Blackfeet used buffalo jumps, lighting fires to stampede bison over a cliff in order to process the animals for tools, clothing, and food. (*Siksika*, or "black feet," may have referred to moccasins ashdarkened from these prairie fires.) When the Blackfeet acquired horses in the 1700s and later guns from French fur traders, their hunting methods altered.

The 1800s brought devastating misery to the Blackfeet. A smallpox epidemic in 1837 killed 6,000 people. The buffalo population declined by two-thirds, which led to Starvation Winter in 1884, claiming the lives of 600 Blackfeet. By the middle of the 19th century, the first treaty with the U.S. government defined Blackfeet territory as two-thirds of eastern Montana, starting at the Continental Divide. White settlers arrived, rankling the Blackfeet, who raided settlements. To squelch hostilities, in 1870 the U.S. Army sent Colonel E. M. Baker to kill the raid leader, Mountain Chief. But Baker mistakenly attacked Heavy Runner's peaceful band, slaughtering 200 and capturing 140 women and children.

Blackfeet leaders, desperate to help their destitute people, negotiated with the U.S. government for their survival. They sold off portions of the reservation in trade for tools, equipment, and cattle. Glacier, from the Continental Divide to the eastern boundary, was one of these trades, purchased by the U.S. government for a mere $1.5 million in 1896. Still in dispute today are Indigenous hunting and fishing rights in Glacier. These were retained as part of the terms of the sale, but revoked when Glacier became a national park in 1910.

Today, the Blackfeet economy is based mostly on cattle ranching and agriculture. While making strides to preserve its language and culture, the Blackfeet Nation struggles with unemployment and poverty. In recent years, Blackfeet initiatives have seen success. In 2016, the Blackfeet began re-introducing bison, so you may get a glimpse of the herds, especially on U.S. 2. In 2020, after a 30-year struggle, the Blackfeet finally gained protection for the sacred Badger-Two Medicine area with the cancellation of illegal oil and gas leases.

EXPERIENCE BLACKFEET CULTURE

The Blackfeet refer to themselves as "Niitsitapi" (nee-itsee-TAH-peh), which translates to "the real people." You can learn about the Blackfeet by visiting Browning, which is the center of Blackfeet culture, education (including a community college), and governance. In Browning, you can tour the **Museum of the Plains Indian,** sleep in a tepee at the **Blackfeet Culture Camp,** and attend **North American Indian Days** in July.

Two Medicine Lake. In September, the aspens turn bright yellow, almost emitting a light of their own. **Scenic Point** rises across the lake, and red rocks flank **Rising Wolf.** At 3 miles (4.8 km), the road crosses over a cattle guard and passes the entrance sign, but you won't reach the entrance station until 4 miles (6.4 km). At 5.2 miles (8.4 km), stop to see **Running Eagle Falls** interpretive site. Then, the road lined with blue camas in July climbs into the Two Medicine basin. Once in the basin, the peaks of Two Medicine pop out: Sinopah, Lone Walker, and Rising Wolf. After passing the ranger station and entrance to the picnic area and campground (7.1 mi/11.4 km), the road terminates in the parking lot at **Two Medicine Lake.** Check the park's **Recreational Access Display** (www.nps.gov/applications/glac/dashboard/) for real-time status of Two Medicine Road and parking lots before driving.

LOOKING GLASS HILL-BROWNING LOOP

From East Glacier, a 49-mile (79-km) scenic drive twists up MT 49 (open May-Oct.) and loops through Browning. State law restricts the size of trailer combinations and RVs to 21 feet (6.4 m) on MT 49, and motorcycles should use caution. Expect chewed-up pavement, potholes, gravel portions, and slumps. As the road climbs to a high vantage point on Looking Glass Hill above **Lower Two Medicine Lake,** 3 miles (4.8 km) past the Two Medicine junction, find unmarked pullouts overlooking the valley for great photo ops before descending to Kiowa Junction.

Drive slowly: "Open range" means no fences. Cattle wander willy-nilly. You may have to wait for cows standing in the middle of the road. Give them room, as they can dent your car with a good kick. Because the road is narrow and curvy, take it slow. You'll have less chance of putting a cow imprint across your grille.

At Kiowa, turn right onto U.S. 89 toward **Browning** to make the loop through the Blackfeet Reservation. At the Museum of the Plains Indian, turn back to East Glacier on U.S. 2 past the Blackfeet Nation Bison Reserve. From Kiowa, an alternate tour continues north on U.S. 89 to St. Mary along the Rocky Mountain Front on a scenic but narrow, curvy drive.

Sights

TWO MEDICINE LAKE

The largest of three lakes, **Two Medicine Lake** is the highest road-accessible lake in Glacier, sitting almost 1 mile (1.6 km) high and flanked by peaks rich in Blackfeet history. Its waters collect snowmelt from peaks over 8,000 feet (2,438 m) high but devoid of glaciers. The lakes are all that remain of the 1,000-foot-thick (305-m) ice field that filled the valley and flowed out onto the prairie past Browning. To explore Two Medicine Lake, jump on the historic *Sinopah* tour boat, or if the waters are calm, paddle its shoreline, swim in its chilly clear waters, or fish for brook trout.

TWO MEDICINE CAMPSTORE

Little remains of Two Medicine Chalets, but the dining hall, now operating as the **Two Medicine Campstore,** is designated a National Historic Landmark. Built in 1912-1913, the chalets replaced the original tepee camp. The log two-story chalet was once the hub of the small colony, the first stop on the Inside Trail horse trip with the Park Saddle Horse Company in the 1920s. The dining hall hosted Franklin Delano Roosevelt when he addressed the nation from here in an unofficial fireside chat in 1934.

★ RUNNING EAGLE FALLS

A short **nature trail** (0.6 mi/1 km rt, 15 min, easy) leads to **Running Eagle Falls,** formerly known as Trick Falls. In high runoff, water gushes over the top of the falls, spraying those standing nearby. But in lower flows, you can see the trick. Part of the falls runs underground and spits out through a cavern halfway down the cliff face. Running Eagle, the Blackfeet name for the falls, honors a female warrior named Pitamakin who had her vision quest here. She gained renown for stealing horses from the Kootenai but was eventually killed during a raid.

★ GLACIER PARK LODGE

In East Glacier, **Glacier Park Lodge** (1 Midvale Rd., 844/868-7474 or 406/226-5600, www.glacierparkcollection.com) stands as the headliner hotel for the historic chain of Great Northern Railroad hostelries built throughout Glacier. On land purchased from the Blackfeet Nation, the 155-room hotel, built in 1913-15, started its life providing train visitors with a first taste of Glacier. The posh lodge touted high-class amenities: a plunge pool, electric lights, and steam heat. The nine-hole golf course followed 14 years later. Road access

into the park stole much of the lodge's thunder. Now listed on the National Register of Historic Places, the lodge is worth a look. Walk the gardens leading up to the front door, lounge in its massive lobby held up by 500- to 800-year-old Douglas firs, and peruse the historical photo display chronicling the hotel's glory days.

BLACKFEET SENTRIES

Blackfeet artist Jay Laber gives new life to garbage in what he calls "reborn Rez Wrecks." Using farm tools, jewelry, hubcaps, and barbwire, he sculpted a not-to-be-missed sculpture series. The *Blackfeet Reservation Sentries* are posted on the reservation's four boundaries. Each pair of life-size sentries rides atop horses. Posted in East Glacier, one pair guards the reservation's western entrance (U.S. 2, 0.2 mi/0.3 km west of town).

BLACKFEET NATION BISON RESERVE

While driving between East Glacier and Browning, you may catch sight of the **buffalo herd** managed by the Blackfeet. Bison provided food, shelter, and clothing for the nomadic Blackfeet until the buffalo were exterminated in the 1800s.

Running Eagle Falls in late summer

Two Medicine and East Glacier Hikes

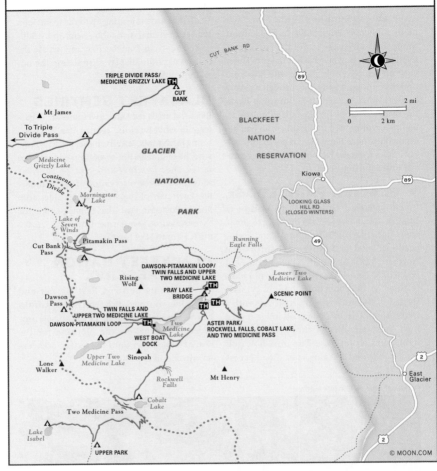

★ MUSEUM OF THE PLAINS INDIAN

Located adjacent to the roundabout at U.S. 2 and 89 in Browning, the **Museum of the Plains Indian** (406/338-2230, www.doi.gov/iacb/museum-plains-indian, 9am-4:45pm Tues.-Sat. June-Sept., adults $5, seniors $4, kids $1, under age 6 free, cash only; 10am-4:30pm Mon.-Fri. Oct.-May, all ages free winter) is a tiny but informative center for Blackfeet culture and history. Displays cluster phenomenal beadwork, leather, tools, and clothing to tell the story of the Northern Plains Indigenous people. Seeing the life-size beaded ceremonial regalia is worth the price of admission. The museum also exhibits its contemporary artists and craftspeople. Periodically, it hosts events for the summertime Native America Speaks program.

Two Medicine and East Glacier Hikes

Trail	Effort	Distance	Duration
Scenic Point	moderate-strenuous	7.4 mi (11.9 km) rt	4 hr
Aster Park	easy	3.8 mi (6.1 km) rt	2 hr
Rockwell Falls, Cobalt Lake, and Two Medicine Pass	easy-strenuous	6.8-15.8 mi (10.9-25.4 km) rt	4-8 hr
Two Medicine Lake Loop, Twin Falls, and Upper Two Medicine Lake	easy-moderate	2-10.7 mi (3.2-17.2 km) rt	1-5 hr
Dawson-Pitamakin Loop	strenuous	15.3 or 17.6 mi (24.6 or 28.3 km)	7-9 hr
Medicine Grizzly Lake	moderate	12 mi (19.3 km) rt	6 hr
Triple Divide Pass	strenuous	14.8 mi (23.8 km) rt	7.5 hr

Recreation

DAY HIKES

Hiking at Two Medicine is in a class by itself. Except for a few short hikes from the lake's upper boat dock, hikers here find solitude even on the busiest summer days.

With a maze of trail junctions breaking off the north-shore and south-shore Two Medicine Lake trails, the park's non-topographic trail map can be helpful. Find these at the ranger station and the Glacier Park Lodge activity desk. For longer hikes, such as the Dawson-Pitamakin Loop, take a good topographic map; you can buy one in the Two Medicine Campstore. Hikers use the Two Medicine Lake tour boat as a shuttle to prune miles off hikes.

Two Medicine trailheads usually can be accessed mid-May-October, or as long as the road is open. Lower-elevation trails melt out by late May, but higher elevations retain snow through June. Use ice axes and caution on high-angled snowfields in early summer. Seasonal bridges are usually installed in May and removed in late September. Consult the ranger station or look online (www.nps.gov/glac) for trail status updates. Check the **Recreational Access Display** (www.nps.gov/applications/glac/dashboard/) for parking lot availability.

★ Scenic Point

Distance: 7.4 miles (11.9 km) round-trip
Duration: 4 hours
Elevation gain: 2,124 feet (647 m)
Effort: moderate-strenuous
Trail surface: narrow dirt path with roots and rocks
Trailhead: milepost 6.9 up Two Medicine Road (see map p. 194)

Scenic Point is one short climb with big scenery. The trail launches up through a thick subalpine fir forest. A short side jaunt en route allows a peek at Appistoki Falls. As switchbacks line up like dominoes, stunted firs give way to silvery dead and twisted limber pines. Broaching the ridge, the trail enters seemingly barren alpine tundra. Only alpine bluebells and pink mats of several-hundred-year-old moss campion cower in crags.

Scenic Point

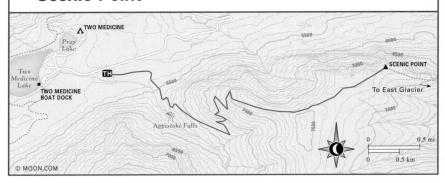

© MOON.COM

On the ridge, the trail traverses a north-facing slope; avoid the early summer steep snowfield by climbing a worn path that goes above it before descending to Scenic Point. To reach the actual Scenic Point above the trail, cut off at the sign, stepping on rocks to avoid crushing fragile alpine plants. At the top, views plunge several thousand feet straight down to Lower Two Medicine Lake and across the plains. Return the way you came, or drop 7 miles (11.3 km) to East Glacier, passing outside the park boundary, where cow pies buzz with flies. The latter half of the Scenic Point-East Glacier trail requires a Blackfeet recreation permit ($10), available at the Two Medicine Ranger Station or Bear Track Travel Center (Exxon gas station) in East Glacier.

Aster Park

Distance: 3.8 miles (6.1 km) round-trip
Duration: 2 hours
Elevation gain: 610 feet (186 m)
Effort: easy
Trail surface: narrow dirt path with roots and rocks
Trailhead: adjacent to Two Medicine boat dock (see map p. 196)

Beginning on the South Shore Trail, Aster Park is reached via a spur trail just past Aster Creek. About 1.2 miles (1.9 km) southwest of the boat dock, turn left at the signed junction and follow the trail past Aster Falls as it switchbacks up to a flower-covered knoll.

This overlook provides grand views of Two Medicine Lake and Rising Wolf.

Rockwell Falls, Cobalt Lake, and Two Medicine Pass

Distance: 6.8-15.8 miles (10.9-25.4 km) round-trip
Duration: 4-8 hours
Elevation gain: minimal-2,518 feet (minimal-767 m)
Effort: easy-strenuous
Trail surface: narrow dirt path with roots and rocks
Trailhead: adjacent to Two Medicine boat dock

Follow the gentle South Shore Trail along Two Medicine Lake past beaver ponds and bear-scratched trees to Paradise Creek, crossing on a swinging bridge. At 2.3 miles (3.7 km), turn left at the signed junction. The trail wanders through avalanche paths with uprooted trees shredded like toothpicks. At 3.4 miles (5.5 km), you reach Rockwell Falls. Spur trails explore the falls.

Continuing on to Cobalt Lake, the trail climbs up several switchbacks into an upper basin, crossing the creek. It ascends at a moderate pitch for the last 2 miles (3.2 km). Tucked in the uppermost corner of the basin, Cobalt Lake sits below mountain-goat cliffs.

Another 2.2 miles (3.5 km) climbs above the tree line through alpine tundra along the windblown Two Medicine Pass. From the high point atop Chief Lodgepole Mountain, you'll stare straight down a dizzying drop to Cobalt Lake with Two Medicine Lake in the distance.

Blackfeet Peaks

The most prominent feature in Two Medicine Valley is the hulking 9,513-foot (2,900-m) **Rising Wolf Mountain.** It is named for the first person of European descent to meet the Blackfeet. Born Hugh Monroe in Quebec, Canada, in 1798, the 16-year-old traveled west as an apprentice for the Hudson's Bay Company. With an intense interest in the Indigenous population, he was sent to live with the Small Robes band of Piegans, one nation of the Blackfeet, to learn their language and to find beaver-trapping territory. The band's chief, **Lone Walker,** took a liking to the congenial Monroe. After several seasons with the Piegans, Monroe married **Sinopah,** Lone Walker's daughter. When officially admitted to the band, Monroe was given the name Rising Wolf. He served as a guide and interpreter for territorial survey teams and early reconnaissance of Glacier National Park. Despite discrepancy as to Monroe's birth date, he lived to a ripe old age, even after losing sight in one eye in a fight with a Sioux. He died in 1892, just as Great Northern Railway laid tracks over Marias Pass. Many of Monroe's descendants still live on the Blackfeet Reservation. How can you enjoy these peaks?

- From the beach at Two Medicine Lake (Sinopah across the lake, Lone Walker in the distance behind the lake's head, and Rising Wolf on the north shore)

- From the tour boat or paddling

- Hiking to Upper Two Medicine Lake to see Lone Walker

- Hiking the South Shore of Two Medicine Lake Trail and Cobalt Lake Trail along the base of Sinopah

- Hiking the North Shore of Two Medicine Lake Trail along the base of Rising Wolf

- Hiking Dawson-Pitamakin for a complete loop around Rising Wolf to see all sides

Two Medicine Lake Loop, Twin Falls, and Upper Two Medicine Lake

Distance: 2-10.7 miles (3.2-17.2 km) round-trip
Duration: 1-5 hours
Elevation gain: none-424 feet (none-129 m)
Effort: easy-moderate
Trail surface: narrow dirt path with roots and rocks
Trailhead: North Shore Two Medicine Lake trailhead at Pray Lake Bridge in Two Medicine Campground, South Shore Two Medicine Lake trailhead near boat launch, or Two Medicine Lake west boat dock (see map p. 196)

Two Medicine and Upper Two Medicine Lake are a set of subalpine lakes formed by the immense Two Medicine Glacier. As an added treat for hikers, the trail also takes in Twin Falls, a double flume of cascades. The North Shore and South Shore Trails connect at the west end of Two Medicine Lake to form the loop, a route that cuts through forest, avalanche chutes, huckleberry bushes,

and meadows. The South Shore Trail takes in beaver ponds, a swinging bridge over Paradise Creek, and the precipitous slopes of Mount Sinopah, while the North Shore Trail trots along the base of Rising Wolf, the biggest peak in the area, and captures views of Pumpelly Pillar. A spur trail at the west end of the lake leads to Twin Falls and Upper Two Medicine Lake below Lone Walker Mountain. In early summer, water floods the upper lake's beach, leaving only a brushy shoreline. For lunch, help maintain the safety of those sleeping in the backcountry campground by sitting in the cooking area to eat.

To hike the Two Medicine Lake Loop, Twin Falls, and Upper Two Medicine Lake (10.7 mi/17.2 km), go either direction starting at the North Shore trailhead or South Shore trailhead, connecting the two trailheads with 0.8 mile (1.3 km) of road walking. Other routes vary depending on starting trailheads, ending points, and whether or not you opt to use the

Two Medicine Lake Trails

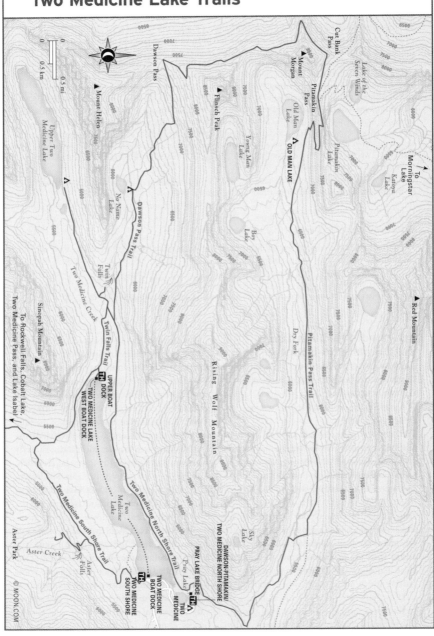

© MOON.COM

Two Medicine Lake boat as a shuttle. Taking the boat round-trip across the lake makes for the shortest hikes (2 mi/3.2 km round-trip for Twin Falls and 4.2 mi/6.8 km round-trip for Upper Two Medicine Lake). Hiking the North Shore Trail, Twin Falls, and Upper Two Medicine Lake to end at the west boat dock for a one-way shuttle (pay cash when boarding, $7 adults, half price for children) across the lake makes for mid-sized hikes (4.6 mi/7.4 km for Twin Falls and 7.2 miles (11.6 km) for Upper Two Medicine Lake). All trail junctions have signage, but maps help with clarifying routes.

TOP EXPERIENCE

★ Dawson-Pitamakin Loop

Distance: 15.3 or 17.6 miles (24.6 or 28.3 km)
Duration: 7-9 hours
Elevation gain: 2,909 feet (887 m)
Effort: strenuous
Trail surface: narrow dirt path with roots and loose rocks
Trailhead: Two Medicine Lake west boat dock, or Pray Lake Bridge in Two Medicine Campground (see map p. 196)

Although this loop can be done from either direction, both with the same elevation gain up to 8,000 feet (2,438 m), the approach to Dawson Pass is much steeper than to **Pitamakin Pass.** It crams all the elevation gain within a shorter distance, while Pitamakin Pass spreads it out over more than double the miles. So pick your route based on your preference or aversion to uphill grunts and knee-pounding descents. Taking the Two Medicine boat one direction or the other shortens the route to 15.3 miles (24.6 km).

In its loop around Rising Wolf, the route actually crosses three passes: Pitamakin, Cut Bank, and Dawson. The latter two passes have frequent winds that are sometimes strong enough to knock you off-balance. Much of the route crosses through bighorn sheep summering terrain, offering opportunities to see newborns. Going counterclockwise from the Pray Lake Bridge in Two Medicine Campground, the trail climbs the southeast flank of Rising

Wolf and drops to cross Dry Fork Creek before ascending the valley through forests and meadows to the Old Man Lake junction at mile 6.1 (km 9.8). The lake contains cutthroat trout that will steal flies off an angler's lines. From the lake, climb switchbacks to Pitamakin Pass at mile 7.6 (km 12.2) to cross the narrow arête perched 700 feet (213 m) above Pitamakin Lake. The climb continues through alpine tundra overlooking **Lake of the Seven Winds** to reach the high point at the south end of Cut Bank Pass. A top-of-the-world traverse heads south to Dawson Pass at 10.9 miles (17.5 km). Those with a fear of heights will be uncomfortable, but it's the best part of the trail, walking a tightrope between vertigo and soaring. Midway, between Mount Morgan and Flinsch Peak, the trail overlooks **Old Man Lake** and Dry Fork Valley. From Dawson Pass, the trail plunges to the North Shore Trail, at mile 14.3 (km 23), along Two Medicine Lake. Go left for 3.3 miles (5.3 km) to complete the loop or go right, and then left at all junctions, to reach the boat dock in 1 mile (1.6 km).

Medicine Grizzly Lake

Distance: 12 miles (19.3 km) round-trip
Duration: 6 hours
Elevation gain: 540 feet (165 m)
Effort: moderate
Trail surface: narrow dirt path with roots and rocks
Trailhead: terminus of Cut Bank Road
Directions: Locate the signed Cut Bank Road 6 miles (9.7 km) north of Kiowa Junction on U.S. 89. Follow the narrow dirt road over cattle grates into the park and past the ranger station. The trailhead is about 4 miles (6.4 km) up, just before the campground.

Fewer people populate this trail due to its off-the-beaten-path location. For anglers, Medicine Grizzly Lake harbors 12-inch (30.5-cm) rainbows, but expect to battle a brushy shoreline for casting. Check with the ranger station before leaving, as bear activity frequently closes the lake and its spur trail.

The trail follows Atlantic Creek up a forested drainage to a signed junction at 4 miles (6.4 km). Turn right, climbing past the Atlantic Creek Campground for 0.6 mile (1 km) to the junction for the lake or Triple Divide Pass. Continue straight for 1.4 miles (2.3 km) to reach Medicine Grizzly Lake, set below high cliffs of the Continental Divide.

★ Triple Divide Pass

Distance: 14.8 miles (23.8 km) round-trip
Duration: 7.5 hours
Elevation gain: 2,223 feet (678 m)
Effort: strenuous
Trail surface: narrow dirt path with roots and rocks
Trailhead: terminus of Cut Bank Road
Directions: Locate the signed Cut Bank Road 6 miles (9.7 km) north of Kiowa Junction on U.S. 89. Follow the narrow dirt road over cattle grates into the park and past the ranger station. The trailhead is about 4 miles (6.4 km) up, just before the campground.

The less-visited Cut Bank location puts fewer people on this trail than Two Medicine trails. The trail is part of the historic Inside Trail that connects Two Medicine and St. Mary. From the trailhead in a meadow, the easy-going route follows Atlantic Creek up a forested drainage to a signed junction (4 mi/6.4 km). Turn right, ascending past the Atlantic Creek Campground for 0.6 mile (1 km) to a second junction. Turn right to begin the climb to the pass.

Soon the trail bursts out of the trees, traversing a rocky face below Mount James as it looks down on Medicine Grizzly Lake. After winding into a large bowl, look for bighorn sheep that summer here. The pass tucks at the base of Triple Divide Peak, a three-way continental watershed to the Pacific Ocean, Atlantic Ocean, and Hudson Bay. The pass actually stands on the split between the Saskatchewan and Missouri River drainages, beginning here as Hudson Bay Creek and Atlantic Creek.

Guides

The National Park Service guides **free hikes** (mid-June-mid-Sept.) to a variety of destinations in Two Medicine: Upper Two Medicine Lake, Aster Park, Dawson Pass, and Cobalt Lake, as well as a daily boat ride and hike

to Twin Falls. (The hike is free, but you still need to pay for the boat ride.) Check the park newspaper or the ranger station for the current schedule.

Glacier Guides (406/387-5555 or 800/521-7238, http://glacierguides.com) leads a weekly **group hike** (Sat. mid-June-late Sept., $120 pp) up Scenic Point. The group meets at its office in West Glacier; transportation, lunch, snacks, and guiding are included in the rate. Custom hikes are also available, where the guide can meet you in East Glacier or Two Medicine. The guide service also has three-to six-day backpacking trips (June-mid-Sept., $225/day) that depart weekly, some on routes out of Two Medicine. Reservations are mandatory.

BACKPACKING

Two Medicine trails offer short trips to lakes perfect for children and longer, high-elevation treks for those looking for higher challenges. Pick up permits (adults $7 pp/night) 24 hours in advance in person at the **Two Medicine Ranger Station** (7am-5pm daily summer), **Apgar Backcountry Permit Office** (406/888-7859 daily May-Oct., 406/888-7800 Nov.-Apr.), or **St. Mary Visitor Center** (406/888-7800, daily late May-early Oct.). For advance reservations, apply online starting in mid-March (www.nps.gov/glac, $40).

Dawson-Pitamakin Loop and Inside Route
18.4-32 MILES (29.6-52 KM)

Although this route can be done as a day hike, you can also stretch it out to make a backpacking trip of it. The Dawson-Pitamakin Loop takes a top-of-the-world Continental Divide traverse between high passes through bighorn sheep summering habitat and alpine tundra. Hike this loop in either direction, starting from the trailhead at Two Medicine Campground. For an 18.4-mile (29.6-km),

1: Two Medicine Pass Trail 2: Old Man Lake on Dawson-Pitamakin Loop 3: backpacker climbing to Pitamakin Pass

three-day trip, camp a night at **Old Man Lake** (OLD) and a night at **No Name Lake** (NON). For four days and 25 miles (40 km), add a night at **Morning Star Lake** (MOR) in the middle, but be prepared for the plunge to the lake and a 2,000-foot (610-m) climb back up the next day. The route is snow-free some summers by early July, but advance reservations are not available until July 15.

To extend this hike up the historic Inside Route (32 mi/52 km total, 4-5 days), head north from Pitamakin Pass to Morning Star Lake (MOR), Triple Divide Pass, and Red Eagle Lake (REH or REF) to reach St. Mary. The east-side shuttle aids in returning to your vehicle.

Cobalt Lake and Lake Isabel
28-31 MILES (45-50 KM)

Cobalt Lake and Lake Isabel anchor both sides of the lofty Two Medicine Pass. A 28-mile (45-km), four-day backpacking trip leads to prime fishing at Lake Isabel with utter solitude. The long trek across Two Medicine Pass goes through alpine tundra surrounded by jagged peaks; it's worth doing both directions. Camp on the first and third nights at Cobalt Lake (COB) and the second night at Lake Isabel (ISA). Snow can melt from the route by mid-July, allowing for walk-in permits, but advance reservations are not available for Cobalt until August 1.

A one-night trip to Cobalt is a good destination for kids. An alternative point-to-point route from Isabel descends down Park Creek 17 miles (27 km) to Essex with or without an additional night at Lower Park camp (PAR); the 31-mile (50-km) route avoids the return climb over Two Medicine Pass, but requires a shuttle.

BIKING

Bicycling around the park's southeast corner is usually restricted to narrow, curvy, shoulderless roadways. Be prepared to have large RVs nearly shove you off the road, simply due to their size in comparison to the skimpy pavement. It's an area where you may encounter bears on the roadway, especially on Two Medicine Road; on MT 49, with open range, you can round a corner into a small herd of cows. For some reason, no matter which direction you're riding, a strong head-wind always blasts.

Glacier's trails do not permit bikes, but campground loops work well for kids. Two Medicine Campground has shared **hiker-biker campsites** ($5-8 pp) with bear-resistant food storage containers. Bike rentals are not available.

HORSEBACK RIDING

Glacier Gateway Trailrides (520 Third Ave./MT 49, 406/226-4408, June-early Sept., $40-200) leads trail rides and cowboy-style horseback rides; the latter tour cross-country rather than riding single file. Led by Blackfeet guides, the tours roam on the Blackfeet Reservation. Rides last 1-3 hours or all day. Wear long pants and sturdy shoes (no sandals). Kids must be at least seven years old and have some experience riding. Reservations are recommended.

WATER SPORTS
Boating and Paddling

On calm days, kayaks, canoes, and paddle-boards tour the shoreline of **Two Medicine Lake**. But it is one of the windiest lakes in the park, so boaters need to keep an eye on waves; if whitecaps pop up, get off the lake. Some paddlers prefer the tiny **Pray Lake** in the campground for its more protected water instead. Two Medicine Road terminates at the public boat ramp, so it's easy to find. Hand-propelled watercraft and non-trailered electric-powered boats are allowed, but Jet Skis and gas-engine motorboats are not.

Glacier has instituted strict boating and paddling guidelines in order to protect its pristine waters from aquatic invasive species. Stop at the **Two Medicine Ranger Station** (7am-4:30pm daily) to get your watercraft inspected and get your **permit** (free) before launching. Boating season runs June-late September.

Leave No Trace

To keep Glacier pristine, visitors to this unique park need to take an active role in maintaining its well-being.

- **Plan ahead and prepare.** Hiking in Glacier's backcountry is inherently risky. Three miles (4.8 km) here may be much harder than 3 miles through your neighborhood park back home. Choose appropriate routes for mileage and elevation gain with this in mind, and carry hiking essentials.

- **Travel and camp on durable surfaces.** Always camp in designated sites. Protect fragile plants by staying on the trail, refusing to cut switchbacks, and walking single file on trails even in the mud. If you must walk off the trail, step on rocks, snow, or dry grasses rather than wet soil and delicate plants.

- **Leave what you find.** Flowers, rocks, and goat-fur tufts on shrubs are protected park resources, as are historical cultural items. For lunch stops and camping, sit on rocks or logs where you find them rather than moving them to accommodate your camp. Avoid building rock cairns.

- **Properly dispose of waste.** Whatever you bring in, you must pack out. Pack out all garbage. If toilets are not available, pack out toilet paper. Urinate on rocks, logs, gravel, or snow to protect soils and plants from salt-starved wildlife, and bury feces 6-8 inches (15-20 cm) deep at least 200 feet (61 m) from water.

- **Minimize campfire impacts.** Make fires in designated fire pits only. Be aware that fires and collecting firewood are not permitted in many places in the park.

- **Respect wildlife.** Bring along binoculars, spotting scopes, and telephoto lenses to aid in watching wildlife. Keep your distance. Do not feed any wildlife, even ground squirrels. Once fed, they become more aggressive.

- **Be considerate of other visitors.** Where cell service is available, be considerate to others around you who are trying to enjoy the quiet.

For more information, visit Leave No Trace online at www.LNT.org.

Located at the Two Medicine boat dock, **Glacier Park Boat Company** (406/257-2426, www.glacierparkboats.com, $16-23/hour) rents canoes, single and double kayaks, rowboats, and small motorboats. Life jackets and paddles are included.

Fishing

In the Two Medicine Valley, brook trout populate the lakes. To fish **Upper Two Medicine Lake,** hike about 2 miles (3.2 km) after taking the boat shuttle across Two Medicine Lake. It's an attractive lake to fish, but with a brushy shore and outlet clogged with downed timbers. For **Two Medicine Lake,** anglers have more success tossing a line from a boat rather than fishing from the heavily timbered and brushy shore. On the valley's south side,

Paradise Creek harbors some trout, but Aster and Appistoki Creeks are empty. Other area lakes, such as **No Name** and **Old Man,** support trout, but Cobalt is barren. In the Cut Bank Valley, **Medicine Grizzly Lake** lures anglers, but reality doesn't live up to legend, and the lake is frequently closed due to bear activity. No fishing license is required inside Glacier; pick up fishing regulations at Two Medicine Ranger Station.

GOLF

Built in 1927, the **Glacier Park Lodge Golf Course** (844/868-7474, tee times 406/226-5642, www.glacierparkcollection.com, early June-mid-Sept., $40 with cart) is the oldest grass greens in Montana. The nine-hole course winds through aspen groves with views

of the Dancing Lady, Henry, Calf Robe, and Summit peaks. Don't be surprised if bears (or, more commonly, stray dogs) roam across the course. Each hole is named after a former Blackfeet Nation chief: Rising Wolf, Bad Marriage, Long Time Sleeps, and Stabs-by-Mistake. If weather permits, the course can open earlier in spring.

A public nine-hole pitch-and-putt miniature golf course covers half of the front lawn of Glacier Park Lodge. Pick up gear ($10 pp) at the front desk. Ground squirrel holes add challenge to the course.

WINTER SPORTS

Cross-country skiers can tour roads late December-April. But because winds can scour the road free of snow in places, you may need to take your skis off and walk portions. Headwinds also frequently blow in both directions. **Two Medicine Road** (15 mi/24 km rt) makes a delightfully moderate ski to frozen Two Medicine Lake. Snow piles up enough to bury the restrooms. With relatively little avalanche danger, the gentle terrain undulates a long climb into the spectacular lake basin. From the junction with Two Medicine Road, a ski tour up **Looking Glass Hill** (8 mi/12.9 km rt) on MT 49 goes to spectacular overlooks of Two Medicine Valley.

No equipment **rentals** are available in East Glacier; the nearest rentals are at the **Izaak Walton Inn** (milepost 179.7, U.S. 2, Essex). Be prepared for winter travel: Do not venture out without a complete pack full of emergency gear, ready for self-rescue.

Entertainment and Shopping

RANGER PROGRAMS

On summer evenings, National Park Service naturalists present free 45-minute **talks** (8pm daily) on natural history and wildlife in the Two Medicine Campground Amphitheater. Presentations frequently feature storytellers via the **Native America Speaks** program. They tell about the history of local Indigenous people and their connection with Glacier. Native America Speaks programs also run periodically at different locales on the Blackfeet Reservation in summer. For a current schedule, check the park newspaper or stop at Two Medicine Ranger Station.

From time to time, **Glacier Park Lodge** sponsors entertainers and musicians. Check the sign in the lobby near the front desk for the current schedule.

★ NORTH AMERICAN INDIAN DAYS

Over four days beginning the second Thursday in July, **North American Indian Days** (406/338-7521, https://blackfeetcountry.com) celebrates Native American culture in vibrant, stunning color. In Browning, behind the Museum of the Plains Indian, the **powwow grounds** (4th Ave. NW and Boundary St.) become home to tepees, dancing, drumming, singing, games, rodeos, horse racing, sporting events, food, and crafts. Hosted by the Blackfeet, this family event draws regional Indigenous people from the United States and Canada. Traditional regalia show off exceptional craftsmanship with feathered headdresses and beadwork. Nonnative people are welcome to attend, and it's free to watch the performances and events. No alcohol is sold on the reservation during North American Indian Days.

SHOPPING

East Glacier has a few gift shops in summer to browse. It is home to the unique **Spiral Spoon**

1: the Glacier Park Lodge Golf Course 2: rental boats on Two Medicine Lake 3: bike on Two Medicine Road

(1012 MT 49, 406/226-4558, 9am-9pm daily May-Oct.), which creates artfully hand-carved spoons from different woods. The old post office converted into the **Rock 'n Roll Bakery: Gear and Goodness** (34 Dawson Ave., 406/226-5553, www.seeglacier.com, 7:30am-2pm daily summer), which stocks a small selection of quality-brand backpacking and hiking essentials. Pick up hiking poles, rain gear, socks, maps, hydration packs, and hats.

For the largest collection of Native American art, stop in Browning at the **Blackfeet Heritage Center and Art Gallery** (333 Central Ave., 406/338-5661, 9am-6pm daily June-Oct.). It houses the beadwork, jewelry, paintings, and sculptures of more than 500 artists and craftspeople. Some art comes on rawhide, buffalo hides, and bison skulls. The center also has on display a baby Tyrannosaur skeleton that was found on the reservation.

CASINOS

Gaming and slot machines on the Blackfeet Reservation are at **Glacier Peaks Casino** (46 Museum Loop, Browning, 406/338-2274, www.glacierpeakscasino.com, 10am-2am daily), located at the roundabout junction of U.S. 2 and 89. It has 300 slot machines, live poker, a lounge, and a restaurant.

Food

Two Medicine has only a tiny café, and eateries in Browning are fast food. Most visitors hit East Glacier to dine out. During special days on the Blackfeet Reservation, such as graduation and North American Indian Days, none of the restaurants, groceries, or bars serves alcohol, including East Glacier. The four-day celebration is usually scheduled beginning the second Thursday in July.

INSIDE THE PARK

On the shore of Two Medicine Lake, **Two Medicine Campstore** (end of Two Medicine Rd., 8:30am-6pm daily summer) operates in what used to be the historic dining hall for Two Medicine Chalets. A tiny café in the back of the store sells espresso, soft-serve ice cream, cold drinks, muffins, cinnamon rolls, breakfast burritos, soup, bison chili, and several types of pasties.

Two Medicine has the only **picnic area,** adjacent to the campground. With running water and flush toilets, it is in a scenic spot right on the shore of Two Medicine Lake amid cottonwoods. Most of the sites have some trees, which provide a good windbreak on days when the wind howls, but scant shade on hot days. Sites include a picnic table and a fire ring with a grill. Buy firewood from the campstore; it's illegal to gather wood here.

OUTSIDE THE PARK
East Glacier

Given the small size of the town, you can walk to most of the restaurants from your accommodations.

CASUAL DINING

In the historic Glacier Park Lodge, the **Great Northern Dining Room** (1 Midvale Rd., 406/892-2525, front desk 406/226-5600, www.glacierparkcollection.com, daily late May-late Sept.) has the best views of any restaurant in town. Ask to be seated near the west windows facing Dancing Lady Mountain and Mount Henry: The sunrise smears them orange, and the sunset backlights them with a pink glow. The view and the historical ambience draw diners to the restaurant, which doesn't take reservations. Breakfast (6:30am-10am, $10-17) is frequently a huge buffet ready for those with big appetites, or a la carte breakfast dishes. Dinner (5pm-9:30pm, $18-35) has steak, fish, and vegetarian dishes. Order bag lunches one day in advance. Adjacent to the restaurant with an equally good view, the **Empire Bar** (11:30am-midnight) serves Montana microbrews, wine, cocktails, appetizers, lunch, and dinner.

MEXICAN

Waiting lines on the front porch of ★ **Serrano's Mexican Restaurant** (29 Dawson Ave., 406/226-9392, www.serranos-mexican.com, 5pm-10pm daily May-Sept., $10-21) attest to its tasty food. The made-from-scratch Veggie Delight and Enchilada Especial top the choices of house specialties. Nachos as appetizers and huge plate-loads of food pacify hungry hikers. The building is the oldest house in East Glacier; you can eat inside its cozy dining room with wooden booths or sit on the deck out back while watching the sunset. Either way, the margaritas go down easy.

CAFÉS

Opposite the train station, ★ **Two Medicine Grill** (314 U.S. 2, 406/226-9227, www.seeglacier.com, 6:30am-9pm daily spring-fall, closes earlier in winter, $6-15) is a local hangout for diner-type meals, espresso drinks, gooey homemade cinnamon rolls, wild huckleberry shakes, bison burgers, and pie made with a butter crust. You can sit on one of the eight stools at the bar, or eat in the tiny dining room. Built in Choteau in 1935, the funky diner building moved to East Glacier where it serves as a year-round place to eat and where locals connect.

North of the railroad tracks, the **Whistle Stop Restaurant** (1024 MT 49, 406/226-9292, 7am-9pm daily June-Sept., $7-28) serves up the breakfast specialties of huckleberry-stuffed French toast and baked oatmeal. Lunch and dinner serve small or large Barbecue platters, plus burgers including bison. Top it off with huckleberry pie.

Look for the colorful pink and purple trailer for the family-run **Burger Box** (219 U.S. 2, 406/450-6134, 11am-8pm daily summer, $4-12) for lunch and dinner stops. Order burgers on fry bread and Indian tacos to go or sit on their outdoor picnic table to eat.

BAKERIES

The **Rock 'n Roll Bakery: Gear and Goodness** (34 Dawson Ave., 406/226-5553, www.seeglacier.com, 7:30am-2pm daily May-Sept.) serves up baked goods, including pesto popovers, braids, and muffins. The bakery also scored with hiring premier pie baker Kathryn Hiestand. Her double butter crust triple berry and huckleberry pies can be purchased whole at the bakery or by the slice à la mode at Two Medicine Grill.

Brownie's Bakery and Deli (1020 MT 49, 406/226-4426, https://brownieshostel.com, 7am-9pm daily May-Sept.) churns out muffins, bagels, cookies, breads, and brownies, pizza, plus espresso and ice cream. Pick up deli sandwiches or wraps for hiking, and take home a bottle of their huckleberry habanero sauce.

GROCERIES

Most grocery stores are open daily year-round, except where noted seasonally. Be aware that on the Blackfeet Reservation, alcohol sales are banned during graduation, North American Indian Days, and other holidays.

In East Glacier, **Glacier Park Trading Company** (316 U.S. 2 E., 406/226-9227, www.seeglacier.com, 8am-9pm summer, 9am-8pm winter) sells fresh veggies, dairy products, wine, meat, and staples. It also carries a broad selection of Montana microbrews. The deli makes sandwiches for hiker lunches, plus pizzas to go. The **Bear Track Travel Center** (Exxon station, 20958 U.S. 2, 406/226-5504, 7am-10pm summer, 7am-8pm winter) sells convenience-store foods, ice, firewood, camping and fishing supplies, beer and wine, propane, and fishing licenses. **Brownie's Bakery and Deli** (1020 MT 49, 406/226-4426, www.brownieshostel.com, 7am-9pm May-Sept.) carries a few groceries, too.

For a full-size grocery store, go to Browning for **Glacier Family Foods** (601 SE Boundary St., 406/338-7283, 7am-10pm Mon.-Sat., 8am-8pm Sun.).

Accommodations

OUTSIDE THE PARK

In this section of Glacier, all accommodations are outside the park. Browning, the cultural and leadership center of the Blackfeet Reservation, has minimal tourist amenities: Lodging includes the **Holiday Inn Express and Suites** (50 Museum Loop, 406/338-2400 or 866/264-5744) adjacent to Glacier Peaks Casino, and the smaller, family-owned **Going-to-the-Sun Inn and Suites** (121 Central Ave. E., 406/338-7572).

East Glacier

Outside the park boundary on the Blackfeet Reservation, **East Glacier** caters to tourists with multiple restaurants, motels, cabins, a lodge, and hostels. Bring earplugs for the clatter of passing trains and highway trucks. On the west side of the railroad tracks, historic Glacier Park Lodge is on MT 49 along with a compact strip of motels—think very rustic, not a highway megastrip. On the east side of the tracks along U.S. 2, East Glacier has several motels within a few blocks of restaurants. All fill completely in midsummer, so reservations are strongly advised. Add on a 7 percent tax to all rooms. **VRBO** (www.vrbo.com) lists vacation rentals that range from small cabins to large homes in the East Glacier vicinity and on the Blackfeet Reservation.

LODGE

Historic **Glacier Park Lodge** (1 Midvale Rd., 844/868-7474, www.glacierparkcollection.com, early June-late Sept., $150-450) is right across from the train depot. It's the only historic park lodge with an outdoor swimming pool (heated, but still chilly), golf course, and pitch-and-putt. In the gigantic lobby, huge Douglas firs hold aloft a multistory ceiling. The main lodge connects to guest rooms in the west wing via a scenic enclosed walkway. Get a room facing the mountains to enjoy the sunrises and sunsets casting orange glows. Lodge rooms, suites, and family rooms are available, along with a chalet and home. West-wing guest rooms tend to be larger. Expect rustic: tiny baths converted from original closets, thin walls, slanted floors, cantankerous hot water, and no TV, air-conditioning, or elevators. The lobby has limited Wi-Fi. Revel in the historical ambience instead. Make reservations a year in advance.

A restaurant, lounge, snack shop, and gift shop surround the lobby. Red bus tours depart from the hotel, and trail riding is across the street. Trails to Scenic Point and Firebrand Pass depart nearby.

CABINS

On the east edge of town amid aspen trees, ★ **Travelers Rest Lodge** (20987 U.S. 2 E., 406/226-9143 summer, 406/378-2414 winter, www.travelersrestlodge.net, May-mid-Oct., $129-179) has roomy log cabins with gas fireplaces and fully equipped kitchenettes. Each is positioned so that its covered deck has privacy and views of the Bob Marshall Wilderness. The nicely decorated cabins sleep 2-4 in log-hewn beds; there are TVs and CD players but no phones (a phone is available in the office). In one of the cabins, owners Diane and Bob Scalese have their engraving workshop.

Located 1.5 miles (2.4 km) from East Glacier, **Bison Creek Ranch B&B** (milepost 207.4, 20722 U.S. 2, 406/226-4482, www.bisoncreekranch.com, mid-May-Sept., $118-242) combines rustic cabin stays with a hot breakfast. Remodeled one-bedroom Gandy Dancer cabins (built as bunkhouses for railroad repair workers) and two-bedroom A-frame chalets are spread among the firs and meadows. It appeals to those who want real quiet without phones, internet, or TVs but with electricity and private baths.

1: Serrano's Mexican Restaurant 2: Glacier Park Trading Company and Two Medicine Grill

MOTELS

East Glacier has seven basic, older family-run motels, some with cabins and all within walking distance to restaurants, stores, and the train station (you'll hear train noise almost everywhere). Advance reservations in midsummer are wise. Some motels offer pickups at the train depot.

Several summer-only older motels line MT 49's strip north of Glacier Park Lodge adjacent to restaurants. Rates are lowest in spring and fall. The ★ **Mountain Pine Motel** (909 MT 49, 406/226-4403, www.mtnpine.com, May-late Sept., $82-142) offers 25 tidy guest rooms lined up surrounding a lawn tucked under tall, shady trees. The nonsmoking guest rooms have queen beds, wireless internet access, and adjoining rooms for families. Two small cabin complexes have older facilities, some with kitchenettes: **East Glacier Motel and Cabins** (1107 MT 49, 406/226-5593, www.eastglaciermotelandcabins.com, May-mid-Oct., $120-349) and **Jacobson's Cottages** (1204 MT 49, 406/226-4422, http://jacobsonscottages.com, May-Sept., $140-200).

Three year-round motels are in "downtown" East Glacier, south of the tracks. Rates are highest in summer and lowest in winter. The **Whistling Swan Motel** (512 U.S. 2, 406/226-4412 or 406/226-9227, www.seeglacier.com, $65-160) is run by the same family that owns the Two Medicine Grill, Glacier Park Trading Company, and Rock 'n Roll Bakery. Its 10 pine-walled guest rooms offer various bed configurations, and you can get loads of advice from the owners, who are avid hikers. The **Dancing Bears Inn** (40 Montana Ave., 406/226-4402, dancingbearsinn.com, $84-230) has 16 guest rooms with continental breakfast and Wi-Fi;

some guest rooms have kitchenettes. The **Circle R Motel** (406 U.S. 2, 406/226-9331, www.circlermotel.net, $94-222) has newer rooms, older rooms, and nearby cabins.

GUESTHOUSE

Art aficionados can rent a room from a professional potter and sculptor at ★ **The Brown House** (402 Washington St., 406/226-9385, June-Sept., $90-100), which has three nonsmoking guest rooms, each furnished with antiques. Each room has a private entrance and bath. The upstairs guest room has a view of the park's peaks. Originally a 1920s store, the building still has some of the fixtures from that era. The gift shop also sells the works of local artisans.

HOSTELS

For budget travelers, East Glacier has two hostels open May-September. Located one block from the train depot, **Backpacker's Inn** (29 Dawson Ave., 406/226-9392, www.serranos-mexican.com) has three dorms ($20 pp, bring sleeping bags), plus two cabins ($50, queen bed) located in the backyard of Serrano's Mexican Restaurant. A little outdoor oasis serves as a common area for these tiny renovated original 1920 prefab cedar Sears and Roebuck homes. **Brownie's Hostel** (1020 MT 49, 406/226-4426, https://brownieshostel.com) is in a renovated old two-story 1908 building that used to house railroad workers. A six-block walk from the train station and adjacent to restaurants, the hostel has a fully equipped communal kitchen, co-ed dorms ($25 pp), private bedrooms ($49-74), and a deli, convenience store, and internet. Cinnamon rolls scent the morning air from the downstairs bakery.

1: garden walkway to Glacier Park Lodge
2: Travelers Rest Lodge **3:** Two Medicine Campground

Camping

RVers requiring hookups will need to stay in East Glacier, as Glacier National Park campgrounds have no hookups. If the campgrounds are full, check the Marias Pass and Essex districts.

INSIDE THE PARK

Two National Park Service campgrounds are in Glacier's southeast corner. Campsites have picnic tables and fire rings with grills. Campground hosts usually sell firewood. All campsites are first-come, first-served. Historic and current fill times are posted online: www. nps.gov/glac. Use the previous few days to gauge when to arrive to claim a site.

Two Medicine Campground

★ Two Medicine Campground (406/888-7800, late May-late Sept., $20) yields views of bears foraging on Rising Wolf Mountain, especially from the A and C loops. Riverfront sites are 95, 99, and 100. In early summer, ruby-crowned kinglets call out "teacher, teacher" from the trees. The campground surrounds the calmer waters of small Pray Lake, a good place for paddling, fishing, or chilly swimming. With 99 sites, the campground may have availability later than campgrounds nearer Going-to-the-Sun Road, but it can fill up midsummer before 11am. Tenters should choose sheltered sites due to abrupt high winds that can flatten poles. Flush toilets, water, and a dump station are provided. The North Shore Trail departs right from the campground, leading in both directions around Rising Wolf Mountain. A seven-minute walk or a few-minute drive connects with the boat tour and rental dock. Only 13 sites can handle RVs up to 32 feet (9.7 m). Primitive camping (late Sept.-Oct., $10) has pit toilets and no water.

Cut Bank Campground

Located 19 miles (31 km) north of East Glacier off U.S. 89, Cut Bank Campground (406/888-7800, June-mid-Sept., $10) is at the end of a 5-mile (8-km) potholed dirt road. The ultra-quiet campsites can only fit very small RVs, and trailers are not recommended. The campground has pit toilets and no running water. Atlantic Creek runs nearby, but you'll need to filter the water or boil it for five minutes. With only 14 sites set in deep shade under large firs, it's a great place to escape the crowds. Atlantic Creek has fishing, and a nearby trailhead departs to Medicine Grizzly Lake and Triple Divide Pass. To locate the road, look for the campground sign 6 miles (9.7 km) north of the junction of MT 49 and U.S. 89.

OUTSIDE THE PARK
East Glacier

A small 3-acre (1.2-hectare) campground on the Blackfeet Reservation, Y Lazy R RV Park (junction of Lindhe Ave. and Meade St., 406/226-5505, mid-May-Sept., tents $25, hookups $30) is two blocks off U.S. 2. With only a few aspen trees, its open, rough grass-and-dirt setting overlooks Midvale Creek and affords big views of surrounding mountains. Amenities include flush toilets, picnic tables, coin-op showers, a dump station, a large laundry, and hookups for electricity, water, and sewer. The campground is an easy few blocks' walk from restaurants. Bring earplugs for the hoards of nearby trains.

Browning

On a prairie wildflower knoll west of Browning in view of Glacier's peaks, the ★ Lodgepole Gallery and Tipi Village (U.S. 89, 2.5 mi/4 km west of Browning, 406/338-2787, www.blackfeetculturecamp. com, May-Sept., $80 first person, $10-16 pp for extras) provides an authentic experience in 10 traditional double-walled canvas tepees with inside fire pits and the ground for the floor. Supplied wood heats the tepees on cooler nights. Bring your sleeping bag, air mattress, and flashlight, or rent them ($12). A central bathhouse has flush toilets and showers. A Blackfeet art gallery and art classes are on-site, and the owners can arrange Blackfeet-guided tours, fishing trips, and horseback riding.

Transportation and Services

TRANSPORTATION
Driving and Parking
Two-lane roads are ubiquitous. Some are very narrow and curvy. In East Glacier, find parking streetside or in a potholed dirt parking lot south of the train depot. In Browning, find parking at businesses. In Two Medicine, find parking at the road terminus at Two Medicine Lake, in the picnic area, and at trailheads.

Shuttles
Pursuit Glacier Park Collection (844/868-7474, www.glacierparkcollection.com, June-Sept., $15-30 one-way) runs shuttles on the east side of the park between East Glacier, Two Medicine, and St. Mary, where you can connect with the park shuttle on Going-to-the-Sun Road. Reservations are recommended 24 hours in advance or more; you can also pay when boarding for last-minute seats if they are available.

SERVICES
Car rentals are available in East Glacier May-September through **Avis** at **Glacier Park Trading Company** (316 U.S. 2, 406/226-9227, www.seeglacier.com).

Other services in East Glacier include **ATMs** at Glacier Park Trading Company and Glacier Park Lodge. There is a **post office** (15 Blackfoot Ave., East Glacier, 8:30am-noon and 1:30pm-5pm Mon.-Fri.). The area's daily newspaper is the *Great Falls Tribune*. A **launderette** is at **Y Lazy R RV Park** (Lindhe Ave. and Meade St.); it offers **coin-op showers** on a drop-in basis.

Gas and Repairs
Two Medicine has no gas station, but East Glacier has two: an **Exxon** at the **Bear Track Travel Center** at the east end of town on U.S. 2 and **Grizzly Gas** on MT 49 at the Sears Motel. Browning has several gas stations, plus repair locations.

Cell Phone and Internet Access
Some cell phones have reception in East Glacier, Browning, and Cut Bank Campground. No reception is available at Two Medicine. In East Glacier, internet access is available at Brownie's, Bear Track Travel Center, and some accommodations.

Emergencies
Call 911 in emergencies. To contact a park ranger, call 406/888-7800. You can also walk into the **Two Medicine Ranger Station** (7am-5pm daily summer), on Two Medicine Road at the campground junction. The nearest hospital is on the **Blackfeet Reservation** (Blackfeet Community Hospital, 760 Blackweasel Rd., Browning, 406/338-6154).

Marias Pass and Essex

The Theodore Roosevelt Highway (U.S. 2) runs

2,119 miles (3,410 km) from Minnesota to Washington, with 57 miles (92 km) bordering Glacier National Park. The Rocky Mountain corridor's history, as much as its scenery, adds to its appeal.

Tiny, rustic mountain enclaves dot the route. Both Marias Pass and Essex gained their notoriety through the railroad: Marias Pass as the route chosen for the railroad to cross the Continental Divide, Essex as a train community to tend the tracks.

Running through John F. Stevens Canyon, the year-round highway accesses wild country. With 1.5 million acres (0.6 million hectares) of the Bob Marshall Wilderness Complex to the south and Glacier's 1 million acres (0.4 million hectares) to the north, the road bisects the

Highlights

Look for ★ to find recommended sights, activities, dining, and lodging.

★ **Drive over Marias Pass:** From this pass, peaks tower about you, revealing remarkable geology (page 217).

★ **See the Lewis Overthrust Fault:** Sixty-five million years ago, the Lewis Overthrust pushed ancient rock on top of younger sediments. Look for it in the cliff face along Summit and Little Dog Mountains (page 217).

★ **Watch for mountain goats:** These shaggy white beasts congregate May-early July at the **Goat Lick.** Bring your binoculars to see them strutting across sheer cliffs (page 218).

★ **Ski at the Izaak Walton Inn:** Don cross-country skis and glide across the groomed trails at this historic inn. Warm up with a hot lunch in the dining room before tackling more trails in the afternoon (page 218).

★ **Climb to Firebrand Pass:** Trek uphill through wildflowers and circle around Calf Robe Mountain to reach this pass. Keep your eyes peeled for bighorn sheep (page 221).

★ **Ascend Elk Mountain:** Climb this steep, little-traveled trail to the summit. A sea of peaks stretches north into Glacier and south into the Bob Marshall Wilderness (page 221).

★ **Hike to Stanton Lake:** This popular, family-friendly jaunt leads to a subalpine lake in Flathead National Forest (page 224).

★ **Go River Rafting and Kayaking:** Float the Middle Fork of the Flathead River as it cuts between Glacier National Park and the Great Bear Wilderness (page 228).

largest grizzly bear habitat in the Lower 48. The Middle Fork of the Flathead River, designated a Wild and Scenic River, races through the canyon, creating a playground for rafters, kayakers, and anglers. The canyon also draws mountain goats in search of minerals and bighorn sheep and elk for wintering. From this passageway, most of Glacier is only accessible on foot. Hikers soak up solitude on remote trails, while horseback riders, anglers, and hunters dive into the Bob Marshall Wilderness.

Backwoodsy and removed from the accoutrements of civilization, the southern route around Glacier is devoid of stores and fast-food restaurants. Services are few and far between. Most visitors just drive through, but for hikers, anglers, and river floaters, it's an area rich with recreation.

PLANNING YOUR TIME

If you just want to sightsee, you can do it in **less than three hours** with stops at Izaak Walton Inn, a river access, the Goat Lick, and Marias Pass. For hiking, a **one-day excursion** can take you to a lake, pass, or lookout. Or the area can be a base camp for **3-5 days,** yielding a calmer summer experience compared to frenzied inside-park locales. However, you will tack on more driving time to go to other park regions. Essex serves as a winter recreation destination for **1-3 days.**

Summer temperatures usually average 65-80°F (18-27°C) during days and 40-43°F (4.5-6°C) at night. Hiking and backpacking into higher elevations will encounter temperatures often 10-15°F (6-8°C) cooler. Winter temperatures waffle between -10°F (-23°C) in Arctic cold fronts accompanied by frigid wind chills to 35°F (2°C).

HISTORY
Marias Pass

When Lewis and Clark passed through Montana in 1805, they failed to find Marias Pass. They came within 25 miles (40 km) but swung south on the Missouri River to cross the Continental Divide on a much higher and more difficult pass. Lewis named the Marias River, calling it "Maria's River" after his cousin. The apostrophe got lost through history, much like Marias Pass with the same name.

Reports of a "lost" pass filtered through the ranks of fur traders and mountain men. Government-funded expeditions went looking, but to no avail. Mountain men and Indigenous people wandered through the real Marias Pass, yet "undiscovered." Rumors of the pass reached Great Northern Railroad developer J. J. Hill, prompting him to dispatch railroad engineer John F. Stevens and his Flathead guide Coonsa to see if the fable was true. While temperatures plummeted to -40°F (-40°C) in December 1889, the pair traveled on rawhide snowshoes through deep snow. Unable to slog on, Coonsa stayed behind at the fire as Stevens ventured on solo. He found the lost pass, deeming it appropriate for the railroad crossing. Within two years, Hill had a line built across the Continental Divide at Marias Pass in his push to complete his transcontinental railroad.

Automobiles and Inns

As auto travel enchanted Americans, the demand for a road through John F. Stevens Canyon rose to a clamor. To transport an auto over the Continental Divide, you had to cough up $12.50 to put your car on a Great Northern Railway flatbed. While building Going-to-the-Sun Road dragged on for 20 years, the road over Marias Pass went through in a jiffy, finishing in 1930 due to the easier terrain.

Later, in 1939, the railway constructed Izaak Walton Inn to house railroad workers who cleared the tracks of snow in winter, planning to convert it to guest lodging when the park service built a southern road entrance

---

Previous: Bluebells; mountain goats at the Goat Lick; Elk Mountain summit.

Marias Pass and Essex

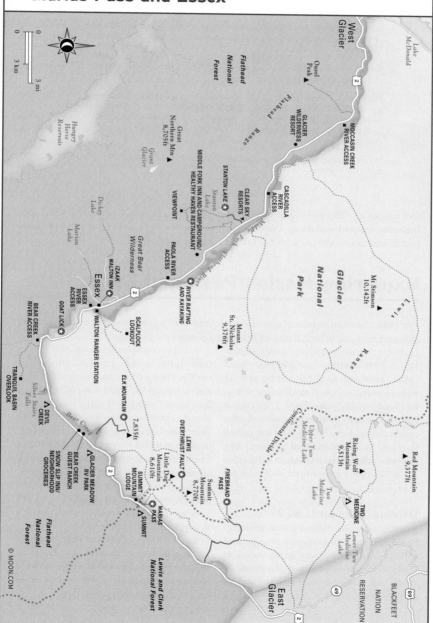

© MOON.COM

Where Can I Find...?

- **Cell reception:** Because of surrounding steep mountains, cell service is **nonexistent** on U.S. 2, but you can stop to use public **pay phones** at **Izaak Walton Inn** and **Snow Slip Inn.**

- **Gas:** You won't find gas stations between **East Glacier** and **West Glacier.** Fill up in either of those towns before you leave.

- **Restrooms:** Even though U.S. 2 lacks many services, public restrooms are plentiful. Most are **vault toilets** with no running water and are open spring to fall. Find these at all **river access points** (Bear Creek, Paola, Cascadilla, and Mocassin Creek), Walton Picnic Area, the Goat Lick, and Marias Pass (use the last one only in a pinch as it receives less regular maintenance).

- **Wi-Fi:** Internet services are only available for guests at **private campgrounds** and **inns** along the highway.

into Glacier. The Depression and World War II plummeted park visitation, scrapping the south entrance. Today, Glacier's southern valleys remain remote bastions of wilderness, accessible only by trail, some only after fording the Middle Fork.

Exploring Marias Pass and Essex

The public lands of Glacier National Park, Helena-Lewis and Clark National Forest, Flathead National Forest, and the Bob Marshall Wilderness Complex surround U.S. 2. They add up to 2.5 million acres (1 million hectares). Only small strips of private land line the valley floor. The result is a necklace of tiny mountain blink-and-miss communities, none barely large enough to warrant the title of "village." Midway, the highway enters Glacier National Park for 3.5 miles (5.6 km) with no entrance fee required.

Driving Tour on U.S. 2

After driving the dramatic Going-to-the-Sun Road, most visitors are less impressed with this southern highway. But this two-lane road still has gorgeous scenery. The drive between East Glacier to West Glacier takes 70 minutes or so. Large RVs and trailers must use this route, as they are banned from driving Going-to-the-Sun Road.

U.S. 2 is considerably easier to maintain than Going-to-the-Sun Road. It is wider, more gradual, and, for the most part, follows a fairly long, gentle 2,000-foot (610-m) ascent from West Glacier to Marias Pass. However, even though Marias Pass is 1,500 feet (457 m) lower than Logan Pass, winter still poses difficulties. While plows clear and sand the road frequently to keep it passable for winter travel, cornices thousands of feet above break loose, sending avalanches careening down across its path. In some winters the highway is closed for several days while road crews clear a path through ice, rock, and tree debris.

You'll see several white crosses along this highway for traffic fatalities. The American Legion-sponsored program works with the Montana Department of Transportation to use the crosses as safety reminders.

Public Lands

Many people find it confusing to differentiate the various types of public land. In the greater Glacier ecosystem, national park lands border national forests and wilderness areas. National parks, national forests, and wilderness areas are each managed with different purposes:

- **National parks** fall under the U.S. Department of the Interior. Parks are set aside for their historical, geological, cultural, or biological significance and are geared toward public recreation. Hunting is not permitted, nor is picking mushrooms or berries for commercial use. Mining and logging are also taboo. Leases for developing recreation like ski resorts are not available. Generally, dogs are not allowed on trails; neither are mountain bikes. Permits are needed for backcountry camping.

- **National forests** come under the U.S. Department of Agriculture. Hunting, timber harvesting, and commercial berry picking are generally allowed by permit. National forest land is leased for recreational development, such as ski areas. Your pooch can go with you on hikes; you can mountain bike as long as no special designation says otherwise. Permits are not needed for backcountry camping.

- **Wilderness areas** are administered usually by the national forest that contains the wilderness boundaries. Two concepts set wilderness apart: no mechanical transportation and no permanent human inhabitants. Wilderness areas do not have roads inside them. While hunting is permitted and Fido can go along on the trail, mountain biking is not allowed. Permits are not needed for backcountry camping.

Sights

U.S. 2 sights are listed here from East Glacier to West Glacier.

HELENA-LEWIS AND CLARK NATIONAL FOREST

From south of East Glacier to Marias Pass, U.S. 2 passes through the **Helena-Lewis and Clark National Forest** (www.fs.usda.gov). Its 1.7 million acres (0.7 million hectares) serve as the headwaters for the mighty Missouri River. High prairies at 4,500 feet (1,372 m) in elevation climb up to Rocky Mountain Peak, at 9,362 feet (2,854 m), along the Rocky Mountain Front in an extremely diverse ecosystem that is home to species like lynx and grizzly bears. Around milepost 198, you'll see remnants from the 2007 Skyland Fire.

★ MARIAS PASS

At 5,220 feet (1,591 m), **Marias Pass** (milepost 197.9) is the lowest **Continental Divide** **saddle** north of New Mexico. Two monuments mark the pass: A statue of John F. Stevens commemorates his discovery of the route for the railroad, and a tall obelisk stands in memory of Theodore Roosevelt, for whom the highway is named. At the pass, the 3,100-mile (4,989-km) Continental Divide Trail crosses into Glacier National Park, where hikers and skiers launch onto Autumn Creek Trail. With the area's broad flat forest, you'd be hard-pressed to realize you were crossing the Continental Divide. Bypass the ill-kept restrooms here in favor of the ones at the Goat Lick or Walton Picnic Area.

★ LEWIS OVERTHRUST FAULT

Opposite Marias Pass, the **Lewis Overthrust Fault** shoved older 1.6-billion-year-old rocks on top of 80-million-year-old stones. This fault exposed some of the oldest sediments in North America; these ancient Precambrian rocks formed as Belt Sea sediments solidified. On the face of Summit and Little Dog Mountains, look for an obvious upward line where the younger Cretaceous rock from the dinosaur age shows up as black or brown. This is the site where in the 1890s geologists discovered the Lewis Overthrust Fault, which extends into Canada and sets Glacier apart as a World Heritage Site.

SILVER STAIRS FALLS

An unmarked and unsigned **pullout** (milepost 188.2) on the highway's south side stares up **Silver Stairs Falls.** Tumbling thousands of feet, the waterfall cascades down stair steps created from eroding sedimentary layers. In June-July, water rages down in torrents, but by late August it slows to a trickle. You can catch a glimpse with a drive-by, but with trees surrounding the falls, you'll get a better view by stopping.

★ GOAT LICK

Much of Glacier National Park's wildlife tends to be mineral deficient. Because their bodies crave minerals from their winter-deprived condition, during spring and early summer, mountain goats congregate at the **Goat Lick** (milepost 182.6). The lick is actually a huge mass of gray rock cliffs, an exposed fault containing salts like calcium, magnesium, and potassium. Goats hop sure-footedly along the steep cliff faces as if they were on flat land to slurp the minerals. The well-marked overlook has a couple of viewing areas: one at the interpretive sign and the other at the end of a short, wheelchair-accessible walkway. Bring your binoculars for better viewing. You can also catch sight of the goats on the slopes above the Goat Lick bridge on the highway.

BOB MARSHALL WILDERNESS COMPLEX

While Glacier rises to the north of U.S. 2, to the south the **Bob Marshall Wilderness Complex** spans nearly 1.5 million acres (0.6 million hectares). It actually is three wilderness areas combined: the **Bob** (as locals call it), the **Great Bear,** and the **Scapegoat.** The Great Bear is the section bordering U.S. 2.

The Bob was one of the country's first wilderness areas, dedicated in 1964 concurrent with the Wilderness Act. While roads do not enter the wilderness areas and mechanized vehicles are prohibited (this means no mountain bikes or snowmobiles), over 1,000 miles (1,610 km) of trails criss-cross the Bob, a world-class area for hiking, backpacking, horse packing, fishing, and big-game hunting. The Bob also contains 110 miles (177 km) of the Continental Divide Trail. The wilderness complex is managed jointly by Flathead, Helena-Lewis and Clark, and Lolo National Forests.

The Bob is home to a huge ungulate population of deer, elk, moose, mountain goats, and bighorn sheep. They feed predators like lynx, grizzlies, black bears, mountain lions, and wolves. Its peaks reach 9,000 feet (2,743 m) high with the 1,000-foot-high (305-m) Chinese Wall escarpment running for 22 miles (35 km) along the Continental Divide.

Here are some tips for where to start your exploration of The Bob:

- Admire views from U.S. 2, especially at Bear Creek River Access on the Middle Fork of the Flathead River.
- Hike Grant Ridge Loop, Stanton Lake, Marion Lake, Dickey Lake, or Ousel Peak.
- Fish Stanton Lake, Marion Lake, or Dickey Lake.
- Raft the Upper Middle Fork of the Flathead River through the Great Bear Wilderness.

★ IZAAK WALTON INN

Listed on the National Register of Historic Places, **Izaak Walton Inn** (milepost 179.7, 290 Izaak Walton Inn Rd., 406/888-5700, www.izaakwaltoninn.com) is opposite the southernmost point of Glacier National Park at Essex. The hotel stands adjacent to the train tracks, luring train aficionados and

1: Marias Pass at the Continental Divide **2:** Mount St. Nicholas **3:** Lewis Overthrust Fault

those looking for something a bit different, like sleeping in a renovated caboose. In the winter, it becomes a cross-country skiing destination. Loaded with historical photos and memorabilia, the inn makes you feel almost like you've been transported back to a different era. In the downstairs bar, check out photos of avalanches burying the railroad tracks. Cozy up to the warm lobby fire.

MOUNT ST. NICHOLAS

The toothy 9,376-foot (2,858-m) spire of **St. Nicholas** is easy to pick out on the skyline, especially when rimmed with winter snow. Look for a notched spire with precipitous cliffs on its southern face. Get good views of this forbidding-looking peak driving eastward on U.S. 2. For more in-your-face views, hike Grant Ridge Loop counterclockwise or climb to Scalplock Lookout.

JOHN F. STEVENS CANYON

Named for the Great Northern Railway engineer who verified the feasibility of Marias Pass as a railroad route, **John F. Stevens Canyon** begins just west of the pass and follows Bear Creek and the Middle Fork of the Flathead until its terminus near West Glacier. U.S. 2 and the railroad traverse the canyon's entire 40-mile (64-km) distance. In places the canyon broadens into wide valleys; in others it tightens up into narrow channels, frothing with wild waters. Although its more dramatic sections are best seen from a raft or kayak on the river, several highway pullouts offer good photo ops.

FLATHEAD NATIONAL FOREST

From the Continental Divide west past Flathead Valley and extending 120 miles (193 km) south of the Canadian border, **Flathead National Forest** (www.fs.usda.gov) is broken up by state and private land but still tallies up a healthy 2.3 million acres (0.9 million hectares). Within its glaciated mountains, it has 2,600 miles (4,184 km) of trails. Over 46 percent of the forest is designated as the Bob Marshall Wilderness Complex. Spruce, Douglas fir, lodgepole, larch, and pine cover its slopes, which house wolverines, grizzly bears, and wolves.

MIDDLE FORK OF THE FLATHEAD RIVER

Draining Glacier National Park and the Bob Marshall Wilderness Complex, the **Middle Fork of the Flathead River** is no small tributary. Designated a Wild and Scenic River, its 95-mile (153 km) length is known for some of the best white-water rafting and kayaking in Montana. Dropping at 35 feet (10.7 m) per mile, the Great Bear section teems with Class III-IV rapids; the lower waters break up long, scenic floats with Class II-III rapids with such names as Jaws and Bonecrusher. Hook up with one of the four West Glacier rafting companies to splash in its waves, or float it yourself.

WINTERING RANGE

Belton Mountain, to the road's north (mileposts 155-157), is quite a different ecosystem from the heavily forested south slopes. Fires, winds, and a dry exposure have minimized forest growth. Winds create a lower snowpack, and south-facing slopes melt off early. Those are factors that make the area a prime **wintering range** for ungulates such as deer, elk, and bighorn sheep. Grizzly and black bears also forage on its slopes. Even in summer, it's worth a stop at one of the several pullouts to scan the slopes with binoculars.

Recreation

DAY HIKES

U.S. 2 is one road where hiker shuttles are not available; you must get to the trailheads on your own. Most of Glacier's trails on the south end are long valley hikes accessing little-used areas. Additional short hikes, mostly in the Great Bear Wilderness, round out the options, especially for hikers with Fido. While trails within Glacier do not allow dogs, canine friends can tag along on a leash south of the highway in the national forests and wilderness.

While trails within Glacier National Park are well signed and frequently maintained, trails in the wilderness areas are not; signs, if any, may be just a wooden trail number or name nailed to a tree. Don't expect to see mileages. Take a good topographic map, which you can purchase from the **Hungry Horse Ranger Station** (10 Hungry Horse Dr., Hungry Horse, 406/387-3800, www.fs.usda.gov/flathead), and know how to read it. Be prepared to encounter deadfall, downed trees, and heavy brush. Trail crews in the national forests do not have the staff numbers of the national park trail crews; it takes them longer to get to damaged or buried trails. Unlike in Glacier, bear-warning signage does not exist, except in extreme cases. Make noise and take precautions in bear country.

While snow melts from most lower-elevation trails such as Stanton Lake in May, it hangs on the upper elevations of Firebrand Pass, Elk Mountain, Marion Lake, Dickey Lake, Scalplock Lookout, and Grant Ridge Loop through June. Snow reappears on those trails in October. Check on trail status for Firebrand, Elk, and Scalplock online (www.nps.gov/glac); call Hungry Horse Ranger Station for the status of Flathead National Forest trails.

★ Firebrand Pass

Distance: 9.6 miles (15.4 km) round-trip

Duration: 4.5 hours

Elevation gain: 2,210 feet (674 m)

Effort: moderate

Trail surface: narrow dirt path with roots; rocky

Trailhead: at milepost 203 on the north side of U.S. 2 (see map p. 224) in Glacier National Park

From the trailhead, the path crosses into Glacier, wanders by beaver ponds, passes the old Lubec ranger station site, and follows Coonsa Creek northward. At 1.4 miles (2.3 km), turn right at the Autumn Creek Trail junction and ascend through aspens and meadows thick in July with valerian, lupine, paintbrush, and penstemon to another junction about a mile (1.6 km) later. Take a left, gaining elevation as the trail circumvents Calf Robe's lower slopes. Make noise, for this is prime bear country.

As the trail breaks out of the trees, you'll have views of Dancing Lady Mountain and East Glacier. The trail rounds Calf Robe into a hanging basin and then ascends to the pass, where you can look down Ole Creek and into Glacier's remote southern peaks. Scrambles up Calf Robe or Red Crow lend even better views, but don't go off-trail unless you're ready to deal with steep scree hillsides.

★ Elk Mountain

Distance: 7.4 miles (11.9 km) round-trip

Duration: 6 hours

Elevation gain: 3,326 feet (1,014 m)

Effort: strenuous

Trail surface: narrow dirt path with roots and loose rocks

Trailhead: Turn north off U.S. 2 at Fielding (milepost 192) and follow the dirt Forest Road 1066 about 0.5 mile to the trailhead, which links with Glacier National Park across the railroad tracks.

Hike up through private logged land to the railroad tracks and cross into Glacier. The trail starts off deceptively easy enough, but shortly after turning right at the junction near a ranger cabin, the trail climbs and climbs.

Marias Pass and Essex Hikes

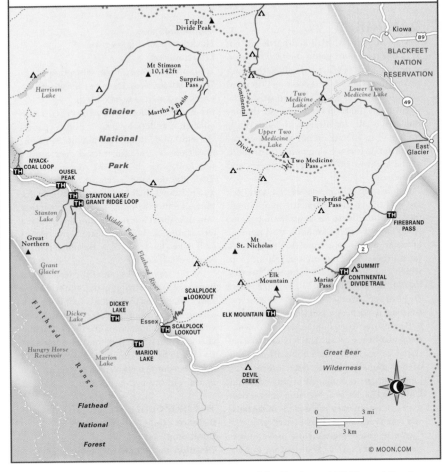

Steep does not come close to describing the pitch as it ascends to an open saddle, where it climbs sharply across a talus slope to the summit. No wonder you have so much solitude here.

From the top, among debris from what was once the lookout, the views make the grunt worthwhile. Panoramas both north and south line up peak tops for miles into Glacier's remote southern sector and the Bob Marshall Wilderness Complex. A knife ridge leads east toward the Continental Divide, and the view down Autumn Creek is dizzying.

Scalplock Lookout

Distance: 9.4 miles (15.1 km) round-trip
Duration: 5 hours
Elevation gain: 3,079 feet (938 m)
Effort: strenuous
Trail surface: narrow dirt path with roots and rocks
Trailhead: Walton Picnic Area (milepost 180.5) in Glacier National Park

Marias Pass and Essex Hikes

Trail	Effort	Distance	Duration
Firebrand Pass	moderate	9.6 mi (15.4 km) rt	4.5 hr
Elk Mountain	strenuous	7.4 mi (11.9 km) rt	6 hr
Scalplock Lookout	strenuous	9.4 mi (15.1 km) rt	5 hr
Marion Lake	strenuous	3.4 mi (5.5 km) rt	2 hr
Dickey Lake	moderate	4.8 mi (7.7 km) rt	2.5 hr
Stanton Lake	easy	2 mi (3.2 km) rt	1 hr
Grant Ridge Loop	strenuous	10.2-mi (16.4-km) loop	5 hr
Ousel Peak	very strenuous	5.2 mi (8.4 km) rt	3.5 hr

Snow lingers on top in June, but by early July, bluebells fill the high meadows. Beginning in the Walton Picnic Area, the trail wanders along the Middle Fork of the Flathead in the first mile, crossing Ole Creek on a swinging bridge over a small gorge and ascending to the Ole Creek Trail. Turn west onto this trail for 0.4 mile (0.6 km) to a second junction where the climb begins. In the remaining 3 miles (4.8 km), the trail grunts up switchbacks at nearly 1,000 feet (305 m) per mile as the sounds of the highway and trains reverberate from below.

Peekaboo views of the Middle Fork of the Flathead River are the only respite from the relentless ascent. Soon, the trail breaks out of the trees to climb up a ridge flanked with wildflower meadows. At the top, Scalplock Lookout has a commanding view of the entire Middle Fork drainage, including Mount St. Nicholas's spire.

Marion Lake

Distance: 3.4 miles (5.5 km) round-trip
Duration: 2 hours
Elevation gain: 1,739 feet (530 m)
Effort: short but strenuous
Trail surface: narrow dirt path with roots and rocks
Trailhead: Turn south onto Dickey Lake Road (milepost 178.7 on Forest Rd. 1640) at Essex and follow the left fork 2.3 miles (3.7 km) to the signed trailhead in Flathead National Forest.

The trail is popular and sees quite a bit of summer traffic, making it well-worn and quite obvious to follow until you encounter heavy foliage. From the start, it taxes your lungs on its steep climb up Marion Creek Valley. You will encounter thick, heavy brush in the trail's midsection. Cow parsnip, nettle, elderberry, and false huckleberry nearly suffocate the trail. Make noise here to avoid surprising a bear.

You know you're nearing the lake when the trail assumes a more moderate pitch. Marion Lake sits in a photo-worthy glacial cirque surrounded by cliffs with its outlet congested with logs. Anglers should bring rods, as the lake harbors westslope cutthroat trout up to 12 inches (30.5 cm) long.

Dickey Lake

Distance: 4.8 miles (7.7 km) round-trip
Duration: 2.5 hours
Elevation gain: 1,446 feet
Effort: moderate
Trail surface: narrow dirt path with roots and loose rocks
Trailhead: Turn south onto Dickey Lake Road (milepost 178.7 on Forest Rd. 1640) at Essex and follow the right fork 3 miles (4.8 km) to an unmarked spur where the trail begins in Flathead National Forest.

This short trail in the Great Bear Wilderness gives rather decent rewards for its efforts. After wading Dickey Creek, the forested trail

Firebrand Pass

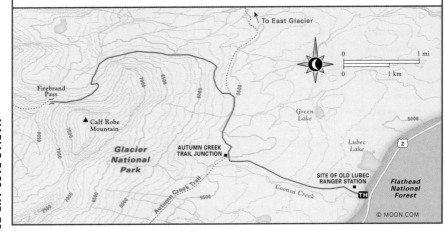

climbs up a large bowl riddled with avalanche paths, which means deadfall, limbs, and up-rooted and downed trees. In places, thick brush chokes the path, but you can still follow it to the headwall near the basin's end. From here, a rock cairn, which may be buried in snow that hangs late in the season, marks the trail, ascending steeply through false huckle-berry bushes dangling with pale apricot blos-soms and into a hanging valley.

Upon reaching the upper basin, the trail pops out on the edge of Dickey Lake. The shallow tarn, flanked by meadows and steep talus slopes, is a scenic lunch spot. You'll most likely find solitude here.

★ Stanton Lake

Distance: 2 miles (3.2 km) round-trip
Duration: 1 hour
Elevation gain: 600 feet (183 m)
Effort: easy
Trail surface: dirt path with roots and rocks
Trailhead: Stanton Lake trailhead on U.S. 2 at milepost 169.9 in Flathead National Forest (see map p. 226)

A favorite of families with little kids, this trail takes hikers and anglers to the shores of Stanton Lake in the Great Bear Wilderness.

From the trailhead, a steep grunt heads straight uphill. But it soon levels out into a nice forested walk that leads into the basin cradling Stanton Lake. From the foot of the lake, you can see Great Northern Mountain. Anglers should bring rods to fish for westslope cutthroat, rainbows, and mountain whitefish in the outlet creek.

Grant Ridge Loop

Distance: 10.2-mile (16.4-km) loop
Duration: 5 hours
Elevation gain: 3,605 feet (1,099 m)
Effort: strenuous
Trail surface: narrow dirt path with roots and loose rocks
Trailhead: Stanton Lake trailhead on U.S. 2 at milepost 169.9 in Flathead National Forest (see map p. 226)

This loop explores the scenic Grant Ridge in the Great Bear Wilderness. You can hike this loop in either direction, starting with the as-cent to Stanton Lake but turning left at the first junction to ford Stanton Creek, or hik-ing 0.5 mile (0.8 km) east along the highway

---

1: view from Scalplock Lookout **2:** fall hiking to Firebrand Pass **3:** Elk Mountain Trail

to where the trail dives into the forest for a switchback ascent of the ridge. Soon, rest stops yield peekaboo views into Glacier. When the trail breaks out of the forest, it climbs through steep wildflower meadows with frontal views of Grant Peak and Grant Glacier. Turn around for spectacular views of Glacier's southern monoliths and the Middle Fork of the Flathead River far below. On the descent, the trail cuts toward Great Northern, the highest peak in the Great Bear Wilderness, before a long, forested descent to ford Stanton Creek and join the Stanton Creek Trail back to the trailhead.

Ousel Peak

Distance: 5.2 miles (8.4 km) round-trip
Duration: 3.5 hours
Elevation gain: 3,818 feet (1,164 m)
Effort: very strenuous
Trail surface: narrow dirt path with roots and loose rocks
Trailhead: milepost 159.6 on U.S. 2 in Flathead National Forest

Do the math: This trail gains well over 1,000 feet (305 m) per mile, and from the first minute it makes no bones about heading straight uphill. If the uphill doesn't tax your lungs, the downhill will pound your knees. Nevertheless, the view from the top is outstanding and well worth the effort or pain. Sitting on the northern edge of the Great Bear Wilderness, the trail climbs through a forest canopy littered with various microclimates, from wet seeps to dry, arid slopes. The path finally breaks out of the forest with glimpses of Glacier's peaks. At the top, remnants of the old lookout scatter across the hillside amid tiny yellow stonecrop. Look into Glacier to see Mounts Jackson and Stimson along with Harrison Glacier.

Guides

Glacier Guides (11970 U.S. 2 E., West Glacier, 406/387-5555, http://glacierguides. com, mid-May-Sept.) leads a few day hiking and backpacking trips that depart from U.S. 2 into Glacier National Park. Solo travelers can hook up with weekly Sunday hikes

Stanton Lake and Grant Ridge Loop

to Firebrand Pass (start dates vary pending snowpack, $120 pp). Families and small groups can arrange for guided hikes ($560 for up to five people). Reservations are required. Plan to tip your guides at least 15 percent for day trips.

BACKPACKING

Backpacking from U.S. 2 offers two different experiences, depending on whether you hike north or south. Trails north go into Glacier National Park, which require backcountry camping **permits** ($7 pp/night). Get them 24 hours in advance in person at the **Apgar Backcountry Permit Office** (406/888-7859 May-Oct., 406/888-7800 Nov.-Apr.) or **St. Mary Visitor Center** (406/888-7800, late May-early Oct.). You can also get them at **Two Medicine Ranger Station** (406/888-7800, daily late May-mid Sept.). For advance reservations, apply online starting in mid-March (www.nps.gov/glac, $40). Trails heading south of the highway go into the Bob Marshall Wilderness, where no permit is required. Consult **Hungry Horse Ranger Station** (406-387-3800, www.fs.usda.gov/flathead) or *Hiking Montana's Bob Marshall Wilderness* by Erik Molvar.

Nyack-Coal Loop
46 MILES (74 KM)

Prepare for wild on this lengthy, forested, old Kootenai trail in southern Glacier National Park. It starts and ends with fording the Middle Fork of the Flathead River at Nyack Creek or Coal Creek, or adding more miles to start at Walton Ranger Station. The route, which can be done in either direction, circles Stimson Peak, a monolith over 10,000 feet (3,048 m). Route-finding skills are required; the trail can be overgrown, washed out, and buried in downfall. Many creeks with no bridges require fording. Due to its difficulty, it guarantees solitude. Plan to camp at Coal Creek (COA), Beaver Woman Lake in Martha's Basin (BEA), Upper Nyack (UNY), and Lower Nyack (LNY). High water in June precludes access and makes for treacherous stream crossings; therefore, advance reservations are not available until July 15. Only those with experienced backcountry savvy should tackle its primitive isolation, but wilderness solitude is the reward.

Continental Divide Trail
117 MILES (188 KM)

Of the 3,100 miles (4,989 km) of the Continental Divide National Scenic Trail (CDT), the northernmost miles are in Glacier National Park. Strong backpackers can cover Glacier's CDT in a week, but most prefer at least 10 days. Weaving together backcountry campsites (by permit) and shared hiker campsites in front-country campgrounds, you can launch a CDT trek from Marias Pass and finish by hiking across the border at Waterton Lake into Canada. En route, the trail crosses high vistas usually snow-free after mid-July: Scenic Point, Pitamakin Pass, Triple Divide Pass, Piegan Pass, Swiftcurrent Pass, and Northern Highline. Because the route uses popular backcountry campsites, apply for an advance reservation permit mid-March.

On the north side of Marias Pass, embark on the CDT via the Autumn Creek Trail, heading 14 miles (22.5 km) to East Glacier or 24 miles (39 km) to Two Medicine. Many hikers opt to stay their first night in East Glacier hostels before climbing over Scenic Point to Two Medicine. Portions of this trail require a Blackfeet Tribal Conservation Permit ($10). At Two Medicine Campground, stay in a shared hiker campsite and augment food supplies at the camp store. Going north, camp at Old Man Lake (OLD), Morning Star Lake (MOR) or Atlantic Creek (ATL), Red Eagle Lake Head (REH) or Foot (REF), and Reynolds Creek (REY). After climbing over Piegan Pass to Many Glacier, camp in a shared hiker campsite at Many Glacier Campground, take a break from trail food by dining at 'Nell's in the Swiftcurrent Motor Inn, and resupply at the camp store. After departing Many Glacier, overnight at Granite Park (GRN), Fifty Mountain (FIF), and Kootenai Lakes (KOO). Finish the route by hiking the Waterton Lakeshore Trail across the boundary to the Waterton Townsite in Canada. Passports are required.

For those without passports or when snow clogs the Northern Highline in early summer or late fall, an official alternate route diverges from Many Glacier over Red Gap Pass for a total of 107 miles (172 km). Camp at Poia Lake (POI), Elizabeth Lake Foot (ELF), and optionally at Gable Creek (GAB) to reach the border and trailhead at Chief Mountain Customs.

BIKING

Cross-country cyclists use U.S. 2 to cross the Continental Divide when Going-to-the-Sun Road is not open. Many use it also to make a big loop through and around Glacier (Going-to-the-Sun Rd., U.S. 89, MT 49, and U.S. 2). Compared to the rest of Glacier's roads, U.S. 2 is definitely an easier ride, because it has shoulders in some sections and is a bit wider and less curvy. However, due to heavy traffic in summer, it can be downright dangerous, with large rigs that nearly blow cyclists off the road. Tackle it only if you can handle riding with semis and RVs whipping by your elbows at 60 mph (97 kph).

Be prepared for winds, especially at Marias Pass. They are usually blowing eastward, so those riding toward West Glacier encounter substantial headwinds. Also, be extra cautious in the 5 curvy miles (8 km) east of West Glacier, as severe turns reduce the visibility of drivers on the road. Even though no law requires wearing a helmet, think twice about leaving your brain bucket off. Most drivers here are gawking at scenery or trying to spot wildlife rather than keeping their attention totally on the road.

Mountain biking is not permitted on trails in the wilderness areas or in Glacier National Park.

WATER SPORTS
★ River Rafting and Kayaking
Designated as a Wild and Scenic River, the **Middle Fork of the Flathead River** is the local hot spot for rafting and kayaking. It has a wild section above Bear Creek and a recreational section along the highway below Bear Creek. **Flathead National Forest** (10 Hungry Horse Dr., Hungry Horse, 406/387-3800, www.fs.usda.gov/flathead) manages the river. Stop in the ranger station, located 9 miles (14.5 km) west of West Glacier, for assistance in planning self-guided overnight trips, get information for day trips, or to check on conditions. The Forest Service is considering a permit system for rafting the river starting in 2021.

Above Bear Creek, the wild, upper Middle Fork headwaters start in the Great Bear Wilderness and run 26 miles (42 km) of Class III-IV whitewater ending at Bear Creek River Access. To access this section requires a flight into Schaeffer Meadows or packing in on a horse. The normal float season lasts from mid-May to mid-July. During peak runoff in May, the trip can often be more challenging,

with several rapids becoming Class V and spring snows chilling the air. Only one raft company in West Glacier guides overnight trips on this section: **Glacier Raft Company** (406/888-5454 or 800/235-6781, https://glacierraftco.com).

From Bear Creek downstream to the confluence with the North Fork of the Flathead, the river runs 46 miles (74 km), with easy river access sites from locations on U.S. 2: **Bear Creek** (milepost 185), **Essex** (milepost 180), **Paola** (milepost 175.2), **Cascadilla** (milepost 166), **Moccasin Creek** (milepost 160.5), and **West Glacier** (follow signs past the golf course). With the float season running mid-May through early September, the river accesses make for easy half-day or full-day float trips. Between Bear Creek and Cascadilla, rapids rate Class III-IV. Waters flatten to a float trip from Cascadilla to Moccasin Creek, but be wary of deadly log jams. From Moccasin to West Glacier, rapids range Class II-III, with some Class IV stretches during late May high water. The average float time in July from Bear Creek to Cascadilla is usually 6.5 hours, and from Moccasin Creek to West Glacier 2.5 hours.

For overnight trips, toilet systems and fire pans are recommended or required, depending on where you are on the river. Rafters and kayakers should purchase the *Three Forks of the Flathead Floater's Guide* ($13), available through the ranger station or downloadable free online, for locations of rapids and public land for camping. No camping is allowed on the Glacier National Park side. In the Great Bear Wilderness, sites are not restricted, but in the section below Bear Creek, private land abuts national forest land, much of it unmarked.

GUIDES, RENTALS, AND SHUTTLES
Four local river companies operate out of West Glacier, guiding half-day, full-day, and overnight trips on the Middle Fork of the

1: rafting Middle Fork of the Flathead River
2: fishing in the Middle Fork of the Flathead

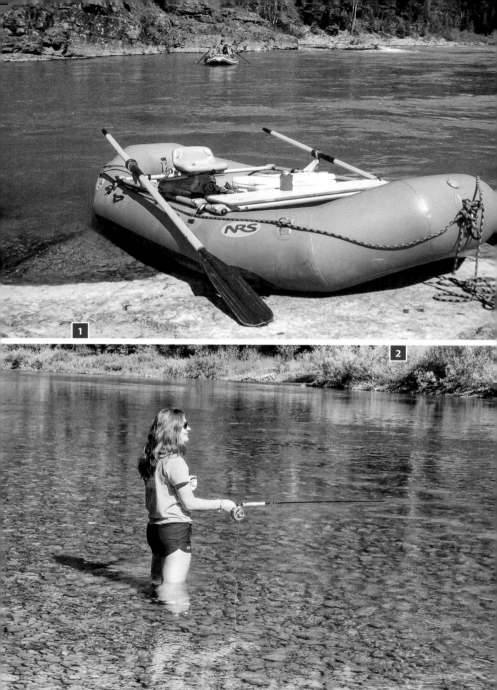

Flathead. In addition to guiding river trips, **Glacier Raft Company** (406/888-5454 or 800/235-6781, https://glacierraftco.com) and **Montana Raft Company** (406/387-5555 or 800/521-7238, http://glacierguides.com) rent rafts, kayaks, camping gear, toilet systems, and fire pans and provide shuttle services along the Middle Fork. **Great Northern Whitewater** (406/387-5340 or 800/735-7897, http://greatnorthernresort.com) and **Wild River Adventures** (406/387-9453 or 800/700-7056, www.riverwild.com) also guide rafting trips.

Fishing
RIVERS AND STREAMS
In Glacier National Park, Ole, Park, Muir, Coal, and Nyack Creeks are closed to fishing. However, anglers can drop lines in Summit, Railroad, and Badger Creeks, which flow from Marias Pass east through Helena-Lewis and Clark National Forest and onto the Blackfeet Reservation. **Badger Creek,** in particular, has a good reputation for rainbow trout. **Bear Creek,** good for westslope cutthroat, mountain whitefish, and some rainbow trout, drops west from Marias to its confluence with the Middle Fork of the Flathead River. The **Middle Fork** has plenty of river accesses for fishing: Bear Creek, Essex, Paola, Cascadilla, and Moccasin.

LAKES
Inside the park, good cutthroat trout fishing lakes such as Ole, Harrison, and Isabel usually require backpacking or fording the Middle Fork of the Flathead. It's actually easier to get to lakes in the Great Bear Wilderness on the south side of the highway. **Stanton Lake** is a quick destination with westslope cutthroat trout, mountain whitefish, and rainbow trout, but it's somewhat overfished because of its ease of access. Dickey and Marion Lakes also harbor cutthroat.

GUIDES
For guided fishing on Blackfeet Nation lands, contact **Blackfeet Fish and Wildlife**

(406/338-7207, blackfeetfishandwildlife. net) for a list of licensed outfitters. From West Glacier, four fishing companies guide fly-fishing trips on the Middle Fork of the Flathead River: **Glacier Guides** (406/387-5555 or 800/521-7238, http://glacierguides. com), **Montana Fly-Fishing Guides** (406/387-5340 or 800/735-7897, http:// greatnorthernresort.com), **Wild River Fishing Guides** (406/387-9453 or 800/700-7056, www.riverwild.com), and **Glacier Anglers** (406/888-5454 or 800/235-6781, http://glacierraftco.com).

LICENSES AND REGULATIONS
Fishing regulations along U.S. 2 vary depending on land ownership. Check carefully where you are before dropping a line into the water; the road passes through Blackfeet land, Glacier National Park, and national forests. No licenses are required inside Glacier, although you must be aware of fishing regulations. Elsewhere you'll need to plan ahead to get the appropriate fishing licenses, as none are available along the highway. Purchase Blackfeet fishing permits ($20 one day, $45 three days, $75 season) at **Bear Track Travel Center** (20958 U.S. 2, East Glacier, 406/226-5504). **Montana fishing licenses** (Montana residents: $21-31 season, $15 for 2 days; non-residents: $50 for 2 days, $81 for 10 days, $111 season) are required for ages 12 through adults; get them at **Glacier Outdoor Center** (11957 U.S. 2 E., West Glacier, 406/888-5454 or 800/235-6781, https://glacierraftco.com).

HUNTING
Hunting is illegal in Glacier National Park, but south of U.S. 2, the famed Bob Marshall Wilderness boasts world-renowned big-game hunting for bighorn sheep, elk, and black bears. East-side grasslands are also famous for bird hunting. For hunting in the Bob Marshall Wilderness or in national forests, get regulations and license info from **Montana Fish, Wildlife, and Parks** (406/444-2535, www. fwp.mt.gov). The **Blackfeet Reservation** (406/338-7207, blackfeetfishandwildlife.net)

has separate regulations and licenses for its land. Check also with each entity for the names of licensed outfitters.

WINTER SPORTS
Cross-Country Skiing and Snowshoeing

In winter, ski and snowshoe routes off U.S. 2 are popular for their ease of access. Trails, groomed snowmobile routes, and roads turn into popular trails.

IZAAK WALTON INN

With 20 miles (32 km) of track groomed daily for skate and classic skiing late November-mid-April, **Izaak Walton Inn** (290 Izaak Walton Inn Rd., Essex, 406/888-5700, www.izaakwaltoninn.com) becomes a great cross-country skiing destination in winter. At the inn, trails range from easy meanders to steep grunts. One short section of trail is lit for night skiing. Although the area never feels crowded, the most popular time is late December-late February. Lessons are available from the lodge as well as ski and snowshoe rentals, and the rentals can be taken elsewhere to use. **Trail passes** ($18 adults, $10 kids) are required; rentals cost $15-30.

AUTUMN CREEK TRAIL

One of the most popular ski trails in Glacier is **Autumn Creek Trail** at Marias Pass, which can be skied point-to-point if you set up a car shuttle or hitchhike, which is legal in Montana. Park for the west trailhead at milepost 193.8 on U.S. 2, and ski up the railroad access road and across the tracks. Park for the other trailhead at Marias Pass and locate the trailhead north of U.S. 2 and the railroad tracks. Orange markers on trees denote the 6-mile (9.7-km) trail. Beginners will find the Marias Pass section easier than the steep Autumn Creek section. To avoid the narrow, steep 660-foot (200-m) downhill plummet, begin on the west end and finish at the pass.

GUIDES

Guided cross-country skiing, backcountry skiing, and snowshoeing tours are available by reservation through **Glacier Adventure Guides** (406/892-2173, www.glacieradventureguides.com, Dec.-Mar.). The avalanche-certified guides lead single- or multiday trips; rates vary. Lunch, snacks, park entrance fees, and equipment are included. Plan on tipping the guide 15-20 percent.

Izaak Walton Inn offers groomed ski trails in winter.

Snowmobiling

Snowmobilers gravitate to groomed and ungroomed roads in **Helena-Lewis and Clark National Forest** (406/791-7700) and **Flathead National Forest** (406/758-5204). The most popular snowmobiling is in the Marias Pass and Skyland-Challenge complex, both straddling the Continental Divide south of U.S. 2. The Cut Bank Snowgoers and Flathead Snowmobile Association groom about 40 miles (64 km) of trail December-mid-May. Contact them via the **Montana Snowmobile Association** (www.snowmobilemt.org). Snow depths in both of these snowmobiling areas vary 150-250 inches (381-635 cm). Some restrictions apply to the designated connecting trails, so get a good snowmobile map from the Forest Service. The nearest rentals are in Flathead Valley.

Food

OUTSIDE THE PARK

Restaurants along U.S. 2 vary from old dives to family cafés and a couple of casual-dining restaurants. Off-season, don't be surprised if one is closed when its hours say otherwise; if the fish are biting, the owners may lock up.

Casual Dining

Travelers can once again enjoy the 1906 Summit Station that used to be the train stop at Marias Pass. The ★ **Summit Mountain Lodge** (16900 U.S. 2, 406/226-9319, https://summitmtnlodge.com, 5pm-9pm daily mid-June-mid-Sept., $12-38) has an intimate dining room and enlarged deck with outstanding views of Summit and Little Dog Mountains. It's known for steaks, but also serves pasta and fish.

At Izaak Walton Inn, the ★ **Dining Car Restaurant** (290 Izaak Walton Inn Rd., Essex, 406/888-5700, https://izaakwaltoninn.com, 7:30am-8pm daily, $10-30) serves up scrumptious meals as trains rumble past the window. The cozy restaurant serves breakfast, lunch, and dinner with a menu that changes with the seasons and includes vegetarian and kid options. Dinners feature meats, fish, and pasta. Leave room for the huckleberry desserts. Be sure to head downstairs to the Flagstop Bar for a nightcap or at least to look at the historical photos of local railroad disasters.

Cafés

Inexpensive family-run cafés, favorites for locals and good for after-hike burgers, are the mainstay of U.S. 2. Lighter meals at these establishments run $7-10; full dinners run $15-25. Located 6 miles (9.7 km) west of Marias Pass, the **Snow Slip Inn** (15644 U.S. 2 E., Essex, 406/226-4400, 8am-10pm daily) bases its home-style cooking on local, fresh products as much as possible. It offers live music on Saturday nights in summer in its 1945 historic bar. On the west side of Essex, the three-generation family-run ★ **Healthy Haven Café** (14305 U.S. 2 E., 406/888-5720, www.glacierhaveninn.com, 6pm-8pm Tues.-Sat. mid-June-Aug.) serves home-style dinners with fresh ingredients including buffalo burgers and huckleberry pie.

Groceries

You can pick up a few groceries at the small Neighborhood Grocery store at the **Snow Slip Inn** (15644 U.S. 2 E., Essex, 406/226-4400). To stock up for camping or traveling, find seasonal grocery stores in East Glacier and West Glacier. Larger food markets are in Browning on the east side or Hungry Horse and Columbia Falls on the west side.

Picnic Areas

There is only one designated picnic area on U.S. 2, and that is **Walton** (milepost 180.5).

Behind the Walton Ranger Station, the small picnic area is under thick trees adjacent to the Middle Fork River. Picnic tables, pit toilets, and fire rings with grills are available. Trails to Ole Creek, the Middle Fork, and Scalplock Lookout depart from the picnic area.

With several **river accesses** along the Middle Fork of the Flathead, there are plenty of additional places sans tables for picnicking at a scenic spot and soaking your feet in cold water. **Cascadilla** and **Paola** offer the best beaches.

Accommodations

OUTSIDE THE PARK

Along U.S. 2, lodging includes historic inns, cabins, train cabooses, and unique domes and tree cocoons. All charge a 7 percent **bed tax.** Bring earplugs due to the proximity of the railroad. Most places have Wi-Fi for guests. Many lodging properties boast of being near Glacier, but on U.S. 2, the only access is on foot, horseback, or by raft, with the exception of Walton Picnic Area and the Goat Lick. You must go to the east side or west side to drive into the park.

Izaak Walton Inn

With some of the most unique lodging around Glacier, ★ **Izaak Walton Inn** (290 Izaak Walton Inn Rd., Essex, 406/888-5700, http://izaakwaltoninn.com, $110-400) celebrates its railroad heritage with accommodations in historic lodge rooms, cabooses, a luxury locomotive, log cabins, and an old school house. From the lobby fireplace to the Dining Car Restaurant and the swinging seat on the porch, the National Historic Landmark is a place to relax. The inn maintains its historical ambience with no TVs, in-room phones, air-conditioning, or elevators; a pay phone is off the lobby. Lodge guest rooms vary in size, although most baths are fairly small. A short walk over a footbridge above the railroad tracks leads to four heated cabooses set in the trees that sleep four each, with kitchenettes and full baths. In the same glen, six log cabins with kitchens sleep up to six in bedrooms and lofts. One locomotive and three additional cabooses offer luxury accommodations.

caboose room at Izaak Walton Inn

Two nights minimum are required for the cabooses, locomotive, and cabins.

Amenities include a sauna, hot tub, coin-op laundry, wireless internet in the main lodge, restaurant, cross-country ski trails in winter, walking trails, rental cars, and railroad ambience. You can arrive and depart by train, as it's an Amtrak stop. Winter has ski or snowshoe rentals, groomed trails, lessons, and guided adventures. In summer, hiking trails depart from the inn.

Motels

Located about midway between West and East Glacier, **Glacier Haven Inn** (14305 U.S. 2, Essex, 406/888-5720, www.glacierhaveninn. com, May-Sept., $100-350) is a family-run place with an on-site restaurant. It has eight small motel rooms with a queen bed and a double or twin, a camping cabin with separate bathroom and showerhouse, and cabins with two or three bedrooms and equipped kitchens.

Cabins and Resorts

The 1906 Summit Station used to serve as the depot at Marias Pass before Glacier Park Lodge and its depot in East Glacier attracted more visitors. Summit's use died, and it was moved to its present location to become ★ **Summit Mountain Lodge** (16900 U.S. 2, 406/226-9319, https://summitmtnlodge. com, mid-May-Sept., $160-470). Named for park peaks, the cabins with private bathrooms and log beds come in various sizes for couples or families up to eight people. Smaller cabins have mini-fridges and microwaves, while large cabins have full kitchens. Some cabins require two-night minimum stays. Sinopah and Running Rabbit cabins garner superb mountain views of Summit and Little Dog. The main lodge houses the restaurant.

Flathead National Forest (406/387-3800, www.fs.usda.gov/flathead) rents two quiet, rustic **cabins** (reservations 877/444-6777, www.recreation.gov, $10 reservation fee) with three-night maximum stays and no pets. Both are accessible from U.S. 2 and must

be reserved. Decked out with propane, mattresses, and kitchen utensils, the cabins are warmed with either propane heat or woodstoves (wood is supplied). A 7-mile (11.3-km) ski or snowmobile ride up Skyland Road (milepost 195.8 on U.S. 2), tiny one-room **Challenge Cabin** (Dec.-Mar., $50) sleeps six people stacked like sardines. A much larger two-bedroom cabin that sleeps eight, **Zip's Place** (June-Mar., $70) is off U.S. 2; turn at milepost 191.9 and drive 2 miles (3.2 km), following the signs. In winter, it requires a ski or snowshoe trip to reach the front door. Bring your own food and sleeping bags.

Located adjacent to the Stanton Lake trailhead, the Stanton Creek restaurant, bar, and cabins were renovated by new owners in 2019 to become ★ **Clear Sky Resorts** (13951 U.S. 2, 406/219-7811, https://clearskyresorts.com, June-Sept., $119-300). The resort has four styles of cabins. You may want to try sleeping in a tree cocoon—a steel-framed canvas bubble suspended in trees accessed by wooden stairs. Private bathrooms with showers are nearby. For stargazers, 16 sky domes (with bathrooms) come with telescopes for enjoying celestial activity through sky portals; some even have swinging beds. Both of these unique lodgings are heated and come with high-end bedding. A welcome dome serves as a lounge with a stargazing telescope, too.

The closest lodging to West Glacier, **Glacier Wilderness Resort** (milepost 163 on U.S. 2, 406/888-5664, www. glacierwildernessresort.com, $225-300, 3-night min.) is a time-share property that also rents cabins in a woodsy setting. With an indoor heated pool, its log cabins sleep 4-6 people and come with fireplaces, satellite TV, fully equipped kitchens, and private hot tubs. Summer adds an outdoor picnic pavilion and walking trails. Winter has cross-country skiing and snowshoeing trails.

Bed-and-Breakfasts

If you prefer horseback riding, **Bear Creek Guest Ranch** (milepost 192, U.S. 2, 406/226-4489, www.bearcreekguestranch.com,

June-mid-Sept.) specializes in riding clinics, cattle drives, and adventure weeks. But the ranch, which has been operating since 1933, also serves as a B&B ($270 for two people, $40/ extra person) with lodging in rustic log cabins with private baths.

Camping

OUTSIDE THE PARK

U.S. 2 has no drive-in national park campgrounds; to camp in Glacier requires backpacking. U.S. Forest Service and private campgrounds line the highway, where noise from trains and trucks permeates the night (bring earplugs).

U.S. Forest Service Campgrounds

Two smaller, summer-only Forest Service campgrounds are adjacent to U.S. 2, tucked in dog-hair timbers and monitored by campground hosts. Expect to find picnic tables (some wheelchair accessible), fire rings with grills, vault toilets, drinking water, bear-proof food storage boxes, but no hookups. Pack out your trash. No firewood is provided, but you can collect it in the woods.

At Marias Pass, the **Summit Campground** (Helena-Lewis and Clark National Forest, 406/466-5341, June-Sept., $10) has 16 sites that are first-come, first-served, so get there by early afternoon in high season, especially if you want to nab one of the campsites farthest from the highway. Across the highway and railroad tracks, the Autumn Creek Trail tours below Glacier's peaks.

At milepost 190, **Devil Creek Campground** (Flathead National Forest, 406/387-3800, late May-Sept., $14) has 14 sites, a few of which can handle up to 40-foot (12.2-m) RVs. From the campground, a trail leads 5.9 miles (9.5 km) up to Elk Lake or 8.2 miles (13.2 km) to Moose Lake. Make reservations for midsummer (877/444-6677, www.recreation.gov).

Private Campgrounds

Two private campgrounds line U.S. 2. If these fill up, a couple of restaurant-bar-cabin businesses also offer a few campsites. The 7 percent Montana bed tax is added to the rates, which usually cover two people; each additional person is $5-10.

Located 16 miles (26 km) west of East Glacier between mileposts 191 and 192, ★ **Glacier Meadow RV Park** (15735 U.S. 2, 406/226-4479, https://glaciermeadowrvpark. com, mid-May-Sept., tents $32, RV hookups $35-60) has 41 sites on a 58-acre (23.5-hectare) meadow and forest setting with a dump station, laundry, a playground, full hookups, flush toilets, showers, and wireless internet access. All the sites are open, providing good satellite dish reception, but not much privacy from the highway and neighboring campers. The trail to Elk Mountain is nearby.

Between mileposts 173 and 174 west of Essex, **Glacier Haven Campground** (14297 U.S. 2 E., 406/888-5720, www.glacierhavenrv-campground.com, Apr.-Oct., tents $30-35, RV hookups $60-66) is part of the Glacier Haven Inn. The treed campground snuggles between the highway and the railroad tracks, with 19 RV hookup campsites, including three that can accommodate large RVs, and room for four tents in a large camping zone. Facilities include flush toilets, showers, full hookups, and launderette. Kids nine and under are free.

Transportation and Services

TRANSPORTATION
Driving and Parking

U.S. 2 is a narrow, curvy, two-lane mountain highway. Because it's a trucking route, large semis will whiz by and press behind you. This is the route for **RVs,** as they are not permitted across Going-to-the-Sun Road.

Find parking only at signed river accesses, trailheads, and businesses.

SERVICES

While you can find some newspapers sold in the inns and restaurants along the highway, you'll need to head to East Glacier or West Glacier for **ATMs, laundry services,** and **groceries.** The closest **post offices** are in East Glacier and West Glacier. For **hot showers** ($5-10), you can pop in to Glacier Meadow RV Park or Glacier Haven Campground. A few of the inns and restaurants sell the *Great Falls Tribune, Hungry Horse News,* and Flathead Valley's *Daily Interlake.*

Even though U.S. 2 lacks many services, **public restrooms** are plentiful. Most are vault toilets with no running water and are open spring-fall. Find these at all river access points, Walton Picnic Area, the Goat Lick, and Marias Pass (use the last one only in a pinch as it receives less care).

Gas and Repairs

This 60-mile (97-km) corridor through wild, untamed wilderness is a road where the usually expected conveniences of civilization are not available. You won't find gas stations between East Glacier and West Glacier; fill up in either of those towns before you leave. For car repairs, call mobile repair services in Flathead Valley.

Cell Phone and Internet Access

Because of surrounding steep mountains, you'll find cell reception nonexistent on U.S. 2, but you can stop to use old-fashioned **public pay telephones** at Izaak Walton Inn and Snow Slip Inn. Internet services are only available for guests at a few private campgrounds and inns.

Emergencies

For highway, river, or wilderness emergencies, call 911. A seasonal **urgent-care clinic** (100 Rea Rd., West Glacier, 406/888-9224, 9am-4pm daily Memorial Day-Labor Day) operates in West Glacier. Regional hospitals in Flathead Valley include **Kalispell Regional Medical Center** (310 Sunny View Ln., Kalispell, 406/752-5111) and **North Valley Hospital** (1600 Hospital Way, Whitefish, 406/863-3500). The east side is served by the **Blackfeet Community Hospital** (760 Blackweasel Rd., Browning, 406/338-6154).

The **Walton Ranger Station** (milepost 180.5, U.S. 2, 406/888-7800), at Walton Picnic Area on the southernmost tip of Glacier National Park, is staffed only in summer, and not full time, as the rangers patrol miles of backcountry trails. If you need assistance, use the pay phone at **Izaak Walton Inn** (0.8 mi/1.3 km west of the Walton Ranger Station) to call Glacier National Park **headquarters** (406/888-7800). For maps, guidebooks, and information on outdoor activities in the Great Bear Wilderness and the Bob Marshall, contact the **Hungry Horse Ranger Station** (10 Hungry Horse Dr., Hungry Horse, 406/387-3800, www.fs.usda.gov/flathead). For Helena-Lewis and Clark National Forest information, call the **Rocky Mountain Ranger Station** (406/466-5341, www.fs.usda.gov/lewisclark).

Waterton

For such a small park, Waterton Lakes National

Park packs a punch. Located at a nexus of major bird migration routes and weather systems, its prairies make for easy wildlife-watching, and wildflowers bloom profusely.

On the Continental Divide's east side, mountains meet the prairie; with no transitional foothills, eastern peaks plummet directly to grass-lands, a phenomenon caused by geological overthrusts that exposed the oldest sedimentary rock in the Canadian Rockies. Although active glaciers vacated Waterton's borders a century ago, the results of ice gnawing on its landscape left lake pockets strewn through the park. A long, glacier-gouged trough forms Upper Waterton Lake, the deepest lake in the Canadian Rockies and one that straddles the U.S.-Canadian

Highlights

Look for ★ to find recommended sights, activities, dining, and lodging.

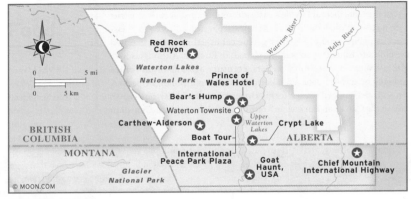

Red Rock Canyon ★
Waterton Lakes National Park
Prince of Wales Hotel ★
Bear's Hump ★
Waterton Townsite ○
Carthew-Alderson ★
BRITISH COLUMBIA
Upper Waterton Lakes
Crypt Lake ★
Boat Tour ★
ALBERTA
MONTANA
International Peace Park Plaza ★
Goat Haunt, USA ★
Chief Mountain International Highway ★
Glacier National Park
Waterton River
Belly River
© MOON.COM
0   5 mi
0   5 km

★ **Take a Boat Tour:** Hop aboard the historic MV *International* for a ride on the deepest lake in the Canadian Rockies. You'll float across the international boundary to Goat Haunt, USA (page 245).

★ **Drive Chief Mountain International Highway:** Cross into Canada to reach Waterton on this two-nation scenic road that circles around a mountain sacred to the Blackfeet (page 245).

★ **Visit Prince of Wales Hotel:** This 1927 hotel maintains a British ambience with its kilt-wearing bellhops and afternoon high tea (page 247).

★ **Trek to Goat Haunt, USA:** Launch into Glacier's remote northern trails via Goat Haunt, accessible only by boot (page 247).

★ **Stroll through International Peace Park Plaza:** Tour the outdoor exhibits, plaza, pier, and waterfront viewing area of Waterton Lake (page 249).

★ **Hike to Crypt Lake:** Follow switchbacks up to what looks like impassable cliffs. A hidden tunnel curls into a hanging valley holding an idyllic lake (page 253).

★ **Climb up Bear's Hump:** This short hot grunt of a hike leads to a grand panoramic view of Waterton Townsite and Lake (page 254).

★ **Ascend the Carthew-Alderson Trail:** Cross over a high, windswept alpine pass and you'll be wowed by peaks and icy blue jewels (page 255).

★ **Wander through Red Rock Canyon:** This brilliant colorful mosaic of sediments is evidence of the canyon's origins as an ancient inland sea (page 258).

border. The lake frequently kicks up with winds, proving the park's ranking as the second-windiest place in Alberta.

Dominated by the Prince of Wales Hotel and Waterton Lake, the park serves as a destination itself as well as an entrance to Glacier's remote north country. On any summer day, the Waterton Townsite bustles with shoppers, bicyclists, backpackers, boaters, and campers. It's a quintessential Canadian mountain town that embodies what Banff used to be before booming commercialism. The MV *International* shuttles hikers and sightseers across Waterton Lake and the international boundary to Goat Haunt, USA. Only two roads pierce the park's remarkable interior, both gateways to lakes, waterfalls, canyons, peaks, and wildlife.

PLANNING YOUR TIME

The park centers around the **Waterton Townsite,** a tiny year-round town that is home to about 100 people in winter with minimal services, but balloons in summer to nearly 2,000 residents. Summer brings on all town services plus lodging, restaurants, and shopping.

From Glacier's east side, you can explore Waterton for **one day** with an early start. You'll be able to take the boat tour, drive one of the short scenic roads, walk along the lake, tour the townsite, and dine early in town before the evening drive back to Glacier. Be aware of the hours at the border, so you can get back across before customs closes.

To see more of Waterton, plan a minimum of **three days** to hike a few short trails, drive both scenic drives, golf or bike, and visit Goat Haunt. If you choose to base your whole trip out of Waterton, you can easily devote a one-day trip to Glacier. You can spend a day driving Going-to-the-Sun Road or head to Many Glacier to hike one of the park's trails.

Due to the 2017 Kenow Fire, the park will be doing repairs through 2021; be aware that some areas may be inaccessible or nonoperational. Verify the status of all elements of your international trip before starting travel.

In the townsite, summer temperatures usually average 18-29°C (65-85°F) during days and dipping to 4.5°C (40°F) or cooler at night. Hiking and backpacking into higher elevations will encounter chillier temperatures by 6-8°C (10-15°F). Strong winds can blow year-round averaging 30 km/hr (20 mph) but gusting to 100 km/hr (60 mph). Winter temperatures waffle between -40°C (-40°F) and 10°C (50°F).

HISTORY

The press westward for a railroad route through the Canadian Rockies brought Lieutenant Thomas Blakiston to Alberta in 1858. Arriving at Waterton Lakes, the ancestral home of several Blackfoot First Nations, he named the lakes for a British naturalist who never visited the area. By the end of the century, the area became Canada's fourth national park. The legendary Kootenai Brown took the reins as Waterton's first superintendent.

Waterton produced western Canada's first oil well in 1902, but within four years the site closed down when it trickled to nothing. Another oil well near Cameron Falls produced one barrel a day and prompted building the Waterton Townsite. When oil riches dissipated in 1910, tourism arrived, fueled in part by Great Northern Railway's Glacier development. The Townsite sprouted cottages, a hotel, a golf course, packhorse outfitters, and boating. As the railway company scouted Waterton for a hotel site to add to its collection, World War I and a proposed dam delayed construction. Ironically, Prohibition in the United States prompted the hotel to be built. Alcohol, after all, was still legal in Canada, attracting scads of Montanans for thirst quenching. In 1927 the Prince of Wales Hotel finally opened on the wind-battered

WATERTON

Previous: Red Rock Canyon; International Peace Park Plaza; Carthew Summit on the Carthew-Alderson Trail.

Waterton

BRITISH COLUMBIA

Akamina-Kishinena Provincial Park

Continental Divide

Upper Kintla Lake

Goat Lake

Lost Lake

Twin Lakes

Newman Peak 8,600ft

Lone Mountain 7,950ft

Anderson Peak 8,701ft

Mt Glendowan 8,770ft

Forum Peak

Mt Custer 8,883ft

Wall Lake

Forum Lake

Lineham Lakes

Mt Lineham 8,000ft

Mt Blakiston 9,581ft

Blakiston Falls

Mt Dungarvan 8,419ft

Mt Galwey 7,799ft

RED ROCK CANYON

Cameron Lake

Brown's Pass

Akamina Pass

Rowe Lakes

AKAMINA PKWY

Carthew Lakes

Mt Carthew 8,650ft

CARTHEW-ALDERSON

RED ROCKS PKWY

Waterton Lakes National Park

MONTANA

CANADA

Lake Wurderman

Mt Alderson 8,832ft

Bertha Lake

Crandell Lake

SEE "WATERTON TOWNSITE" MAP

CRANDELL MOUNTAIN

Campbell Mountain 8,245ft

Waterton Townsite

Mt Crandell 7,812ft

PASS CREEK WINTER

BISON PADDOCK

PARK ENTRANCE

Rainbow Falls

GOAT HAUNT, USA

GOAT HAUNT OVERLOOK

Upper Waterton Lake

Middle Waterton Lake

Mt Boswell 7,841ft

Hell Roaring Falls

Vimy Peak 7,825ft

Lower Waterton Lake

To Pincher Creek

6

5

UNITED STATES

Glacier National Park

CRYPT LAKE

Lewis Range

Sofa Mountain 8,266ft

CHIEF MOUNTAIN

Muskinge Lake

6

INTERNATIONAL HWY (SEASONAL)

CHIEF MOUNTAIN INTERNATIONAL HIGHWAY

CROOKED CREEK

Waterton River

ALBERTA

BELLY RIVER

Belly River

5

To Cardston

Chief Mountain 9,080ft

CHIEF MOUNTAIN CUSTOMS

To Hwy 89 and St. Mary

17

To Kootenai Lakes

0

2 km

0

2 mi

© MOON.COM

Kenow Fire

Much of the landscape in Waterton Lakes National Park looks different now due to the Kenow Fire, an extreme fire that swept through the park in fall 2017. It started from lightning in neighboring Akamina-Kishinena Provincial Park, but moved fast to eat up 193 square kilometers (75 sq mi) inside the park. Its aggressive behavior gobbled up 39 percent of the park, 70 percent of the park's forest, and 80 percent of the trails. While the vegetation has changed, the glacier-carved mountains remain ruggedly beautiful.

You will see effects of the fire's severity along roadways: skeletons of burned aspen groves and conifers. However, some charred timbers have already turned silver, and wildflower lovers are in luck: In the first several years following wildfires, wildflowers go crazy due to the nitrogen put back into the soil. Moose, elk, bighorn sheep, and bears have returned into the affected areas, and bird counts in 2019 were near normal. The fire also revealed scads of unknown 7,000-year-old Blackfoot trails and camps that are now protected archaeological sites.

While the fire spared the Townsite's hotels, restaurants, shops, and campground, it burned Crandell Campground, the visitors center, and the park's two scenic parkways. Repairs will be underway into 2021.

knoll above the town, and the 22-meter (72-ft) MV *International* took its first sightseers up Waterton Lake.

Within five years the park gained status in conjunction with Glacier as **Waterton-Glacier International Peace Park.** Sharing the 49th parallel, which includes forests, mountains, and water, the parks are the world's first with that designation. Later, Waterton-Glacier became a **Biosphere Reserve** and **World Heritage Site.** Most recently, they have been recognized as the world's first **International Transboundary Dark Skies Preserve.**

ECOLOGICAL SIGNIFICANCE

Despite its tiny size at 135 square kilometers (52 sq mi), Waterton is a nexus. The park is on a narrow north-south wildlife corridor and is at the axis of two major migratory bird flyways. Over 250 **bird species** nest or use the park's rich habitat for migration stopovers. Rare trumpeter swans nest here, as do Vaux's swifts. It is one of the last places in North America where grizzly bears roam into the fringes of their original grassland habitat.

Because arctic and Pacific weather systems collide at Waterton, a breadth of vegetation abounds. It is home to more than half of Alberta's plant species, 179 of which are considered rare and 22 of which are found nowhere else in the province. Moonwort, a small fern, grows in eight varieties; one is found only in Waterton. The park's diminutive acreage has more plant diversity than the much larger Banff, Jasper, Kootenay, and Yoho parks combined. Waterton is known for extensive **wildflower blooms** from prairies to peaks; wildflower season rolls out mid-June through July. Part of its diversity is due to its huge span in elevation, from 1,280 meters (4,200 ft) around the Townsite to 2,743 m (9,000 ft) at peak tops.

Where Can I Find...?

- **ATMs:** ATMs will dispense **Canadian dollars,** so only withdraw as much as you will use. ATMs are located at Pat's Gas Station, The Tamarack, Rocky Mountain Food Mart, Mountain Spirits Liquor Store, Bayshore Inn, and the Prince of Wales Hotel.

- **Best exchange rates:** Use a **credit card,** rather than cash, as much as possible to get the best exchange rate. Waterton has no banks; the nearest banking services are in **Cardston** and **Pincher Creek.**

- **Cell reception:** Telus, Bell, and some Verizon cell phones can get service in the **Townsite,** but not on Red Rocks or Akamina Parkway roads or at Goat Haunt.

- **Gas:** The only gas in town is at **Pat's Gas Station.** It's more expensive than gas purchased in the United States. Fill up your tank in **Babb** or **St. Mary** before driving to Waterton.

- **Restrooms:** Waterton has **plentiful** restrooms. All **picnic areas** along the Entrance Road, Red Rocks Parkway, Akamina Parkway, and lakefront around the Townsite have restrooms. In addition, parking lots at the end of Red Rocks and Akamina Parkways also have restrooms as does the visitors center, boat dock, campground, and Cameron Falls. If you need a toilet just before crossing the border into Canada, stop at **Chief Mountain Customs Trailhead.**

- **Wi-Fi:** The Townsite offers **Waterton Wi-Fi,** which services restaurants, motels, and the Townsite campground with two options. The **free service** offers limited speeds and intermittently cuts out. The **fee service** has faster speeds and is more dependable.

Exploring Waterton

VISITORS CENTERS

Due to the Kenow Fire burning down the visitors center, the **Waterton Lakes Visitor Information Centre** is in a temporary facility in **Lions Hall** (Fountain Ave., 403/859-5133, www.pc.gc.ca, 9am-5pm daily mid-May-Sept.). It provides information, wilderness-use permits, road conditions, fishing licenses, and maps. These services will move to the new permanent visitor center slated to open in 2021. The new $7.6 million **Waterton Lakes National Park Visitor Information Centre** (Windflower Ave., 9am-5pm daily open year-round) features a theater and interpretive displays on the Blackfoot Confederacy of First Nations people, biodiversity, park flora and fauna, and some hands-on activities. Outdoors, kids will have a natural-features playground. With its new location, you can settle in to your campsite or hotel and walk to the visitors center.

ENTRANCE STATIONS

The **entrance gate** is **open 24-7 year-round,** but only staffed early May-early October. Glacier and U.S. park passes are not valid in Canadian parks, although many Americans expect them to be. Even though Waterton-Glacier is an International Peace Park, no combined park pass is sold. To enter Waterton, you must purchase a separate **Parks Canada day pass** valid until 4pm the following day (C$7-8 pp or single-vehicle C$16, May-Oct.; C$5-6 pp or single-vehicle C$12, Nov.-Apr.). A **Parks Canada Discovery Pass** is valid for one year for entry to 80 Canadian national parks and sites (C$58-68 or single-vehicle C$137). Children under 17 are admitted free. Admission to the park is free on Canada Day (July 1) and Parks Day (July 17). Seniors get a discounted rate.

No entrance fees are charged to hike into Waterton from Glacier National Park or to enter Glacier from Waterton Lakes National Park by foot or on the tour boat. The tour boat, however, charges a fee.

INTERNATIONAL BORDERS

To drive to Waterton from Montana requires crossing through **Chief Mountain Customs** (mid-May-Sept., hours vary) on Chief Mountain International Highway. You can also drive north of Babb on US 89 through **Piegan-Carway Port of Entry** (open year-round, 7am-11pm daily). Passports and/or international travel IDs are required.

You can also cross the border on the tour boat (fee) on **Upper Waterton Lake.** The tour boat goes to **Goat Haunt** in Glacier National Park in the United States. Visitors may debark the boat to tour the **Peace Park Pavilion** and walk to the **Goat Haunt Pavilion** and back without going through U.S. or Canadian customs.

From Waterton, **hikers** walking the Lakeshore Trail to Goat Haunt or taking the tour boat to Goat Haunt to hike the trails there must report in electronically to U.S. Customs on the morning of your departure. You'll need appropriate **passports** or **passport cards.** Before hiking from Waterton or taking the boat to Goat Haunt to hike, file trip plans at the **CBP ROAM kiosks** at the tour boat dock and other locations around town; a CBP ROAM app is also available for smartphones. Hikers entering Canada from Glacier via the Goat Haunt-area should register plans on the **CB ROAM app,** too.

SHUTTLES AND TOURS
Shuttles
OVERLAND SHUTTLES

Waterton Outdoor Adventures (214 Mount View Rd., 403/859-2378, www.hikewaterton.com, daily June-Sept., C$20-50 pp) runs hiker shuttles from The Tamarack. They run scheduled and custom shuttles to trailheads; make reservations to be guaranteed a seat. For point-to-point backpacking trips, they run shuttles to the Tamarack Trail. The 30-minute **Chief Mountain Connector** (departs noon from Tamarack, departs Chief Mountain Customs at 12:30pm) is for backpackers starting or exiting from Chief Mountain Trailhead in Glacier. The shuttle goes to the Canadian side of the border; hikers walk through the customs station into the United States and the trailhead less than five minutes away. Shuttle riders returning to Waterton must pay their own park entry fees. Mountain bikers can take the shuttle to ride the Akamina trails and then ride back to town. Reservations are a good idea midsummer and are required for cyclists.

WATER SHUTTLES

Waterton Shoreline Cruises (403/859-2362, www.watertoncruise.com) operates two boat services that serve as hiker shuttles to trailheads. The **Crypt Lake Water Shuttle** (daily late May-early Oct., adults C$26 round-trip, children C$13) departs from the marina for a 15-minute ride across Upper Waterton Lake to Crypt Landing, where the Crypt Lake trail begins. Shuttles depart the marina at 10am; earlier departures are added to the schedule June-early September at 8:30am and 9am. Return boats leave Crypt Landing at 5:30pm, with a 4pm boat added in summer. Purchase tickets a day in advance, or arrive at least 20 minutes before departure to buy tickets.

The tour boat to **Goat Haunt** (daily June-late Sept., adults one-way C$33, children C$13-17) also functions as a hiker shuttle. It accesses trailheads in northern Glacier and provides transportation back to Waterton after hiking the Lakeshore Trail to Goat Haunt. Buy your return ticket in the morning before hiking down the lake. Day hikers bound for Goat Haunt trails need two one-way tickets: one for the 10am boat and a reserved spot for a selected return boat. Hikers using the boat need to bring passports and file trip plans with CBP ROAM in Waterton the morning of their scheduled hike.

Waterton Townsite

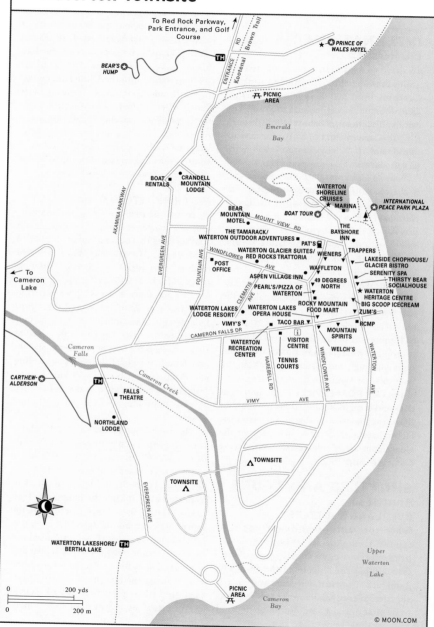

To Red Rock Parkway, Park Entrance, and Golf Course

★ PRINCE OF WALES HOTEL

BEAR'S HUMP

TH

ENTRANCE RD
Kootenai Brown Trail

🌲 PICNIC AREA

Emerald Bay

BOAT RENTALS
CRANDELL MOUNTAIN LODGE

WATERTON SHORELINE CRUISES
MARINA

★ INTERNATIONAL PEACE PARK PLAZA

BEAR MOUNTAIN MOTEL

BOAT TOUR

AKAMINA PARKWAY

MOUNT VIEW RD

THE TAMARACK/ WATERTON OUTDOOR ADVENTURES
PAT'S

THE BAYSHORE INN

EVERGREEN AVE

FOUNTAIN AVE

WATERTON GLACIER SUITES/ RED ROCKS TRATTORIA
WIENERS
TRAPPERS

WINDFLOWER AVE

POST OFFICE

WAFFLETON

LAKESIDE CHOPHOUSE/ GLACIER BISTRO

To Cameron Lake

ASPEN VILLAGE INN

49 DEGREES NORTH

SERENITY SPA
THIRSTY BEAR SOCIALHOUSE

CLEMATIS AVE

PEARL'S/PIZZA OF WATERTON

★ WATERTON HERITAGE CENTRE
BIG SCOOP ICECREAM

WATERTON LAKES LODGE RESORT
WATERTON LAKES OPERA HOUSE
ROCKY MOUNTAIN FOOD MART
ZUM'S

VIMY'S
TACO BAR
RCMP

Cameron Falls

CAMERON FALLS DR

MOUNTAIN SPIRITS

★ CARTHEW-ALDERSON

Cameron Creek

ℹ️ VISITOR CENTRE

WELCH'S

WINDFLOWER AVE

WATERTON AVE

TH

FALLS THEATRE

WATERTON RECREATION CENTER

HAREBELL RD

TENNIS COURTS

NORTHLAND LODGE

EVERGREEN AVE

VIMY   AVE

⛺ TOWNSITE

⛺ TOWNSITE

WATERTON LAKESHORE/ BERTHA LAKE
TH

🌲 PICNIC AREA

Upper Waterton Lake

Cameron Bay

0   200 yds
0   200 m

© MOON.COM

Akamina-Kishinena Provincial Park

Where Waterton Lakes National Park meets the Continental Divide, Akamina-Kishinena Provincial Park begins. It flanks the international boundary of Montana's Glacier National Park and runs westward to the North Fork of the Flathead River. This remote 27,000-acre park is accessible only on foot from Akamina Parkway in Waterton Lakes or on trails from the end of a 109-kilometer (68-mi) dirt road that starts 16 kilometers (10 mi) south of Fernie, British Columbia.

The small park is part of the same slice of the Rockies that provides corridors for grizzly bears and wolves. Geologic wonders display themselves in Forum Peak's 1.3-billion-year-old sedimentary rocks, and rare plants like the pygmy poppy grow here.

From Waterton, hikers and mountain bikers can access the park via a circa-1920 trail that connects the Cameron Valley to the North Fork of the Flathead Valley. At Akamina Pass, the boundary between Waterton National Park and the provincial park, you can mountain-bike to Wall Lake or hike to Forum Lake and the Akamina Traverse.

On both sides of the international border, a growing movement is lobbying to make Akamina-Kishinena a national park. The addition would complete the protection of the "Crown of the Continent" ecosystem, matching the entire distance of Glacier's international boundary with lands protected under the Canadian national park system.

Contact **British Columbia Parks** (205/489-8540, www.gov.bc.ca/bcparks) for information on visiting the park.

★ Boat Tour

Waterton Shoreline Cruises (at the marina at junction of Mount View Rd. and Waterton Ave., 403/859-2362, www.watertoncruise.com, 10am, 1pm, 4pm, and 7pm daily July-Aug., 10am and 1pm daily May-June and Sept.-early Oct., adults C$51 round-trip, kids C$17-25, under age 4 free) operates the historic *International* on Upper Waterton Lake. During the two-hour tour on the wooden 200-passenger boat, which has been cruising here since 1927, knowledgeable guides punctuate their patter with humor. For the best views, go for a sunny seat on the boat's top deck. If the weather is brisk, just bundle up. June-late September, the boat usually docks for 30 minutes at Goat Haunt, allowing enough time to walk to the ranger station pavilion to see the full length of the lake. Shoulder season launches, which are often on the *Miss Waterton* instead, do not stop at Goat Haunt. Buy tickets at least one hour in advance; to guarantee space, buy them a day in advance.

Driving Tours

★ CHIEF MOUNTAIN INTERNATIONAL HIGHWAY

The **Chief Mountain International Highway** provides a connection between Glacier and Waterton National Parks. Its season and hours are linked to the Canadian and U.S. immigration and customs stations at the border (daily mid-May-Sept., 7am-10pm June-Labor Day, 9am-6pm May and Sept.). You may want to top off on gas in the United States since gas is generally more expensive in Canada. The nearest gas is in Babb, Montana, or in Waterton Townsite. The 30-mile (48-km) road undulates over rolling aspen hills and past beaver ponds as it curves around Chief Mountain, imposing and alone on Glacier's northeast corner. A few unmarked pullouts offer good photo ops. Drive this open range carefully, for cows wander the road. Your car also may need a good cleaning if wet cow pies litter the road, but the 2016 repaving of the Waterton section smoothed out the tread.

From the United States, as the road rounds

Chief Mountain, it enters Glacier National Park. There is no entrance station here, and no payment is required. The road reaches the international border and Chief Mountain border crossing at 18.6 miles (30 km). After crossing the border, the road enters Alberta and Waterton Lakes National Park, but you won't reach a park entrance station until nearly at the Townsite. After the road crosses the Belly River, it briefly exits the park, crossing the Kainai Reserve, before reentering the park. Regrowth from the 1998 Sofa Mountain Fire lines both sides of the road. As you crest a big rise, stop at the overlook (45 km/28 mi) to gaze at the Waterton Valley. For the descent, shift into second gear to avoid burning your brakes.

PARK ENTRANCE ROAD

From Highway 6, the 8-kilometer (5-mi) year-round road connecting the park entrance station with Waterton Townsite is worth a drive with a pair of binoculars. Linnet, Maskinonge, and Lower Waterton Lakes attract scads of birds as well as moose, bears, elk, and smaller wildlife. Stop at a picnic area along the route for wildlife-watching: Knight's Lake (1 km/0.6 mi), Hay Barn (4 km/2.5 mi), or Marquis (6.5 km/4 mi). You will drive through the Kenow Fire zone.

Stop at Kootenai Brown's gravesite for a good view and to pay tribute to the park's first superintendent and local legend. Brown's escapades include reputedly pulling an arrow out of himself and cleaning the wound with turpentine, escaping from the Sioux, serving as a pony express rider and a scout for Custer in Montana, and being acquitted of murder charges. He built a cabin by Upper Waterton Lake, working as a guide, commercial fisherman, hunter, rancher, trader, and scout. When Canada established the Kootenay Lake Forest Reserve in 1885, Brown became its first game warden. When Waterton Lakes became a national park, he stepped in as its first superintendent.

AKAMINA PARKWAY

The 16-kilometer (10-mi) **Akamina Parkway** underwent major reconstruction after the 2017 Kenow Fire and is expected to re-open by spring 2021. West of the Prince of Wales Hotel, the signed Akamina Parkway climbs steeply from Waterton Townsite as it curves above Cameron Creek Gorge. It passes trailheads to Crandell Lake, Lineham Falls, Rowe Lakes, Akamina Pass, and Forum Lake and several picnic areas. From Waterton Townsite, the route climbs along the base of Crandell

Chief Mountain International Highway connects Glacier and Waterton.

Mountain to **Cameron Lake.** For the return descent to the Townsite, shift into second gear; you can always smell the hot brakes of those who don't.

RED ROCK PARKWAY

Red Rock Parkway (open May-Oct.) travels through the 2017 Kenow Fire zone to terminate at Red Rock Canyon. Locate the signed turnoff on the park entrance road (3.5 km/2.2 mi north of the Townsite; 4 km/2.5 mi south of the park entrance station). The 15-kilometer (9.3-mi), narrow road climbs through grasslands, squeezes through a canyon, and opens up into meadows along Blakiston Creek. Early July often brings on a wildflower show. Bring binoculars for watching bears and bighorn sheep. The road is quite narrow but passable for trailers and RVs. It passes Crandell Mountain Campground about midway and several picnic areas. The parkway ends at two parking areas, which have restrooms. A self-guided trail leads around **Red Rock Canyon.**

Sights

CHIEF MOUNTAIN

Located along Chief Mountain Highway, **Chief Mountain** abruptly rises to 9,080 feet (2,768 m) from aspen parklands and prairie. It is the northeasternmost peak in Glacier National Park. Legend tells of a young Flathead brave who carried a bison skull to its summit and remained there for four nights wrestling the Spirit of the Mountain. When he finally prevailed, the spirit gave him a protection totem to keep him safe in battle and hunting.

★ PRINCE OF WALES HOTEL

Designated a Canadian National Historic Site, the 37-meter-tall (122-ft), seven-story, 90-room **Prince of Wales Hotel** (844/868-7474 or 403/859-2231, www.glacierparkcollection. com, daily early June-mid-Sept.) took more than a year to build. Constructed by the Great Northern Railway as a link in its Glacier chain, the hotel opened its doors in 1927. Even if you are not staying here, drop in to see its massive lobby with floor-to-ceiling windows looking down Waterton Lake. Kilt-wearing bellhops haul luggage, and the lobby serves high tea in the afternoon. Walk out on the bluff for the best photographic views of Waterton Lake. Beware the howling winds that can rip off hats.

WATERTON LAKE

Set in a north-south trough gouged by Pleistocene ice age glaciers, **Waterton Lake** is the deepest lake in the Canadian Rockies. (It's actually Upper Waterton Lake, which feeds Middle and Lower Waterton Lakes, but no one calls it that.) Its 149-meter (487-ft) depths hold 23-kilogram (50-lb) lake trout and opossum shrimp, which are tiny relics of the ice age. Spanning the international boundary, the 0.8-kilometer-wide (0.5-mi) and nearly 11.3-kilometer-long (7-mi) lake conveys visitors over its waters in the 1927 wooden *International* tour boat.

THE U.S.-CANADIAN BORDER

For Waterton visitors, the **border** inside the park is an attraction. The long, straight swath is cleared every 20 years by the International Boundary Commission. The boat tour down Waterton Lake crosses this unnatural forest line en route to Goat Haunt, where visitors can debark for 30 minutes without going through customs. Hikers can also walk over the border swath on the Waterton Lakeshore Trail.

★ GOAT HAUNT, USA

A tiny seasonal enclave housing rangers, **Goat Haunt, USA,** is at Waterton Lake's southern end in Glacier National Park. Accessed only

by boat or on foot, Goat Haunt sees hundreds of visitors per day in midsummer. Most arrive via the *International* tour boat. Goat Haunt's International Peace Park Pavilion displays tell the story of the peace park. Trailheads depart to Goat Haunt Overlook, Kootenai Lakes, Rainbow Falls, and beyond. Hikers can reach Goat Haunt from Waterton via the Lakeshore Trail.

★ INTERNATIONAL PEACE PARK PLAZA

Together, Waterton and Glacier became the first International Peace Park in the world. The **International Peace Park Plaza,** an outdoor interpretive site, celebrates this recognition plus the honoring of the pair as a World Heritage Site and International Biosphere Reserve. In the Townsite, tour the plaza and paved walkway between the Bayshore Inn and the marina. The walkway loops around the pier with interpretive signs, providing views of Prince of Wales Hotel and the expanse of Upper Waterton Lake southward into Glacier.

CAMERON LAKE

Tucked in a glacial cirque at the terminus of Akamina Parkway, **Cameron Lake** reflects the steep slopes of Mount Custer. Across the glacially fed lake sit the remnants of Herbst Glacier in Montana, where avalanches preen the slopes into good bear habitat. Rent a rowboat or canoe to paddle around the lake's shoreline, or saunter the Lakeshore Trail along the west shore, watching for moose, shorebirds, and bears. From here, hikers also climb the Carthew-Alderson trail to trek to the Townsite.

CAMERON FALLS

Picturesque **Cameron Falls** is on the edge of Waterton Townsite on Evergreen Avenue. In June, water roars through its slots, but the flow drops substantially by August. Cameron Creek has eroded a massive fold

of the Waterton Formation, a 600-million-year-old rock layer, which makes the water plunge in multiple directions. Sit on a bench at the base, or climb the short, steep trails on both sides of the creek to reach overlooks. Opt for the north-side switchback trail for better views.

WATERTON TOWNSITE

A quaint little tourism town frequented by bighorn sheep and deer, **Waterton Townsite** is in a dramatic location at the foot of Waterton Lake. Paved walking trails lead through the town, connecting the few-blocks-long shopping district with the campground, beach accesses, and picnic areas. Waterton Townsite hums in summer with visitors riding surrey bikes but is quiet in winter under the snow. New streetlights in town provide dark skies for spotting the Milky Way.

MASKINONGE LAKE

Birders and wildlife-watchers migrate to **Maskinonge Lake** for its rich diversity. Located east of the park entrance, the aspen-rimmed lake attracts waterfowl, ospreys, trumpeter swans, yellow-headed blackbirds, and kingfishers. Because Waterton is on the axis of two migratory flyways, it sees over 250 species of birds. The lake also attracts huge Shiras moose, weighing 680 kilograms (1,500 lb), plus muskrats, mink, and tiny vagrant shrews. When rare trumpeter swans nest here in midsummer, some of the area closes to protect their offspring. Bring binoculars and spotting scopes for wildlife-watching. Rent binoculars at **Pat's Gas Station** (224 Mount View Rd., 403/859-2266, www.patswaterton.com, $15/day).

BISON PADDOCK

Roaming the plains in vast numbers 150 years ago, wild bison all but vanished from North America. Two kilometers (1.2 mi) west of the park entrance road on Highway 6, the **Bison Paddock** had contained a small herd until the 2017 Kenow Fire swept through the paddock. Don't worry: The bison were moved to

---

1: historic Prince of Wales Hotel **2:** Goat Haunt, USA **3:** International Peace Park Plaza **4:** Cameron Falls

safety. Parks Canada plans to return them to the paddock as soon as native fescue grows back enough to sustain them. When they are returned, you can see them from a viewing area or via a 4-kilometer (2.5-mi) rough road looping through the paddock. No trailers are allowed on this road. Ask about the status at the visitors center.

Recreation

DAY HIKES

Waterton has more than 200 kilometers (124 mi) of trails. Among them, 3 kilometers (1.8 mi) of paved and dirt walking trails connect sights, restaurants, lodging facilities, the campground, and picnic areas in Waterton Townsite. From the marina to Cameron Bay, the trail follows the shoreline. Trails also connect to the Falls Theater, Cameron Falls, Bertha Lake and Waterton Lakeshore trailheads, Emerald Bay, and the Prince of Wales Hotel. Contrary to Glacier's backcountry rules, Waterton's trails permit dogs on a leash, but keep your pet under control and away from wildlife.

Be aware that almost all trails except for Crypt Lake and the south end of the Waterton Lakeshore Trail burned in the 2017 Kenow Fire. Shade is now minimal. Check ahead for **access to trailheads** on **Akamina Parkway,** which is slated to re-open in 2021.

Lower-elevation trails (Bear's Hump, Waterton Lakeshore) usually become snow-free in May. Snow melts off other trails in June, but can linger on high-elevation trails (Avion Ridge, Carthew Pass, Bertha Lake, Lineham Ridge) into early July. Use ice axes for crossing steep snowfields. For current trail conditions, look on the Parks Canada website (www.pc.gc.ca) or stop by the visitors center. The **Waterton Lakes National Park Gem Trek map** (877/921-6277, www.gemtrek.com, C$15) includes trail descriptions for easy, moderate, and strenuous hikes, plus trails in Akamina-Kishinena Provincial Park and at Goat Haunt.

Shuttles by water and land aid trailhead access. **Waterton Shoreline Cruises** (403/859-2362, www.watertoncruise.com) operates the Crypt Lake and Goat Haunt boats. **Waterton Outdoor Adventures** (The Tamarack, 214 Mount View Rd., 403/859-2378, www.hikewaterton.com) operates the land shuttles. **Pat's Gas Station** (224 Mount View Rd., 403/859-2266, www.patswaterton.com, C$7-15/day) rents bear spray and hiking poles.

Hikers going to Goat Haunt trails on foot or by boat must have **passports;** register the morning of your departure with the **CBP ROAM** via a smartphone app you can download before arrival. Look online (www.nps.gov/glac) for updated status reports for trails in Glacier National Park.

Bertha Lake

Distance: 11.4 kilometers (7 mi) round-trip
Duration: 3-4 hours
Elevation gain: 451 meters (1,480 ft)
Effort: strenuous
Trail surface: Dirt path with rocks and roots
Trailhead: southwest corner of Waterton Townsite off Evergreen Avenue (see map p. 254)

From the parking lot, the trail starts with a gradual climb along the western shore of Waterton Lake. Just before the junction, an overlook with a bench takes in the view south to Mount Cleveland, the highest peak in Glacier National Park. Taking the right fork at the junction, head across a steep hillside to Lower Bertha Falls, where pounding waters crash through bedrock. For a destination, the falls is 6.4 kilometers (4 mi) round-trip.

To continue to Bertha Lake, cross the bridge below the falls and climb incessant switchbacks up through the burned forest

---

1: walking trails in Waterton 2: pier near International Peace Park Plaza

Waterton Hikes

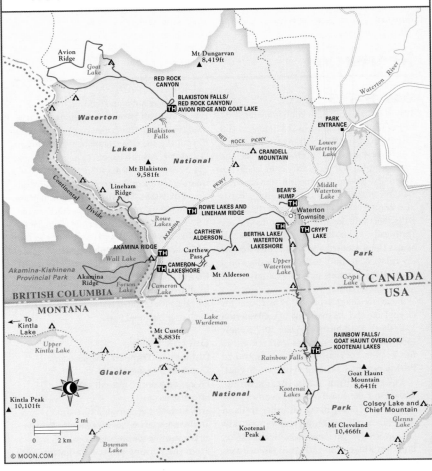

WATERTON
RECREATION

hillside beside Upper Bertha Falls, a larger sister of the lower falls. Soon the trail crests a knoll high above narrow Bertha Lake for the best view of the lake. To reach the shore, descend 160 meters (525 ft) to the campground near its outlet.

Waterton Lakeshore Trail

Distance: 13 kilometers (8 mi) one-way
Duration: 4 hours
Elevation gain: minimal

Effort: easy by elevation gain, moderate by length
Trail surface: narrow dirt path with roots and rocks
Trailhead: southwest corner of Waterton Townsite off Evergreen Avenue (see map p. 254)

Bordering the west lakeshore of Waterton Lake, the trail begins at the Bertha Lake trailhead. After 1.5 kilometers (1 mi), the trails diverge, with the Waterton Lakeshore Trail dropping in a quick, steep descent to Bertha Bay Campground on the lake. The trail climbs up and down with intermittent lake views

Waterton Hikes

Trail	Effort	Distance	Duration
Bertha Lake	strenuous	11.4 km (7 mi) rt	3-4 hr
Waterton Lakeshore Trail	easy	13 km (8 mi) one-way	4 hr
Crypt Lake	moderate-strenuous	17 km (10.6 mi) rt	5.5-8 hr
Bear's Hump	strenuous	2.8 km (1.7 mi) rt	1.25 hr
Rowe Lakes and Lineham Ridge	moderate-strenuous	8.4-17.2 km (5.2-10.6 mi) rt	2.5-6 hr
Cameron Lakeshore	easy	3.2 km (1.9 mi) rt	1 hr
Carthew-Alderson	moderate-strenuous	18 km (11.2 mi) one-way	6 hr
Akamina Ridge via Wall and Forum Lakes	strenuous	8.8-18.3 km (5.4-11.4 mi) rt	6-7 hr
Blakiston Falls	easy	2 km (1.2 mi) rt	45 min
Red Rock Canyon	easy	1 km (0.6-mi) loop	30 min
Avion Ridge and Goat Lake	moderate-strenuous	12.6-22.5 km (7.8-14 mi) rt	4-7 hr
Rainbow Falls	easy	2.3 km (1.4 mi) rt	1 hr
Goat Haunt Overlook	very strenuous	3.2 km (1.9 mi) rt	2 hr
Kootenai Lakes	easy	9 km (5.6 mi) rt	3-3.5 hr

until the international boundary at 6.1 kilometers (3.8 mi). The dock at Boundary Bay makes an idyllic lunch spot.

After the trail crosses the border, it becomes more level until entering the well-signed maze of trails at the end of Waterton Lake. Follow signs to Goat Haunt and catch the boat back to the Townsite. Before you leave in the morning, buy your return ticket with Waterton Shoreline Cruises. Bring your passport and file your trip with CBP ROAM app in Waterton before departing in the morning.

★ Crypt Lake

Distance: 17 kilometers (10.6 mi) round-trip
Duration: 5.5-8 hours
Elevation gain: 701 meters (2,300 ft)
Effort: moderate-strenuous

Trail surface: narrow dirt path with roots and loose rocks; metal stairs
Trailhead: Crypt Landing, accessible by boat from Waterton (see map p. 255)

From the marina in the Waterton Townsite, catch the water taxi operated daily by **Waterton Shoreline Cruises** (403/859-2362, www.watertoncruise.com, late May-early Oct., adults C$26 round-trip, kids half price) to cross Upper Waterton Lake to Crypt Landing. July-early September, it departs the marina at 8:30am, 9am, and 10am and Crypt Landing at 4pm and 5:30pm. Spring and fall boats go only at 10am and 5:30pm. The startup date in May depends on snowmelt on the trail. Buy tickets the day before or at least one hour in advance.

From Crypt Landing, the climb bolts up 19 switchbacks through a wooded hillside along

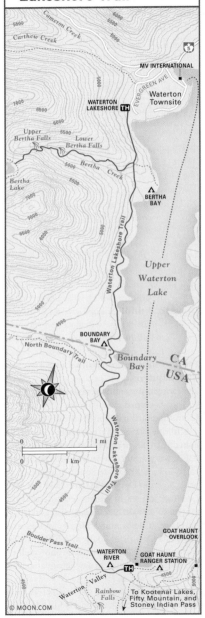

Waterton Lakeshore Trail

(Map labels:) Cameron Creek · Carthew Creek · MV INTERNATIONAL · EVERGREEN AVE · Waterton Townsite · WATERTON LAKESHORE TH · Upper Bertha Falls · Lower Bertha Falls · Bertha Creek · Bertha Lake · Waterton Lakeshore Trail · BERTHA BAY · Upper Waterton Lake · BOUNDARY BAY · North Boundary Trail · Boundary Bay · CA USA · Waterton Lakeshore Trail · Boulder Pass Trail · GOAT HAUNT OVERLOOK · WATERTON RIVER · GOAT HAUNT RANGER STATION · Waterton Valley · Rainbow Falls · To Kootenai Lakes, Fifty Mountain, and Stoney Indian Pass · © MOON.COM · 0 1 mi · 0 1 km

WATERTON
RECREATION

Hellroaring Creek. At the sixth switchback, an alternate, steeper route drops and climbs the edge of Hellroaring Creek to see its waterfalls; you can take one route up and one down. Soon the trail passes Twin Falls, and lodgepole pines give way to open meadows and boulder fields at Burnt Rock Falls, where the trail shoots up another 18 switchbacks. This exposed climb can be a scorcher, but yields a full view of 183-meter-high (600-ft) Crypt Falls.

The trail appears to dead-end in the headwall, but a hidden route leads to a narrow, 16.1-kilometer (10-ft) steel ladder that climbs up to a tunnel. Its 6.4-kilometer (4-ft) height demands an awkward walk or crawl. The 97-meter-long (60-ft) tunnel emerges on a cliff with a steel cable to hold onto when crossing. The trail breaks into a tight cirque housing Crypt Lake, which drains from an underwater channel. The international boundary crosses the lake's southern end. To catch the return boat, hikers jump up to speed down the trail en masse. Take the earliest and latest boats (8:30am, 5:30pm) to have the maximum time for hiking, especially if you want to add on the 1.8-kilometer (1.1-mi) loop around the lake. For wildflowers, the trail is best in early July.

★ Bear's Hump

Distance: 2.8 kilometers (1.7 mi) round-trip
Duration: 1.25 hours
Elevation gain: 168 meters (550 ft)
Effort: strenuous but short
Trail surface: narrow dirt path with rocks and stair steps
Trailhead: Bear's Hump trailhead parking lot across from the turnoff to Prince of Wales Hotel

This short grunt up to an overlook yields exceptional views, but prepare for heat due to the Kenow Fire stripping away shady vegetation. For cooler temperatures, go in early morning or evening after the hump shades the east-facing slope.

The rebuilt route promptly climbs upward, gaining elevation rapidly, some in steep steps. As the trail switchbacks up to pop out on the Bear's Hump, a rocky outcropping on Mount Crandell's ridge, it offers one of the best views

Crypt Lake

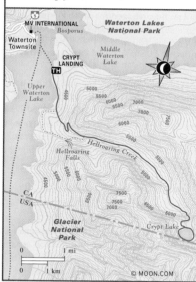

MV INTERNATIONAL
Waterton Lakes
National Park
Bosporus
Waterton
Townsite
Middle
Waterton
Lake
CRYPT
LANDING
TH
Upper
Waterton
Lake
Hellroaring
Falls
Hellroaring Creek
CA
USA
Glacier
National
Park
Crypt Lake

0   1 mi
0   1 km
© MOON.COM

trail splits off to Lower Rowe Lake, a destination for those wanting the shortest trek. Continuing on from the junction, the trail ascends into a broad meadow at the base of a giant cirque. After you cross the creek at 5.2 kilometers (3.2 mi), the left fork climbs steep switchbacks to Upper Rowe Lakes, a pair of scenic shallow lakes fringed with alpine larch.

For Lineham Ridge, the right fork after the creek crossing swings around the cirque to climb from subalpine wildflower meadows into alpine tundra. Red argillite colors the mountainside. From the ridge, Lineham Lakes appear below. At the saddle below Mount Lineham, you can opt to climb off-trail east to the peak or continue on the rugged trail west up Lineham Ridge to look down Blakiston Creek.

of the Waterton Townsite, the Prince of Wales Hotel, the prairie, and Middle and Lower Waterton Lakes. On top, views extend down Upper Waterton Lake into Glacier National Park. The return is a knee-pounding descent.

Rowe Lakes and Lineham Ridge

Distance: 8.4 kilometers (5.2 mi) round-trip to Lower Rowe Lake; 12.8 kilometers (7.9 mi) round-trip to Upper Rowe Lakes; 17.2 kilometers (10.6 mi) round-trip to Lineham Ridge
Duration: 2.5-6 hours
Elevation gain: 950 meters (3,116 ft)
Effort: moderate-strenuous
Trail surface: narrow dirt path with roots and loose rocks
Trailhead: Rowe Tamarack trailhead, 10.9 kilometers (6.7 mi) up Akamina Parkway

In July this trail bursts with wildflowers: yellow arnica, paintbrush, and purple lupine. The climb starts through thin forest broken by avalanche paths, following Rowe Creek. At 3.9 kilometers (2.4 mi), a 10-minute spur

Cameron Lakeshore

Distance: 3.2 kilometers (1.9 mi) round-trip
Duration: 1 hour
Elevation gain: none
Effort: easy
Trail surface: dirt path with roots and rocks
Trailhead: end of Akamina Parkway (see map p. 256)

This short trail follows the lake's western shoreline to a small interpretive display called Grizzly Gardens, due to the abundance of bears in the basin. Although the trail is flat, watch your footing on tree roots. Several points reach the shoreline for photos of Mount Custer and the remains of Herbst Glacier. At the trail's terminus, scan the avalanche slopes for grizzly bears feeding on glacier lilies. Do not continue farther; bears depend on quiet here for denning, feeding, and rearing cubs.

★ Carthew-Alderson

Distance: 19.3 km (12 mi) from Townsite return or 20 kilometers (12.5 mi) one-way from Akamina Parkway
Duration: 6-8 hours
Elevation gain: 439-1,023 meters (1,440-3,356 ft)
Effort: strenuous
Trail surface: narrow dirt path with roots and rocks
Trailhead: Next to Cameron Falls in the Townsite or from Cameron Lake at the end of Akamina Parkway (see map p. 256)

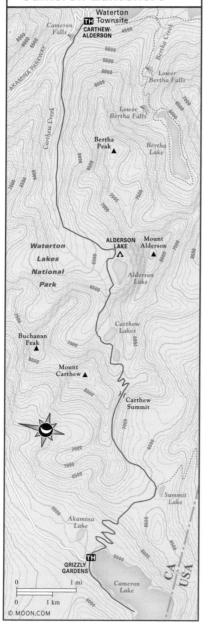

Carthew-Alderson and Cameron Lakeshore

One of the most popular hikes in Waterton, the trail climbs to **Carthew Summit,** where alpine tundra stretches along a windswept ridge. Be prepared for strong winds, even on a sunny summer day. Some winds may even force you to crawl over the pass. From the summit, views span deep into Glacier National Park's interior.

From the Townsite, the trail grunts up to Alderson Lake before climbing along a cliff wall to reach a pair of tarns rimmed with wildflowers in late July. The final ascent to Carthew Summit creeps into alpine tundra inhabited only by tiny wildflowers. Enjoy the view and return via the same route.

For a point-to-point route from Cameron Lake to the Townsite, the trail switchbacks above the east side of Cameron Lake to a plateau containing Summit Lake. The path then arcs around a large basin gaining elevation until cresting Carthew Summit for expansive views. That's where the plunge begins, dropping steeply to the pair of tarns and then steeply again to Alderson Lake. Once you depart the lake, avalanche chutes cut through the burned timbers en route to Cameron Falls at Waterton Townsite. For this route, catch the **Cameron Express hiker shuttle** (www.hikewaterton.com, mid-June-Sept., reservations required) to Cameron Lake or set up your own shuttle.

Akamina Ridge via Wall and Forum Lakes

Distance: Akamina Ridge Loop, 18.3 kilometers (11.4 mi); 8.8 kilometers (5.4 mi) round-trip to Forum Lake; 10.4 kilometers (6.4 mi) round-trip to Wall Lake
Duration: 6-7 hours
Elevation gain: 975 meters (3,199 ft)
Effort: strenuous
Trail surface: narrow dirt path with roots and rocks
Trailhead: Akamina Pass trailhead, 14.8 kilometers (9.2 mi) up Akamina Parkway
This hike begins in Waterton Park, but within 0.6 kilometer (1 mi) reaches low Akamina

1: ladder on Crypt Lake Trail **2:** wildflowers in early summer

Pass, where it crosses over the Continental Divide and into Akamina-Kishinena Provincial Park. Hikers looking for shorter adventures can choose either Wall or Forum Lake as a destination, but the longer loop hike gets the views. Continue 700 meters (0.4 mi) to the Forum Lake junction, turning left; Wall Lake is to the right, and it's the way you will return. The trail climbs to the snowmelt-fed Forum Lake, surrounded by steep talus and larch slopes. From the lake, follow the rough unmaintained trail that ascends the western ridge up through a 26-meter (16-ft) rock band where you'll need to use your hands for climbing. Once above the band, the ridge walk begins.

The 5-kilometer (3.1-mi) Akamina Ridge walk is truly spectacular. Rolling over peaks and knolls, the alpine tundra is devoid of trees but rampant with miniature plants like pink moss campion struggling to survive. To the south, Glacier's remote Kintla Peak stands with Agassiz Glacier while a sea of peaks stretches in all directions. At the end of the ridge, the trail drops steeply back into forest to Wall Lake, a dramatic cirque tucked against abrupt limestone walls. From Wall Lake, hike 3 kilometers (1.8 mi) back to the Forum Lake junction and return to the trailhead over Akamina Pass.

Blakiston Falls

Distance: 2 kilometers (1.2 mi) round-trip
Duration: 45 minutes
Elevation gain: 30.5 meters (100 ft)
Effort: easy
Trail surface: narrow dirt path with roots, rocks, and stair steps
Trailhead: end of Red Rock Parkway

Turn left just after you cross Red Rock Canyon. After crossing Bauerman Creek, turn right and ascend through the forest above Blakiston Creek. At Blakiston Falls, stair steps and several platforms overlook the roaring falls with Mount Blakiston looming above.

★ Red Rock Canyon

Distance: 1 kilometer (0.6 mi) loop

Duration: 30 minutes
Elevation gain: 40 meters (130 ft)
Effort: easy
Trail surface: narrow, rough pavement; dirt with roots and rocks
Trailhead: end of Red Rock Parkway

From the bridge over Red Rock Canyon, walk down and up either side of the loop. Water chiseled the canyon, exposing the lustrous red mudstone. Iron-rich argillite sediments are layered on top of each other, some turning red from oxidization, others remaining green. Evidence of the ancient Belt Sea appears in mud cracks and ripple marks. These are some of the region's oldest exposed sedimentary rock, created 1.5 billion years ago. At the top of the loop, you'll stare down a dizzying drop more than 23 meters (75 ft) to the creek, a distance that took up to 10,000 years to carve.

Avion Ridge and Goat Lake

Distance: Avion Ridge Loop, 22.5 kilometers (14 mi); 12.6 kilometers (7.8 mi) round-trip to Goat Lake
Duration: 4-7 hours
Elevation gain: 533 meters (1,750 ft)
Effort: moderate-strenuous
Trail surface: narrow dirt path with roots and loose rocks
Trailhead: end of Red Rock Parkway

The Avion Ridge Loop begins and ends on the Snowshoe Trail, an old dirt roadway that permits bicycles. It's easiest done clockwise, but some hikers prefer the vertical ascent via Goat Lake in favor of a less-steep descent. At 4 kilometers (2.5 mi) up the Snowshoe Trail, you'll reach the Goat Lake junction. Those heading to Goat Lake abruptly climb a relentless uphill into the hanging valley above Goat Lake, known for its rainbow trout.

For Avion Ridge Loop, continue up the Snowshoe Trail from the Goat Lake junction. At 8.2 kilometers (5.1 mi), you'll reach the Snowshoe Warden Cabin and campsites. Take the trail heading north toward Lost Lake and climb to Avion Ridge. An 8-kilometer (5-mi) unmaintained trail ascends along a barren, windswept ridge. The trail circles above

Goat Haunt Trails

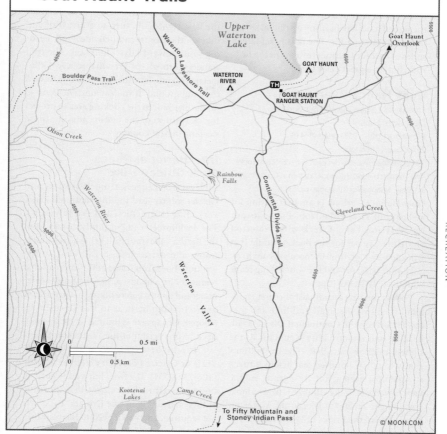

Upper
Waterton
Lake

Goat Haunt
Overlook

Waterton Lakeshore Trail

GOAT HAUNT

WATERTON
RIVER

TH

GOAT HAUNT
RANGER STATION

Boulder Pass Trail

Olson Creek

Rainbow
Falls

Continental Divide Trail

Cleveland Creek

Waterton River

Waterton Valley

0   0.5 mi

0   0.5 km

Kootenai
Lakes

Camp Creek

To Fifty Mountain and
Stoney Indian Pass

© MOON.COM

a cirque right on the boundary of Waterton National Park (you'll see signs). Endless peaks parade in all directions. As the trail swings north, it descends to a saddle, traverses a steep sidehill, and reaches a pass above Goat Lake. A knee-pounding descent through wildflower meadows plummets to the lake and then to the Snowshoe Trail junction. Turn left to return to the trailhead.

Rainbow Falls

Distance: 2.3 kilometers (1.4 mi) round-trip
Duration: 1 hour

Elevation gain: minimal
Effort: easy
Trail surface: narrow dirt path with roots and rocks
Trailhead: behind the ranger station at Goat Haunt in Glacier National Park (see map p. 259)

Rainbow Falls is one option for a short hike from the boat tour on Waterton Lake. Check with Waterton Shoreline Cruises for the boat schedule that will allow enough time to complete your hike. Take your passport and file your hiking plans with the CBP ROAM app.

Follow the paved trail to the first junction, taking the right fork onto dirt. The trail wanders through thick forests, filled with mosquitoes in early summer. Just before reaching the Waterton River, take a left turn at the signed junction, heading up the east bank toward Rainbow Falls. The falls is actually a series of cascades cutting troughs in the bedrock, but it's a great place to sit.

Goat Haunt Overlook

Distance: 3.2 kilometers (1.9 mi) round-trip
Duration: 2 hours
Elevation gain: 257 meters (844 ft)
Effort: very strenuous
Trail surface: narrow dirt path with roots and rocks
Trailhead: behind the ranger station at Goat Haunt in Glacier National Park (see map p. 259)

Goat Haunt Overlook is another option for a short but steep hike from the boat tour on Waterton Lake. Check with Waterton Shoreline Cruises for the boat schedule that will allow enough time to complete your hike. Take your passport and file your hiking plans with the CBP ROAM app.

Follow the paved trail past the first right-hand turn to a dirt trail and hike 160 meters (525 ft) on the Continental Divide Trail, heading south toward Fifty Mountain. At the signed junction, turn left. The trail climbs gently for a few hundred feet before it turns straight up a steep uphill. It's a grunt, but the view is well worth the climb. At the overlook, you can gander down-lake to the Waterton Townsite and the Prince of Wales Hotel.

Kootenai Lakes

Distance: 9 kilometers (5.6 mi) round-trip
Duration: 3-3.5 hours
Elevation gain: minimal
Effort: easy
Trail surface: narrow dirt path with roots and rocks
Trailhead: behind the ranger station at Goat Haunt in Glacier National Park (see map p. 259)

Kootenai Lakes attracts hikers for its often-seen moose and sometimes-seen nesting trumpeter swans. Access is via the tour boat. Catch one of the earlier Waterton Shoreline Cruises boats, and schedule your return boat with enough time to complete your hike. Take your passport and file your hiking plans with the CBP ROAM app.

At Goat Haunt, follow the paved trail past the first right-hand turn to a dirt trail and hike on the Continental Divide Trail, heading south toward Fifty Mountain. The trail wanders through old-growth forest. At 4 kilometers (2.5 mi), take the right junction toward the campground. If you eat lunch here, do so on the beach or in the cooking area to protect the cleanliness of the tenting sites for those sleeping in bear country.

International Peace Park Guided Hike

Interpretive rangers from Waterton and Glacier jointly lead the International Peace Park Hike (10am Tues. and Fri. July-Aug.). The 14-kilometer (8.7-mi) hike leaves from the Bertha Lake trailhead. Bring a sack lunch, water, and extra clothes, and wear sturdy walking shoes. You'll stop at the international boundary for a hands-across-the-border ceremony and photos before hiking to Goat Haunt and returning by boat to the Townsite by 6:30pm. Group size is limited to 30, so you'll need to preregister at the **Waterton Lakes Visitor Information Centre** (403/859-5133) or Glacier's **St. Mary Visitor Center** (406/732-7751). It's free, but you'll need to buy your return boat ticket that morning with Waterton Shoreline Cruises. Passports are required, and you'll need to file your hiking plans with CBP ROAM.

Guides

Parks Canada naturalists guide free hikes to several destinations, usually Wednesday-Monday in summer. Destinations include Crandell Lake, Bertha Falls, and Blakiston Falls, which are suitable hikes for families with children. Check at the visitors center for the current schedule or look online (www.pc.gc.ca/waterton). Before the 2019 closure of Goat Haunt (due to staffing shortages), interpretive rangers from Glacier led free hikes (passports required) to Goat Haunt locales such as Kootenai Lakes. To find out if the hikes are running again, consult the park newspaper or go online (www.nps.gov/glac).

The Baker family has been hiking in Waterton for more than 90 years, and the youngest generation now operates the commercial guide service **Waterton Outdoor Adventures** (The Tamarack, 214 Mount View Rd., 403/859-2379, www.hikewaterton.com, June-Sept.). The guides provide interpretive services, trail knowledge, and ground transportation to the trailhead. Reservations are required. Half- and full-day hikes start at C$80-95 per person (at least three people). Bring your own trail snacks, lunches, and water, or add on lunches for a fee.

BACKPACKING

Backpackers in Waterton have two route options: routes in Waterton Lakes National Park or routes in Glacier National Park accessed through Waterton, most starting at Goat Haunt. Both require permits that backpackers can get at the Waterton visitors center. For Glacier's trails, the center can only issue permits for trips launching from Chief Mountain or Goat Haunt trailheads; payment must be by credit card.

For backcountry camping in Waterton, **Wilderness Use Permits** ($10 pp/night, free kids 16 and younger) can be picked up at the Waterton Lakes Visitor Centre 24 hours or less before your trip. Make advance reservations ($12) up to 90 days prior to the trip, starting April 1, by calling the visitors center (403/859-5133). For kids, the easiest backpack trip is the Waterton Lakeshore Trail, camping at Bertha Bay or Boundary Creek.

Tamarack Trail
39 KILOMETERS (24 MI)

A few lakes tuck under the Continental Divide on the boundary of Waterton and Alberta. Launch from the Red Rock Canyon trailhead, hiking west along Bauerman Creek to Twin Lakes for the first night. Then go south to Lone Lake for the second night. The final day climbs over the knife-edged Lineham Ridge to round through a glacier-scoured cirque before descending Rowe Creek to the exit at the Rowe Lakes trailhead. Set up shuttles for the three-day trip through **Waterton Outdoor Adventures** (403/859-2379, www.hikewaterton.com).

Stoney Indian Pass
47 KILOMETERS (29 MI)

Hiking the Waterton Lakeshore Trail launches this four- to six-day backpacking trip over Stoney Indian Pass in Glacier National Park. Lop off walking down Waterton Lake to Goat Haunt by hopping the boat run by **Waterton Shoreline Cruises** (403/859-2362, www.watertoncruise.com). Pick up a permit in Waterton, file trip plans with CBP ROAM, and take your passport. Spend the first night at Kootenai Lakes (KOO) watching moose. Then climb to Stoney Indian Pass (STO) for the second night, tucked below the Stoney Indian parapets. Split your remaining nights in campsites at lakes in the Mokowanis Valley: Mokowanis Lake (MOL), Glenns Lake Head (GLH) or Foot (GLF), Cosley Lake (COS), and Gable (GAB). Exit at Chief Mountain Customs. Make reservations for the shuttle from **Waterton Outdoor Adventures** (403/859-2379, www.hikewaterton.com) to return to Waterton.

BIKING

All roadways in Waterton offer good cycling, but ready to ride with cars at your elbows on narrow-cornered roads with minimal shoulders, especially Red Rocks Parkway and Akamina Parkway. Be prepared to encounter bears on both roads. Red Rock Parkway offers a unique cycling opportunity in spring and fall, when it is closed to vehicles. The 7-kilometer (4.3-mi) paved **Kootenai Brown Trail** connects the park entrance with Waterton Townsite, offering the best family-friendly bicycling option with big scenery. For campers traveling by bicycle, campgrounds have bear resistant storage containers.

Parks Canada levies heavy fines of up to C$2,000 for riding on sidewalks, grass, or trails designated for hiking only. Alberta law requires children under age 18 to wear a helmet while bicycling. Given the narrow roads and the fact that most drivers are gaping at the scenery or looking for bears, and that winds can gust riders off bikes, it's a wise idea for riders of all ages to wear helmets.

Mountain Bike Trails

Four rough, unpaved trails in Waterton permit mountain biking. For current trail conditions, check with the visitors center. Get a complete list of all mountain biking trails at the visitors center; here are two of the best:

Near the end of Akamina Parkway, **Akamina Pass Trail** climbs a stiff, steep 1.3 kilometers (0.8 mi) on a forested trail to the Continental Divide, which is the boundary of Waterton National Park, Akamina-Kishinena Provincial Park, Alberta, and British Columbia. From there, it rambles to Wall Lake (10.4 km/6.4 mi round-trip).

At the end of Red Rock Parkway, the **Snowshoe Trail** is 16.4 kilometers (10.2 mi) round-trip along Bauerman Creek to the Snowshoe Warden Cabin. An abandoned fire road with a fairly wide berth, the trail has some steep sections and creek fords for spice.

Rentals

Pat's Gas Station (224 Mount View Rd., 403/859-2266, www.patswaterton.com, C$20-30/hr) rents mountain bikes, tandem bikes, and e-bikes. Helmets come free with rentals. Pat's also rents its famous two-person four-wheel surrey bikes for tootling around the Townsite; they're fun for a spin on the flat roads, but hills are difficult with only one gear. **Blakiston and Company** (102 Mountainview Rd., 800/456-0772, www.blakistonandcompany.com, 9am-8pm daily mid-May-mid-Sept., shorter hours in shoulder seasons, C$30/hr) rents e-bikes.

HORSEBACK RIDING

Waterton's open grassland prairies flanking the mountains make a big view backdrop for trail rides with **Alpine Stables** (off the park entrance road opposite the golf course, 403/859-2462 summer or 403/653-2089 winter, www.alpinestables.com, 9am-5pm daily May-Sept., C$45-200). With small saddles, the stables can take kids as young as five years old. Reservations are highly recommended. Wear long pants and sturdy shoes or boots. One-hour rides depart on the hour for meadow and lakeshore tours, with 1.5- and 2-hour versions offered less frequently. Three-hour rides head

bicycling the Kootenai Brown Trail

to the Bison Paddock or Bertha Falls, and longer rides tour trails for 4-8 hours. Kids can get 15-minute pony rides for C$10.

WATER SPORTS
Boating, Paddling, and Windsurfing

Waterton Lakes National Park bans all motorized boats (except for those that are sealed and quarantined for 90 days). Parks Canada instituted the ban to protect the lakes and downstream waterways from aquatic invasive species. Hand-launched, human- or wind-powered watercraft are still allowed with a free required permit after a self-inspection; you can pick one up at the visitors center.

CAMERON LAKE

Cameron Lake is the ideal spot for paddling your own rig or a rental boat. Winds are often less cantankerous than on the larger lakes, and the views are tantalizing, especially with glassy water reflecting the mountains on the border of Canada and the United States. Avoid beaching at the southern half of the lake to protect the prime grizzly bear habitat there. **Cameron Lake Boat Rentals** (403/627-6643, www.cameronlakeboatrentals.com, 9am-5pm daily mid-June-mid-Sept., shorter hours in shoulder seasons, C$30-45/hour) rents canoes, kayaks, paddleboards, paddleboats, and rowboats. Rates include life jackets and paddles.

WATERTON LAKES

A few paddlers tackle **Upper Waterton Lake**, hugging shorelines because of the wind or paddling only when waters are calm. However, be aware that whitecaps are common, with an average wind speed of 32 km/h (20 mph). Novice paddlers will find calmer, more sheltered water on **Emerald Bay,** a block from the Blakiston rental shop. Strong paddlers can overnight at backcountry camps at Bertha Bay and Boundary Creek in Waterton, and Goat Haunt in Glacier. Get required wilderness camping permits and advanced reservations at the **Waterton Lakes**

Visitor Centre (403/859-5133) for Bertha Bay and Boundary Creek (adults C$10 pp/night, ages 16 and under free, $12 advance reservation) and for Goat Haunt (adults $7 pp/night, $40 advance reservation). All three campsites have docks, but you'll need to completely beach and secure boats at night due to high winds.

Because winds on Upper Waterton Lake often rage, expert sailboarders, kite surfers, and windsurfers launch from **Windsurfer Beach** on Waterton Avenue. No rentals are available, so bring your own gear including wet suits or dry suits, as the glacier-fed lake is freezing cold. You should know how to water-start and self-rescue; it's not a place for beginners.

Middle Waterton Lake, the **Dardanelles** (the waterway connecting the two lakes), and **Lower Waterton Lake** have exceptional wildlife-watching, birding, and less-hefty gales. Hay Barn and Marquis Picnic Areas offer good put-ins for paddling these sections.

Rent canoes, kayaks, and paddleboards from **Blakiston and Company** (102 Mountainview Rd., 800/456-0772, www.blakistonandcompany.com, 9am-8pm daily June-mid-Sept., shorter hours in shoulder seasons, C$30-60/hour). **Pat's Gas Station** (224 Mount View Rd., 403/859-2266, www.patswaterton.com, C$30/hr) rents single-person kayaks.

Fishing

Fish are no longer stocked in Waterton Lakes National Park; however, introduced species still populate the waterways: arctic grayling, British Columbia and Yellowstone cutthroat, and rainbow, eastern brook, and brown trout. Conscientious anglers practice catch-and-release, especially to protect 17 species of native fish, including bull trout, ling, lake chub, deepwater sculpin, northern pike, pygmy whitefish, and spottail shiner. Bull trout are a protected species. Follow the adage "No black, put it back."

In **Upper Waterton Lake,** home to

rainbow trout, whitefish, and pike, fish feed on the tiny opossum shrimp, a crustacean that is a relic of pre-ice age days. The record lake trout caught in Waterton Lake was 23 kilograms (51 lb). Some hiking destinations, like **Goat Lake,** offer decent rainbow trout fishing. At **Cameron Lake** (Cameron Lake Boat Rentals, 403/859-2396, www.cameronlakeboatrentals.com, C$12 half day), anglers can rent fishing poles and buy licenses.

LICENSES AND REGULATIONS

Waterton Park requires a **fishing permit** (daily C$10, annual C$35) to fish within park boundaries. Purchase one at the visitors center, campground kiosks, Cameron Lake Boat Rentals, or Pat's Gas Station. Kids under age 16 can either purchase their own permit to catch a full limit or share limits with an adult. Check for species limits when you purchase fishing licenses. Anglers planning to fish Wall and Forum Lakes in Akamina-Kishinena Provincial Park need British Columbia provincial fishing licenses.

The general fishing season runs **July-October,** but anglers may fish Upper and Middle Waterton Lakes, Crandell Lake, Cameron Lake and Creek, and Akamina Lake mid-May-early September. Waters closed year-round include Maskinonge Lake and inlet, plus several creeks: Blakiston, Bauerman, Sofa, Dungarvan, and the North Fork of the Belly River.

Scuba Diving

Scuba divers go after a spot in **Emerald Bay** where a sunken circa-1900 paddle steamer, *The Gertrude,* provides exploration at a depth of 20 meters (66 ft). For the clearest waters, early spring and fall are best for diving. Just remember that historic artifacts, which include anything on the wreck, are protected by the park; leave everything where you find it. Bring your own gear.

1: windsurfer at Upper Waterton Lake 2: trail ride with Alpine Stables 3: Waterton Lake

Swimming

Beaches at Waterton Lake attract swimmers, but the water is chilly, and winds can howl. Most families head to **Emerald Bay** where the water is more protected. The indoor **Waterton Health Club and Recreation Centre** (Waterton Lakes Lodge, 101 Clematis Ave., 403/859-2150 or 888/985-6343, 7am-10pm daily, shorter hours in winter, C$8) includes a hot tub, 18-meter swimming pool, sauna, and fitness equipment. Pay for entry at the front desk at Waterton Lakes Lodge Resort. For kids, an outdoor **spray and splash park** is located outside the Waterton Community Center (201 Cameron Falls Dr.).

GOLF

Focusing on your putting can be difficult with huge scenery. Not only are sand traps a hazard, but sometimes grizzly bears, too. Located 3 kilometers (1.8 mi) north of the Townsite, the 18-hole **Waterton Golf Course** (403/859-2114, www.golfwaterton.com, dawn-dusk May-Oct., C$75-85 with cart, C$50 without cart) is an original Stanley Thompson design like the Banff Springs and Jasper courses. The pro shop rents clubs, and a licensed clubhouse keeps guests fed and watered on its patio, which has outstanding views. Many of Waterton's hotels offer golf packages in May and after mid-September.

TENNIS

There are four hard-surface outdoor public tennis courts (Cameron Falls Dr. and Harebell Dr.). The free unlit courts, which are snow-covered in winter, are available on a first-come, first-served basis. **Pat's Gas Station** (224 Mount View Rd., 403/859-2266, www.patswaterton.com, C$3/hour) rents tennis rackets.

SPA

Part of the Bayshore Inn, **Serenity Spa** (111 Waterton Ave. #103, 403/859-2404, www.serenityspawaterton.com, C$20-310) offers day spa services. Relax with massages, manicures, pedicures, facials, and body wraps.

WINTER SPORTS

In winter, when heavy snows render many of the roads impassable by vehicle, the parkways become ideal **cross-country ski trails** with guaranteed quiet and solitude. Skiers can also glide down Waterton Lake after it freezes. Rent cross-country ski and snowshoe gear through **Waterton Lakes Lodge** (101 Clematis Ave., 403/859-2150 or 888/985-6343, C$15-20).

Waterton is a land of winter extremes. It records the highest precipitation levels in Alberta, much of it as snowfall. It also records winter winds over 97 kph (60 mph), which can plummet windchills. With winter chinooks, the park is also one of Alberta's warmest areas, with an average of 28 days above freezing in winter. With this diversity, snow varies from dry light powder to heavy wet glop. Conditions can change within an hour. Most cross-country skiers sacrifice speed for reliable glide by using waxless skis.

Two designated ski trails are marked: **Cameron** and **Dipper Ski Trails,** both off Akamina Parkway, which is plowed to the trailheads at Little Prairie. Other trails such as Crandell Lake, Rowe Trail, and Akamina Pass offer more options, but be prepared with avalanche gear. Popular **snowshoe trails** lead to Bertha Falls and Crandell Lake. Contact the **Waterton Lakes Visitor Center** for avalanche conditions.

Entertainment and Shopping

ENTERTAINMENT

Parks Canada offers evening slide shows and indoor interpretive programs (8pm daily summer, free) at the **Falls Theater** (across Evergreen Ave. from Cameron Falls) and Crandell Mountain Campground. Programs cover wildlife, ecology, and geology. Call 403/859-2445 for a current schedule, which is also posted in the visitors center and campgrounds. **Waterton Lakes Opera House** (309 Windflower Ave., 403/859-2466) shows movies in summer and sometimes has concerts.

EVENTS

Waterton celebrates **nature festivals** (877/780-1998, http://mywaterton.ca). The **Waterton Wildflower Festival** is usually in June and the **Waterton Wildlife Festival** in July. Consult the online calendar for current dates and schedules.

The **Blackfoot Arts and Heritage Festival** stages exhibition powwows for several days in late July. You can watch the dancing for free on the Community Center greens.

SHOPPING

Shopping in Waterton features Canadian souvenirs, with moose and T-shirts with red maple leaves. Most shops are open daily May-September but close in winter. During shoulder seasons, hours are shorter, often 10am-5pm daily, but in midsummer shops stay open until 8 or 9pm.

If you need outdoor gear, **The Tamarack** (214 Mount View Rd., 403/859-2378, www.hikewaterton.com, early May-Sept.) can outfit you from head to toe with hiking, backpacking, camping, and fishing gear. The shop carries good reputable brands at reasonable prices as well as topographic maps for hiking. Chocoholics and kids revel in **Welch's Chocolate Shop** (401 Windflower Ave., 403/859-2363), a sister shop to one in Banff. It stocks international chocolates and makes its own candy.

Food

In this remote resort oasis in a national park, food prices can be exorbitant. Plus, the 5 percent GST gets slapped on every bill. But an influx of less-expensive eateries have moved into town in recent years. If you're camping or backpacking, consider bringing supplies with you, as groceries are limited. In late summer, blackflies descend for several weeks on the Townsite, even in restaurants. Just think of them as small wildlife. No dressing up is required for dining; casual clothes, including hiking attire, are acceptable.

With a few exceptions, restaurants in the Townsite cluster along Waterton and Windflower Avenues. The two streets have a European feel with patio and sidewalk dining. Only Vimy's and Red Rocks Trattoria stay open year-round; all other restaurants are open daily May-September. In spring and fall, some restaurants often shorten their hours or days. For the trail, many restaurants sell hiker lunches at C$16-20.

INSIDE THE PARK
Resort Dining

Located in the Bayshore Inn, the ★ **Lakeside Chophouse** (111 Waterton Ave., 403/859-2211, www.bayshoreinn.com, 7am-10pm daily) packages up scenery with fine dining. It is the only restaurant with outdoor patio seating on Waterton Lake. The dining room serves breakfast, lunch, dinner, international wines, and cocktails. Breakfast (C$10-22) brings on eggs Benedict and a daily buffet. Lunch and dinner (C$13-33) feature burgers, sandwiches, salads, and an eclectic global cuisine. The after-5pm menu also adds on grilled aged AAA Alberta beef and bison steaks (C$30-50). Be sure to save room for wild Saskatoon berry pie. Reservations are recommended. The adjoining **Fireside Lounge** (noon-1am daily) also serves pizza, burgers, sandwiches, salads, and pastas.

At Waterton Lakes Lodge Resort,

Vimy's Lounge and Grill (101 Clematis Ave., 403/859-2150 or 888/985-6343, www.watertonlakeslodge.com, 7am-10pm daily, shorter hours in winter) offers four dining options in summer: a lounge downstairs, an outside patio, upstairs dining with a view of Mount Cleveland, and outside upper deck dining. Breakfast (C$10-18) includes multiple variations on eggs Benedict, while lunch and dinner (C$19-38) has burgers, sandwiches, and salads plus, after 5pm, Alberta steaks and dinner entrées that rotate seasonally. It's also one place you can get the Canadian classic appetizer of *poutine*: homemade french fries drowning in cheese curds and gravy.

The historic **Prince of Wales Hotel** (844/868-7474, front desk 403/859-2231, www.glacierparkcollection.com, daily early June-mid-Sept.) puts on a regal view of Waterton Lake from massive floor-to-ceiling windows in the **Royal Stewart Dining Room.** Breakfast (6:30am-10am, C$12-17) specializes in eggs Benedict and omelets, while the lunch (11:30am-2pm, C$12-17) and dinner (5pm-9:30pm, C$18-34) menus introduce classics from Great Britain such as bangers and mash and Canadian prime rib. Reservations are recommended in midsummer. The British atmosphere goes into full swing with **afternoon tea** (1pm-5pm daily, adults C$33, kids C$18) in the hotel lobby overlooking Waterton Lake. Make reservations for this full meal of finger sandwiches and a sugar-fest of desserts: pastries, fruits, and berries. Pour your tea from signature porcelain servers. It's a unique experience, but mostly about the atmosphere. You can also enjoy the hotel views down-lake with a lighter meal and cocktail from the **Windsor Lounge** (11:30am-10pm).

Italian

In Waterton Glacier Suites, with a contemporary vibe, ★ **Red Rock Trattoria** (107 Windflower Ave., 403/859-2004, www.

redrockcafe.ca, 5pm-9pm daily, $18-40) serves up classic Italian appetizers, pastas, and entrées built with fresh and sometimes local ingredients. Order a bottle of fine Italian wine to accompany your multi-course meal and top it off with tiramisu. Make reservations as seating is limited.

Two pizza restaurants, which sit next to each other on Windflower Avenue, offer seating indoors or outdoors. They also make to-go pizzas for your motel, beach, or campsite. ★ **49 Degrees North** (303 Windflower Ave., 403/859-3000, www.49degreesnorthpizza. com, noon-10pm, C$12-30) makes pizza and calzone doughs fresh daily, including gluten-free, and bakes in a stone-deck-fired oven. It also serves soup, salads, and appetizers, plus weekend breakfasts. Next door, the long-time Waterton staple **Pizza of Waterton** (305 Windflower Ave., 403/859-2660, www. pizzaofwaterton.com, 7am-9pm daily, C$12-30) serves handcrafted pizzas and calzones, lasagna, salad, beer, wine, and cocktails out of Pearl's Café.

Mexican

In a tiny, graffiti-walled café, the **Taco Bar** (310 Windflower Ave., 403/915-2294, http://watertontacos.wixsite.com/thetacobar, 11:30am-9:30pm daily, shorter hours spring and fall, C$5-15, cash only) brings the flavors of Mexico to Canada with burritos, tacos, and bowls filled with choices of meats, beans and cheese or veggies, gluten-free, and kid-sized options. Crisp citrus slaw and fresh-made salsas add zing.

Pubs

With indoor or patio seating, the **Thirsty Bear Kitchen & Bar** (111 Waterton Ave., 403/859-2211, www.thirstybearwaterton.com, 11am-1am Sun.-Thurs., 11am-2am Fri.-Sat., $16-40) serves pub fare, Alberta craft beers, and Caesars. It doubles as the town's only nightclub, with live music and dancing usually on weekends.

Cafés

Waterton is full of tiny eateries where you can enjoy varied flavors for dining in or grabbing portable food to go for the road or trail. A local favorite with outdoor picnic tables for seating, ★ **Wieners of Waterton** (301 Windflower Ave., 403/859-0007, www. wienersofwaterton.com, 7am-9pm daily) knows how to pile large, high-end sausages with choose-your-own fresh toppings on homemade buns. Hot dogs come from local butchers, and sweet potato fries are served with tasty homemade sauces.

With the scent of sweet waffles wafting out into the street, ★ **Waffleton** (301 Windflower Ave., 403/339-0226, 8am-10pm daily) tops fresh-baked buttermilk and Belgian liege waffles with fruits, whipped cream, ice cream, frozen Greek yogurt, Nutella, or multiple other toppings.

The **Glacier Bistro Starbucks** (111 Waterton Ave., 403/859-2211, 7am-11pm daily) serves light meals, croissants and baked goods, wraps, sandwiches, and soups, plus a selection of dessert goodies and espresso.

Family Dining

Two family restaurants anchor opposite ends of the same block. Their appeal comes from large, diverse menus with broad Canadian choices for breakfast, lunch, and dinner plus indoor or shaded outdoor sidewalk dining, and beer, wine, and cocktails. To decide between them, browse their outdoor menus and assess waiting lines. Both serve up omelets, sandwiches, salads, burgers, kids' meals, gluten-free and vegetarian options, and lighter or heavier meals. **Zum's Eatery** (116 Waterton Ave., 403/859-2388, https://zums. ca, 8am-9:30pm daily, C$12-26) specializes in crispy fried chicken, pub-style fish-and-chips, and baby back ribs in its house Guinness barbecue sauce. The signature dessert is a tasty saskatoon berry pie. In addition to lighter meals, **Trappers Mountain**

1: Lakeside Chophouse 2: Vimy's Lounge and Grill
3: Thirsty Bear Kitchen & Bar

Grill (106 Waterton Ave., 403/859-2445, 8am-8pm daily, C$12-45) serves up barbecue with a smokehouse process that finishes with broiling.

Coffee, Pastries, and Ice Cream

Espresso and ice cream outlets are ubiquitous in Waterton. You can linger over your favorite cappuccino or latte or get it to go at multiple locations on Waterton and Windflower Avenues. **Pearl's Café** (305 Windflower Ave., 403/859-2260, http://pearlscafe.ca, 7am-10pm daily) is a locals' fave for a sit-down coffee shop with internet access. Chow down on a gooey cinnamon bun, sipping espresso and connecting with wireless internet to catch up on email. Hikers can grab to-go fresh-baked goods and lunches to hit the trail.

The number of ice cream shops comes in a close second behind espresso outlets. For the biggest flavor selections, house-made waffle cones, and fruit-filled frozen yogurts, go to **Big Scoop Ice Cream Parlor** (114 Waterton Ave., 10am-10pm daily).

Groceries

While several outlets in town carry convenience foods, only the **Rocky Mountain Food Mart** (307 Windflower Ave., 403/859-2121, 8am-8pm daily May-Sept.) stocks fresh produce, meats, dairy, and deli and baked goods. It's tiny, so expect limited selection, and prices can be high. It also carries ice, firewood, and camping supplies. Off-season, find the closest grocery stores in Pincher Creek. Go to **Mountain Spirits Liquor Store** (504 Cameron Falls Dr., 403/859-2337, 11am-10:30pm Mon.-Thurs., 10am-11pm Fri.-Sat., 1pm-10:30pm Sun.) for beer, wine, and liquor.

Picnic Areas

Waterton has **14 picnic areas.** Those on Waterton Lake have shelters, which offer a place to hunker away from raging winds. Find six along the park entrance road and several located on the lakes. Red Rock Parkway and Akamina Parkway each have three picnic areas. In the Townsite on Waterton Lake, two picnic shelters are located near the end of Waterton Avenue and one at the end of Evergreen Avenue.

Accommodations

In Waterton, all hotels sit within walking distance in the compact town. No matter where you stay, you can walk to restaurants, shopping, boat tours, or hiking. (Staying at Prince of Wales Hotel requires a 15-minute walk to town; all others are within a block or two of restaurants.) All hotels have wireless internet access. Six hotels (except Prince of Wales and Northland Lodge) outfit rooms with televisions, but channels are limited to just a handful. Waterton hotels are all smoke-free, and reservations are absolutely mandatory for midsummer. Only two hotels have views of Waterton Lake: Prince of Wales and Bayshore Inn. Only Waterton Lakes Lodge and Waterton Glacier Suites are open year-round; all others are summer only.

All accommodations have the 5 percent GST and the 4 percent tourism tax added to the rates; together they add up. Rates are highest in July and August. Many of the hotels offer golf, seasonal activity packages, and shoulder season specials; ask or check their websites for current deals. You'll get better deals in Waterton in the off-season (May-early June, late Sept.-Oct., and winter), when most lodging properties drop their rates substantially, making travel cheaper at a crowd-free time. Waterton lodging is at a premium in midsummer during the big visitor season. If you don't want to pay the high rates, drive 35 minutes north to Pincher Creek for less-expensive chain motels.

INSIDE THE PARK
Lodges
PRINCE OF WALES HOTEL

Located on a bluff above Waterton Lake, historic ★ **Prince of Wales Hotel** (7.6 km/4.7 mi south of the park entrance station, 844/868-7474 or 403/859-2231, www.glacierparkcollection.com, late May-late Sept., C$250-350, suite C$600-800) is a seven-story wonder named for the prince who later became King Edward VIII. Kilted bellhops greet visitors, and high tea is served in the afternoon. Its lobby, with floor-to-ceiling windows, swings with a huge rustic chandelier. Lakeview rooms allow you to shower while looking into Glacier National Park, and mountain-view guest rooms let you spy on bighorn sheep. But despite its grand facade, the building is old, creaky, and thin-walled, and the upper stories seem to sway in high winds. Be prepared for tiny sinks and small baths, many installed in what were once closets. The guest rooms have phones but no other amenities. A cantankerous elevator accesses upper floors but requires a bellhop to run, rendering it unavailable at all hours. Top-floor lodgers get a workout climbing the stairs. A restaurant, a gift shop selling English bone china and Waterford crystal, and a lounge surround the lobby. You can reach town via a 5-minute drive or a 15-minute walk down a trail.

WATERTON LAKES LODGE RESORT

With mountain views from many of the rooms, the **Waterton Lakes Lodge Resort** (101 Clematis Ave., 403/859-2150 or 888/985-6343, www.watertonlakeslodge.com, C$170-360 summer, $120-270 winter) has 80 modern, air-conditioned guest rooms. Some include kitchenettes, suites, fireplaces, jet tubs, or are pet-friendly. The pleasant accommodations are in 11 two-story chalets. For 2nd-floor units, you'll need to climb the stairs, but some upstairs rooms include skylights and vault ceilings. Guests get free use of the on-site Waterton Health Club and Recreation

Centre pool, hot tub, and workout room. The resort also has a restaurant and bar.

CRANDELL MOUNTAIN LODGE

The 17-room **Crandell Mountain Lodge** (102 Mount View Rd., 403/859-2288 or 866/859-2288, www.crandellmountainlodge.com, mid-Apr.-mid-Oct., C$110-350) is tucked beneath its namesake peak. The two-story circa-1940 inn has a variety of country-themed guest rooms, from standard rooms up to three-room suites with full kitchens and fireplaces. In a private garden area, a huge deck with a barbecue and lounge chairs begs for afternoon relaxation.

Motels
THE BAYSHORE INN

One of only two hotels on Waterton Lake, ★ **The Bayshore Inn** (Mount View Rd. and Waterton Ave., summer 403/859-2211 or 888/527-9555, www.bayshoreinn.com, May-early Oct., C$160-460) offers lakefront guest rooms with prime views from private balconies. Family rooms, deluxe suites, and pet-friendly rooms are available, along with less-pricey guest rooms with mountain views. The complex has a lounge, a saloon, restaurants, a hot tub, a gift shop, satellite internet access, an ice cream shop, and the Serenity Spa. Located adjacent to the marina, it sits on the Townsite's main block that houses most of the shopping. Lakeside rooms overlook the Townsite Loop trail, lawn, trees, and the lake.

WATERTON GLACIER SUITES

With mountain views and large rooms, ★ **Waterton Glacier Suites** (107 Windflower Ave., 403/859-2004 or 866/621-3330, www.watertonsuites.com, C$175-380 summer, C$130-200 winter) has 26 units with private balconies for enjoying the mountain scenery. Room amenities include fridges, microwaves, air-conditioning, and whirlpool tubs. Some guest rooms have gas fireplaces, and 2nd-floor units require walking stairs.

ASPEN VILLAGE INN

Sporting red metal roofs (you won't get lost looking for these), the aging **Aspen Village Inn** (111 Windflower Ave., 403/859-2255 or 888/859-8669, www.aspenvillageinn.com, May-early Oct., C$120-350) combines a two-story motel with 16 cottages that accommodate 2-8 people. Some are pet-friendly or come with kitchens. The units surround mowed lawns, a playground, and an outdoor barbecue picnic area. Complimentary access to the Waterton Health Club and Recreation Centre is included.

BEAR MOUNTAIN MOTEL

The ★ **Bear Mountain Motel** (208 Mount View Rd., 403/859-2366, www.bearmountainmotel.com, mid-May-early Oct., C$115-260), a 1960s wood-and-masonry motel, has 36 small one- and two-bedroom units, several of which have tiny kitchenettes and living rooms with hide-a-beds. Expect clean, basic guest rooms with no frills and a pay phone near the office; these are the most affordable rooms in town. A shared patio has a microwave, grills, and picnic tables.

Bed-and-Breakfast

NORTHLAND LODGE

For park-history buffs, the quiet **Northland Lodge** (408 Evergreen Ave., 403/859-2353, www.northlandlodgecanada.com, mid-May-early Oct., C$150-275, two-night min. in summer) holds appeal. Louis Hill, builder of the Prince of Wales Hotel and many of Glacier National Park's historic hotels, constructed the Swiss-style lodge as his private residence circa 1948, although he never lived here. Two of the lodge's nine guest rooms share a bath, and the rest have private baths; guest rooms are split among three levels. A large balcony is great for soaking up the views with coffee and homemade muffins with Saskatoon-berry jam in the morning. A 10-minute walk leads to shopping and restaurants via the scenic Townsite Loop trail, just across the street. Some interiors were spritzed up in 2016.

Camping

INSIDE THE PARK

Waterton Lakes National Park campgrounds have flush toilets, drinking water, kitchen shelters, and bear-resistant food storage lockers. With the exception of the Townsite campground, most campground sites have fire rings, and firewood is supplied, but you pay C$9 per site for a burning permit in addition to the campground fee. Check online (www.pc.gc.ca) for campground details.

Waterton Townsite Campground

With the entrance on Evergreen Avenue, the ★ **Waterton Townsite Campground** (Apr.-Oct., unserviced sites C$23-28, electrical or full hookups C$23-40) is citified with a mowed lawn, but it sits on prime real estate with gorgeous views and within walking distance to restaurants in town. The huge campground borders the Townsite Loop trail and the beach. A few trees shade some sites, but most are open, offering little privacy. Go for spots nearest the lake in the G loop but be prepared for winds. For more sheltered scenery, go for the Cameron Creek E loop sites. Fires are only permitted in the kitchen shelters, but the campground includes hot showers, dishwashing stations, a dump station, and several new restroom buildings and electrical upgrades. In midsummer, the campground fills early; plan on arriving by noon to claim a site, or make reservations (C$12) starting in January through the **Parks Canada Campground Reservation Service** (877/737-3783, https://reservation.pc.gc.ca). You can sometimes have your pick of sites without a reservation until June and after mid-September.

Crandell Mountain Campground

On the opposite side of Crandell Mountain from the Townsite and 6.8 kilometers (4.2 mi) up the Red Rock Parkway, **Crandell Mountain Campground** (mid-May-early Sept., C$23-28) nestles along Blakiston Creek with mountain views. Due to significant damage from the 2017 Kenow Fire, the campground is under construction with the aim of re-opening in spring 2022. Check online status of this popular campground including RV limits and new facilities. From the campground, you can hike 2 kilometers (1.2 mi) to Crandell Lake.

Belly River Campground

On Chief Mountain Highway and 26 kilometers (16 mi) from Waterton Townsite, the **Belly River Campground** (mid-May-early Sept., C$16) has 24 pleasant sites for small RVs and tents in aspen groves with hand-pumped well water and both pit and flush toilets. Some sites are shaded, and some are in meadows. It is a good location for watching wildlife and birding, and it is the closest campground to the Chief Mountain border crossing for those who want to scamper across the boundary first thing in the morning.

Pass Creek Winter Campground

In winter, when all other campsites have closed, free sites are available at **Pass Creek Winter Campground** (mid-Oct.-mid-Apr.). Located on the entrance road 5 kilometers (3.1 mi) from the Townsite, the eight sites offer primitive camping with only a pit toilet and a woodstove in the kitchen shelter. Water from the creek may be boiled or purified for use.

OUTSIDE THE PARK

Often windy, **Crooked Creek Campground** (6 km/3.7 mi east of the park entrance road, 403/653-1100, https://crookedcreekcampground.ca, mid-Apr.-early Oct., C$25 tents, C$28-42 for hookups) has 80 close-knit campsites adjacent to the highway in a grassy setting. Amenities include flush toilets, showers, Wi-Fi, a dump station, a cook shack, laundry, ice, fire rings, and firewood.

Waterton Townsite Campground

Tips for Waterton Travel

- **GST:** Everywhere in Canada, a 5 percent **Goods and Services Tax** (GST) is applied to some purchases and services. In most cases, it is added onto your bill, not already included. In general, groceries, prescription drugs, health care, and medical devices are not taxed. But you will pay GST on motels, campground fees, restaurant bills, souvenirs, clothing, gas, recreation rentals, and tours.

- **Gas:** Gas up before you head north across the border as gas in Canada is usually $0.50-0.80 per gallon more expensive than in the United States. Also, be aware that gas is sold by the liter in Canada, so the price on the pump will look pretty darn good. To convert the price, remember 3.8 liters equals one U.S. gallon.

- **Coins:** Canada has $1 Loonies, named for the loons on the coins, and $2 Toonies, named for its two-dollar value and to match the Loonie.

- **Tips:** Tipping in Canada is comparable to the United States. Tip 15-20 percent in restaurants, $2 per bag for bellhops, $2-5 per day for housekeeping, and 15-20 percent for guides.

- **Kids:** Ice cream, short trails, renting surrey bikes, and a play park with water-spray features attract families with kids.

- **Credit Cards:** For the best exchange rate, use credit cards rather than cash.

- **ATMs:** Remember that ATMs will give you Canadian dollars. Only withdraw as much as you will use. ATMs are located at Pat's Gas Station, The Tamarack, Rocky Mountain Food Mart, Mountain Spirits Liquor Store, Bayshore Inn, and the Prince of Wales Hotel.

- **U.S. Currency:** Most businesses, including restaurants, shops, and lodges, will accept U.S. currency; however, return change will be given in Canadian currency. For conversions, most businesses use the bank exchange rate, but some have their own policies.

- **For the best exchange rates:** Use a credit card as much as possible to get the bank exchange rate. Waterton has **no banks;** the nearest banking services are in Cardston and Pincher Creek.

Transportation and Services

DRIVING AND PARKING

Waterton roads are all two-laners. Highways 5 and 6 are **open year-round,** as is the main road into Waterton Townsite. But Chief Mountain International Highway, part of Akamina Parkway, and Red Rock Parkway **close for the winter.** For **road conditions,** call 511 in Alberta.

In Waterton Townsite, find public parking lots at the marina, visitors center, streetside, picnic areas, trailheads, and Cameron Falls. Large public lots sit at the ends of Akamina Parkway and Red Rock Parkway.

SERVICES

The Townsite has a coin-op **launderette** (302 Windflower Ave., 7am-9pm daily May-Oct.). Showers (C$7) are available at the **Waterton Health Club and Recreation Centre** (101 Clematis Ave., 403/859-2150 or 888/985-6343).

The Townsite has a **post office** (102 Windflower Ave., 8am-4:30pm Mon.-Fri. year-round). Remember to use Canadian postage stamps rather than U.S. stamps to send mail from Canada. The *Calgary Herald* carries regional, national, and international news. The *Lethbridge Herald* covers local and regional news.

The official travel planning website run by the **Waterton Chamber of Commerce** (https://mywaterton.ca) offers more information on lodging, activities, dining, events, services, shopping, and the community.

Gas and Repairs

Pat's Gas Station (224 Mount View Rd., 403/859-2266, www.patswaterton.com) is much more than a place to gas up or buy propane for the RV. Pat can magically perform minor car repairs, but go to Pincher Creek for serious vehicle repairs.

Cell Phone and Internet Access

Telus, Bell, and some Verizon cell phones can get service in the Townsite, but not on the internal parkway roads or at Goat Haunt.

Waterton Wi-Fi services restaurants, motels, and the campground with two options. The **free service** offers limited speeds and intermittently cuts out, but it's enough to get a few emails and look up the weather; the **fee service** has faster speeds and is more dependable.

Emergencies

For emergencies, dial 911 or contact the **Royal Canadian Mounted Police** (RCMP, 202 Waterton Ave., 403/859-2244 or 403/627-2113) during summer months or **Parks Canada Wardens** (215 Mount View Rd., 403/859-2224) year-round. The nearest hospitals are 50 kilometers (31 mi) away: **Pincher Creek Hospital** (1222 Bev McLachin Dr., Pincher Creek, 403/627-1234) and **Cardston Health Centre** (144 2nd St. W., Cardston, 403/653-5234). To contact the park's emergency ambulance, call 403/859-2636.

Flathead Valley

Surrounded by mountain ranges and abundant

lakes, the Flathead Valley is an outdoor recreation paradise offering fishing, skiing, hiking, hunting, biking, paddling, and boating.

With 2.5 million acres (1 million hectares) of wilderness and national parklands, there's no shortage of space to get away from it all. One of the country's largest national forests fringes the valley floor, which is dotted with lakes, including Flathead, the largest freshwater lake west of the Mississippi. Summer brings flat-water kayaking and river floating. Anglers drop lines from drift boats, golfers hit the links, and hikers climb to wildflower-strewn heights with huge views of the valley.

Strip-mall culture has made some inroads into the valley, paving

Highlights

Look for ★ to find recommended sights, activities, dining, and lodging.

★ **Go play in Whitefish:** Romp through this train town turned resort town for shopping, art galleries, restaurants, and bar-hopping (page 280).

★ **Explore Bigfork:** Join the summer bustle of restaurants, shopping, theater… and whitewater kayaking (page 280)!

★ **Admire Flathead Lake from land or water:** Sail the blue waters or drive around the perimeter of the largest freshwater lake west of the Mississippi (page 280).

★ **Plunge into Whitefish Lake:** Cool off on hot summer days in this lake hopping with water-skiers, boaters, paddlers, anglers, and swimmers (page 281).

★ **Find year-round fun at Whitefish Mountain Resort:** Ski or snowboard this winter wonderland, or find summer adventures: mountain biking, zipline tours, an aerial park, an alpine slide, and scenic chairlift rides (page 281).

★ **Climb Mount Aeneas:** Hike the short trail up the highest peak in Jewel Basin. From the summit are views into the Great Bear Wilderness, down onto Flathead Lake, and north to Glacier (page 283).

★ **Go biking or hiking on the Whitefish Trail:** This extensive trail system is accessible from multiple trailheads outside Whitefish (page 284).

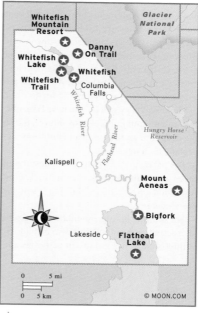

★ **Hike down Danny On Trail:** Ride a chairlift to the top of Big Mountain to hike down the most popular trail in the Flathead. It's a romp through mounds of wildflowers with panoramic views (page 286).

once pastoral farmlands. Housing developments sprout between towns, blending the borders of one with another. People who want to create another Aspen have thrown up multimillion-dollar mansions on the hillsides. But an underlying culture remains: Ripped Carhartts and a duct-taped jacket rank as fashion. Rather than hit the nine-to-five office hours, lots of folks work seasonally in Glacier National Park or Flathead National Forest and at ski areas.

When snow falls, logging roads and golf courses become ski and snowshoe trails, while two alpine ski areas rack up the vertical for skiers and snowboarders. Many in the valley adhere to the six-inch rule: If 6 inches (15 cm) or more of snow falls, call in late for work.

PLANNING YOUR TIME

Flathead Valley has four major towns. You can make a base camp in one town and still visit the others as they are 15-40 minutes apart. **Whitefish** is a year-round resort town while **Bigfork** is a summer resort town on Flathead Lake. **Columbia Falls,** which is the closest town to Glacier Park, and **Kalispell** are working towns. A minimum of **three days** in Flathead Valley will let you have lake, hiking, and mountain biking adventures, but to dig deep into recreation, plan **five days,** especially for winter.

For packing, don't bother with a suit and tie or fancy dinner dress, even in the priciest restaurants. Recreational clothing is suitable everywhere.

For summer hiking, mountain biking, and lake activities, head to Whitefish or Bigfork. Whitefish also has mountain activities and sightseeing at Whitefish Mountain Resort, plus winter sports. All four Flathead Valley towns have golf courses, although Whitefish has the most popular course in the state. To be closest to Glacier Park, Columbia Falls can be a home base.

Summer temperatures usually average 75-85°F (24-29°C) during days and around 50°F (10°C) at night. Winter temperatures average 29-40°F (-2 to -8°C) during days and 14-26°F (-10 to -3°C) at night. Hiking or skiing into higher elevations will encounter temperatures often 10-15°F (6-8°C) degrees cooler than towns in the valley. Snow falls November-April, and June sees the most rain.

HISTORY

Originally the home of the Flathead, Salish, and Kootenai people, the Flathead Valley saw its first person of European descent, the explorer David Thompson, in 1809. Within 40 years, trappers, homesteaders, and ranchers arrived. By the end of the 19th century, the Great Northern Railway had laid tracks through the Flathead, prompting Kalispell to be plotted for township to become the next St. Paul.

But in 1901, Great Northern Railway rerouted its tracks through Whitefish to access Canadian coal, transforming the tiny lakefront community into a railroad town. By the mid-1900s, the construction of the Hungry Horse dam spawned an aluminum plant and Whitefish Mountain Ski Resort. Today, while ranching, farming, and timber still support many families, some of the Flathead's 100,000 residents rely on technology industries and tourism.

Previous: Flathead Lake; gondola at Whitefish Mountain Resort; Danny On Trail in fall.

Flathead Valley

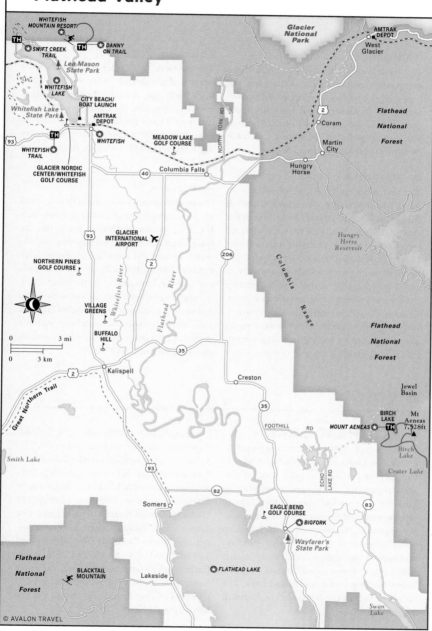

WHITEFISH MOUNTAIN RESORT
TH SWIFT CREEK TRAIL
TH DANNY ON TRAIL
Lee Mason State Park
WHITEFISH LAKE
Whitefish Lake State Park
CITY BEACH/ BOAT LAUNCH
AMTRAK DEPOT
93
WHITEFISH TRAIL
TH WHITEFISH
GLACIER NORDIC CENTER/WHITEFISH GOLF COURSE
MEADOW LAKE GOLF COURSE
NORTH FORK RD
Columbia Falls
40

Glacier National Park
AMTRAK DEPOT
West Glacier
2
Coram
Martin City
Hungry Horse
Flathead National Forest

GLACIER INTERNATIONAL AIRPORT
93
2
NORTHERN PINES GOLF COURSE
VILLAGE GREENS
BUFFALO HILL
Whitefish River
Flathead River
206
Hungry Horse Reservoir

Columbia Range

35
Kalispell
2
Great Northern Trail
Smith Lake
93

Flathead National Forest
Jewel Basin

Creston
35
FOOTHILL RD
MOUNT AENEAS
BIRCH LAKE
TH
Mt Aeneas 7,528ft
Birch Lake
Crater Lake

ECHO LAKE RD
82
Somers
EAGLE BEND GOLF COURSE
BIGFORK
Wayfarer's State Park
83

Flathead National Forest
BLACKTAIL MOUNTAIN
Lakeside
FLATHEAD LAKE
Swan Lake

0   3 mi
0   3 km

© AVALON TRAVEL

Exploring Flathead Valley

Kalispell

The nucleus of Flathead Valley, with three golf courses, restaurants, and shopping, the area's largest town has moved beyond its cowtown past. In historic downtown Kalispell, you can tour the pre-1900s Conrad Mansion and unique art spots. In August, catch the Northwest Montana Fair and Rodeo.

★ Whitefish

The year-round cultural and recreation capital of Flathead Valley, downtown Whitefish fits compactly into several blocks next to the Amtrak station. A railroad town transformed into a resort town, Whitefish boasts shops, boutiques, restaurants, bars, art galleries, and theaters. In the summer, downtown streets crowd with shopping tourists, especially during the Tuesday evening farmers market. In winter, its ski town heritage emerges in early February with the Winter Carnival. The town also serves as a springboard for boating, paddling, golfing, hiking, mountain biking, and skiing.

Columbia Falls

The gateway to Glacier, Columbia Falls never had a waterfall of its own until the town built one. A recent boom in restaurants has upgraded the quality of dining. In summer, it has a public outdoor swimming pool, Big Sky Waterpark, and a Thursday night farmers market with music, food, and family fun.

★ Bigfork

A summer resort town, Bigfork is a small yet charming cultural and recreation hub. Bigfork Summer Playhouse dominates the town, packing restaurants before nightly shows. Quaint gift shops and art galleries fill its several-block-long village, and its historic one-lane steel bridge crosses the Swan River. Recreation combines easy access to the Swan Mountains, golfing, and boating on Flathead Lake. In early June, the town hops with the Bigfork Whitewater Festival, when kayakers shoot the Swan's Wild Mile.

Sights

★ FLATHEAD LAKE

Stretching 28 miles (45 km) long and 15 miles (24 km) wide, **Flathead Lake** is the largest freshwater lake west of the Mississippi. Its 188 square miles (487 sq km), six state parks, islands, deep fishing waters, and wildlife refuges make it a summer play land. Highways circle the lake with public access at 13 different points. Paddlers and boaters can explore **Wild Horse Island State Park,** home to wild horses, bighorn sheep, and big views of Flathead Lake. The southern half of the lake is in the Flathead Nation Reservation.

From Bigfork, **Flathead Lake Sailing Charters** (150 Flathead Lake Lodge, 406/837-5569, www.flatheadlakesailing.com, 1pm, 3pm, and 6:30pm daily mid-June-Aug., $45-60) launch from Flathead Lake Lodge's dock for two-hour cruises. Two restored 1928-1929 Q-class sloops each carry 10 passengers. The sunset cruise includes beer, wine, and appetizers. From Lakeside, **Far West Boat Tours** (7135 U.S. 93 S., 406/844-2628, www.flatheadlakeboattour.com, late June-early Sept., 1pm daily, 7pm Sun.-Wed., $10-22) launches a cabin cruiser. Sit upstairs in the sun for bigger views.

★ WHITEFISH LAKE

Whitefish Lake buzzes in summer. Anglers hit the lake in early morning and evening, while midday is a frenzy of water-skiers, Jet Skiers, party barges, kayakers, and canoers. Swimmers cool off at Whitefish State Park, City Beach, and Les Mason State Park. In winter, when ice covers the lake, hockey players make their own rinks, and anglers ice fish.

FLATHEAD RIVER

In Hungry Horse, the South, Middle, and North Forks of the Flathead River converge. The **Flathead River** then snakes 55 miles (89 km) across the valley to Flathead Lake. Seven river access points allow anglers, canoers, and floaters to get onto its meandering pace through Columbia Falls and Kalispell. Toward Flathead Lake, the river takes several sharp S-turns in sloughs and estuaries, bird habitat for ospreys and waterfowl.

★ WHITEFISH MOUNTAIN RESORT

Whitefish Mountain Resort (end of Big Mountain Rd., 406/862-2900, www. skiwhitefish.com) is a two-season recreational resort. In winter (daily Dec.-early Apr.), skiers and snowboarders arc turns down all sides from Big Mountain's summit where snow ghosts, or ice-encrusted bent firs, compete with the view of Glacier National Park. Thirteen lifts access 105 named runs that see an average of 320 inches (762 cm) of snow per year.

During summer (10am-5:30pm daily mid-June-Labor Day and Fri.-Sun. early June and Sept.) the resort's **scenic lift rides** ($12-20) whisk riders via gondolas or open chairs to the summit of Big Mountain for views of Flathead Valley and Glacier National Park. You can eat lunch in the Summit House and visit the **US Forest Service Summit Nature Center** (10am-5pm daily mid-June-Labor Day, free)

for hands-on exhibits. Kids can do a Junior Ranger program, and families can check out Outdoor Adventure Packs for exploring. The **Danny On hiking trail** also connects with the summit; you can ride the lift one direction ($12) and hike the other. The lifts also access downhill and cross-country mountain bike trails.

Other summer activities take place out of the base lodge at the resort. **Zipline Tours** ($60-96) let you sail through the air 20-300 feet (6-91 m) above the ground on a six-line tour, with the AdrenaLine stretching the longest at 1,900 feet (579 m). The **Alpine Slide** ($10/ride) offers speed thrills sledding down two different tracks. Even little kids can ride with adults. For a physical challenge, tackle the **Aerial Adventure Park** ($32-60) to traverse bridges, cables, and ziplines suspended 10-50 feet (3-15 m) above the ground in courses of varied difficulty. Safety comes from being clipped in with a harness. Several activities target younger kids ($10-12): **Summer Tubing, Spider Monkey Mountain,** and **Strider Bike Park.** Several adventure packages include multiple activities with a discount on rates.

MUSEUMS

In Kalispell, the historic Victorian **Conrad Mansion** (330 Woodland Ave., 406/755-2166, www.conradmansion.com, by tour only, Wed.-Sun. mid-May-early June, Tues.-Sun. early June-mid-Oct., adults $15-18, kids $8-10) preserves 26 rooms with their original 1895 furniture, clothing, and toys. Drop in for docent-led tours that go on the hour 10am-4pm.

Also in Kalispell, the **Hockaday Museum of Art** (302 2nd Ave. E., 406/755-5268, www. hockadaymuseum.org, 10am-5pm Tues.-Sat., adults $2-5, kids free) features Montana pottery, jewelry, and paintings, particularly by Native American and Glacier National Park artists.

SIGHTS

FLATHEAD VALLEY

Flathead Valley Hikes

Trail	Effort	Distance	Duration
Mount Aeneas	moderate-strenuous	5.9-mi (9.5-km) loop	3-4 hr
Birch Lake	moderate	6 mi (9.7 km) rt	3 hr
Danny On Trail	moderate	4 mi (6.4 km) one-way	2 hr
Lion Mountain Trail	easy-moderate	3-mi (4.8-km) loop	1.5 hr
Swift Creek Trail	easy-moderate	1-5 mi (1.6-8 km) rt	1-3 hr

Recreation

DAY HIKES

Since Flathead National Forest surrounds Flathead Valley, hikers have no shortage of trails within spitting distance of the back porch. Dogs are welcome on most trails if they're on-leash.

Jewel Basin

In the Swan Mountains above Bigfork, **Jewel Basin** has 50 miles (81 km) of hiking trails. Accessible late June through October, depending on snow, the 15,349-acre (6,212-hectare) hiker-only area is called "the Jewel" for the 27 alpine fishing lakes that sparkle in its basins. Paths tromp across huckleberry meadows and high ridges with top-of-the-world views. Weekends crowd with cars at the Camp Misery Trailhead, which usually becomes snow-free in late June. Snow lingers on some trails into July. Trail signage is scanty, so take a good map, which are sold in local sports shops or contact **Flathead National Forest** (406/758-5208, www.fs.usda.gov/flathead) or **Swan Lake Ranger Station** (200 Ranger Station Rd., Bigfork, 406/837-7500).

★ MOUNT AENEAS

Distance: 5.9-mile (9.5-km) loop
Duration: 3-4 hours

Elevation gain: 1,779 feet (542 m)
Effort: moderate-strenuous
Trail surface: wide roadbed, then narrow dirt path with roots and loose rocks
Trailhead: Camp Misery trailhead in Jewel Basin

Mount Aeneas, at 7,528 feet (2,295 m), is the highest peak in the Jewel and offers big views for little work, but don't expect solitude at the summit. From the top, you'll see Flathead Lake, Glacier National Park, the Bob Marshall Wilderness Complex, and the Swan Mountains. It yields a lot of scenery for a short hike.

Combined with Picnic Lakes, the trail loops on a ridge and through a lake basin. Begin hiking up Trail 717, a wide roadbed. In 1.5 miles (2.4 km), the trail reaches a four-way junction. Stay on 717, heading uphill. After a few switchbacks, you'll pass an ugly microwave tower before waltzing with the mountain goats along an arête to the summit. From the summit, drop down through the Picnic Lakes Basin. At the lakes, take Trail 392, then turn right onto Trail 68 and left onto Trail 8. At 1.7 miles (2.7 km) from Camp Misery, Picnic Lakes makes a good little-kid destination; just reverse the route.

BIRCH LAKE

Distance: 6 miles (9.7 km) round-trip
Duration: 3 hours
Elevation gain: 800 feet (244 m)

1: scenic lift at Whitefish Mountain Resort
2: Whitefish's City Beach

Huckleberry Mania

The huckleberry is a small, dark-purple fruit about the size of the tip of your little finger. It resembles a blueberry but is much sweeter and more flavorful. It grows only in the wild on low deciduous bushes with leaves that turn red in fall. Growing mostly at elevations above 4,000 feet (1,219 m), the berries ripen late July-September.

The berry has yet to be successfully cultivated. In Flathead Valley, you'll find berry stands selling hucks that have been picked by commercial permit in national forests or on private lands. Expect to pay near $50 per gallon for the precious purple gems (now you know why huckleberry pie is so expensive). Be cautious when purchasing berries in early summer, as you may be buying frozen berries from last year rather than freshly picked ones. The frozen berries are still yummy but are a little softer when they thaw. Fresh ones start hitting the stands in late July.

You can pick your own huckleberries to eat; no permit is needed. You'll find them on many trails in Glacier National Park and Flathead National Forest. While locals don't usually divulge their prized secret stashes, you can usually find good huckleberry picking on Big Mountain at Whitefish Mountain Resort.

Two mammals crave the berries: bears and humans. High in vitamin C, the berries are healthy and low in fat. They enliven any pastry, pie, sauce, or fruit concoction. They're tasty in smoothies and delightful on pancakes.

You'll find huckleberries in everything from ice cream to beer; syrup, jam, and jelly top everyone's favorites. Hucks also flavor and scent chocolate, honey, cocoa, barbecue sauce, tea, salad dressing, ice cream toppings, a daiquiri mix, lotion, lip balm, bubble bath, shampoo, soap, and more.

One word of advice: Avoid using huckleberry shampoo before hiking in bear country.

Effort: moderate

Trail surface: narrow dirt path with roots and rocks

Trailhead: Camp Misery trailhead in Jewel Basin

A short hop over a ridge along with a skip down a trail puts hikers on the shore of Birch Lake, a great destination for kids. Swim in the lake's west end, but don't expect balmy waters. This clear snowmelt pond retains its chill even in August. For those with more gumption, another 2.5 miles (4 km) puts you on the boulder shoreline of Crater Lake.

Begin hiking up the broad roadway of Trail 717 to the four-way junction. Take the right fork onto Trail 7. The trail curves around the lower flanks of Mount Aeneas as it descends to Birch Lake; you'll have to hike up this on the way out. A trail circles the lake, but the best place to stop is on its clearly visible peninsula.

★ Whitefish Trail

With year-round hiking (use snowshoes or cleats in winter), the **Whitefish Trail** (www.whitefishlegacy.org) has more than 43 miles (69 km) of paths and 14 trailheads.

The multiuse trails allow hikers, mountain bikers, equestrians, snowshoers, and skiers. Download maps and get directions to trailheads online.

LION MOUNTAIN TRAIL

Distance: 3-mile (4.8-km) loop

Duration: 1.5 hours

Elevation gain: 260 feet (79 m)

Effort: easy-moderate

Trail surface: narrow dirt path with roots and rocks

Trailhead: Lion Mountain Trailhead of the Whitefish Trail

Directions: Take U.S. 93 North from downtown Whitefish for 2.2 miles (3.5 km) and turn right on Lion Mountain Loop Road to reach the trailhead on the left. This short, logged forest loop ambles up gentle grades. The route starts with an ultra-short loop perfect for families with small kids. From the top of the family loop, continue straight ahead for the ascent up throughs several

1: larch trees in fall on Whitefish Trail **2:** hiker on Danny On Trail

DANNY ON MEMORIAL TR. NO. 370 1/2
⤆ EAST RIM LOOP 4
⤆ VILLAGE SHORT ROUTE
VILLAGE VIA FLOWER POINT 6

basins to a signed four-way junction at the top. Turn right for the short summit loop to overlook Skyles Lake and return to the junction. From the junction, the trail heading south drops for the return loop on an old road to the family loop. From the four-way junction, the Whitefish Trail also continues northwest to several other trailheads.

SWIFT CREEK TRAIL

Distance: 1-5 miles (1.6-8 km) round-trip
Duration: 1-3 hours
Elevation gain: 260 feet (79 m)
Effort: easy-moderate
Trailhead: Swift Creek trailhead of the Whitefish Trail
Trail surface: wide, packed gravel and dirt surface to Swift Creek, then narrow, dirt, roots, and rocks
Directions: From Whitefish, drive Wisconsin Avenue and East Lakeshore Drive for 8.3 mile (13.4 km) around the north side of Whitefish Lake to the trailhead on the right.

From the trailhead, walk about 100 yards (91 m) to a three-way junction. From this point, an ADA-accessible pebble trail goes left through a beautiful old growth forest to a scenic overlook of Swift Creek. Those wanting to stay on the accessible trail should return the way they came. From near the overlook, a dirt trail with roots and rocks continues northward through the forest to a second three-way junction. Turn left for a short descent before the trail climbs to a plateau, circles through a logged zone, crosses a gravel road, and climbs steeply up several switchbacks. At the top, the trail undulates up and down across ridges until cruising around the south side above Smith Lake to the Smith Lake Trailhead. Return the way you came, and veer left at both three-way junctions to complete a loop.

★ Danny On Trail

Distance: 4 miles (6.4 km) one-way
Duration: 2 hours
Elevation gain: 2,400 feet (732 m)
Effort: moderate
Trailhead: Whitefish Mountain Resort
Trail surface: narrow dirt path with roots and rocks

Directions: Drive 7 miles (11.3 km) north of Whitefish, following signs.

The Danny On Trail hosts over 14,000 hikers annually. At Big Mountain's summit, the US Forest Service Summit Nature Center provides interpretive resources for the trail. Catch the chairlift up to hike down or hike up and then ride down (daily mid-June-Labor Day, Fri.-Sun. Sept., $8 pp one-way). While you can hike with a leashed pooch, dogs may not ride up or down the chairlift. Even without the chair ride, you can hike this trail through October.

After beginning in Whitefish Mountain Resort Village, the hiker-only trail switchbacks up through a forested slope and crosses ski runs as it sweeps around the mountain. Snow hangs in the upper back slopes through June; valerian and penstemon bloom in July; huckleberries scent the air in August. Junctions are marked: Stay left at both to go directly to the top. You can also loop through Flower Point for a 5.6-mile (9-km) hike. At the East Rim junction, turn left for a gentle, scenic loop before the final steep ascent. Panoramas at the top span Glacier National Park to Flathead Lake.

BIKING

Oodles of two-lane highways and paved country lanes make long loops around Flathead Lake or short farmland tours for roadies, and there are many single-track and dirt-road choices for mountain bikers. For the best list of itineraries to suit your interests and abilities, check **Glacier Cyclery's website** (www.glaciercyclery.com) for popular area routes: paved roads, dirt roads, and single-track. The shop also maintains a ride board with recent trail updates.

Around Whitefish, the expanding **Whitefish Trail** (www.whitefishlegacy.org) at more than 43 miles (69 km) provides a curvy, multiuse dirt single-track trail with fun terrain for mountain bikers. Current maps to its 14 trailheads can be found online. Most routes are cross-country trails; find the downhill thrills at Spencer Mountain trailhead. For single-track lift-served mountain biking, **Whitefish Mountain Resort** (end of Big Mountain Rd., Whitefish, 406/862-2900, www.skiwhitefish.com, 10am-5:30pm daily mid-June-Labor Day and Fri.-Sun. Sept., $25-41 depending on age and duration) hauls bikes and riders up two chairlifts. Twenty-two downhill routes descend the mountain in three zones for different abilities. Lower-mountain trails allow for skill building, while the Kashmir Flow Trail and cross-country trails work for intermediates. Steep, hair-raising downhill descents with natural obstacles cater to advanced riders. The resort rents bikes ($36-85) and downhill protective gear ($33). Learn to downhill in beginner programs (daily 11am and 2pm, $114, including rental gear).

In Kalispell, the **Great Northern Historical Trail** (www.railstotrailsofnwmt. com) runs 12 miles (19.3 km) of paved bike trail from Meridian Street to Smith Lake in Kila. Another 12-mile (19.3-km) segment links Meridian with Somers for those who want to enjoy Flathead Lake. Find trailhead parking for both at Meridian Road and Derns Road. Maps are online.

Rentals and Repairs

Flathead Valley also has multiple bike shops that rent, sell, and repair bikes. Bike rentals usually run $45-75 per day, including helmets. Weekly rates are available, too. In Whitefish, **Glacier Cyclery** (326 E. 2nd St., 406/862-6446, www.glaciercyclery.com) rents touring bikes, roadies, hybrids, mountain bikes, fat bikes, e-bikes, plus car racks, utility trailers, and Burleys. In Kalispell, closest to the rail trails, **Sportsman** (145 Hutton Ranch Rd., 406/755-6484, www.sportsmanskihaus. com) rents mountain and road bikes. In Bigfork, rent mountain bikes at **Base Camp Bigfork** (8525 MT 35, 406/871-9733, www. basecampbigfork.com).

Whitefish Shuttle (406/212-0800, www. whitefishshuttle.com) runs bike shuttles to the Whitefish Trail trailheads, hotels, or up to Lake McDonald Lodge or Avalanche during spring biking season on Going-to-the-Sun Road in Glacier. They also guide bike tours. Call for rates and schedules.

Mountain Bike Center

Tucked in the woods north of Whitefish, the **Whitefish Bike Retreat** (855 Beaver Lake Rd., 406/260-0274, www.whitefishbikeretreat.

mountain biker at Whitefish Mountain Resort

com, year-round) is a unique trailside biker haven operated by Cricket Butler, a Great Divide record holder. Day passes ($10) access the skills park, flow and berm trails, pump track, disc golf, and two bike-washing stations. Trails connect to the Whitefish Trail system near the Beaver Lake trailhead. The camp store rents bikes ($35-55) and paddleboards ($35-55). It also sells snacks and bike packing supplies. Lodging is in the large bunkhouse with repurposed bicycle parts as fixtures and railings. It has private rooms ($120-175) or shared bunkrooms ($55 pp), a large furnished kitchen, shared bathrooms with showers, an outdoor patio with fire pit, laundry, sauna, and a workroom and secure storage for bikes. Campsites ($50) have picnic tables, bear-resistant food storage, a dishwashing station, flush toilets, and showers. Summer shuttles run to Glacier Cyclery (several times daily, free) or other destinations (fees vary).

HORSEBACK RIDING

Hop in the saddle for horseback adventures. In Whitefish, **The Bar W** (Flathead Lake Lodge Rd., 406/863-9099, www.thebarw.com, summer, $50-110) leads one-, two-, and four-hour trail rides. Kids under seven can get a cowpoke ride ($35). Make reservations up to seven days in advance for weekends and select weekdays.

WATER SPORTS
Boating
Popular boating lakes dot Flathead Valley. The two largest are Flathead and Whitefish Lakes. Both have several launch sites, and rentals are available at marinas. Before launching private boats, boats must pass inspections for aquatic invasive species. Whitefish also has a decontamination station, if you need to clean your boat before an inspection. For rentals, expect to pay hourly rates at $90 for Jet Skis and $125-160 for water-ski boats, pontoon fishing boats, and party barges. In addition to your rental fee, you'll need to pay for the gas you use. Hand-propelled craft like canoes, kayaks,

paddleboards, and rowboats rent for $25-40 per hour. Most launch sites charge $5-10 for launching private boats.

For launching boats on Whitefish Lake, find public ramps at **Whitefish Lake State Park** and **City Beach.** For rentals, mooring, and fuel service, go to **Whitefish Lake Lodge Marina** (1390 Wisconsin Ave., 406/863-4020, mid-May-Sept.).

On Flathead Lake's north end, Bigfork, Somers, and Lakeside serve boaters with boat launches open May-October. The lake also has 13 public access points, six of which are state parks maintained by **Montana Fish, Wildlife, and Parks** (stateparks.mt.gov). Find boat rentals at **Wild Wave** (130 Bills Rd., Lakeside, 406/844-2400 and 180 Vista Ln., Bigfork, 406/837-4843, www.wildwaverentals.com) and **Marina Cay** (180 Vista Lane, Bigfork, 406/837-5861, https://marinacay.com).

Waterskiing
Most vacationers don't come to the Flathead solely for waterskiing since glacial-fed lakes are downright cold. Wetsuits are advised for those used to warm water Whitefish Lake and Flathead Lake offer water-skiing. The marinas rent water skis and wakeboards ($25-50/hour); boats and gas are extra.

Paddling and Rafting
Sea kayakers, canoers, and paddleboarders have multiple places to launch. **Flathead** and **Whitefish Lakes** provide flat water, although Flathead can kick up with big winds. The most popular Flathead Lake paddling destination is **Wild Horse Island,** launching from the public beach in Dayton. Ambling portions of the **Flathead, Whitefish,** and **Swan Rivers** also flow slowly enough for flat-water paddling and adept paddleboarders.

White-water kayakers wearing dry suits gravitate to the freezing cold water of the Swan River outside Bigfork. For Class IV-V rapids, the **Swan River Wild Mile,** a short 1.25-mile (2-km) stretch that drops 100 feet (30.5 m) below Bigfork Dam, sees its best

Clean Your Boat

Montana has some of the last invasive-free water in the country, and the state is trying to keep it that way. If you are bringing motorized or nonmotorized boats into Montana, you'll need to pass an aquatic invasive species (AIS) inspection. This applies to all boats, including canoes, kayaks, paddleboards, and rafts. For full details, go to http://cleandraindry.mt.gov.

BEFORE LEAVING HOME OR ARRIVING:

- Wash and clean every surface of your boat, trailer, and gear to remove all mud, vegetation, and water.
- Drain all boats, water holds, and equipment.
- Dry all surfaces, boats, and equipment. (This can take time; plan ahead.)

INSPECTION STATIONS:

- Find these along highways and at lakes, usually signed as "watercraft inspection."
- You are required to stop at open inspection stations (daily, summer). Consult the online list of all watercraft inspection sites in Montana.
- Some Flathead Valley lakes have inspection stations (daily, summer) at launch sites. Both launches at Whitefish Lake have inspection stations: **City Beach** (6am-10pm, shorter hours May and Sept.) and **Whitefish Lake State Park** (7am-10pm).
- Whitefish has a free decontamination station (Don K Chevrolet lot, corner of U.S. 93 and JP Rd.) if you need to clean your boat before an inspection.

water May-July, especially Wednesday nights when the dam releases flows.

Rentals usually run $25-65 per day. Life jackets and paddles are included in the rates. Find them at marinas on Whitefish and Flathead Lakes. In addition, **Sportsman** (145 Hutton Ranch Rd., Kalispell, 406/755-6484; Mountain Mall, Whitefish, 406/862-3111, www.sportsmanskihaus.com) rents canoes, kayaks, tandem kayaks, and paddleboards. In Bigfork, rent canoes, single and tandem kayaks, and paddleboards from **Base Camp Bigfork** (8525 MT 35, 406/871-9733, www.basecampbigfork.com). **Marina Cay** (180 Vista Lane, Bigfork, 406/837-5861, https://marinacay.com) also has canoes and paddleboards. In Whitefish, rent paddleboards from **Paddlefish Sports** (105 Wisconsin Ave., 406/260-7733, www.whitefishpaddleboards.com). You can also rent at Whitefish Lake State Park and Les Mason Park on Whitefish Lake.

For floating the Flathead River, **Cloud 9 River Rentals** (350 U.S. 2 E., Columbia Falls, 406/871-8001, https://cloud9riverrentals.com) rents river rafts, fishing pontoons, kayaks, and paddleboards.

Fishing

Lakes, estuaries, and rivers abound for fishing in Flathead Valley. Because of dam control and cold glacial water, do not expect blue-ribbon trout fishing. The **Flathead River,** a giant highway for migrating fish, carries many nonnative species, especially northern pike lurking in larger southern sloughs. Seven river access points offer places to fish or launch boats downstream: Blankenship Bridge, the U.S. 2 bridge at Hungry Horse, a spur road at Bad Rock Canyon's west end, Kokanee Bend, Pressentine Bar, the Old Steel Bridge, and the Stillwater mouth. Most anglers hit the stretch between Columbia Falls and the Old Steel Bridge in Kalispell. **Flathead Lake** teems with cutthroat, giant trophy lake trout, mountain and lake whitefish, largemouth bass, bull trout, and yellow perch. It's good for all types of fishing: bait, lure, fly-fishing, and trolling. Montana fishing licenses are only valid on the north half of the lake due to the Flathead Reservation on the south end. **Whitefish Lake** draws anglers for its lake trout and whitefish. During winter, some anglers ice fish. Northern pike, lake trout, and kokanee are common, and it is regularly stocked with westslope cutthroat trout.

Montana fishing licenses (fwp.mt.gov, Montana residents: $17-31 season, $11-15 for 2 days; nonresidents: $43 for 2 days, $74 for 10 days, $104 season) are required for ages 12 through adults. Purchase them at fly shops, outdoor gear stores, and online.

FLY SHOPS AND GUIDES

Hit up fly-fishing shops in the Flathead for locally made, hand-tied flies and tackle as well as advice on where the fish are biting. Guided fishing trips usually run $450-550 for two people for a full day; add on a 15-20 percent tip. Rates do not include Montana fishing licenses. **Lakestream Fly Shop** (669 Spokane Ave., Whitefish, 406/862-1298, www.lakestream.com) guides fly-fishing trips on the main Flathead River plus all three tributaries and a private lake. For guided fishing on the Swan or Flathead Rivers, head to **Bigfork Anglers** (405 Bridge St., Bigfork, 406/837-3675, http://bigforkanglers.com).

CHARTER FISHING

Charter fishing services on Flathead Lake operate June-September. **Howe's Fishing** (Marina Cay, Bigfork, 406/257-5214, www.howesfishing.com, $400-800 for 4-6 people) launches fishing trips by reservation.

Swimming

Find beaches with buoyed swimming zones at six Flathead Valley **state parks** (stateparks.mt.gov, Montana residents free, $8/vehicle for nonresidents). The best state park swimming

beach is at the north end of **Flathead Lake** at **Wayfarers** (8600 MT 35, mid-Mar.-mid Nov.). **Whitefish Lake** has two state parks with swimming: **Les Mason** (2650 E. Lakeshore Dr., Apr.-Nov., summer rentals: paddleboards, kayaks, canoes) and **Whitefish Lake** (1615 W. Lakeshore, year-round). **City Beach** on Whitefish Lake (406/863-2475, free) is a kid favorite due to sand imported decades ago. These beaches are swim at your own risk; no lifeguards are on duty.

Two seasonal **outdoor pools** (mid-June-late Aug., $1-8 pp) attract families. The **Pinewood Family Aquatic Center** (925 4th Ave. W., Columbia Falls, 406/892-3500, Mon.-Sat.) has a bromine 25-meter pool and kids' play pool. In Kalispell, **Woodland Park** (Woodland Park Dr. and Shady Glen Dr., 406/758-7718, daily June-Aug.) has two water slides, a lap pool, a floating stream, and kiddie pool.

Big Sky Waterpark (7211 U.S. 2 E., Columbia Falls, 406/892-5025, www.bigskywp.com, 11am-7pm daily mid-June-Labor Day, $22-27) is a great place to take the kids to unwind after a hot day and a long drive. The park has 10 big and little slides along with a wading pool, hot pool, mini golf, and bumper cars. After 3pm, rates drop.

Flathead Valley has two large physical-fitness complexes that include weights, cardio machines, indoor swimming pools, and hot tubs. Drop-in rates are available per day: adults $10-15, children $5-12. **The Summit** (205 Sunnyview Ln., Kalispell, 406/751-4100, www.krh.org/summit) also has a climbing wall. **The Wave** (1250 Baker Ave., Whitefish, 406/862-2444, www.whitefishwave.com) has a fun kids' pool with a slide and a water fountain.

HUNTING

With Flathead Valley surrounded by Flathead National Forest, it is popular for hunting big game and birds. Get hunting regulations, seasons, and license info from **Montana Fish, Wildlife, and Parks** (406/752-5501, www.fwp.mt.gov).

GOLF

Golf Digest rated Flathead Valley one of the world's 50 greatest golf destinations. The recognition is due to the scenery, reasonable prices, and championship courses. With daylight lasting 16 hours in June, courses are open dawn-dusk, adjusting tee times as daylight hours wane. Depending on snow, most courses are open April-October. All of the Flathead courses have rentals, pro shops, instruction, driving ranges, restaurants, and lounges.

Flathead Valley summer greens fees run $57-115 for 18 holes, but you can get cheaper greens fees in spring, fall, daily after 3pm, and for only 9 holes. Club rentals for 18 holes range $16-70 and carts $20-40.

Courses

With the highest greens fees, **Eagle Bend Golf Course** (279 Eagle Bend Dr., Bigfork, 406/837-7310 or 844/780-9945, https://eaglebendgolfclub.com) is ranked among the top 50 public courses in the country. The challenging 27-hole course is a Jack Nicklaus design with big variety in its fairway layouts. From different tees, you can see Flathead Lake, the Swan Mountains, and Glacier National Park. The clubhouse burned down in 2019, but they have temporary facilities while they rebuild.

Four courses offer summer greens fees in the $60-75 range. The city-owned **Whitefish Lake Golf Course** (1200 U.S. 93 N., Whitefish, 406/862-4000, https://golfwhitefish.com) is Montana's only 36-hole course and has the most rounds played in the state. The north course tours through large cedars and firs; the south course runs past Lost Loon Lake. Both have mountain views. **Meadow Lake Golf Course** (490 St. Andrews Dr., Columbia Falls, 406/892-2111, www.meadowlakegolf.com) has 18 holes among woods, with some tight fairways and lots of adjacent houses. A couple of ponds and a creek separate the fairways, and some trees shade the course. **Northern Pines Golf Club** (3230 U.S. 93 N., Kalispell, 406/751-1950, https://northernpinesgolfclub.com) is a Scottish links-style course. Since its 18 holes sit mid-valley, with few trees, views open up to Big Mountain and Glacier National Park. The Stillwater River runs adjacent to the back nine. **Buffalo Hill** (1176 N. Main St., Kalispell, 406/756-4530 or 888/342-6319, www.golfbuffalohill.com) combines an older course with a newer course for 27 holes. The older Cameron Nine abuts the highway; the newer 18-hole course is moderately difficult with a lot of terrain variety.

With the least expensive greens fees, **Village Greens** (500 Palmer Dr., Kalispell, 406/752-4666, https://montanagolf.com) surrounds its bent-grass greens with a few trees, ponds, and houses. The 18 holes afford a pleasant place to play on one of the easier courses.

WINTER SPORTS
Downhill Skiing

Located 7 miles (11.3 km) north of Whitefish, **Whitefish Mountain Resort** (end of Big Mountain Rd., 406/862-2900, www.skiwhitefish.com, early Dec.-early Apr., $42-83, discounts for online advance purchase and beginner lifts) lives up to its former name of Big Mountain with 3,000 acres (1,214 hectares) of skiing terrain, 2,353 feet (717 m) of vertical drop, 12 lifts plus a carpet, 4 terrain parks, and more than 105 named runs. Big bowls, glades, and long cruisers head off the summit in every direction, and views from the summit on sunny days yield the entire panorama of Glacier's peaks. You can even find good tree skiing in the mountain's famous fog. The resort's village contains restaurants, shops, rental gear, a ski school, day care, and lodging from economy to upscale.

Sitting above Flathead Lake, **Blacktail Mountain** (end of Blacktail Mountain Rd., Lakeside, 406/844-0999, www.blacktailmountain.com, Wed.-Sun. and holidays mid-Dec.-early Apr., $22-45, discounts for half day) attracts families for its smaller 1,000 acres (405 hectares), four lifts, and family-friendly pricing.

Cross-Country Skiing

Several small cross-country ski areas dot Flathead Valley, with trails groomed for classic and skate skiing mid-December-early March. **Glacier Nordic Center** (1200 U.S. 93, 406/862-9498, www.glaciernordicclub. com, shop 9:30am-5:30pm daily, $6-12 trail fee, $10-25 rentals, $35 lessons) grooms 7.5 miles (12 km) on Whitefish Lake Golf Course and 14.3 miles (23 km) at the Big Mountain trailhead. The club's website has grooming updates and information on other Flathead Valley ski trails, such as Round Meadows, Herron Park, Blacktail, and Bigfork. Additional ski rental shops include **Sportsman** (145 Hutton Ranch Rd., Kalispell, 406/755-6484, and Mountain Mall, Whitefish, 406/862-3111, www. sportsmanskihaus.com) and **Glacier Cyclery and Nordic** (326 E. 2nd St., Whitefish, 406/862-6446, www.glaciercyclery.com).

Snowmobiling

Flathead Valley is surrounded by 200 miles (320 km) of groomed snowmobile trails open December-mid-April (some trails close Apr. 1). **Flathead Valley Snowmobile Association** (www.flatheadsnowmobiler. com) maintains the grooming on nine popular trails near Whitefish, Columbia Falls, and Bigfork. For those striking out on their own, check conditions with **Flathead Avalanche Center** (406/257-8402, www. flatheadavalanche.org). Rentals and guides are available through **Swan Mountain Snowmobiling** (406/387-4405 or 877/888-5557, www.glaciersnowmobile.com) and **J & L Rentals** (7356 U.S. 2 E., Columbia Falls, 406/890-9431, www.jandlsnowmobile.com).

SPAS

Flathead Valley has no shortage of day spas, but the best one is on Whitefish Lake, where you can enjoy other amenities before or after your visit. In an upscale setting, the **Spa at Whitefish Lake** (1380 Wisconsin Ave., 406/863-4050, www.lodgeatwhitefishlake. com) offers facials, waxing, massage, scrubs, wraps, manicures, pedicures, and hot river stone therapy.

Entertainment and Shopping

ENTERTAINMENT

In Bigfork, the **Bigfork Summer Playhouse** (526 Electric Ave., 406/837-4886, www. bigforksummerplayhouse.com, mid-May-Aug.) presents five shows in repertory during each summer, from Broadway musical favorites to comedies. In Whitefish, **Whitefish Theatre Company** (1 Central Ave., 406/862-5371, www.whitefishtheatreco. org) sponsors plays, concerts, speakers, and art films year-round in the O'Shaughnessy Center. Broadway veterans formed the acclaimed **Alpine Theatre Project** (Whitefish, 406/862-7469, www.atpwhitefish.org), which has summer productions at Whitefish Performing Arts Center (600 E. 2nd St.). Beloved musicals, classic comedies, and plays highlight its summer schedule, with actors imported from Broadway.

EVENTS

Attracting hundreds of spectators even in soggy weather, the **Bigfork Whitewater Festival** (www.bigforkwhitewaterfestival. com) runs kayakers down the Class IV Wild Mile of the Swan River at the peak of spring runoff. Traditionally held over Memorial Day weekend, competitions run from slalom to boater-cross with hordes of onlookers lining the riverbanks. Local pubs and restaurants party with nightly entertainment. In August, the annual seven-day **Festival**

1: Whitefish Lake Golf Course **2:** Whitefish Mountain Resort **3:** cross-country skiers at Glacier Nordic Center

Take Montana Home

Want local souvenirs to take home? Look for the blue "Made in Montana" logo. Only arts, crafts, food, and other products made by Montana residents and grown or produced within the state can use the label. More than 2,600 businesses, including single-item production, use the distinctive marker.

Find the "Made in Montana" logo on foods like coffee, jams and jellies, preserves, teas, pasta, salad dressings, barbecue sauces, herbs, cheese, jerky, and cookies. There are also personal health-care products ranging from soaps and shampoos to lotions and oils. Toys, games, pet goodies, furniture, and clothing also may sport the logo, as can arts and crafts like photography, music, lithographs, paintings, candles, and more.

For a Made in Montana product fix after you get home, check https://madeinmontanausa.com for companies that sell Made in Montana products online.

While in Montana, look for two other labels that identify Montana-made. The "Grown in Montana" label is used on fresh produce, eggs, honey, meats, grains, and other products. The "Native American Made in Montana" includes handicrafts, jewelry, art, beadwork, and apparel made by Indigenous people on one of Montana's reservations.

Amadeus (https://glaciersymphony.org) celebrates Mozart's music with guest artists, chamber concerts, and orchestra productions, with nightly performances in Whitefish at the Whitefish Performing Arts Center (600 2nd St.) or O'Shaughnessy Center (1 Central Ave.).

In the doldrums of winter, Whitefish celebrates its wacky **Winter Carnival** (406/862-3501, https://whitefishwintercarnival.com), a three-day spree of ski races, ice hockey, the penguin plunge, figure skating, a torchlight parade, fireworks, and skijoring, held the first weekend in February. Hundreds of people line the few blocks of downtown Whitefish for an old-fashioned "drive the old tractor down main street" parade disrupted by raucous yetis and Viking women kissing onlookers.

Art and cultural events abound in the Flathead. Whitefish hosts its **Gallery Nights** (https://whitefishgallerynights.org) on the first Thursday of each month May-October. Whitefish (www.whitefishchamber.org) also sponsors the **Huckleberry Days Arts Festival** (Depot Park, mid-Aug., three days), **Oktoberfest** (Depot Park, late Sept-early Oct., two weekends), **Feast of Whitefish** (varied venues, mid-May, 5 days), and the **Christmas Stroll** (downtown, early Dec., one evening). Kalispell celebrates its three-day **Arts in the Park** (www.hockadaymuseum.org) in mid-July in Depot Park. The **Bigfork**

Festival of the Arts (https://bigfork.org, 2 days) takes place in early August on the town's main street.

Two farmers markets (5pm-7:30pm weekly late May-late Sept.) have grown into outdoor affairs with fresh local produce and food truck vendors. On Tuesdays, find the **Whitefish Farmers Market** (https://whitefishfarmersmarket.org) in Depot Park and Main Street in front of O'Shaughnessy Center with music and craft stalls. On Thursdays, the outdoor venue at O'Brien's Liquor Store hosts the **Columbia Falls Community Market** (830 1st Ave. W., www.cfcommunitymarket.com) with bands, dancing, a beer garden, and kids' attractions such as a climbing wall and bungee jump. On Saturday mornings, the more traditional **Kalispell Farmer's Market** (777 Grandview Dr., kalispellfarmersmarket.org, 9am-12:30pm early May-mid-Oct.), which has local produce and crafts, takes place at the Flathead Valley Community College.

RODEOS AND FAIRS

Located mid-valley between Whitefish and Kalispell, **Majestic Valley Arena** (3630 U.S. 93 N., 406/755-5366, https://majesticvalleyarena.com) is the hub for events: concerts, rodeos, equestrian competitions, and shows. For cowpoke wannabes, the annual five-day **Northwest Montana Fair** opens in mid-August at the Flathead County Fairgrounds (265 N. Meridian, Kalispell, 406/758-5810, nwmtfair.com) with exhibits, rides, and rodeos.

CASINOS AND BARS

While gambling is legal in Montana, casinos haven't rocketed to Las Vegas style. Most Flathead bars have a few slot machines squirreled away in a corner; some even run a card table or two.

The best place for anything approximating nightclubbing is old-fashioned bar hopping in downtown Whitefish. Friday and Saturday nights usually feature dancing and live bands at **Great Northern** (27 Central Ave., 406/862-2816, https://greatnorthernbar.com), **Casey's Bar** (101 Central Ave., 406/862-8150, www.caseyswhitefish.com), and **The Craggy Range Bar & Grill** (10 Central Ave., 406/862-7550, www.thecraggyrange.com).

SHOPPING

While Flathead Valley thankfully has no Mall of America clone or factory outlet mall, it does have its share of strip malls and chain stores, mostly located on U.S. 93 north of Kalispell. Bigfork, Kalispell, and Whitefish each have a few blocks of gifts shops and art galleries.

With shops in Kalispell and Whitefish, stop in **Imagination Station** (221 Central Ave., Whitefish, 406/862-5668, and 132 Main St., Kalispell, 406/755-5668, https://montanatoys.com, 9:30am-6pm Mon.-Sat., 11am-5pm Sun.) for classy, inventive, classic, and educational toys. The store will even ship your toys home for you so you don't have to haul everything on the airplane. Pick up handmade soaps at **Sage and Cedar** (214 Central Ave., Whitefish, 406/862-9411, and 227 Main St., Kalispell, 406/890-2299, www.sageandcedar.com, 10am-5pm Mon.-Sat.), including huckleberry-scented products.

In Kalispell, visit **Sassafras** (120 Main St., 406/752-2433, www.sassafrasartcoop.com, 10am-5:30pm Mon.-Sat.), an artists and antiques co-op, featuring the works of 30-40 local northwest Montana artists. Pieces range from watercolors and cards to pottery, jewelry, clothing, furniture, and sculptures.

In Whitefish, browse Central Avenue for most shops. But then go to the **Nancy Cawdrey Studio and Gallery** (204 Wisconsin Ave., 406/755-2727, https://nancycawdrey.com, 10am-6pm Tues.-Sat., noon-6pm Sun.) for her colorful Montana wildlife art.

Outdoor Gear, Maps, and Guidebooks

For outdoor gear for camping, backpacking, skiing, snowboarding, and fishing gear, several shops carry good brand-name selections and know how to fit equipment to individual people. **Rocky Mountain Outfitter** (135 Main St., Kalispell, 406/752-2446, https://rockymountainoutfitter.com, 9:30am-6pm Mon.-Fri., 9am-5:30pm Sat.) specializes in hiking, backpacking, climbing, and skiing. **REI** (2270 U.S. 93 N., Kalispell, 406/755-4839, www.rei.com, 9am-8pm Mon.-Sat., 10am-6pm Sun.) carries hiking and backpacking gear. Both of these shops also sell maps and outdoor books.

With two stores, **Sportsman** (145 Hutton Ranch Rd., Kalispell, 406/755-6484, 9am-9pm Mon.-Sat., 10am-6pm Sun.; 6475 U.S. 93, Whitefish, 406/862-3111, 9am-8pm Mon.-Sat., 10am-5pm Sun.; www.sportsmanskihaus.com) carries gear and clothing for skiers, snowboarders, hikers, backpackers, anglers, hunters, campers, tennis players, and cyclists. They also sell maps and a few outdoor books. In two locations, **Stumptown Snowboards** (128 Central Ave., Whitefish, 406/862-0955, https://stumptownsnowboards.com) are the local experts in snowboarding and skateboarding, with full equipment and clothing lines.

Books

You can find guidebooks and books on natural history, Lewis and Clark, Montana history, and field guides for flowers, birds, and animals at **Bookworks** (244 Spokane Ave., Whitefish, 406/862-4980, 10am-6pm daily).

Whitefish Food, Lodging, and Camping

Bustling with summer lake fun and winter skiing, Whitefish is a resort town loaded with lodging and restaurants. It sits 15-20 minutes west of Glacier Park International Airport (on U.S. 2) and 45 minutes west of Glacier National Park. It garners the most visitors in the Flathead. Expect to see 3 percent tax added on to restaurant bills and 10 percent onto lodging and camping.

FOOD

As a resort town, Whitefish is overloaded with outstanding restaurants. Because of the crowds, make reservations to avoid long waits in summer or winter. In spring and fall, a few restaurants alter their hours.

Cafés

Zucca Marketplace Bistro (Stumptown Marketplace, 12 Spokane Ave., 406/862-4646, www.zuccamarketplacebistro.com, 8am-4pm Mon.-Sat., $9-12) has attracted a loyal clientele due to its fresh organic paninis, wraps, and salads with a Mediterranean flair. With the appeal of a classic patisserie, **Fleur** (103 Central Ave., 406/730-8486, www.fleurbakeshop.com, 7am-4pm Sun.-Wed., 7am-4pm and 5pm-9pm Thurs.-Sat.) you can have an espresso with fresh breads, French pastries, desserts, and small plates.

Two local faves have broad menus, beer, and wine. You might have to arm wrestle a local's claim to a daily seat at **The Buffalo Café** (514 3rd St. E., 406/862-2833, https://buffalocafewhitefish.com, 7am-2pm and 5pm-9pm Mon.-Sat., 8am-2pm Sun., $6-18). Start the day with Buffalo Pie—hash browns piled with eggs and goodies. Finish the day with fish tacos or bison meatloaf. **Loula's Café** (300 2nd St. E., 406/862-5614, www.whitefishrestaurant.com, 7am-3pm Sun.-Mon., 7am-3pm and 5pm-9:30pm Tues.-Sat., $6-13) starts the day with lemon-stuffed french toast followed by fresh salads or sandwiches. Top your meal with one of Mary Lou and Laura's trademark fresh-baked fruit pies, or buy one to go.

Whitefish has no shortage of coffee shops. **Montana Coffee Traders' Whitefish Coffeehouse** (110 Central Ave., 406/862-7667, www.coffeetraders.com, 7am-6pm Mon.-Sat., 8am-4pm Sun.) offers pastries and desserts as well as *bocadillos* (Spanish sandwiches), in addition to espresso. **Wild Coffee Company** (309 Central Ave., 406-730-2833, www.wildcoffeecompanymt.com, 6:30am-9pm) serves topped toasts, stuffed biscuits, and sandwich melts.

Pubs and Bars

Whitefish is the party town. For cheap burgers and beers, head to the **Bulldog Saloon** (144 Central Ave., 406/862-5636), but be warned: some bathroom stalls are decorated with X-rated pics. The downtown bar-hopping scene heats up with locals dropping in after work, dining, and dancing to weekend bands at **Great Northern** (27 Central Ave., 406/862-2816, https://greatnorthernbar.com). **Casey's Bar** (101 Central Ave., 406/862-8150, www.caseyswhitefish.com) mixes together the works on multiple stories: a restaurant, bar, casino, dance hall, and summer rooftop dining for the best view in downtown Whitefish. With outside seating in summer, **The Craggy Range Bar & Grill** (10 Central Ave., 406/862-7550, www.thecraggyrange.com) added a frost bar to the lounge and has live music. Outside downtown, **Montana Tap House** (845 Wisconsin Ave., 406/862-6006, montanatap.com) has 58 taps pumping out mostly Montana beers, but also Pacific Northwest brews, wine, and specialty sodas.

1: Rocky Mountain Outfitter in Kalispell **2:** Pescado Blanco **3:** Whitefish Farmers Market

FLATHEAD VALLEY
WHITEFISH FOOD, LODGING, AND CAMPING

Flathead Breweries and Distilleries

LIBATIONS AND DINING:

- **Bonsai Brewing Project** (549 Wisconsin Ave., Whitefish, 406/730-1717, noon-8pm Tues.-Sun., $8-14) launched as a Kickstarter-funded project to become a Whitefish institution in an old house with a dog-friendly outdoors, five regular and five rotator beers on tap, and a grill serving gumbo, kabobs, burgers, rice bowls, and salads.

- **Backslope Brewing** (1107 9th St. W., Columbia Falls, 406/897-2850, https://backslopebrewing.com, 11am-8pm Mon.-Sat., $10-14) serves locally sourced burgers, bowls, fresh salads, and small plates. Taps pour four crafted beers plus seasonal rotators.

- **Flathead Lake Brewing Co. Pubhouse** (116 Holt Dr., Bigfork, 406/837-2004, https://flatheadlakebrewing.com, 11am-10pm daily, $10-22) brews a full lineup of IPAs, porters, and fruity flavors. With a deck overlooking Flathead Lake, upstairs dining, and downstairs Chicago pizza cellar, it serves a humungous menu of pub specialties, burgers, sandwiches, and salads.

- **Tamarack Brewing** (105 Blacktail Rd., Ste. #1, Lakeside, 406/844-0244, www.tamarackbrewing.com, 11am-10pm daily, $9-25) puts out about a dozen beers, including the light golden Bear Bottom Blonde, a robust amber Yard Sale Ale (named after ski lingo for someone who crashes hard, littering the hill with skis and poles), and a smooth Switchback Stout. Pair with a big menu of pub food, including pizza. Inside seating can be noisy; outside patio seating abuts the creek.

- **Bias Brewing** (409 1st Ave. E., Kalispell, 406/730-3020, www.biasbrewing.com, noon-8pm daily) partners with Heck's Kitchen for on-site food service (bowls, sandwiches, shared foods) with their small selection of craft beers.

- **Sacred Waters** (3250 U.S. 2 E., Kalispell, 406/257-1992, www.sacredwatersbrewing, noon-8pm daily) pairs with the restaurant next door for dining with their beers, which include IPAs and stouts.

- **SunRift Beer Company** (55 1st Ave. W. N., Kalispell, 406/314-6355, sunriftbeer.com, noon-8pm daily) rolls out craft beers accompanied by smoked meats and beer biscuits.

NO FOOD, JUST THE DRINKS:

- **Spotted Bear Spirits** (503 Railway St., Whitefish, 406/730-2436, www.spottedbearspirits.com, 3pm-8pm Mon.-Thurs., noon-8pm Fri.-Sat., 2pm-6pm Sun.) inhabits a downtown location prime for popping in on farmers market nights for artsy seasonal cocktails of fresh, lively, organic ingredients with vodka or gin.

- **Kalispell Brewing Company** (412 Main St., Kalispell, 406/756-2739, www.kalispellbrewing.com, noon-8pm Mon.-Sat.) serves up German-style lagers and ales in a building that once served as a car dealership. It has a rooftop deck for outside seating.

- **Whistling Andy** (8541 MT 35, Bigfork, 406/837-2620, https://whistlingandy.com, noon-8pm Mon.-Sat.) sources local botanicals, grains, and cherries for whiskeys, gins, and rums.

Italian

Lilting to tunes of Frank Sinatra and Andrea Bocelli, **Ciao Mambo** (234 E. 2nd St., 406/863-9600, www.ciaomambo.com, 5pm-10pm Mon.-Sat., 5pm-9pm Sun., $12-32) transports diners beyond the Flathead to Italy in a cramped, noisy dining room with an open kitchen. Start with Tootsie Roll appetizers of ricotta-cheese-stuffed phyllo on marinara, choose from multiple homemade pastas for entrées, and finish with tiramisu or cannoli. The wine list contains plenty of Italian options.

Abruzzo Italian Kitchen (115

Central Ave., 406/730-8767, www. abruzzoitaliankitchen.com, 4pm-10pm Mon.-Thurs., 4pm-10:30pm Fri.-Sat., 4pm-9:30pm Sun., $12-31) serves fresh house-made pastas, specialty Italian meats, and wood-fired pizza.

Great for families, Montana's home-grown chain **MacKenzie River Pizza** (9 Central Ave., 406/862-6601, www. mackenzieriverpizza.com, 11am-10pm daily, $10-22) serves up traditional and eclectic (chicken fajita, Thai) pizzas with sourdough, natural-grain, or gluten-free crusts. Local microbrews are on tap.

Sushi

Wasabi Sushi Bar and Ginger Grill (419 2nd St., 406/863-9283, www.wasabimt.com, 5pm-10pm daily, $8-22/roll) is the longtime fave. Fusion rolls, *nigiri*, sashimi, sake, and grilled Asian specialties are served in a relaxed, bright atmosphere surrounded by wasabi-green walls. **Indah Sushi** (250 E. 2nd St., 406/730-6001, www.indahsushi.com, 11am-10pm Mon.-Sat., $8-30) has scrumptious sashimi and rolls, plus poke, bowls, and takeout.

Cajun and Creole

At ★ **Tupelo Grille** (17 Central Ave., 406/862-6136, www.tupelogrille.com, 5pm-10pm daily, $14-42), the flavors come from New Orleans with gumbo, Andouille sausage, and shrimp and grits. The Zydeco Combo combines a crawfish-shrimp cake, fried catfish, crawfish étouffée, and jambalaya. The eatery also serves grilled steaks, and nightly specials usually include fish. Top off dinner with their yummy bread pudding.

Mexican

More than a cute variation on the name of Whitefish, **Pescado Blanco** (235 E. 1st St., 406/862-3290, www.pescadoblancorestaurant. com, 5pm-10pm daily, $11-24) excels at locally sourced mountain Mexican cuisine: bison enchiladas, halibut tacos, and house elk chorizo. Salsas and tortillas are hand-made. Signature margaritas are made with fresh lime and a

14 percent distilled agave wine, and the bar serves a full range of south-of-the-border beers and wines.

Fine Dining

Whitefish has more than its share of fine restaurants that specialize in Montana game, fish, and steaks accompanied by extensive wine lists. At Whitefish Lake Golf Course, **Whitefish Lake Restaurant** (1200 U.S. 93 N., 406/862-5285, www. whitefishlakerestaurant.com, daily) offers historical ambience in a renovated 1937 log building. Lunch (11am-5pm during golf season, $11-28) is served on the deck or in the clubhouse. Dinner (5:30pm-10pm, $19-48) is served in the dining room. The New Zealand mussels appetizer can lead into roast duckling, steaks, or prime rib. Smaller-portioned plates are available, too.

Only one restaurant overlooks Whitefish Lake. Settle in for the romance of watching the sunset across the water at ★ **The Lodge at Whitefish Lake Boat Club** (1380 Wisconsin Ave., 406/863-4040, www. lodgeatwhitefishlake.com, daily). Dinner (5pm-10pm, $28-72) is served in the dining room or on the deck with specialties of fish, elk, and steaks that take on seasonal flavors. The restaurant also serves breakfast (7am-11am, $8-15). The adjacent lounge with an outdoor deck serves lunch and dinner (11am-9pm, $10-22). Summer adds a pool and lakeside Tiki Bar.

Ice Cream

Sweet Peaks Ice Cream (419 E. 3rd St., 406/862-4668, www.sweetpeaksicecream. com, 11:30am-11pm daily, winter hours shorten) is the purveyor of locally-made ice cream, sorbets, and frozen yogurts in eclectic flavors from its headliner shop.

Groceries

Whitefish has two large grocery stores, several small groceries, plus convenience marts. Find organic, healthy, and local foods at **Third Street Market** (244 Spokane Ave.,

406/862-5054, thirdstreetmarket.com, 8:30am-7pm Mon.-Sat.).

ACCOMMODATIONS

Whitefish is the only Flathead Valley town that offers luxury lodging, but it also has a myriad of less-pricey options, including chains and independent hotels. Several offer packages, including golfing and skiing. Find a full listing at https://explorewhitefish.com. You can also locate vacation homes and cabins to rent through **Lakeshore Rentals** (406/863-9337 or 877/817-3012, www.lakeshorerentals.us) or from individual owners through **VRBO** (www.vrbo.com) or **AirBnB** (www.airbnb.com).

Reservations in town are mandatory in summer, but when town books out, rooms are usually still available at Whitefish Mountain Resort. In town, summer has the highest rates with the second-highest rates in winter; Whitefish Mountain Resort has its highest rates in winter. Find off-season deals in spring and fall.

Hotels

With a two-story lobby draped with a giant wrought-iron chandelier and a river-rock fireplace, ★ **The Lodge at Whitefish Lake** (1380 Wisconsin Ave., 406/863-4000 or 877/887-4026, https://lodgeatwhitefishlake.com, $115-1,200) is the only hotel on the lake. Premier, upscale guest rooms overlook the water, facing the sunset; other guest rooms have mountain views. Viking Lodge rooms are across the street, accessed via an enclosed bridge. The lodge also has spacious 2-3-bedroom suites and condos with balconies, fireplaces, slate floors, granite countertops, fridges, and tubs and walk-in showers. The lodge has an indoor hot pool fed by a waterfall, indoor hot tub, summer outdoor pool and year-round outdoor hot tub, full-service marina, boat rentals, day spa, several restaurants, and a lounge. A walking trail tours the neighboring Viking Creek.

Located in town, the ★ **Firebrand Hotel** (650 E. 3rd St., 406/863-1900 or 844/863-1900, https://firebrandhotel.com, $119-450) has 81 rooms and five suites with queen or king beds, spa and concierge services, and a fitness center. Rooms have large windows that open for fresh air, mini-fridges, USB charging ports, and accents from burnished steel, reclaimed wood, and tile. For families, some rooms adjoin. Elevators access all floors. The two-story lobby with a restaurant has floor-to-ceiling windows to take in views, as well as a rooftop patio with a hot tub overlooking town.

Located 1 mile (1.6 km) from downtown restaurants and nightlife, **Grouse Mountain Lodge** (2 Fairway Dr., 844/868-7474, www.glacierparkcollection.com, $115-300) sits on the golf course, which turns into a groomed Nordic ski center in winter. It has an indoor pool, outdoor hot tubs, and restaurant. Guest rooms come in six configurations, including basic hotel rooms and upscale suites with rain showers. A complimentary shuttle accesses the town, airport, and ski resort.

Bed-and-Breakfasts

A three-minute drive from downtown and 10 minutes from the ski resort, the spacious ★ **Good Medicine Lodge** (537 Wisconsin Ave., 406/862-5488, https://goodmedicinelodge.com, $135-395) provides six rooms and three suites with private baths. Two of the suites sleep four people. The gourmet breakfast consists of three or four courses, including a hot entrée, often with local ingredients, and a buffet of cereals, breads, and yogurts. Light hors d'oeuvres and wine are served in the evening. Amenities include an outdoor hot tub, ski storage room, outdoor seating patios, several restful common areas, and cookies.

With modern log architecture, **Hidden Moose Lodge** (1735 E. Lakeshore Dr., 406/862-6516 or 888/733-6667, https://hiddenmooselodge.com, $109-319) centers around a spacious great room and an outdoor sitting deck overlooking gardens and woods. Both have river-rock fireplaces. Montana-themed rooms and suites have a queen or king bed and large bathrooms, some with Jacuzzi tubs. Amenities include breakfasts, complimentary evening drinks, outdoor hot tub, and nearby SNOW bus to the ski resort.

One block from downtown Whitefish, the circa-1920 **Garden Wall Inn** (504 Spokane Ave., 406/862-3440 or 888/530-1700, https://gardenwallinn.com, $225-425) is furnished with antiques, historical photos of Glacier, and warmth from a real log-burning fireplace in the living room. Five guest rooms have private baths, some with oversize claw-foot tubs. In the morning, awake to room delivery of a coffee tray followed by breakfast downstairs.

The new **Farmhouse Inn and Kitchen** (28 Lupfer Ave., 406/862-4211, www.thefarmhouseinnandkitchen.com, $76-300) operates in a small historic house two blocks from the town's bars, shops, restaurants, and train depot. Three high-end rooms and a small café give an intimate feel.

Resorts

Located 7 miles (11.3 km) above town, ★ **Whitefish Mountain Resort** (406/862-2900 or 877/754-3474, www.skiwhitefish.com) has a broad range of options from budget to luxury, motels and condos ($125-680), and vacation homes ($230-1,400). Winter sees the highest room rates when restaurants, shops, and lifts open for the ski season. July through August runs a close second, with hiking, chairlift sightseeing, ziplining, mountain biking, and summer activities. Fall and spring are very inexpensive, but lodging options are limited, and no lifts, shops, or restaurants are open. For upscale condos, go for Morning Eagle, and for budget rooms, stay in the Hibernation House.

Guest Ranches

Adjacent to a small lake and Spencer Mountain, **Bar W Guest Ranch** (2875 U.S. 93 W., 409/863-9099 or 866/828-2900, https://thebarw.com) houses guests in a western lodge, cabin suites, and glamping in upscale canvas tents. Ranch activities pile on trail rides, fishing, rodeo, canoeing, archery, and campfires. Three- and six-night packages include meals, lodging, and ranch activities ($920-2,454 double occupancy packages). In winter, the lodge serves as a nightly bed-and-breakfast ($85-243).

CAMPING

Set in the woods right on Whitefish Lake, **Whitefish Lake State Park** (1615 W. Lakeshore, 406/862-3991, stateparks.mt.gov, Apr.-Nov., $18-28) is perfect for swimming

The Lodge at Whitefish Lake

and launching boats but not for sleeping, as trains frequently rumble on the tracks crossing the park. With a good set of earplugs, you can survive the night. Amenities include flush toilets, showers, picnic tables, fire rings with grills, firewood, running water, bear-resistant storage lockers, and a shared biker-hiker site ($8 pp). Water is only turned on May-September.

Two miles (3.2 km) south of town, **Whitefish KOA** (5121 U.S. 93 S., 406/862-4242 or 800/562-8734, www.glacierparkkoa.com, mid-Apr.-mid-Oct., tents $50-72, RV hookups $72-93, $6-9 pp for more than two campers) sits shielded from the highway by thick forest. The outdoor pool attracts kids, while oldsters gravitate to the adults-only hot tub. Amenities include flush toilets, showers, picnic tables, fire rings, cabins, hookups, laundry, a dump station, a camp store, wireless internet access, free mini golf, and a restaurant.

Columbia Falls Food, Lodging, and Camping

Sprawling along the highway, Columbia Falls is the closest town to Glacier and Glacier Park International Airport. The town is 18 minutes from West Glacier and 12 minutes from the airport. Sales taxes include 3 percent on restaurant orders and 10 percent on lodging and camping.

FOOD

Columbia Falls has never been known as a dining mecca until recently. New restaurateurs have ushered in fresh tastes, catapulting the cuisine beyond the fast-food enterprises along the highway.

Cafés

Uptown Hearth Bakery (619 Nucleus Ave., 406/897-5555, www.uptownhearth.com, 7am-3pm Wed.- Sun., $4-13) bakes fresh breads, true French pastries, and specialty frittatas. The bakery also serves espresso.

Frequently crowded, **Montana Coffee Traders' Columbia Falls Cafe** (30 9th St. W., 406/892-7696, www.coffeetraders.com, 6am-3pm Mon.-Sat., 7am-2pm Sun., $7-12) serves huge breakfast omelets, muffins, scones, salads, wraps, and deli sandwiches, with plenty of vegetarian options and espresso.

Pizza

North Fork Pizza (605 Nucleus Ave., 406/897-5000, www.northforkpizza.com, 3pm-9pm Tues.-Sun., $5-25) serves pizza by the slice, calzones, build your own, and specialty pies. Delivery is available, too.

Casual Dining

With attention to atmosphere and flavors, ★ **Three Forks Grille** (729 Nucleus Ave., 406/892-2900, www.threeforksgrille.com, 5pm-close daily, $10-31) sprinkles the menu with burgers, bowls, salads, steaks, and Italian flavors. Sunday brunch (9am-1pm) rolls out eggs Benedict.

With indoor and outdoor seating plus live music, **Gunsight Bar and Grill** (624 Nucleus Ave., 406/897-2820, www.gunsightbar.com, 11:30am-8:30pm, bar closes later, $8-16) transformed this former dive into a place with a modern-historical vibe. The family-friendly restaurant serves big burgers and sandwiches, salads, and appetizers. The bar has 20 beers on tap mostly from Montana, plus specialty cocktails.

An old-school barbecue, **The BackRoom Restaurant** (522 9th St. W., 406/892-3131, www.niteowlbackroom.com, 4pm-9pm daily, $10-25) serves gooey ribs and broasted chicken. Fry bread with honey, coleslaw, and homemade french fries overflow the plate. To clean up, you'll need the roll of paper towels instead of napkins.

Groceries

Columbia Falls has two large groceries. For organic foods, stop in at **Sundrop Health Foods** (639 9th St. W., 406/892-9295, 9:30am-6pm Mon.-Sat.).

ACCOMMODATIONS

Good for those on a budget, the town has two small independent motels located on U.S. 2 near the waterslide and the Flathead River. Surrounding Columbia Falls, cabins and vacation homes are scattered in the woods and along the Flathead River. Locate properties rented by their owners via **VRBO** (www.vrbo.com) and **AirBnB** (www.airbnb.com). Summer rates are highest, but you can find lower rates and deals during the rest of the year. Contrary to Glacier, Wi-Fi is common in Columbia Falls lodging.

Hotels

Owned by Xanterra, which runs the Glacier National Park lodges, ★ **Cedar Creek** Lodge (930 2nd Ave. W., reservations 855/733-4522, front desk 406/897-7070, www.glaciernationalparklodges.com, $90-360) has environmentally friendly elements while tipping its hat to Glacier with cedars and park artwork in the lobby. In three floors with elevator access, it has king, queens, and family suite rooms, plus an indoor pool and fitness center. It is within walking distance to restaurants. Rates include a complimentary hot breakfast buffet and free shuttles to West Glacier (summer) and Whitefish Mountain Resort (winter).

Cabins

Located between Whitefish and Columbia Falls, **North Forty Resort** (3765 MT 40 W., 406/862-7740 or 800/775-1740, https://northfortyresort.com, $120-340) clusters 23 log cabins and one glamping tent under tall evergreens with community hot tubs and saunas. Sleeping 5-10 people, the cabins have log furnishings, kitchens, barbecues, and picnic tables.

Bed-and-Breakfasts

In a quiet area 10 minutes from town, **Bad Rock Bed and Breakfast** (480 Bad Rock Dr., 406/892-2829, www.badrock.com,

Three Forks Grille in Columbia Falls

June-mid-Sept., $189-260) has nine rooms, some in log cabins and others in a river-rock and log-frame house. All have private baths. Breakfast is a large Montana-style affair, sometimes featuring Belgian waffles heaped with fruit.

Resorts

Outside Columbia Falls, among big trees and quiet, **Meadow Lake Resort** (100 St. Andrews Dr., 406/892-8700 or 800/321-4653, https://meadowlake.com) is on an 18-hole golf course, with indoor and outdoor swimming pools, a spa, and tennis courts. The resort has hotel rooms ($90-260) and vacation rentals (condos with 1-3 bedrooms and homes).

In winter, a ski shuttle runs to Whitefish Mountain Resort.

CAMPING

Right in town in a manicured grass setting surrounded by trees, **Columbia Falls RV Park** (103 U.S. 2 E., 406/892-1122 or 888/401-7268, https://columbiafallsrvpark.com, early Apr.-early Oct.) is near the waterslides, an outdoor community swimming pool, and grocery stores. A few blocks' walk puts you at the restaurants in town. It has hookups for electricity, sewer, and water and can accommodate big rigs with slideouts. Amenities include flush toilets, hot showers, dump stations, wireless internet, cable TV, and laundry. Rates start at $49 for RVs and $28 for tent sites.

Kalispell Food, Lodging, and Camping

Built at highway crossroads, Kalispell is Flathead Valley's largest town. Most of the hotels and restaurants are located 15 minutes south of Glacier Park International Airport (on U.S. 2), the opposite direction from Glacier National Park and almost one hour from West Glacier. Add 7 percent tax to lodging and camping.

FOOD

Kalispell has common national chain restaurants along U.S. 93, but not in the few blocks of the downtown area. For a 1950s soda fountain throwback with huge scoops of ice cream, candy racks, and hot dogs, drop in at **Norm's News** (34 Main St., 406/756-5466, www.normssodafountain.com, 9am-7pm Tues.-Sat., 10am-5pm Sun.). Stop by **Ceres Bakery** (318 S. Main St., 406/755-8552, www.ceresbakerymt.com, 7am-6pm Mon.-Fri., 8am-3pm Sat.) for an espresso with a sticky sweet potato roll, croissant, or savory treat. Kalispell has an outpost of **Sweet Peaks Ice Cream** (343 S. Main St., 406/257-1102, www.sweetpeaksicecream.com, noon-9pm Sun.-Thurs, noon-10pm Fri.-Sat.), which

uses locally sourced ingredients for its eclectic flavors.

Cafés

Bonelli's Bistro (38 1st Ave. E., 406/257-8669, www.bonellisbistro.com, 8am-3pm Mon.-Sat., $7-16) dishes up Mediterranean breakfasts, lunches, espresso, and homemade desserts with fresh local ingredients, many organic. House specialties include lasagna and eggplant Parmigiana. Many menu items come gluten-free, dairy-free, egg-free, or low-calorie, and the kitchen will accommodate allergies. **Montana Coffee Traders' Kalispell Cafe** (111 Main St., 406/756-2326, www.coffeetraders.com, 7am-3pm Mon.-Sat., $8-13) serves breakfast scrambles and wraps, lunch sandwiches and salads, pastries, and espresso.

Pizza

For old-style Montana atmosphere, visit **Moose's Saloon** (173 N. Main St., 406/755-2337, moosessaloon.com, 11am-2am daily, $6-24), where peanut shells and sawdust cover the floor in this funky old-time bar that has been a valley staple since 1957. It will be just what you imagine a Montana bar to be: dark and loud. But the pizza is good and beer prices cheap.

Grills

In an old forge, ★ **DeSoto Grill** (227 1st St. W., 406/314-6095, www.desotogrill.com, 11am-8pm Sun.-Mon. and Wed.-Thurs., 11am-9pm Fri.-Sat., $12-35) barbecues brisket, pork, ribs, chicken, salmon, and elk sausage in sandwiches or platters. À la carte sides include house-made cornbread, pork belly collard greens, baked beans, potato salad, and slaw. Several mac-and-cheese bakes are on the menu, too.

Hops Downtown Grill (121 S. Main St., 406/755-7687, www.hopsmontana.com, 11am-3pm and 4pm-9pm Mon.-Fri., 4pm-9pm Sat.-Sun., $12-30) is the place to go for upscale burgers (beef, elk, and yak) and griddle meatloaf with Moose Drool gravy. Try the duck wings appetizer. Pair the meal with wine or Montana craft beers.

Groceries

Kalispell has many large grocery markets. For organic and healthy foods, go to **Withey's Health Foods** (1231 S. Main St., 406/755-5260, www.witheyshealthfoods.com, 9am-6pm Mon.-Sat.) or **Natural Grocers** (2395 U.S. 93, 406/755-5300, www.naturalgrocers.com, 8:30am-9pm daily).

ACCOMMODATIONS

Kalispell has several chain hotels sprawled on the outskirts of downtown, including hotels around the mall and strip mall areas. You can find them online (https://kalispellchamber.com). Other than chain hotels, the pickings are slim. Rates will be highest in summer, with lower prices fall, winter, and spring. Also consult **VRBO** (www.vrbo.com) or **AirBnB** (www.airbnb.com).

Hostels

Downtown above Wheaton's Cycle, the **Kalispell Hostel** (214 1st Ave. W., 406/270-1653, www.kalispellhostel.com, Apr.-Sept., $50-85) has a historical ambience. Three private bedrooms sleep two people each. Shared amenities include a living room with fireplace, a kitchen, Wi-Fi, bathroom with shower, and laundry.

Hotels

Right in downtown Kalispell's shopping district, the historic **Kalispell Grand Hotel** (100 Main St., 406/755-8100 or 800/858-7422, www.kalispellgrand.com, Apr.-Sept., $75-185) feels like it's a century back in time. The lobby still has a tin ceiling, an ornate pump organ, and the original wide oak-banister stairway. Renovated guest rooms have smaller baths with showers. Although the ambience harks back to 1912, when the hotel opened with room rates at $2, its modern amenities now include an elevator, high-speed internet access, air-conditioning, TVs, continental breakfast, and fresh-baked afternoon cookies.

CAMPING

Commercial campgrounds scatter around Kalispell, all within 30-40 minutes of Glacier and 15-20 minutes to Flathead Lake or golf courses. Standard amenities include hook-ups, flush toilets, hot showers, dump stations, laundries, playgrounds, cable TV, Wi-Fi, fire rings, and picnic tables.

The nearest Kalispell campground to Glacier, **Rocky Mountain "Hi" RV Park and Campground** (825 Helena Flats, 406/755-9573 or 800/968-5637, www.glaciercamping.com, year-round, RV hookups $37-45, tents $27) has grassy sites tucked between large fir trees; a few have Swan Mountain views. The setback from the highway reduces road noise. With swimming, fishing, and canoeing in a wide spring-fed creek, it's a good campground for kids.

The newest campground for RVs opened in 2020. **Montana Basecamp** (1000 Basecamp Dr., 406/756-9999, https://montanabasecamp.com, Apr.-Oct., $56-59) has all paved back-in sites with big views and lawns, and can accommodate the largest RVs. It is adjacent to the paved Great Northern Historical Trail for bicycling and walking.

Bigfork Food, Lodging, and Camping

Bigfork's location on Flathead Lake attracts visitors to the resort town in summer. Lake and river activities are big, along with hiking, golf, and the theater. In the off-season, you may have the town nearly to yourself. Of the major towns in Flathead Valley, Bigfork is the farthest from Glacier (65 minutes) and Glacier Park International Airport (35 minutes).

FOOD

For a tiny town, Bigfork packs in the tasty restaurants, most of which sit downtown within two blocks' walking distance of the theater. On performance nights, you won't get a table before the show unless you make reservations.

Cafés

In downtown Bigfork, the **Pocketstone Café** (444 Electric Ave., 406/837-7223, www.pocketstonecafe.com, 6am-3pm daily, $7-16) serves espresso and inventive twists on café staples from home-baked goods to omelets and sandwiches. The huckleberry jalapeño burger is a house specialty, and the Rueben tops the charts with its house-made sauerkraut, rye bread, corned beef, and sauce. Locals heading to Jewel Basin for hiking always fuel up at the family-run **Echo Lake Café** (1195 MT 83, 406/837-4252, www.echolakecafe.com, 6:30am-2:30pm daily, $9-16), where breakfast and lunch are served all day.

Burgers

In the **Garden Bar and Grill** (451 Electric Ave., 406/837-9914, 11am-2am daily, $7-14, cash only) is the local watering hole with 20 microbrews on tap. You can eat burgers inside or out back in the funky garden, with live music on summer weekend evenings.

Asian

Located upstairs in Twin Burch Square, ★ **SakeTome Sushi** (459 Electric Ave., 406/837-1128, https://saketomesushi.com, 5pm-10pm daily) garners a loyal following. The restaurant includes a bar, indoor seating, and deck seating. Find sashimi, *nigiri,* and *maki* rolls ($7-12), and specialty rolls ($14-25) with fun twists on spicy crab or ahi.

The Garden Bar and Grill is a long-time Bigfork staple.

ACCOMMODATIONS

You can find a full list of Bigfork lodging options at https://bigfork.org. Locate lake, river, or golf vacation homes to rent through **Eagle Bend Flathead Vacation Rentals** (406/837-4942, www.mtvacationrentals. com). Reservations are mandatory in summer, which also has the highest rates. Lodging rates are lowest in late fall, winter, and early spring. Also consult **VRBO** (www.vrbo.com) or **AirBnB** (www.airbnb.com). Properties will add on 7 percent state bed tax.

Motels and Cottages

The town's most economical lodging is **Timbers Motel** (8540 MT 35 S., 406/837-6200, https://timbersmotel.com, mid-May-Oct., $109-169), a Wyndham Travelodge located within a five-minute drive of Eagle Bend Golf Course and a couple of minutes from the Bigfork Summer Playhouse. It and has a heated pool, hot tub, and sauna.

In downtown Bigfork adjacent to the historic steel bridge over the Swan River, ★ **Bridge Street Cottages** (309 Bridge St., 406/837-2785 or 888/264-4974, https:// bridgestreetcottages.com, $125-445) offers upscale lodging. Four of the units overlook the river. Surrounded by small perennial gardens, these well-furnished one-bedroom cottages come with fully equipped kitchens and fireplaces. Suites are smaller, with just a fridge and a microwave. Walk to restaurants and the theater.

Resorts

★ **Averill's Flathead Lake Lodge** (150 Flathead Lake Lodge Rd., 406/837-4391, www.flatheadlakelodge.com, mid-June-Aug.) is a family-owned working dude ranch. Lodging, meals, and activities are all included in one big price for seven days: rates run around $3,199-5,185 per week for adults, depending dates and lodge or cabin accommodations. Rates for children are less. With horseback riding, fishing, swimming, waterskiing, tennis, and sailing, the ranch centers around the classy log lodge and cabins. You can park the car and dive into vacation mode for several days, as the ranch coordinates all the activities.

At the Swan River mouth to Flathead Lake, **Marina Cay Resort** (180 Vista Ln., 406/837-5861, www.marinacay.com, $129-529) has courtyard suites, waterfront suites, and condos. The complex includes a tiki bar and restaurant and a marina with boat rentals.

CAMPING

Located on Flathead Lake, **Wayfarer's State Park** (8600 MT 35, 406/837-3041, stateparks. mt.gov, mid-Mar.-mid-Nov., $18-28) is great for boating, fishing, and sunsets. The park is one of the lake's largest campgrounds, with 40 sites on 67 acres (27 hectares), a boat ramp, a swimming area, and 1.5 miles (2.4 km) of hiking trails. Ten shared campsites are reserved for hikers and bikers ($8). Campground amenities include firewood, a fire grill, flush and vault toilets, showers, picnic tables, drinking water (May-Sept. only), and RV dump station. Maximum length for RVs is 40 feet (12.2 m). Four other state parks also rim the lake. Reservations are available online.

Transportation and Services

TRANSPORTATION
Driving and Parking

Most roads in Flathead Valley are two-laners; main arteries such as U.S. 2 and 93 have four lanes. To bypass the many Kalispell stoplights on U.S. 93, take the **Kalispell Bypass** (U.S. 93 Alternate) with roundabouts at intersections; connect with it south of Kalispell near United Drive or north of Kalispell at West Reserve Drive.

In Flathead Valley towns, most parking is streetside or in small lots for businesses.

Large RVs can find parking at **Kalispell Center Mall** (20 N. Main St.) and **Whitefish Mountain Mall** (6475 U.S. 93 S.). Whitefish has a public parking garage on 2nd and Baker Streets with three-hour free parking. Two additional public parking lots are in Whitefish at First Street-Spokane Avenue and Depot Street-Spokane Avenue.

Buses, Shuttles, and Taxis

Flathead Transit (406/275-2877, www.csktdhrd.org/transportation/flathead-transit, 406/275-2877, $33 one-way) runs one bus daily between Missoula, Kalispell, and Whitefish. It leaves Missoula at 11:30am, arriving at 3:10pm in Whitefish. The return trip departs Whitefish at 4pm to arrive in Missoula at 7:30pm.

Within Flathead Valley, **Eagle Transit** (https://flathead.mt.gov/eagle/, $1-5, cash only, pay upon boarding) runs daily bus routes in Kalispell, Whitefish, and Columbia Falls. Schedules are online.

From Whitefish, the **SNOW Bus** (406/892-3390, https://bigmtncommercial.org) operates several seasonal routes. Free summer (July-early Sept.) and winter (early Dec.-early Apr.) buses run between Whitefish and Whitefish Mountain Resort multiple times daily. The **Whitefish Shuttle** (406/212-0800, www.whitefishshuttle.com) can carry up to 14 people and bikes to Glacier, Whitefish Mountain Resort, or other locales for hiking or biking.

Many hotels have shuttles that will meet you at the airport. Flathead Valley taxis are **Glacier Taxi** (406/250-3603, glaciertaxi.com) and **Arrow Shuttle** (406/300-2301, arrowshuttletaxi.com).

SERVICES
Information

Flathead Valley has multiple visitors information centers, mostly with online information: **Flathead Valley Convention and Visitors Bureau** (406/756-9091 or 800/543-3105, www.fcvb.org), **Kalispell Chamber of Commerce** (406/758-2800, kalispellchamber.com), **Whitefish Convention and Visitors Bureau** (877/862-3548, https://explorewhitefish.com), **Columbia Falls Chamber of Commerce** (406/892-2072, www.columbiafallschamber.org), **Bigfork Chamber of Commerce** (406/837-5888, https://bigfork.org), and **Lakeside Chamber of Commerce** (406/844-3715, lakesidesomerschamber.org).

The **Flathead National Forest** (www.fs.usda.gov) surrounds the Flathead Valley. Pick up maps, current trail and camping information, forest and ski conditions, and camping information in several national forest offices and ranger stations: **Flathead National Forest and Talley Lake Ranger Station** (650 Wolfpack Way, Kalispell, 406/758-5208 or 406/758-5204) and **Swan Lake Ranger Station** (200 Ranger Station Rd., Bigfork, 406/837-7500).

Post Offices

Each major town in Flathead Valley has at least one **post office.** Locations are in Bigfork (265 Holt Dr., 406/837-4479), Columbia Falls (65 1st Ave. E., 406/892-7621), Kalispell (350 N. Meridian Rd., 406/755-6450, and 248 1st Ave. W., 406/755-0187), Whitefish (424 Baker Ave., 406/862-2151), Somers (150 Somers Rd., 406/857-3330), and Lakeside (7196 U.S. 93 S., 406/844-3224).

Banks

Banks and ATMs are common in Flathead Valley, but several banks have branches in more than one town. Find **Glacier Bank** (www.glacierbank.com) in Kalispell (202 Main St., 406/756-4200), Bigfork (8251 MT 35, 406/837-5980), Columbia Falls (822 Nucleus Ave., 406/892-7100), and Whitefish (319 E. 2nd St., 406/863-6300). **First Interstate Bank** (www.firstinterstate.com) is located in Kalispell (2 Main St., 406/751-2500, and 100 Hutton Ranch Rd., 406/751-2522), Bigfork (800 Grand Ave., 406/837-1600), and Whitefish (306 Spokane Ave., 406/863-8888).

Cell Phone and Internet Access

Contrary to Glacier's sketchy cell and internet service, Flathead Valley has ubiquitous coverage. Motels have wireless or DSL internet services. You can also get online in the local county **public libraries** on their computers for a limited amount of time in Kalispell (247 1st Ave. E., 406/758-5820), Columbia Falls (130 6th St. W., 406/892-5919), Bigfork (525 Electric Ave., 406/837-6976), and Whitefish (9 Spokane Ave., 406/862-9914). Each library has its own access policies; call for hours (mostly Mon.-Sat.). You'll also find plenty of coffee shops and cafés that have wireless internet for their customers.

Newspapers and Magazines

The local valley news comes in the *Daily Interlake* (www.dailyinterlake.com) and the free *Flathead Beacon* (https://flathead-beacon.com). Community weeklies include Columbia Falls's *Hungry Horse News* (https://hungryhorsenews.com), the *Whitefish Pilot* (https://whitefishpilot.com), and the *Bigfork Eagle* (www.bigforkeagle.com).

Emergencies

For medical, fire, or police emergencies in Flathead Valley, call 911. For medical emergencies in Whitefish and Columbia Falls, the new **North Valley Hospital** (1600 Hospital Way, Whitefish, 406/863-3500, www.krh.org/nvh) is closest. For emergencies in Kalispell, Bigfork, and Flathead Lake, the larger **Kalispell Regional Medical Center** (310 Sunny View Ln., Kalispell, 406/752-5111, www.krh.org) is closest.

Background

The Landscape

GEOLOGY

Glacier's mountains tell a 1.6-billion-year-old story of geologic history. The mountains reveal three geologic events that sculpted the scenery into its colorful, jagged parapets with swooping valleys: First, sediments layered on top of each other in an ancient sea; then, mountains moved; and, most recently, an ice age gouged vertical formations. Since then, relentless erosion has continued to shape the landscape. Wind and water chip away at peaks. Freeze-melt cycles wreak havoc on cliffs, prying off slabs of rock. And weather leaves its mark on the land.

Ancient Belt Sea

Approximately 1.6 billion-800 million years ago, a shallow lake covered parts of what is now Washington, Idaho, Montana, and British Columbia. The lake, known as the Belt Sea, accumulated sands washing down from adjacent highlands. Through pressure and heat, cake-like layers of dolomites, limestone, argillites, siltites, and quartzites piled one on top of the other. Over eons, the layers built up thousands of feet thick.

You can see these layers today in the mountains of Glacier. In a geologic feat found in very few places in North America, Glacier retained its **sedimentary rock** instead of seeing it metamorphose. Find these colorful layers in the mountainsides around Logan Pass, where multihued sediments stripe Mount Clements. You can also find layering on trails to Iceberg Lake, Grinnell Glacier, Gunsight Pass, and Cobalt Lake. The north entrance to Ptarmigan Tunnel has striking red and white layering. Most of Glacier's lakes and rivers collect a rainbow of rocks from higher elevations, compliments of the Belt Sea layers.

Uplift of Mountains

Between 150 and 60 million years ago, major tectonic movement along massive faults created the northern Rocky Mountains. The Pacific and Continental Plates pushed against each other until the ancient Precambrian rocks of the Pacific Plate slid atop the much younger dinosaur-age rock of the Continental Plate. During this uplift, a several-mile-thick Belt Sea chunk sidled 50 miles (81 km) east and higher in elevation, where it is exposed today for visitors to see. This movement is known as the **Lewis Overthrust Fault.** Look for its evidence where geologists originally discovered the fault in 1890: on the side of Summit Mountain north of Marias Pass on U.S. 2.

During the uplift, rock heated and became pliable like bread dough. Sometimes it simply folded due to the pressure and heat. Find folds on Waterton Lake's east shore, above the Ptarmigan Tunnel Trail, and between Lake Josephine and Bullhead Lake on the Swiftcurrent Trail.

Glaciation

More recently, glaciers carved the landscape. Two million years ago, the **Pleistocene ice age** engraved the park's topography via giant advancing and retreating glaciers. Only the tops of Glacier's highest peaks poked out as nunataks, summits completely surrounded by ice. Glaciers thousands of feet deep gouged out huge U-shaped valleys, which contrast with the V-shaped river-carved valleys such as the Grand Canyon.

These ancient ice rivers left long, finger-like deep waters such as St. Mary Lake and Lake McDonald. In other valleys, such as Swiftcurrent, the large glacier receded in a series of melts, leaving a necklace of smaller lakes instead of one large one.

Glaciers also molded the rugged peaks here. When three or more glaciers gnawed away on a peak, a horn resulted, such as Mount Reynolds or Triple Divide. Sometimes two glaciers chewed ridges paper thin into arêtes (French for "fish bone"), such as the ragged Iceberg-Ptarmigan Wall or the Garden Wall on the Continental Divide. The upper ends of glaciers often carved out cirques, steep-walled round basins such as Avalanche Lake basin.

As glaciers retreated, they left large piles of debris in the form of moraines, where rocks, sand, and gravel collected like dirty laundry. Large moraines, such as Howe and Snyder Ridges flanking Lake McDonald, remain from Pleistocene ice, whereas smaller rubble piles in the Grinnell or Sperry Glacier basins date from the 1850s and later.

After ancient Pleistocene ice melted in Glacier about 12,000 years ago, several

Ancient Rocks

Glacier contains some of the oldest exposed rock in North America.

ARGILLITES

Of Glacier's colorful rock formations, the most striking is the argillite, an iron-rich mudstone formed in layers on the floor of the shallow ancient Belt Sea 800 million-1.6 billion years ago. Its blue-green and purple-red hues leap off mountainsides and intensify under water. This clay and silt contain iron, which changes to red hematite when exposed to oxygen, thus giving Grinnell argillite its burgundy color. The Appekunney argillite did not oxidize, remaining green. Spot the red colors on **Red Eagle Mountain** when driving down the east side of Going-to-the-Sun Road. Find both argillites on the trails to **Grinnell Glacier, Iceberg Lake,** and **Red Rocks Falls,** plus rafting on the **Middle Fork of the Flathead.**

RIPPLE ROCK AND MUD CRACKS

Raindrop impressions, water ripples, and mud cracks remain etched in stone, evidence of their origins in ancient seas. Ripple rocks, found most often in red, blue, or beige layers, look like small wave marks on a beach. As the sea dried up, sediments compacted and cracked, similar to a mud puddle drying up in a driveway. Large blocks show webs of cracks filled in with other sediments, an effect that looks like dull maroon or turquoise tiles. Look for slabs with ripple marks and mud cracks on **Hidden Lake Overlook Trail** and along **Many Glacier Valley** trails.

MAGMA INTRUSIONS

Don't be fooled: Yes, Granite Park and its namesake chalet are dubbed for the igneous rock; however, Glacier has no granite. When early prospectors found rounded blue-gray formations of Purcell lava, or pillow lava, they mistakenly called it granite. This lava intruded up through sediment layers, billowing out in ropey coils and bubbles. Walk over this lava on the **Highline Trail** north of Granite Park Chalet.

miniature ice ages shaped the land. The glaciers currently in the park are products of the last 8,000 years. During the **Little Ice Age** (1500-1850), most glaciers grew. Park tree-ring studies and moraines show evidence that there were more than 150 glaciers in the early 1900s. These are the smaller alpine glaciers in the upper basins of peaks. Some of these glaciers plummeted off cliffs, forming hanging valleys: Bird Woman Falls (492 ft/150 m) dives from a hanging valley suspended between Mount Oberlin and Mount Cannon that was once home to a glacier.

Very few alpine glaciers remain today. The two largest are Harrison Glacier and Blackfoot Glacier, the latter visible from Going-to-the-Sun Road. These are expected to melt within the next decade or so. Waterton no longer has any active glaciers, and neither does Two Medicine.

So where can you get close to a glacier? Grinnell has the shortest trail. From Sperry Chalet, Sperry Glacier is the next shortest. With binoculars, you can view glaciers from Going-to-the-Sun Road.

Moving Ice

It's often hard to tell the difference between a glacier and a snowfield. In early summer, they look the same, covered with fresh snow from winter. But they are distinctly different. It's simple math: When more snow adds than melts annually, glaciers form. The snow transforms into icy grains through freeze-thaw cycles. Snow builds up on the upper end of glaciers and pushes down, compressing ice crystals. Over years, the ice compacts in layers, mounting into a huge mass with a rigid surface and a supple base.

Glaciers are **slow-moving ice.** Aided by

One of the most visible magma intrusions is the diorite, or Purcell, sill. It appears from a distance as a 100-foot-thick (30-m) horizontal black line sandwiched between thinner whitish layers. When magma boiled up between limestone layers 800 million years ago, it superheated the limestone, turning it white. You can see the diorite sill from **Many Glacier Road,** visible as a thick dark line on Mount Gould and Mount Wilbur. Hikers see it as black jagged teeth above **Iceberg Lake** or the solid line above **Grinnell Glacier.** On the **Highline Trail,** hikers walk through the sill approximately 1 mile (1.6 km) beyond Haystack Saddle. Look for a crystallized green sheen covering deep black. When the footing changes from broken scree beds to solid, blocky, volcanic rock, it's the sill.

ripple rock

STROMATOLITES

The Belt Sea became habitat for blue-green algae. Six species of this petite primitive life-form lived in the sea, doing what algae does best: turning carbon dioxide into oxygen. During this process, calcium carbonate formed into stromatolites, a round formation 6-15 inches (15.2-38.1 cm) in diameter that looks like Van Gogh's *Starry Night* swirls. They grew in colonies that made 30-foot (9-m) columns up to 3 miles (4.8 km) wide and solidified into rocks. Find stromatolites along **Going-to-the-Sun Road,** the **Highline Trail,** and **Piegan Pass Trail.** The presence of these algal forms in the Belt Sea produced an oxygen-rich atmosphere that allowed other life-forms to develop, including humans.

gravity, the ice presses down, forming a thin elastic barrier that carries the mass toward the glacier's toe, where it may calve off in chunks. When the ice travels over convex ground features, its surface cracks, forming crevasses sometimes hundreds of feet thick. Hidden crevasses make glaciers deadly for travel, so do not walk out on them without appropriate rescue gear.

For a glacier to move, a certain amount of ice is needed—usually a surface of at least 25 acres (10 hectares) and a minimum depth of 100 feet (30 m). Less than that and the ice becomes a static, permanent snowfield. Moving glaciers behave similarly to a bulldozer, gouging out troughs and picking up rocks from the surrounding mountain. Once the winter season's snow melts, you can recognize glaciers by their telltale debris bands of rock piles lining up on the surface.

Glacier After the Glaciers Melt

Locals often joke about Glacier National Park's name: What should the park be called after its glaciers all melt? Of course, the name will remain the same. Despite the disappearance of the glaciers in future, evidence of their presence will remain. The U-shaped valleys, horns, arêtes, hanging valleys, and moraines retain their formations thanks to glaciers. Smaller evidence of glaciers will remain, too. On the Avalanche Lake or Hidden Lake Trails, look for glacial striations, or large scratches, on rocks where ice abraded the surface. Also, on the Avalanche Trail, large boulders called erratics were strewn about from receding ice.

CLIMATE

Glacier and Waterton live on a collision course for both **arctic continental** and **Pacific maritime** weather. Wet weather

Exploring the Ecosystem

One of the best ways to become intimate with Glacier's wildlife, geology, birds, and cultural history is to join the regionally and nationally recognized experts from the **Glacier Institute** (406/755-1211, www.glacierinstitute.org). Offered year-round, the courses blend in-the-field experiences with hands-on learning. You can learn to bird, watch bears, track animals on snowshoes, photograph wildlife, find herbs and mushrooms, and identify wildflowers. College credit is available for some of the workshops and classes. Adult seminars include wilderness first aid, art, photography, science, and ecology. Youth camps for ages 7-16 emphasize outdoor science. Most single-day courses cost $50-75; most multiple-day courses range $125-725, including lodging and meals.

For an intimate experience in Glacier, **Glacier National Park Volunteer Associates** (406/888-7800, gnpva.org) looks for volunteers each summer for backcountry and front-country projects. Some tasks restore historic log structures, reconstruct damaged trails and campsites, and transplant seedlings from the park's native-plant nursery. Volunteers also staff the Apgar Nature Center and help at visitors centers and permit offices. Work projects are led by a backcountry ranger intern. No special skills are required, just a desire to help.

For those itching to contribute to scientific research in Glacier, the **Crown of the Continent Research Learning Center** (406/888-7800, www.nps.gov/glac) conducts citizen science projects every summer. Since 2008, they have contributed to field studies on common loons, invasive weeds, and high-country species of concern such as mountain goats and pikas. Some training is necessary but is available through the center.

races in from the Pacific with moderate temperatures. Near West Glacier, precipitation results in an annual average 29 inches (73.7 cm) of rainfall and 157 inches (399 cm) of snow. Waterton also sees more precipitation than the rest of Alberta.

Although the east side of the Continental Divide equals the west in terms of precipitation, east-slope winds produce more extremes. Winter winds blow snow from slopes, providing forage for ungulates. Winds also blow trains off their tracks. Several east-side high passes are notorious for raging unpredictable winds causing hikers to crawl on all fours. **Chinook winds,** warm winds with speeds that can exceed 90 mph (145 kph), occur any time of year, but mostly in winter. Blackfeet called them "snow eaters" for the snow they rapidly melted. When a chinook descends the Continental Divide's east side, it blows warm and dry, fooling trees into their spring activity of absorbing water into their cells. When temperatures plummet again, the cold freezes the water in the cells, killing the trees. This "winter kill" accounts for the number of dead silver trunks

dotting east-side forests, especially visible in Two Medicine and Waterton.

Glacier is a land of weather extremes, from a high of 99°F (37°C) to a low of -36°F (-38°C). Elevation makes a huge difference, too: While Lake McDonald beckons swimmers to sunny beaches, frigid winds can rage across Logan Pass. Sometimes you'll experience four seasons in one day, so always dress in layers and carry extra clothing, no matter what the weather looks like in the morning. Rains move in fast, and snow can fall any month of the year.

Spring

While March-May are appealing off-season months to travel, in Glacier they are wet and cold, still clinging to winter. Snow buries the high country and some of the lowlands. May is moody, alternating between warm days and rainstorms or frequent late snows that can cause avalanches in the high country.

Summer

During summer months, June habitually monsoons, but July-August usher in warmer, drier skies. Higher elevations are often substantially cooler—up 15 degrees chillier than valley floors. While cool breezes are welcome on baking summer days, they can also bring snows in August. Drier summers can result in wildfire closures and view-inhibiting smoke in August.

Fall

Autumn begets lovely bug-free warm days and cool nights. While aspen and larch trees turn gold, temperatures bounce through extremes, from highs of 75-80°F (24-27°C) during the day to below freezing at night. During wildfire summers, fire and smoke can persist until the snow flies. The weather is seemingly schizophrenic as rains and snows descend for a few days, followed by clearing and warming trends.

Winter

Winter temperatures in Glacier vary depending on elevation, but mostly hang around 10-25°F (-12 to -4°C), and snowfall is voluminous. Logan Pass is buried under 350-700 inches (889-1,778 cm) of snow per year. Temperatures can spike above freezing, with accompanying rain, or below 0°F (-18°C) with an arctic front. Because Chinooks visit Waterton more than the rest of Alberta, it is one of the warmest places in the province in winter. While the Canadian prairies suffer below-freezing temperatures, Waterton may be reveling in 30-50°F (-1 to 10°C) temperatures.

Daylight

Given Glacier's latitude and placement on the western edge of the Mountain Time zone, hours of daylight fluctuate wildly during the year. In June, about 18 hours of daylight leaves lots of time to play outdoors. First light appears around 5am, and dark doesn't descend until almost 11pm. By late August, dark comes at 9pm, with daylight hours shortening through autumn. At the winter solstice, the sun rises at 8am and sets at 4:30pm.

Plants and Animals

PLANTS

Glacier and Waterton Lakes National Parks have rich floral diversity. That's one of the reasons the parks are UNESCO Biosphere Reserves. Forests, prairies, and peaks have different vegetation specific to elevation, habitat, and weather. Five different floral habitats flank the park's mountains, yielding a rich, broad spectrum of plant life that goes from rainforest to arid alpine tundra.

Glacier is home to rare Montana plants; four are found only in the park. Many species here are at the fringes of their habitats: Great Plains flowers to arctic bulbs. In Lake McDonald Valley, you can find nearly 100 Pacific Coast species.

For a small park, Waterton has a lot of rare plants: 30 grow only within its borders, including the rarest plant, the Waterton moonwort. The tiny park ironically chalks up more plant diversity than its much larger northern national park siblings, Banff and Jasper.

Grasslands

Grassland prairies sprout wildflowers that adapt to dry, shadeless, windy, and warm conditions. More than 100 grass species proliferate across the Glacier-Waterton prairies. These prairies poke into valley drainages on the Continental Divide's east side and have been preserved by natural fires in the North Fork Valley. Waterton also has a large prairie, one of two prairie lands in the Canadian national park system and one of North America's last places where grizzly bears range into their historic grassland habitat.

Aspen Parklands

Aspens dominate east-side valleys of Many Glacier, Belly River, Two Medicine, St. Mary, and Waterton where they harbor elk herds in winter. Broken by wildflower meadows of **arrowleaf balsamroot** and **sticky geranium,** groves of quaking aspen shake their leaves in the slightest breeze, hence their name. They mark the transition between grasslands and coniferous forests. Flowers such as **mountain death camas, paintbrush, pasqueflower, lupine, stonecrop,** and **horsemint** thrive in these parklands.

Montane Forests

In low to mid-elevations, dense forests mix poplars and firs, which vary substantially depending on moisture and winds. **Cedar-hemlock** and **birch** forests dominate wetter western valleys, while drier slopes yield **limber pine, Douglas fir, white spruce,** and **lodgepole pine.** The **western larch,** a conifer that turns gold in fall and loses its needles each winter, also inhabits lower-elevation forests. Below the shade-producing canopy, six-petaled **queen's cup** wildflowers hide for protection from the sun's drying rays, along with fragile **orchids.** Juniper, Pacific yew, thimbleberry, and serviceberry make up the midstory brush.

Subalpine Zone

Between 5,000 and 7,000 feet (1,524 and 2,134 m) in elevation, stately forests surrender to **subalpine firs,** dwarfed and gnarled in their struggle to survive in a short growing season, brutal winds, frigid temperatures, and heavy snows. Trees often develop a bent, stunted krummholz, forming a protective mat rather than growing upright. **Whitebark pine** and **Engelmann spruce** also sneak into the subalpine. Between tree islands, lush mountain meadows bloom with a colorful array of **columbine, bog gentian, valerian, fleabane,** and **bear grass.** Flowers must do their business so fast in the subalpine zone that yellow **glacier lilies** and

spring beauties force their blooms through the snow.

Alpine Tundra

Nearly 25 percent of Glacier and Waterton is alpine tundra. Above tree line, the land appears to be barren rock, but a host of miniature plants adapt to the harsh conditions of high winds, drying altitude, short summers, cold temperatures, and rocky soil that lacks organic matter. Hugging the ground, the miniature wildflowers bloom during a short few-week season. Hairy leaves provide protection from winds and the sun's high-elevation intensity. Mats of pink **moss campion,** delicate **spotted saxifrage,** purple **butterwort,** and **Jones' columbine** fling their energy into tiny flowers.

Huckleberries

Of all Glacier's flora, the huckleberry draws the most attention. While several varieties grow throughout the park, from lowlands to subalpine, they all have one thing in common: a sweet berry. Look for a low-growing shrub with small green to reddish leaves. About the size of a small blueberry, huckleberries ripen into a rich dark purple-blue. Find lowland berries in late July, but mid-August-early September is known as huck season. Grizzly bears carbo-load on hucks to survive winter.

Wildflowers

Glacier's wildflowers peak late June-early August, depending on snowmelt and elevation. Early summer brings on fields of yellow **glacier lilies** and white **spring beauties** poking buds through the snowpack. At lower elevations, the large white heads of **cow parsnip** bloom alongside roads and continue into higher elevations as summer progresses. Some years, **bear grass** blooms so thickly in July that subalpine hillsides look snow-covered. **Paintbrush** spews across fields in yellow, red, fuchsia, white, salmon, and orange. Just a reminder: Picking flowers in national parks is prohibited. Use your camera instead.

Poisonous Plants

Very few plants in Glacier are poisonous. Several can be toxic if eaten, so avoid eating plants or mushrooms. Most of Glacier is inhospitable for poison ivy, poison oak, and poison sumac, but watch for **stinging nettles:** Although not poisonous, they cause obnoxious itching. A few people have allergic reactions to **cow parsnip.** Wear long sleeves and long pants to avoid contact with irritating plants.

ANIMALS

Glacier and Waterton teem with wildlife. The diversity of animal life is one reason the parks have been designated Biosphere Reserves by UNESCO. The Crown of the Continent remains a North American bastion of an intact ecosystem, with many animals present that were here before the massive impact of human activity over the past 150 years. Wolves, eliminated in federally funded programs, migrated from Canada in the late 1980s, adding more original members to Glacier's wildlife family. Only mountain bison and woodland caribou remain extirpated.

Bears

Two bear species roam Glacier's mountains: **black bears** and **grizzly bears.** Omnivores and opportunistic feeders, bears will eat anything that is easy pickings. Intent on gaining 100-150 pounds (45-68 kg) before winter, Glacier's bears feed on a diet heavy in plant matter: bulbs, roots, berries, shoots, and flowers. Ants, insects, carrion, and ground squirrels fill in proteins. Contrary to popular opinion, humans are not on their menu of favorite foods.

Because bears learn fast, they adapt quickly to new food sources, be it a pack dropped by the side of the trail or dog food left out in a campground. For this reason, Glacier imposes strict rules for handling food and garbage in picnic sites, campgrounds, and backcountry areas. All garbage cans and dumpsters are bear resistant. Bears that eat human foods and garbage find themselves moved to a new habitat, or worse, destroyed.

Because grizzly and black bears are integral to Glacier's ecosystem, the National Park Service employs several bear rangers whose jobs entail monitoring and deterring bears from trouble. For bruins that linger near roadways and front-country campgrounds, the bear team uses hazing methods, such as loud noises, gunshots, pellet beanbags, and sometimes Karelian bear dogs, in an attempt to teach bears to stay away. Nuisance bears are transplanted to remote park drainages or destroyed if their offenses warrant. "A fed bear is a dead bear," the truism goes. A bear that dabbles in human food often aggressively seeks more.

Bears are one of the least fertile mammals, giving birth once every two or three years. While black bears have a gestation of 220 days, for grizzlies spring mating season is followed by delayed implantation, in which the fertilized eggs are simply stored until winter. Pending the sow's health, the egg or eggs implant, resulting in 1-3 cubs born during winter's deep sleep. If her health is severely threatened, she may abort the egg instead.

Bears don't actually hibernate, as their respiration and pulse remain close to normal. Instead, they enter a deep sleep in which the body temperature drops slightly. Before crawling into their dens, they scarf down mountain ash berries, rough grasses, and twigs to form an anal plug, which inhibits eating, urinating, or defecating during winter. Bears emerge in the spring ravenously hungry, heading straight for avalanche chutes to rummage for snow-buried carcasses.

Carnivores

Glacier has three elusive members of the cat family: **mountain lions, bobcats,** and **Canada lynx.** Quiet hunters and mostly nocturnal, cats may see you but you'll rarely see them. For mountain lions, deer tops the menu, while lynx favor snowshoe hares. Both cat populations rise and fall with their prey populations. With keen eyesight and hearing, these three cats stalk their prey, the lynx with the help of large snowshoe-shaped feet.

Spectacular Wildflower Spots

Wildflowers do not bloom park-wide all at once. When spring hits lower elevations, popping open buds around Lake McDonald and St. Mary, big Logan Pass alpine meadows cower under snow. As summer progresses, like a mist lifting, higher and higher habitats spread out floral displays. To identify wildflowers, pick up a field guide from **Glacier National Park Conservancy** (406/892-3250, https://glacier.org).

Here are some top places to see Glacier's wildflowers on display:

FROM THE CAR

- **Many Glacier Road:** Late May-early June brings tiny pink shooting stars, followed in July by hot-pink sticky geraniums, purple lupine, and tall light pink hollyhock (page 154).

- **Chief Mountain International Highway:** In June, meadows pop with pink shooting stars. In early July, the few miles between the Waterton Overlook and Highway 5 are lined with tiger lilies (page 154).

- **Two Medicine Road:** Blue camas blooms in early July (page 188).

- **Going-to-the-Sun Road:** Lower elevations bloom with huge white cow parsnip heads in early July. In late July-early August, wildflowers along the road's alpine section bloom with orange paintbrush, purple shrubby penstemon, and yellow columbine. In some years, high meadows' slopes will look snow-covered in mid-July when 3-foot-tall (0.9-m) creamy bear grass blooms prolifically. July also brings on the big sunflower-like arrowleaf balsamroots and dusty pink prairie smoke in Two Dog Flats on the east side of the road along St. Mary Lake (page 109).

- **Logan Pass:** Yellow glacier lilies bloom as the snow melts in early July, but they give way to pink alpine laurel, pale yellow paintbrush, and fuchsia monkeyflower by early August (page 116).

Gray wolf packs inhabit fairly large ranges of 100-300 square miles (259-777 sq km), so chances of seeing a wolf are fairly rare despite their relatively high reproductive potential of 4-7 pups per year. **Coyotes, foxes, wolverines,** and **badgers** round out the list of large carnivores. Although wolverines are the most elusive creatures, Glacier provides prime habitat for them with remote terrain, snowfields, and plentiful ground squirrels. Many hikers spot them along the Highline Trail.

Ungulates

Ungulates crowd Glacier's high and low country. **Moose** feed in streambeds and lakes. Find them in Swiftcurrent Valley, especially around bogs and willow thickets. **Elk, mule deer,** and **white-tailed deer** live throughout the park at the tree line and below, while **mountain goats** and **bighorn sheep** cling to rocky alpine slopes. During late spring, goats congregate at the Goat Lick on U.S. 2, seeking minerals for their depleted systems. They are also a regal staple at Logan Pass.

Small Mammals

Members of the weasel family such as **fishers, pine martens, minks,** and **weasels** inhabit forests and waterways. The short-tailed weasel changes color in winter: Its fur becomes white, except for the small black tip of its tail. Snowshoe hares also change to white in winter, their large feet providing extra flotation on snow. In subalpine country, a chorus of eeks, screams, and squeaks bounce through

ON THE TRAIL

· **Quartz Lakes:** In the North Fork, find fairy-slipper orchids in the rich forest duff in late June (page 83).

· **Scenic Point:** In early July, see several-hundred-year-old mats of pink moss campion, small bluebells, and red king's crown, the miniature plants of the alpine tundra (page 193).

· **Preston Park:** Hikers on the **Piegan Pass** (page 127) and **Siyeh Pass Trails** (page 128) revel in the show of purple fleabane, fuchsia paintbrush, and fuzzy-headed western anemones spread thick across meadows. In early July, rare Jones' columbine blooms on the switchbacks between Preston Park and Siyeh Pass.

· **Fifty Mountain:** Meadows that stretch about 1.5 miles (2.4 km) yield big floral displays, starting with yellow glacier lilies and white spring beauties in early July. Late July–early August brings on a rich palette of wildflowers (page 132).

bog orchids

· **Highline Trail:** Color bursts everywhere along the Garden Wall in late July–early August with yellow arnica, deep blue gentians, creamy death camas, white valerian, and fuchsia monkeyflowers. More than 30 varieties of wildflowers speckle meadows (page 125).

· **Hidden Lake Overlook:** In late July, tall bear grass, fuchsia monkeyflower, and several varieties of paintbrush flank the trail (page 125).

rockfalls. The noisemakers are **pikas,** which look like tailless mice, and the ubiquitous **Columbian ground squirrel,** recognized by its reddish tint. Looking like fat house cat-size fur balls, **hoary marmots** splay on rocks, sunning themselves. Scampering between high alpine rocks, **golden-mantled ground squirrels** look like oversize chipmunks with their telltale gold stripes.

Fish

With 750 lakes and 1,500 miles (2,414 km) of streams, Glacier provides abundant habitat for native and nonnative species of fish. **Bull trout, westslope cutthroat trout,** and **whitefish** are among the 17 native species. To promote recreational fishing, lakes were once stocked with nonnative fish such as rainbow trout, arctic grayling, and kokanee salmon. Introduced species flourished, threatening native fish, whose populations are now waning. Since the 1970s fish are no longer stocked in Glacier or Waterton.

Birds

More than 200 species of birds mean every park visitor can see wildlife. Bird checklists are available at visitors centers and online (www.nps.gov/glac). In summer, trees teem with songbirds: **cedar waxwings, thrushes, chickadees, vireos, sparrows, dark-eyed juncos,** and **finches.** Brilliant-colored **western tanagers** and striking **mountain bluebirds** flit between treetops. Sightings of **rufous** and **calliope hummingbirds** are common. **Woodpeckers,** including the

Bear Country

GRIZZLY BEARS VERSUS BLACK BEARS

Even though colors are used to name the bears, black and grizzly bears display a variety of fur hues. For instance, a black bear can give birth to cubs of different colors: blond, black, red, and brown. Grizzly bears, while their name evokes silver hair, appear in all colors of the spectrum, too. Don't be fooled by color; look instead for body size and shape.

Grizzlies are bigger than black bears, standing on all fours at 3-4 feet (0.9-1.2 m) tall and weighing in at 300-600 pounds (136-272 kg). Black bears average 12-18 inches (30-46 cm) shorter on all fours. Adult females weigh around 140 pounds (63 kg), while males bulk up to 220 pounds (100 kg).

In profile, the grizzly has one notable feature: a hump on its shoulders. The solid muscle mass provides the grizzly's forelegs with power for digging and running. Black bears lack this hump. Their face profiles are also different. On the grizzly, look for a scooped or dished forehead-to-nose silhouette; the black bear's nose will appear straighter in line with its forehead. Note the ears, as the grizzly's will look a little too small for its head while a black bear's ears seem big, standing straight up. Paw prints in mud reveal a difference in their claws and foot structure. Grizzly claws are 4 inches (10 cm) long with pads in a relatively straight line, while black bear claws are 1.5 inches (3.8 cm) long with pads arced across the top of the foot.

Although both bears have mediocre vision, they are fast runners. In three seconds, a grizzly bear can cover 180 feet (55 m).

HIKING IN BEAR COUNTRY

With a few precautions, you can eliminate the scares.

· **Make noise.** To avoid surprising a bear, use your voice. Sing loudly, hoot, or holler. Clap your hands. Bears tend to recognize human sounds as ones to avoid; they'll usually wander off if they hear people approaching. Make loud noise in thick brushy areas, around blind corners, near babbling streams, and against the wind.

· **Hike with other people.** Avoid hiking alone. Keep children near. Very few bear attacks happen to groups of four or more.

large red-capped pileated woodpecker, pound at bark in search of bugs. Ground birds such as the chicken-size **grouse** surprise hikers on trails, while smaller **ptarmigans,** whose plumage turns white in winter, blend with summer coloration into rocks. **Steller's jays** and **Clark's nutcrackers** add to the cacophony.

Because of Glacier's profuse rivers, streams, and lakes, waterfowl find plentiful habitat. **Loons, grebes, mergansers,** and **goldeneyes** fill almost every lake, while **harlequin ducks** migrate to rapidly flowing streams in spring for nesting. **Tundra swans** use Glacier's lakes as a stopping place during their annual migration to and from their arctic breeding grounds. **American dippers,** or

water ouzels, nest near waterfalls: The dark bird's obvious bobbing action is a dead giveaway of the species.

RAPTORS

Nothing is more dramatic than sighting a **golden eagle** soaring along the Continental Divide. Commonly nesting in remote spots, goldens often return yearly to the same location. Glacier also boasts about 10 nesting pairs of **bald eagles,** seen along waterways year-round. Above lakes, ospreys dive for fish from impressive heights, while **red-tailed hawks** and **American kestrels** hover over field mice. Listen carefully, for nights are haunted by the small **pygmy owl**'s "whew" call and the **great horned owl**'s six deep hoots.

- **Avoid bear feeding areas.** If you stumble across an animal carcass, leave the area immediately and notify a ranger. Toward summer's end, huckleberry patches provide high sugars for bears.

- **Hike in broad daylight.** Avoid early morning, late evening, and night.

- **Never approach a bear.** Head swaying, teeth clacking, laid-back ears, a lowered head, and huffing or woofing are signs of agitation: Clear out slowly.

- **If you do surprise a bear, back away.** Contrary to all inclinations, do not run. Instead, back away slowly, talking quietly and turning sideways or bending your knees to appear smaller and nonthreatening. Avoid direct eye contact. Leave your pack on; it can protect you if the bear attacks.

- **Use pepper spray.** If you surprise a bear that attacks in defense, aim pepper spray at the bear's eyes and nose. Watch wind direction, as it may affect the spray's ability to reach the bear.

- **Play dead.** Should a bear attack, protect yourself and your vulnerable parts by assuming a fetal position on the ground with your hands around the back of your neck. Play dead. Move again only when you are sure the bear has vacated the area.

- **If a bear stalks you as food, or attacks at night, fight back.** Bears stalking humans as prey is extremely rare. Use any means at hand, including pepper spray, shouting, waving sticks, or throwing rocks, to tell the bear you are not an easy food source. Try to escape up something, like a building or a tall tree.

- **Pay attention to trail signage.** Special bear signage is used at trailheads to inform hikers of concerns. Yellow **bear warning** signs indicate bears are frequenting the trail; use extra caution and make noise. Orange **bear closure** signs indicate a trail is closed, usually because one has been aggressive or is defending a carcass.

- Two books have accurate information on bears: Bill Schneider's *Bear Aware* and Stephen Herrero's *Bear Attacks: Their Causes and Avoidance.*

Snakes and Spiders

For the most part, Glacier and Waterton are devoid of poisonous snakes and spiders. The climate is too harsh for rattlesnakes. However, you will find **garter** and **bull snakes** on some trails. Due to colder conditions, native spiders are small, although a bite may produce swelling or an allergic reaction.

ENVIRONMENTAL ISSUES
Climate Change

The current increase in global temperatures affects Glacier. Changes seem to be happening fast, which is why Glacier serves as a living laboratory for studying climate change. While glaciers have shrunk since 1850, most of the park's namesakes are destined to melt in the next decade or so. Melting produces not just a loss of ice but a shift in flora and fauna. As temperatures warm, the tree line advances upward in elevation, encroaching on alpine zones. Glacier's tree line was once 3,200 feet (975 m) lower than it is today; how far up it will climb is unknown.

A rising tree line will cause basins scoured clean by ice and blooming with wildflower meadows to succumb to heavy forests of spruce, fir, pines, shrubs, and bushes. Photographs have already recorded significant changes in vegetation in some locations in the park. In addition, after wildfires, studies are showing new trees struggling to survive heat and drought at lower elevations. Plants at the fringes of their habitat may disappear entirely.

Shifts in floral habitat may force

wildlife to change elevation or latitude in search of food sources. Species such as the heat-intolerant **pika** may suffer extinction. Animals adapted to cold winters, waters, or snow, such as **mountain goats, bighorn sheep, bull trout, westslope cutthroat trout, ptarmigan, short-tailed weasels, showshoe hares,** and **wolverines** may disappear if they can't adapt to warmer temperatures and changing vegetation. For two species of stoneflies that reside around the icy runoff from glaciers, the warming waters pose a threat to their survival. Fish and other aquatic wildlife rely on these bottom-of-the-food chain insects. In the past several years, citizen science programs have aided Glacier National Park in collecting population data on several species that may be threatened by climate change. Gathering baseline population counts and following up with monitoring will track how these animals respond.

Because of Glacier's easily accessed alpine areas, scientists are monitoring melt rates of Grinnell and Sperry Glaciers to help predict future impacts on the park's biodiversity. The **Northern Rocky Mountain Science Center** (www.usgs.gov/centers/norock/) has produced a series of repeat photography collections showing changes in glaciers and forest growth, comparing photographs from the last century to the present day. Find these online and in Many Glacier Hotel.

The changing climate in Glacier is also affecting the annual spring plowing of Going-to-the-Sun Road. With warmer nighttime temperatures failing to drop below freezing, the snowpack does not re-solidify in its 24-hour cycle. That in turn creates conditions for heavy, wet slab avalanches to crash onto the Sun Road, endangering plow crews and damaging the already cleared roadway. These conditions make plowing dangerous and, if plowed too early, add to repair costs.

Glacier's warmer climate is also affecting fire behavior. Huge wildfires are becoming more frequent. Unlike in the past when wildfires would abate at night with cooler temperatures and higher humidity, fires now rage through the night. Recent fires like the 2017 Sprague Fire that burned Sperry Chalet or the Kenow Fire in Waterton grew with fast, scary rampages spawned by dry winds to eat up miles of forest in mere hours. Once snows put the fires out, falling trees and landslides become hazards.

Of all the issues facing Glacier, climate change will produce the biggest impact. While all outcomes may not be known, the effects on this ecosystem are already profound.

Endangered Species

In the 1800s, more than 100,000 **grizzly bears** roamed grasslands and foothills in the Lower 48. Today, only a tiny fraction live in less than 1 percent of their historic range. Greater Glacier's grizzly bears are currently listed as threatened on the Endangered Species List, but due to bear management efforts assisting their recovery, plans are afoot for delisting.

In an effort to count the grizzly population, the U.S. Geological Survey conducted two major studies around Glacier and continues with monitoring today. Collecting scat and bear hair via barbwire stapled to rub trees and surrounding scent lures, scientists used tweezers to bag the hairs for DNA genotyping of species, sex, and individual. You may find barbwire on trees along trails where biologists still gather samples. The study documented a rebounding population of grizzlies across 8 million acres (3.2 million hectares) in northwest Montana. Today's population has topped 1,000 with Glacier housing the densest number. A continuing Montana Fish, Wildlife, and Parks study radio-collars female grizzlies to track reproduction and mortality. It found that the grizzly population in the Northern Continental Divide Ecosystem, which includes Glacier, is growing at 3 percent per year. Both studies revealed that grizzlies have exceeded federal recovery targets, so government machinery now churns toward delisting the grizzly bear.

Grizzlies require a large range; many travel outside the park and across international boundaries. Human pressures from road and house building, agriculture and livestock, timber harvesting, and mineral, oil, and gas mining impact their habitat. Just outside Waterton, legal Canadian hunting and predator-control programs subject bears to high mortality rates. In northwest Montana, poaching, management actions, and private landowners account for the deaths of about 30 grizzlies per year. While bad berry crops and encroaching rural development contribute to bears getting into trouble, inappropriate care with attractants such as garbage, livestock grain, pet food, and bird feeders lead to many of the deaths.

Recorded sightings of the **Canada lynx** have declined substantially in the past 40 years, prompting it to be listed as threatened. In coniferous forests, the lynx follows its primary prey, the snowshoe hare; the cat's population rises and falls with hare numbers. Park studies have followed tracks in the snow to ascertain the lynx's status.

Two endemic trout descended from ice age lakes that formed as the glaciers retreated: **westslope cutthroat trout** and **bull trout.** Glacier provides a stronghold for these fish. Bull trout populations have declined 90 percent, forcing it to be listed as an endangered species, but pure westslope cutthroat have yet to be placed on the list. While habitat degradation and overfishing contributed to the demise, another menace came from nonnative lake trout stocked for recreational fishing, turning bull trout into easy prey. But the biggest threat comes from hybridization with other trout such as rainbows.

Other species not officially listed as endangered also suffer threats to their survival. Of all the ungulates, **bighorn sheep** face the greatest risk. Once widely scattered across most western mountain ranges, the sheep today live in fragmented pockets. Hunting, disease, agriculture, mining, competition for food, fire-suppression policies, and habitat destruction forced this grassland forager into the more rugged fringes of its historic range. Today, 400-600 bighorn sheep graze

in Glacier, with an additional population in Waterton. Recent studies used GPS radio collars to track the sheep, and DNA samples revealed two genetically different populations in northern and southern Glacier.

Current research is also monitoring other species of concern. Annual counts of waterbirds, such as **loons** and **harlequin ducks,** are keeping tabs on these small populations. A winter-hair snag study tracked the number of **wolverines,** as Glacier appears to be one of the few strongholds in the Lower 48 for the gluttonous weasel.

While other animals are in danger, **gray wolves** have seen a recovery. Once ranging throughout most of North America, gray wolves disappeared from Glacier-Waterton by 1920 due to predator-control programs. In the 1970s they were placed on the Endangered Species List. In 1986, following the natural migration of the Magic Pack from Canada, Glacier saw its first litter of pups born in over 50 years. By 2009, numbers in the Northern Rockies rebounded to the point where the federal government delisted the wolf. Outside the park, Montana permits hunting and trapping wolves.

Going-to-the-Sun Road Corridor

Glacier National Park faces issues with visitation on the Sun Road. It has an aging shuttle fleet crowded to capacity, lack of funding for shuttle replacements, nonnative noxious weeds proliferating via vehicles, parking lots crammed full by 8am, human-wildlife interactions, overcrowded trails, and increased shoulder season bicycling. Simply adding more parking is not a viable solution to crowding, as the repercussions spin off in excessive traffic on trails. Damage (widening, trampled vegetation) is already visible on trails, such as the Hidden Lake Overlook, Avalanche Lake, Highline, and St. Mary Falls. Some trails have seen a 250 percent increase in traffic. As annual park visitation climbed substantially to waffle around three million annual visitors, more than one million visit in July alone.

The park is developing a management plan for the Sun Road corridor, based on a three-year study. The study also focused on mountain goats at Logan Pass. The goats frequently slurp antifreeze from the pavement, lick railings and urination spots for salts, and approach humans. In 2016, the park launched a pilot "Bark Ranger" program, where a trained border collie herded sheep and goats from the parking lot into adjacent meadows for safety. Biologists also collared 25 mountain goats with radio and GPS transmitters to follow their movements. They discovered the goats hang around humans rather than cliffs for protection from predators.

Historical Protection

Glacier has many cultural and historical resources, but protecting archaeological and historic assets is difficult. At 50 years old, artifacts including garbage dumps are considered historic, according to federal law. To date, Glacier has identified more than 429 archaeological sites. But many have not been cataloged. More funding is needed for adequate protection.

History

Human use of the Crown of the Continent dates back at least 10,000 years. Evidence shows that the Indigenous people living near Glacier and Waterton today have ancestral roots in the two national parks. These are the traditional lands of the Amskapi Piikuni, Kootenai, Selis, and Qlispe peoples.

INDIGENOUS PEOPLES

Spanning what became the U.S.-Canadian border, the **Blackfeet,** or Niitsitapi ("original people"), included three nomadic groups who based much of their livelihood on hunting bison in the vast prairies on the Continental Divide's east side. The most northerly group, the Siksika, or Blackfoot, were the first to meet European traders. (To refer to the group, *Blackfoot* is used in Canada, and *Blackfeet* is used in the United States.) The Kainai and Piegan (or Piikani) make up the southern groups. For thousands of years, their lands ranged from the Saskatchewan to Yellowstone Rivers.

During spring and summer, efforts focused individually on stocking food: hunting, digging roots, and collecting berries. In summer, Blackfeet people convened for the sun dance, a spiritual ceremony. As bison moved northwest to their wintering ranges in fall, groups met at buffalo jumps, where hunters funneled bison over a cliff to slaughter them for food, hides, and bones. Afterward, they returned to their winter camps, sheltered in deep mountain forests.

For the Blackfeet, the Glacier National Park area was known as the "Backbone of the World." Used for spiritual sanctuary, the mountains provided places for prayer, vision quests, and sacred ceremonies. They were a place to gather guidance, holy plants, and roots used for their healing properties. Unfortunately, many of the Blackfeet names used for land features were given other names, but some remain: Going-to-the-Sun Mountain, Two Medicine Lake, Pitamakin Pass, and Running Eagle Falls.

Today, the Blackfeet celebrate their culture during North American Indian Days in Browning. Dressed in regalia, the community takes to the dancing and rodeo arenas to connect with their history.

On the Continental Divide's west side, the **Salish** and **Kootenai** hunted, trapped, and fished. They ventured east over the mountains on annual bison hunts. Known as the Ktunaxa, the Kootenai (in Canada *Kootenay*) comprised seven bands spanning the western Rockies from southern Alberta to Missoula, Montana. The Kootenai typically used mountain passes like Marias, Cut Bank, Red Eagle, and Brown to cross through Glacier and

Waterton to hunt, and the Blackfeet used the same passes for raiding parties. For the Kootenai, the Lake McDonald area was a place for sacred dances, hence its original name of Sacred Dancing Waters.

Two other nations lived in the Glacier-Waterton vicinity: the Assiniboines, or Stoney people, and the Gros Ventre (which means "Big Belly"). Both of these groups find name-sakes in park features: Stoney Indian Pass and Peaks, the Belly River, and Gros Ventre Falls.

As westward expansion brought an influx of nonnative people and mass slaughters of bison, Indigenous peoples were moved into government-planned reservation boundaries: The Siksika were settled near Calgary, the Kainai were moved onto a reserve adjacent to Waterton, and the Piegans, the largest of the three Blackfeet groups, split in two, with the North Piikani settling near Pincher Creek in Alberta and the South Piikani in Montana. Their reservation included Glacier's eastern slopes up to the Continental Divide. The Salish and Kootenai were moved to the Flathead Reservation southwest of Glacier. Smallpox, poverty, starvation, and social problems took their toll on all of these Indigenous groups.

EXPLORERS, TRAPPERS, AND MINERS

In 1803, when **Lewis and Clark** came west, they bypassed Glacier. At Camp Disappointment, located today on the Blackfeet Reservation, they came within 25 miles (40 km) of Marias Pass, one of the lowest passes through the treacherous Rocky Mountains. But they never found it.

Soon, French, Spanish, and English fur trappers entered the Glacier-Waterton area, but the land between the Continental Divide and the plains belonged to the Blackfeet. In 1895 the U.S. government negotiated a settlement with the Blackfeet to purchase the portion of their reservation that makes up Glacier's eastern slopes today. Starving and in dire need of money, the Blackfeet agreed to the terms of the sale, and Glacier became a public **forest reserve.**

Miners arrived, looking for copper and gold. At the turn of the 20th century, mining boomed in Many Glacier and Rising Sun. Oil wells spewed: western Canada's first in Waterton, and Montana's first at Kintla Lake. Neither oil nor mining paid off, both supplanted by burgeoning tourism.

performers dancing at North American Indian Days

BUILDING A PARK

Pressure to find rail passages through the Northern Rockies began in the mid-1800s. When the Great Northern Railway finally succeeded in 1891 to lay track over the Continental Divide, the face of Glacier changed. The railroad company needed a destination to lure wealthy passengers. The railroad's economic needs and preservationists spawned the idea of **Glacier National Park,** which became a reality on May 11, 1910.

William Logan, for whom Logan Pass is named, took the reins as the first superintendent of the nation's 10th park. Charged with building a headquarters, hiring rangers, constructing trails, and surveying for a road through the park's interior, Logan did little his first year but put out fires. Literally. More than 10 percent of the park flamed during one of the West's biggest fire seasons. His second summer finally saw steps toward readying Glacier for visitors.

In order to provide travelers with places to stay and go, the **Great Northern Railway** created many of the park's facilities: hotels, tent camps, chalets, roads, trails, and boats. Competing for travel time and dollars from wealthy Americans taking steamships to Europe, the railroad pitched the slogan "See America First" to lure vacationers to Glacier, which became known as "America's Switzerland." Large hotels such as Many Glacier and Glacier Park Lodge were built to impress. They touted high-end amenities of the era, such as steam heat.

Horse concessionaires operating from every hotel and chalet in the park merged into the Park Saddle Horse Company. By the mid-1920s, the way to see the park was on horseback. At its peak, the company operated more than 1,000 horses and led more than 10,000 visitors through the park each summer.

As the country's infatuation with the automobile grew, the demand for a road bisecting Glacier's interior increased, and the **Transmountain Highway,** named later after Going-to-the-Sun Mountain, altered how visitors toured the park. Although building the western portion of the Sun Road began in 1919, the 50-mile (81-km) project was not completed until 1932. The opening of Going-to-the-Sun Road ushered in a new era of park visitation. A fleet of red buses hit Glacier's roads for touring. With increased motorized travel, camping gained in popularity, and the Great Northern Railway added budget motor inns to its property collection. With the popularity of Going-to-the-Sun Road, saddle trips and the pricey chalets began to meet their demise.

During the Great Depression and World War II, travel restrictions and fuel conservation made park visitation plummet, forcing hotels and chalets to close. Several chalets fell into disrepair and had to be razed. As bus-tour business usurped rail travel and private car travel grew, Park Saddle Horse Company folded. The railroad's hotel business suffered. Finally, in 1954, Great Northern Railway sold Many Glacier Hotel and Lake McDonald Lodge to the National Park Service and unloaded the two remaining chalets for $1. In 1957 the railroad finally sold off the hotel concessions business.

Of the remaining park lodges and chalets, six are listed as **National Historic Landmarks.** Going-to-the-Sun Road was recognized as the first road in the United States to become a National Historic Landmark. It also is the only road in the country to be a National Historic Landmark and a National Civil Engineering Landmark.

SAVING PARK ATTRIBUTES

In the past two decades, ailing park facilities have received facelifts and rehabilitation. The Sperry and Granite backcountry chalets saw restoration after they were both closed in the 1990s. The 2017 Sprague Fire burned Sperry Chalet's dorm, but it has since been rebuilt. Glacier's red jammer buses were also sidelined in the 1990s, but Glacier Park, Inc., the National Park Fund, and Ford Motor Company collaborated on getting them back on the road, and now park concessionaire Xanterra is providing ongoing upgrades while keeping their historical appearance intact.

Two major rehabilitation projects saw completion in 2018 and 2019. A 10-year, $270 million reconstruction of Going-to-the-Sun Road shored up the road against vehicle wear and tear, torrential rains, mudslides, and avalanches. Many Glacier Hotel underwent a multiyear $30 million reconstruction to fix structural issues without damaging the historical appearance.

INTERNATIONAL PEACE PARK

In 1932, Glacier and Waterton made front-page headlines as the world's first **International Peace Park.** The brainchild and work of Rotary International chapters from Alberta and Montana, their lobbying efforts paid off as the Canadian Parliament and U.S. Congress officially recognized the continuity of the parks. With credit to the longest undefended border in the world, the U.S. and Canadian governments dedicated the parks together as **Waterton-Glacier International Peace Park.**

BIOSPHERE RESERVE

In 1976, the United Nations Educational, Scientific, and Cultural Organization (UNESCO) designated Glacier National Park a **Biosphere Reserve.** Three years later, Waterton Lakes received the same recognition. As Biosphere Reserves, the parks are recognized for their huge diversity of wildlife and plants. Part of the designation is also due to the parks functioning as living laboratories for significant scientific research into fire ecology and climate change.

WORLD HERITAGE SITE

In 1995 UNESCO declared Waterton and Glacier a **World Heritage Site.** This designation was assigned for the parks' natural beauty and unique geological features. Their beauty is attributed to the dramatic topography created by sedimentation in the Belt Sea, the Lewis Overthrust, and glaciation. Those three actions exposed some of the oldest sedimentary rock in North America and created unique geological features, such as Triple Divide Peak, from which water flows to the Pacific, the Gulf of Mexico, and Hudson Bay.

INTERNATIONAL DARK SKY PRESERVE

In 2017, Waterton-Glacier received designation as the world's first **International Transboundary Dark Sky Preserve.** It is one of the dwindling places in the world to see the Milky Way due to minimal light pollution. Astronomy programs at Logan Pass, Apgar Visitor Center, and St. Mary Visitor Center provide constellation tours and telescopic views of planets, star clusters, nebulae, and galaxies. Waterton participates in the Great Worldwide Star Count in October.

Essentials

Getting There

AIR

The closest place to fly in to reach the park is **Glacier Park International Airport** (FCA, www.iflyglacier.com) in Kalispell, Montana. With most flights, you can arrive and get into the park on the same day (35 minutes to West Glacier and Apgar, 1.5 hours to East Glacier, 2.5-3 hours to St. Mary and Many Glacier).

Located outside Great Falls, the **Great Falls International Airport** (GTF, 406/727-3404, www.gtfairport.com) is convenient for picking up on-site rental cars but requires hotel shuttles or taxis to reach

Coronavirus in Glacier National Park

At the time of writing in November 2020, Glacier National Park was significantly impacted by the effects of the coronavirus, but the situation is constantly evolving. Visitors were required to wear face masks in public indoor spaces, as well as outdoors when social distancing could not be maintained. Now more than ever, Moon encourages its readers to be courteous and ethical in their travel. We ask travelers to be respectful to residents and mindful of the evolving situation in their chosen destination when planning their trip.

BEFORE YOU GO

- Check local websites for local **restrictions** and the overall **health status** of the destination. (See *Resources* below.) Glacier's Status Update page is especially helpful for providing up-to-date information.

- If you plan to fly, check with your airline and the destination's health authority for updated **travel requirements.**

- Check the website of any venues, activities and tours you wish to patronize to confirm that they're open, if their hours have been adjusted, and to learn about any specific visitation requirements, such as **mandatory reservations** or **limited occupancy.**

- Pack **hand sanitizer,** a **thermometer,** and plenty of **face masks.** Consider packing **snacks,** a **refillable water bottle,** and even a **cooler** to limit the number of businesses you need to visit.

- **Assess the risk** of entering crowded spaces, joining tours, and taking public transit.

- Expect **general disruptions.** Visitors should be aware that park services may be limited. **Entrances** may be closed, **restaurants** may be offering takeout-only options or other modified services, and **transportation** and **tour services** may be suspended altogether. Sections of **Going-to-the-Sun Road** may be closed, and **activities** like boating and paddling may be restricted to certain areas. Additionally, areas that are part of the **Blackfeet Nation reservation** may be closed to non-tribal members and nonresidents.

RESOURCES

- **Glacier National Park Status Update** (www.nps.gov/glac/planyourvisit/statusupdate. htm): This page lists the current status for Glacier's entrances, roads, activities, lodges, restaurants, and campgrounds.

- **COVID-19 Montana Response** (https://montana.maps.arcgis.com/home/index.html): On this map, you can see numbers of current cases of the coronavirus in Montana as well the counties of Flathead and Glacier, which surround Glacier National Park.

- **Blackfeet Nation** (https://blackfeetnation.com/covid19/): This page lists current regulations and resources regarding the Blackfeet reservation and COVID-19.

- **Flathead County Health Department** (https://flatheadhealth.org/novel-coronavirus-covid-19/): Find information about current regulations regarding masks, social distancing, quarantine procedures, current cases, and testing sites on this site.

- **Whitefish COVID Cares** (www.whitefishcovidcares.com): On the website of Explore Whitefish, you can check this page to find current COVID-19 regulations for the town in the Flathead Valley.

Top Sightseeing en Route to Glacier

- **National Bison Range** (Dixon, Montana): One of the oldest national wildlife refuges and home to preserving the American bison (406/644-2211, www.fws.gov/refuge/national_bison_range/).

- **First Peoples Buffalo Jump State Park** (Ulm, Montana): The National Historic Landmark is one of the largest buffalo jumps in the country (406/866-2217, stateparks.mt.gov/first-peoples-buffalo-jump).

- **Lewis and Clark Caverns State Park** (Whitehall, Montana): A limestone cave of fantastical shapes with guided tours (406/287-3541, stateparks.mt.gov/lewis-and-clark-caverns).

- **Lewis and Clark National Historic Trail Interpretive Center** (Great Falls, Montana): A museum with historical displays, live demonstrations, hands-on activities, and multimedia shows (406/727-8733, www.fs.usda.gov/main/hlcnf/home).

- **C. M. Russell Museum** (Great Falls, Montana): Museum celebrates the work of the famous Western painter Charlie Russell (1864-1926), who summered in his cabin on Glacier's Lake McDonald (406/727-8787, https://cmrussell.org).

- **Frank Slide** (Blairmore, Alberta): Interpretive center that commemorates a 1903 rockslide that buried a mining town (403/562-7388, https://frankslide.com).

- **Head-Smashed-In Buffalo Jump** (Fort Macleod, Alberta): A World Heritage Site and museum that shares the early life of Blackfoot peoples (403/553-2731, https://head-smashed-in.com).

lodging and restaurants in town, 10 minutes away. To reach the east side of Glacier Park requires 2.5 hours driving to East Glacier and Two Medicine or 3 hours to St. Mary or Many Glacier.

Another option is **Calgary International Airport** (YYC, 403/735-1200, www.calgaryairport.com). Because Calgary is still 240 kilometers (149 mi) from Waterton, most visitors heading to the parks rent a car. Driving time is three hours to Waterton and four hours to the east side of Glacier Park at St. Mary or Many Glacier. Others chop off part of the distance by flying south to **Lethbridge** (YQL, www.lethbridgecountyairport.com) via **Air Canada** (888/247-2262, www.aircanada.com) to rent a car to drive the 140 kilometers (87 mi, 1.5 hrs) to Waterton or two hours to drive to the east side of Glacier Park at St. Mary or Many Glacier.

Spokane International Airport (GEG, 509/455-6455, http://spokaneairports.net) requires a five-hour drive to reach the west entrance of Glacier Park at West Glacier. While the driving distance is farther, flights are often less expensive.

SUGGESTED DRIVING ROUTES
From Western Montana, Idaho, and Washington

From I-90 west of **Missoula,** take exit 96 onto U.S. 93 north to Flathead Valley (103 mi/166 km). This scenic route passes below the craggy Mission Mountains and along Flathead Lake, the largest freshwater lake west of the Mississippi. Travelers coming from Idaho through **Libby,** Montana, on U.S. 2 will also follow this route starting in Kalispell.

In Kalispell, a confusing highway maze jogs through Flathead Valley. Follow signs to Glacier Park or West Glacier. In downtown Kalispell, turn east onto U.S. 2 (E. Idaho St.). Go 2 miles (3.2 km) and turn left with U.S. 2 heading north 12 miles (19.3 km). At the intersection with MT 40, turn right; follow the highway through Columbia Falls on U.S. 2 to West Glacier (16 mi/26 km). The total time

Suggested Routes

eagle migrations and buttress for the Bob Marshall Wilderness. Stitching together a Yellowstone National Park and Glacier vacation requires an entire day (7-10 hours) to drive from one park to the other. From I-90 in **Butte,** turn north toward Helena onto I-15 (exit 129/227) and drive 101 miles (163 km) to exit 228. Turn north onto U.S. 287.

Along U.S. 287, strong side winds can slow travel with gusts that rock RVs and trailers, but the scenery is worth the drive. Follow the narrow two-lane U.S. 287 north 66 miles (106 km) through Augusta to Choteau (SHOW-toe), the epitome of Rocky Mountain Front towns. The route travels past Freezeout Lake, known for its spring snow goose migration. In Choteau, the road turns left onto U.S. 89 (Main St.). From Choteau, head north 72 miles (116 km) to Browning. Again, narrow curves slow driving time, but Glacier's peaks soon jut up from the plains. Just before Browning, join U.S. 2 heading northwest. At Browning's west end, turn left as U.S. 2 leaves town. It leads 13 miles (21 km) to East Glacier. Total driving time from I-90 to East Glacier is about five hours (253 mi/410 km).

From **Great Falls,** two routes lead to East Glacier, both with spectacular views of the Rocky Mountain Front as it pops above the plains. For easy interstate and highway driving, take I-15 heading north to Shelby and then U.S. 2 west to East Glacier (143 mi/230 km, 2.5 hours).

A much more interesting approach strikes off through small, rural Rocky Mountain Front towns. From Great Falls, head 10 miles (16.1 km) north on I-15 to catch U.S. 89 north toward Browning. Connect with the Butte route in Choteau. While shorter, the narrow road makes for slower driving to reach East Glacier (139 mi/224-km, 2.75 hrs).

from I-90 to West Glacier about three hours (145 mi/233 km), but it can be four hours or more with heavy traffic, snow, or road-construction delays.

From **Spokane,** drivers should exit I-90 at St. Regis and follow MT 135, MT 200, and MT 28 via Paradise and Hot Springs to reach Flathead Lake. Turn north onto U.S. 93 to reach Kalispell. Spokane to West Glacier (271 mi/435 km) is a five-hour drive.

From Eastern Montana or Yellowstone

This long but scenic approach follows the Rocky Mountain Front, a highway for golden

From the Canadian Rockies

Many travelers link Waterton-Glacier with the national parks of the Canadian Rockies: Jasper, Banff, Yoho, and Kootenay. The Flathead Valley connects directly to Banff and the Canadian Rockies via U.S. 93 and BC

93. To get to Glacier, travel south on BC 93 through British Columbia toward Cranbrook. Six kilometers (3.7 mi) before Cranbrook, merge with CA 3 heading 58 kilometers (36 mi) east toward Elko, where roads go east to Waterton and Glacier's east side or south toward West Glacier.

To head to Waterton, stay on CA 3 for 96 kilometers (60 mi) through Crowsnest Pass and turn south onto AB 6 at Pincher Creek. Drive 32 kilometers (20 mi) to Waterton Lakes National Park, where the seasonal Chief Mountain Highway connects with Glacier National Park's east side.

To head to West Glacier, take BC 93 south at Elko for 39 kilometers (24 mi) toward Roosville on the Canadian-U.S. border (open 24 hours daily year-round). After crossing, continue south 63 miles (101 km) on U.S. 93 through Eureka to Whitefish. Drive with caution: Deer frequent the road between Eureka and Whitefish, earning it the nickname "Deer Alley." In downtown Whitefish, U.S. 93 turns south again at the third stoplight. Drive 2 miles (3.2 km) to the junction with MT 40 with signs for Glacier. Turn left onto MT 40 which joins U.S. 2 just before Columbia Falls, goes through several small burgs, and reaches West Glacier. Expect 6.5 hours driving time from Banff.

From Calgary

Speed limits in Canada are posted in kilometers; 80 km/h is 50 mph. As a general rule, speed limits in Alberta tend to be a little lower than in Montana, especially compared to Montana's narrow, two-lane rural highways, which can be posted at 70 mph (113 kph).

From Calgary, head south for 181 kilometers (113 mi) on AB 2 toward Fort Macleod. For Waterton Lakes National Park, turn west onto CA 3 to Pincher Creek. Turn south onto AB 6 for to the park entrance. From Calgary to Waterton take about 3.5 hours (240 km/149 mi).

To head straight to Glacier from Calgary, continue from Fort Macleod south through Cardston to the Carway-Piegan border crossing (open 7am-11pm daily year-round). From Calgary to the border takes about three hours (266 km/165 mi). After crossing the Canadian-U.S. border onto U.S. 89, drive 25 minutes (19 mi/26 km) to St. Mary for Going-to-the-Sun Road's east entrance. To enter the park at Many Glacier instead after crossing the border, drive U.S. 89 to Babb and turn right onto the Many Glacier Road to reach Many Glacier Hotel or Swiftcurrent in 40 minutes (22 mi/35 km). Total drive time from Calgary to Many Glacier or St. Mary is about four hours.

TRAIN ROUTES

In the United States, Glacier is one of the rare national parks serviced by train. In fact, much of the park's development came from the Great Northern Railway, and Amtrak offers an updated way to reach the park on a historic rail line.

Amtrak

Amtrak's daily *Empire Builder* (800/872-7245, www.amtrak.com) stops at several locations at Glacier National Park. Between Seattle and Shelby, Montana, National Park Service guides offer educational services on board. High summer travel volumes make reservations imperative, and riders may need to contend with delays. Heavy freight traffic, spring flooding, and winter avalanches can cause delays, but the on-time performance has improved with a second track in places. Trains that run late can lag by several hours or more.

Three stops are year-round in the Glacier environs: Essex, West Glacier, and Whitefish. East Glacier is a summer-only stop. Check with Amtrak for schedules.

The westbound route originates in Chicago, stopping at Milwaukee, St. Paul-Minneapolis, and Fargo, plus smaller towns on its way to Glacier. The ride from Chicago to East Glacier takes about 30 hours or more. From Chicago, westbound trains arrive in the evening at East Glacier, Essex, West Glacier, and Whitefish.

Eastbound trains starting in Seattle

and Portland join in Spokane and stop in Whitefish before reaching West Glacier in a little more than 15 hours. From West Glacier, the train skirts the southern edge of Glacier, stopping in Essex and East Glacier. The eastbound train lands riders in the Glacier environs in early morning.

VIA Rail Canada

Canada's **VIA Rail** (888/842-7245, www.viarail.ca) jogs far north to Edmonton between Winnipeg and Vancouver. It even bypasses Calgary, the nearest metropolitan city to the Rockies. Most train travelers switch to air or bus travel to reach Calgary and then rent a car to reach Waterton or Glacier.

TRAVEL HUB: FLATHEAD VALLEY

Flathead Valley is the closest, easiest access to Glacier National Park. Flights arriving before evening can put you via shuttle at Lake McDonald in time to catch the sunset in the park. With the exception of one hotel adjacent to the airport, if you arrive on a late flight or want to explore Flathead Valley, you will need to stay in one of four towns. **Columbia Falls** is closest to Glacier, but **Whitefish** is more attractive, with its resort-town atmosphere. **Kalispell** and **Bigfork** are farthest from Glacier.

Airport

Nonstop flights come from about a dozen cities via Alaska, Allegiant, American, Delta/SkyWest, and United to service the closest airport to Glacier National Park, **Glacier Park International Airport** (FCA, www.iflyglacier.com). Some routes are winter or summer only, when rates are highest. Even though the airport has an international designation, the connections are Canadian charter flights. Car-rental desks sit near baggage claim. Prearranged shuttles are right outside.

Train

Amtrak's *Empire Builder* (800/872-7245,

www.amtrak.com) stops in Whitefish twice daily, once eastbound in early morning and once westbound in late evening. Reservations are a must in summer.

Bus

Flathead Transit (406/275-2877, www.csktdhrd.org/transportation/flathead-transit) runs one bus daily between Missoula, Kalispell, and Whitefish.

Within Flathead Valley, **Eagle Transit** (https://flathead.mt.gov/eagle/) runs weekday bus routes in Kalispell, Whitefish, and Columbia Falls. From Whitefish, the free **SNOW Bus** (https://bigmtncommerial.org) goes multiple times daily from Whitefish to Whitefish Mountain Resort July-early September and early December-early April.

Taxi and Shuttle

For visitors staying in Flathead Valley, many hotels have airport shuttles. Otherwise, call **Glacier Taxi** (406/250-3603, glaciertaxi.com). **Arrow Shuttle** (406/300-2301, arrowshuttle-taxi.com) also goes to Flathead Valley towns, plus West Glacier, East Glacier, or Polebridge.

Car Rental

The Glacier Park International Airport terminal has four car-rental agencies with desks in the airport: **Hertz** (406/758-2220 or 800/654-3131, www.hertz.com), **National-Alamo** (406/257-7144 or 800/227-7368, www.alamo.com, www.nationalcar.com), **Avis** (406/257-2727 or 800/331-1212, www.avis.com), and **Budget** (406/755-7500 or 800/527-0700, www.budget.com). Kalispell and Whitefish also have car-rental agencies (check www.iflyglacier.com); they will deliver a car to the airport or pick you up.

RV Rental

No companies rent RVs in Flathead Valley, but you may find rentals through www.rvshare.com. Be aware, however, of Going-to-the-Sun Road's vehicle length restrictions (21 ft/6.4 m). You may need to see the famous road via tour bus or rent a car.

Gear Rentals

Inside the airport near the baggage claim, **Glacier Outfitters** (406/219-7466, www.goglacieroutfitters.com) has an outlet for renting bear spray and hiking gear.

Food and Accommodations

Because Glacier is so close to Glacier Park International Airport, many travelers go directly into the park the day they arrive; likewise with flying out. For those needing adjacent airport lodging for ultra-early or late flights, stay at **Country Inns and Suites** (4150 U.S. 2, 406/751-9000, www.radissonhotels.com).

Flathead Valley lodging varies from inexpensive hostels to upscale, and many hotels offer complimentary airport shuttles. Although the airport is within Kalispell city limits, many visitors are surprised to find Kalispell hotels 15 minutes away in the opposite direction of the park. In fact, the airport is almost equidistant at 15-20 minutes between downtown Kalispell, Whitefish, and Columbia Falls. Columbia Falls is the closest town to the park, although with more limited lodging. Downtown Kalispell and Whitefish are in opposite directions from the airport, although Whitefish is attractive for its resort town atmosphere. Bigfork, another resort town, is furthest away. All four towns have plentiful restaurants.

TRAVEL HUB: GREAT FALLS

Straddling the mighty Missouri River, Great Falls, Montana, is an east-side gateway to Glacier. But the additional distance to Glacier and lack of easy connections with Amtrak and buses make renting a car preferable. With a flight arriving by late afternoon, you can be in East Glacier to watch the sunset that same day, about a 2.5-hour drive.

Airport

Alaska, Allegiant, Delta/Sky West, and United airlines service **Great Falls International Airport** (GTF, 406/727-3404, https://flygtf.com) with nonstop flights from seven cities (some summer only). The airport's international label comes from a couple of Canadian charter flights. Located outside town, the airport is convenient for picking up on-site rental cars but requires hotel shuttles or taxis to reach lodging and restaurants in town, 10 minutes away.

Train and Bus

Greyhound (www.greyhound.com) reaches Great Falls, but no farther. The closest westbound **Amtrak** depot to East Glacier is Shelby, 87 miles (140 km) north of Great Falls. Bus connections between Great Falls and Shelby are not convenient, but **Northern Transit Interlocal** (406/873-2207 or 406/470-0727, https://northern.rural-transit.com) runs buses on Mondays and Thursdays.

Taxi

Some hotels provide airport shuttle service. Otherwise, call **Diamond Cab** (406/453-3241) or use Uber (www.uber.com).

Car Rental

Great Falls has most national car-rental chains. The airport terminal contains **Alamo** (406/727-0273 or 800/462-5266, www.alamo.com), **Hertz** (406/761-6641 or 800/654-3131, www.hertz.com), **Enterprise** (406/216-5001 or 800/325-8007, www.enterprise.com), **National** (406/453-4386 or 800/227-7368, www.nationalcar.com), and **Avis** (406/761-7610 or 800/230-4898, www.avis.com).

RV Rental

No companies rent RVs in Great Falls, but you may find rentals through www.rvshare.com. Be aware, however, of Going-to-the-Sun Road's vehicle length restrictions (21 ft/6.4 m). You may need to see the famous road via tour bus or rent a car.

Food and Accommodations

Great Falls has hotels and motels ranging from low-end to moderately priced accommodations, but nothing upscale. Most national hotel chains are downtown. Check listings with **Great Falls Convention and Visitors Bureau** (800/735-8535, www.genuinemontana.com).

For a filling meal at a reasonable price and a view overlooking the Missouri River, head for **MacKenzie River Pizza Company** (500 River Dr. S., 406/761-0085, 11am-10pm daily, $8-24), Montana's creative answer to pizza chains. The restaurant serves cowboy nachos, giant salads and sandwiches, eclectic pizzas, and Montana microbrews.

TRAVEL HUB: CALGARY

Calgary is the closest metropolitan city to Glacier. If coming in mid-July, you can take in the **Calgary Stampede** (403/269-9822 or 800/661-1767, www.calgarystampede.com), one of the biggest rodeos in the world. With an early afternoon flight arrival, you can be walking the beach at Waterton Lake in the evening with about 3.5 hours of driving. Both St. Mary and Many Glacier are about four hours from Calgary.

Airport

Calgary International Airport (YYC, 403/735-1200, www.yyc.com) bustles with flights from Tokyo, London, and Frankfurt. It has restaurants, shopping, and service from more than 25 airlines. Airport shuttles connect with downtown, hotels, car-rental agencies, and the Greyhound bus terminal. Because Calgary is still 240 kilometers (149 mi) from Waterton, most visitors heading to the park rent a car. Others chop off part of the distance by flying south to **Lethbridge** (YQL, www.lethbridgeairport.ca) via **Air Canada** (888/247-2262, www.aircanada.com), where they rent cars to drive the 140 kilometers (87 mi) to Waterton. From Calgary, you can also reach the east side of Glacier at St. Mary or Many Glacier in about four hours.

Bus, Taxi, and Shuttle

You cannot reach Waterton or Glacier traveling by **Greyhound Canada** (403/265-9111 or 800/661-8747, www.greyhound.ca).

Daily buses run from Calgary International Airport to Pincher Creek, but no farther: From Pincher Creek, make reservations with **Pincher Creek Taxi** (403/627-3114) to get to Waterton.

The **Airport Shuttle Express** (403/509-4799, www.airportshuttleexpress.com) runs a scheduled summer bus service from the Calgary airport to Waterton and East Glacier, Montana. They also have charters.

Car Rental

Most major car-rental chains have desks inside the Calgary Airport terminals or within a shuttle ride down the road. U.S. travelers can book vehicles from home through sister companies: **Alamo** (800/462-5266, www.alamo.com), **Hertz** (800/654-3131, www.hertz.com), **Dollar** (866/434-2226, www.dollar.com), **National** (800/227-7368, www.nationalcar.com), **Budget** (800/219-7992, www.budget.com), and **Avis** (800/230-4898, www.avis.com).

RV Rental

Two RV-rental companies are within 3 kilometers (1.8 mi) of the Calgary Airport: **Canada RV Rentals** (877/778-9569, https://canada-rv-rentals.com) and **CanaDream** (888/480-9726, www.canadream.com). Motorhome RVs start at C$400-600 per day. Be aware of Going-to-the-Sun Road's vehicle-length restrictions (21 ft/6.4 m). You may have to supplement your RV tour with shuttles or red bus tours to see the historic landmark.

Equipment Rental

If you need outdoor gear, **Calgary Outdoor Centre** (2500 University Dr. NW, 403/220-7749, www.ucalgary.ca) rents equipment for camping, backpacking, boating, bicycling, fishing, snowshoeing, climbing, and skiing. Per-day rates ($4-25/item) are charged for tents, backpacks, GPS units, stoves, sleeping bags, clothing, hiking boots, climbing gear, and rain gear. It also rents rafts, kayaks, skis, canoes, mountain bikes, and car racks. Find the complete list of rental gear and rates online. Call to reserve equipment ahead of time, a must during midsummer; a nonrefundable credit card deposit is required. When picking up gear, try it on to be sure it fits, and have the staff demonstrate how to use unfamiliar equipment. You'll need a driver's license or photo ID to rent gear.

Food and Accommodations

The airport terminal houses the extremely convenient **Calgary Airport Marriott In-Terminal Hotel** (403/717-0522, www.marriott.com). Within a few miles of the airport, major chain hotels offer airport shuttles. Find them via the **airport** (www.airporthotelguide.com/calgary) or contact **Tourism Calgary** (800/661-1678, www.visitcalgary.com).

Budget-minded travelers may want to head for a hostel. The revamped **HI-Calgary City Centre Hostel** (403/269-8239 or 866/762-4122, https://hihostels.ca, C$38-42) has dorm beds. A Hostelling International membership ($35) is required; otherwise, rates are 10 percent higher.

For dining, Canadian cuisine has a few Alberta specialties meriting a taste. Calgary is in the heart of cattle country; grass-fed Alberta beef graces menus in all forms, as does bison. At the high end, it's tender and sweet; at the lower end, it's still decent. The doctored-up Canadian french-fry dish called *poutine* comes with a variety of toppings, but the traditional version includes cheese curds and gravy. Contrary to many towns east of the Rocky Mountains where steak-and-potato fare reigns, Calgary is much more cosmopolitan, with a good share of international restaurants. Canada's 5 percent Goods and Services Tax (GST) will be added to lodging and food bills.

Getting Around

ORIENTATION

Getting your bearings in Glacier is not difficult; the park is split along the Continental Divide into the east side and west side, each with several entrances to valley drainages. Two Medicine, St. Mary, and Many Glacier are on the east, while Lake McDonald and the North Fork cover the west. Although U.S. 2 passes briefly through the park's southern tip between East Glacier and West Glacier, southern entrances into the park's core are via foot or on horseback trails. On the north side, Waterton Lakes National Park provides access via boat or on foot across the Canadian-U.S. border into Glacier's interior.

Only one route bisects the entire park: Going-to-the-Sun Road. Rush hour on this road is 8am-5pm seven days a week July-August.

Most summer visitors love the park's expansive east-side views. On a clear day, not much obstructs the view of mountains. By autumn, not many services remain open to take the front's brutal winds.

The park's heavily forested west side balances remote corners of the North Fork with the busy hub of West Glacier. Mountain snows feed large rivers that drain into Flathead Lake. Mixed with farmland, rural pockets, and resort towns, the fast-growing Flathead Valley, anchored in winter by recreational skiing, is a year-round enclave for nearly 100,000 people.

DRIVING

Driving in Glacier National Park is not easy. Narrow roads built for cars in the 1930s barely fit today's SUVs, much less RVs and trailers. With no shoulders and sharp curves, roads require reduced speeds and shifting into second gear on extended descents to avoid burning brakes. Check the park's **Recreational Access Display** (www.nps.gov/applications/glac/dashboard/) for real-time status the roads, weather, parking lots, and campgrounds.

Two roads cross the Continental Divide: Going-to-the-Sun Road bisects the park, while U.S. 2 hugs Glacier's southern border. Both are two-lane roads; however, the seasonal Going-to-the-Sun Road (mid-June-mid-Oct.) is the more difficult drive, climbing 1,500 feet (457 m) higher on a skinnier, snakier road than year-round U.S. 2. The Sun Road does not permit RVs or trailer-combos over 21 feet (6.4 m) long.

Paved two-lane roads also lead to Two Medicine, St. Mary, Many Glacier, and Waterton. But don't be deluded: Just because roads are paved doesn't mean that they are smooth. Frost heaves and sinkholes pock-mark them, bouncing passengers and slowing travel. Montana is also the land of dusty, potholed dirt roads: On the west side, notoriously narrow, bumpy roads lead up the North Fork Valley; on the east side, a dirt road leads into the Cut Bank Valley. In some places they are as bad as they can be without requiring a 4WD vehicle. Larger RVs and those with trailers will not be comfortable on these dirt roads.

Gas

Gas up before you go: Service stations are not on every corner, nor are gas stations inside the park. Find gas in West Glacier, East Glacier, St. Mary, Babb, and Waterton, but few of the stations can repair severely broken-down vehicles. For big vehicle work, hit Browning or Flathead Valley in Montana or Pincher Creek in Canada.

SHUTTLES
Bus Shuttles

Inside Glacier, the National Park Service runs **free Going-to-the-Sun Road shuttles** July-Labor Day and more limited in September. These are shuttles, not guided tours. Between Apgar and St. Mary, they stop at lodges, trailheads, campgrounds, and Logan Pass. Get on or off at any of the stops denoted by interpretive signs. No tickets are needed, and no reservations are taken. Departing every 15-30 minutes, these extremely popular shuttles enable point-to-point hiking on some of Glacier's most spectacular trails. Check schedules and routes online (www.nps.gov/glac).

Two companies operate fee-based shuttles on Glacier's east side. For hikers and backpackers, these aid in doing point-to-point trails, and for travelers without vehicles, they help connect with the Sun Road shuttles. Find schedules, rates, and online. **Pursuit Glacier Park Collection** (844/868-7474, www.glacierparkcollection.com) runs van service daily early June-late September north-south between East Glacier, Two Medicine, and St. Mary. **Xanterra** (855/733-4522, www.glaciernationalparklodges.com) operates daily shuttles July-Labor Day from Many Glacier to St. Mary.

In Waterton, **Waterton Outdoor Adventures** (The Tamarack, 214 Mount View Rd., 403/859-2378, www.hikewaterton.com) shuttles hikers in summer to a few trailheads and to the Chief Mountain border crossing for backpacking Stony Indian Pass to Waterton.

Boat Shuttles

Hikers and backpackers also use tour boats as shuttles to reduce foot miles. In Glacier, **Glacier Park Boat Company** (406/257-2426, https://glacierparkboats.com, June-Sept.) carts hikers across Two Medicine Lake and in Many Glacier across Swiftcurrent Lake and Lake Josephine. Both add early morning Hiker Express shuttles in July-August. Get advance reservations for round-trip shuttles only. No reservations are necessary to catch a return boat; pay cash for a half-price fare upon boarding. Return shuttles run until all hikers are accommodated.

In Waterton, **Waterton Shoreline Cruises** (403/859-2362, www.watertoncruise.com) runs boat shuttles to the Crypt Lake trailhead late May-early October, and the tour boat to Goat Haunt functions as a hiker shuttle June-mid-September for round-trip or one-way rides. Buy tickets a day in advance.

Driving Times

Mileage is an inaccurate way to plan for trips around Glacier, as narrow, curvy, two-lane mountain roads take more time to drive than regular highways do. Instead, you'll need to plan for driving times that reflect real road conditions and summer traffic. For example, Going-to-the-Sun Road is only 50 miles (81 km) long but takes two hours to drive without stops during midday traffic. Logan Pass driving times are the most variable and depend on conditions. Photo stops, sightseeing, traffic delays, entrance station lineups, border crossings, and construction add more time. Add up links from park hubs to get the total driving time to a destination.

WEST GLACIER TO:

- Apgar: 0:08
- Polebridge: 1:00
- Essex: 0:35
- East Glacier: 1:10
- Logan Pass: 1:30
- St. Mary: 2-2.5 (on either Going-to-the-Sun Road or US 2 and 89)

FROM POLEBRIDGE TO:

- Bowman Lake: 0:30
- Kintla Lake: 1:15

FROM EAST GLACIER TO:

- Essex: 0:35
- West Glacier: 1:10
- Two Medicine: 0:25
- Browning: 0:15
- St. Mary via MT 49 and U.S. 89: 0:50
- St. Mary via Browning and Duck Lake Road: 1:05

FROM ST. MARY TO:

- East Glacier via U.S. 89 and MT 49: 0:50

TOURS

Bus Tours

Two bus-tour companies operate in Glacier National Park, both traveling the scenic Going-to-the-Sun Road. You'll get the "inside story" on the park from both companies' guides. Neither include park entrance fees, meals, or guide gratuities.

Departing from East Glacier, Browning, St. Mary, and West Glacier, the Blackfeet-owned and guided **Sun Tours** (406/732-9220 or 800/786-9220, www.glaciersuntours.com) has daily tours mid-June-mid-September over Going-to-the-Sun Road in air-conditioned buses with huge windows. Interpretation is steeped in Blackfeet cultural history and park lore.

The historic **red jammer buses**

- East Glacier via Duck Lake Road: 1:05
- Browning via U.S. 89: 0:40
- Browning via Duck Lake Road: 0:45
- Logan Pass: 0:35
- Many Glacier: 0:35
- Chief Mountain border crossing: 0:35
- Waterton: 1:15

FROM MANY GLACIER TO:
- St. Mary: 0:35
- Waterton: 1:30

TO WEST GLACIER FROM:
- Columbia Falls: 0:25
- Glacier Park Airport in Kalispell: 0:40
- Whitefish: 0:45
- Kalispell: 0:50
- Bigfork: 1:10

FROM GREAT FALLS TO:
- East Glacier: 2:30

FROM CALGARY TO:
- Waterton: 3:20
- St. Mary: 4:00
- Many Glacier: 4:00

with rollback canvas tops are operated by **Xanterra** (855/733-4522, www.glaciernationalparklodges.com). Late May-September, daily tours depart from all the park lodges for Going-to-the-Sun Road, Waterton, and other park destinations.

Boat Tours

Five glacier-carved lakes in Waterton-Glacier International Peace Park have scenic boat tours. Tour boats run daily with multiple departures. Buy tickets at the docks or in advance online. In Glacier, **Glacier Park Boat Company** (406/257-2426, https://glacierparkboats.com) operates June-September boat tours on Lake McDonald, Two Medicine Lake, St. Mary Lake, and in Many Glacier on Swiftcurrent Lake and

Lake Josephine. In Waterton, **Waterton Shoreline Cruises** (403/859-2362, www.watertoncruise.com) travel down Waterton Lake across the international border May-early October. The boats stop at Goat Haunt, USA, June through mid-September.

TRAVELING BY RV

RVing is a great way to travel, but in Glacier it has its limitations. Roads are narrow, curvy, and shoulderless, and many inside-park campsites cannot fit larger RVs. Most of all, RVs are restricted on Going-to-the-Sun Road.

Road Restrictions

Going-to-the-Sun Road restricts RVs and trailers. From bumper to bumper, vehicles including truck-trailer or car-trailer combos must be 21 feet (6.4 m) or shorter to drive the road over Logan Pass between Avalanche Campground on the west and Rising Sun on the east. The maximum width allowed, including mirrors, is 8 feet (2.4 m); maximum height is 10 feet (3 m). Despite meeting width and height requirements, small RV drivers will still feel pinched as they navigate the skinny lanes hemmed in by a 1,000-foot (305-m) vertical wall and oncoming traffic inches away.

RVers shouldn't lose heart. You can still see the famed Going-to-the-Sun Road via Xanterra's red bus tours, Sun Tours, and free park shuttles, or rent a car in West Glacier, East Glacier, or St. Mary.

The North Fork roads inside Glacier also prohibit vehicles and RVs over 21 feet (6.4 m) long, and trailers are not allowed.

Camping

Campsites to fit large RVs are limited inside Glacier. Apgar can handle up to 40 footers (12.2 m). Fish Creek, Many Glacier, and St. Mary can fit RVs up to 35 feet (10.7 m). Two Medicine can accommodate RVs up to 32 feet (9.8 m). Only the shorter RVs can fit into sites at Rising Sun (up to 25 ft/7.6 m), Avalanche (up to 26 ft/7.9 m), and Sprague Creek (up to 21 ft/6.4 m, but no towed units). RVs must

be shorter than 21 feet (6.4 m) for Bowman Lake, Kintla Lake, Logging Creek, and Quartz Creek, and no trailers are permitted.

Campgrounds inside the park do not have hookups, nor do adjacent national forest campgrounds. For hookups, head outside the park to commercial campgrounds in West Glacier, East Glacier, St. Mary, Flathead Valley, and along U.S. 2. In Waterton Lakes National Park, the Townsite Campground has hookups.

Generator use is restricted in campgrounds inside Glacier by hours and campsite location. Find details on generator hours and permitted locations online (www.nps.gov/glac).

Disposal Stations

Six campgrounds inside Glacier have disposal stations: Apgar, Fish Creek, Many Glacier, Rising Sun, St. Mary, and Two Medicine. Many private campgrounds at West Glacier, St. Mary, and East Glacier have disposal stations, too, but the North Fork has none. In Waterton, find dump stations at Townsite and Crandell Mountain Campgrounds and commercial campgrounds outside the park.

Repairs

Should you need repair services, drive to **Blue Dog RV** (3138 U.S. 2 E., Kalispell, 406/351-0132, www.bluedogrv.com) in Flathead Valley. If unable to drive, **Mike's Mobile RV Services** (406/261-7684) can come to you. He can repair many things where you are, even in Glacier, but you'll pay handsomely. In Waterton, **Pat's Gas Station** (224 Mount View Rd., 403/859-2266, www.patswaterton.com) can do minor repairs.

TRAVELING BY BICYCLE

Glacier is a tough place to cycle. There are no shoulders, roads are narrow and curvy, and drivers gawk at scenery instead of the road, all putting cyclists in precarious positions. With that caveat, for a dedicated cyclist, nothing compares with bicycling Going-to-the-Sun Road, one of the country's premier routes. Other roads surrounding Glacier also make good rides, particularly the 142-mile (229-km) loop linking Going-to-the-Sun Road and U.S. 89, MT 49, and U.S. 2. Roadies loop them in one day; tourers ride the loop in 2-3 days. Riders need to be prepared for large trucks and RVs whizzing by their elbows.

Spring bicycle season takes place on vehicle-closed roads currently being plowed. All manner of bikes (roadies, mountain bikes, kiddie trailers, tagalongs, tot striders, and even tricycles) hit the roads on sunny days, especially Going-to-the-Sun Road. Riding starts in mid-April and goes until the roads open, which can be late May to mid-July. You can ride as far as plowing operations and avalanche conditions permit.

Find rental bikes at several locations in Flathead Valley, Apgar, and West Glacier. If you fly in, you can ship your bike to **Glacier Cyclery** (406/862-6446, www.glaciercyclery.com) in Whitefish for reassembly, storage until you arrive, and return shipping.

Bike Trails

Designated bike trails are few and far between in Waterton-Glacier. In fact, Glacier has only two trails, one paved and one dirt in the Apgar area. No bicycles are allowed on any other backcountry trails in Glacier. In Waterton, a paved bike trail and four backcountry paths permit bicycles. Outside Glacier, the 10-mile (16.1-km) **Gateway to Glacier Trail** is a paved pathway paralleling U.S. 2 from Hungry Horse to West Glacier.

Campsites

Glacier's campgrounds designate campsites for cyclists and hikers at Apgar, Fish Creek, Sprague Creek, Avalanche, Rising Sun, St. Mary, Many Glacier, and Two Medicine. Held until 9pm, the sites are shared, holding up to eight people, who pay $6-8 per person. If these sites are full, you must find a regular unoccupied tent site, which is impossible in midsummer or late at night. Hiker-biker sites have special bear-resistant food storage containers.

Safety

Because of the narrow shoulderless roads, cyclists should have some riding ability before hitting Glacier's roads. Drainage grates, ice, and debris can quickly throw bikes off balance, adding to the challenge. Although cyclists on Going-to-the-Sun Road are fairly common, many drivers are so agog at the view that they may not be fully aware of your presence. That's a good reason to wear a helmet and bright colors. Skinny shoulderless roads demand riding in single file. For added protection, be sure your bike has reflectors on both ends, and use lights in fog and at dawn, dusk, or at night.

Restrictions

Because of high traffic volume and narrow lanes, Glacier enforces bicycling restrictions on Going-to-the-Sun Road's west side. Two sections of the road are closed 11am-4pm daily June 15 through Labor Day: between Apgar Loop Road and Sprague Creek Campground, and eastbound (uphill) from Logan Creek to Logan Pass. The ride from Sprague to Logan Creek takes about 45 minutes; the climb from Logan Creek to Logan Pass usually takes at least three hours.

Repairs

Bring spare tubes and brake pads, a pump, and equipment to make minor repairs yourself. The park doesn't have any bike shops to bail you out. For major repairs, head to the bike shops in Flathead Valley.

TRAVELING BY MOTORCYCLE

Motorcyclists relish riding Going-to-the-Sun Road. On sunny days, the ride is unparalleled; on inclement days, it's bone-chilling. The alpine wonderland attracts scads of decked-out Harleys, Goldwings, and motorcycle clubs who come just to tour the Sun Road. Between East Glacier and U.S. 89, MT 49 is posted for motorcycle warnings due to severe uneven pavement and gravel sections.

Many motorcyclists gravitate to Montana

because the state requires helmets only for those under age 18. However, since most drivers on Going-to-the-Sun Road find their attention severely divided between the scenery and the road, you may want to consider head protection. In Waterton, helmets are required.

Missoula has the closest motorcycle rentals at **Grizzly Harley-Davidson** (406/721-2154, www.grizzlyhd.com). If you need repairs, the Flathead Valley has several motorcycle shops that specialize in one brand over another. Check business listings to pick the appropriate service for your machine.

TRAVELING WITH BOATS, CANOES, KAYAKS, AND PADDLEBOARDS

Glacier poses unique issues for those traveling with boats. Trailers are not allowed over Going-to-the-Sun Road, so those towing boats are required to drive U.S. 2 to get from one side of the park to the other. Due to overhangs on the Sun Road, rigs also can be no higher than 10 feet (3 m), so truck-camper combinations with kayaks, canoes, or rafts on top may be too tall. The North Fork inside Glacier prohibits vehicles longer than 21 feet (6.4 m) and trailers; you can only get gear to the lakes if carried on top of your rig.

Due to aquatic invasive species, boating regulations have gotten stricter in Glacier and Waterton. All boats, including kayaks, canoes, and paddleboards, must obtain permits (free). In Glacier, get these from park headquarters in West Glacier, St. Mary Visitor Center, Two Medicine Ranger Station, and Many Glacier Ranger Station. For Waterton, get permits at the park entrance or visitors center.

Glacier allows only non-trailered boats with electric motors on Lake McDonald, Bowman Lake, Two Medicine Lake, St. Mary Lake, and Swiftcurrent Lake. All other lakes are for hand-propelled boats only. Gas-powered boats and their trailers require a 30-day quarantine to receive a permit. Waterton bans all motorized and trailered boats.

Recreation

DAY HIKING
Trail Status

Conditions on Glacier's trails vary significantly depending on the season, elevation, recent severe weather, and bear closures. Swinging and plank bridges across rivers and creeks are installed in late May-June. Some years, bridges are installed and then removed a few weeks later to wait for rivers swollen with runoff to subside. Most years, higher passes are snowbound until mid-July. Steep snowfields often inhibit hiking on the Highline Trail until mid-July or so. Ptarmigan Tunnel's doors are usually open mid-July-early October. Several backcountry campsites are snowbound until August. To find out about trail conditions before hiking, stop at ranger stations or visitors centers for updates or consult trail status reports June-September on the park's website (www.nps.gov/glac). Bear or fire closures are also listed online.

Signage

All park trailheads and junctions have excellent signage. Be prepared to convert kilometers to miles in your head to understand distances. Some signs show both kilometers and miles, others simply kilometers. This is, after all, the International Peace Park, and kilometers are more international. In Waterton, all trail sign distances use kilometers. Pull out your math skills: To convert kilometers to miles, multiply the kilometers listed by 0.6 (example: 3 km x 0.6 = 1.8 miles). To convert miles to kilometers, multiply the miles by 1.6 (example: 2 miles x 1.6 = 3.2 km). These calculations are simple, easy approximations for the trail. For more precise conversions, multiply

Hiking in Glacier demands preparedness. Unpredictable, fast-changing weather can mutate a warm summer day into wintry conditions in hours. Different elevations vary in temperature, wind, and visibility: Sun on the shore of Two Medicine Lake may hide knock-over winds barreling over Dawson Pass 6 miles (9.7 km) away. Hot valley temperatures may give way at Grinnell Lake to chilly breezes blowing down from the Continental Divide across the ice. To be prepared in Glacier's backcountry, take the following:

· **Extra Clothing:** Rain pants and jackets can double as wind protection, while gloves and a lightweight warm hat will save fingers and ears. Carry at least one extra water-wicking layer for warmth. Avoid cotton fabrics, which stay soggy and fail to retain body heat.

· **Extra Food and Water:** Depending on the hike's length, take a lunch and snacks, like compact high-energy food bars. Low-odor foods will not attract animals. Always carry extra water: Heat, wind, and elevation lead quickly to dehydration, and most visitors find they drink more than they do at home. Avoid drinking directly from streams or lakes. Due to the possibility of giardia and illness-inducing bacteria, always filter or treat water sources before drinking.

· **Map and Compass or GPS Device:** Although Glacier's trails are extremely well signed, a map can be handy for ascertaining distance traveled and location. A compass or GPS device will also help, but only if you know how to use it. In deep, heavily forested valleys, a GPS receiver may not pick up the satellites.

· **Flashlight:** Carry a small flashlight or headlamp for after-dark emergencies. Take extra batteries, too.

· **First-Aid Kit:** Two bandages may not be enough. Carry a fully equipped standard first-aid kit with blister remedies. Many outdoor stores sell suitably prepared kits for hiking. Don't forget to add personal items like bee-sting kits and allergy medications.

· **Sun Protection:** Altitude, snow, ice, and lakes all increase ultraviolet radiation. Protect yourself with SPF 30 sunscreen, sunglasses, and a sun hat or baseball cap.

· **Emergency Toilet Supplies:** Not every hike conveniently places a pit toilet at its destination. To accommodate an alfresco toilet stop, carry a small trowel, plastic baggies, and toilet paper, and move at least 200 feet (61 m) away from water sources. For urinating, aim for a durable surface, such as rocks, logs, gravel, or snow. "Watering" fragile plants, campsites, or trails attracts mineral-starved animals that dig up the area. Bury feces 6-8 inches (15-20 cm) deep in soil. Do not bury toilet paper; use a baggie to pack it out.

· **Feminine Hygiene:** Carry heavy-duty zippered baggies and pack out tampons, pads, and everything else.

· **Insect Repellent:** Summer can be abuzz at any elevation with mosquitoes and blackflies. Insect repellents that contain 50 percent DEET work best. Purchase applications that rub or spray at close range rather than aerosols that go airborne onto other people, plants, and animals.

· **Pepper Spray:** If you want to carry pepper spray, purchase an 8-ounce (237 ml) can, as nothing smaller will be effective; however, do not bother unless you know how to use it and what influences its effectiveness. Do not use it like bug repellent.

· **Miscellaneous:** A knife may come in handy, as can a few feet of nylon cord and a bit of duct tape (wrap a few feet around something small like a flashlight handle or water bottle). Many hikers have repaired boots and packs with duct tape and a little ingenuity.

by 0.62 to convert kilometers to miles; to convert miles to kilometers, multiply by 1.61. Some hikers enjoy kilometers: the number is always higher, so the accomplishment feels greater.

Trailheads may also display **yellow warning** or **orange closure** signs to alert hikers to bear or mountain lion activity. Obey the closures! They can mean an animal is guarding prey.

Heavily trampled areas may have a **footprint with a red slash** in fragile alpine meadows and areas of abuse replanted with native vegetation. It means "don't walk here."

Guides

National Park Service naturalists guide free hikes during summer in Glacier and snowshoe excursions in winter. Consult schedules in the park newspaper or online (www.nps.gov/glac) or in visitors centers. Parks Canada naturalists guide free summer hikes in Waterton; find current schedules in the visitors center or online (www.pc.gc.ca). Naturalists from both parks lead the International Peace Park Hike twice weekly in July-August.

One company in Glacier and one company in Waterton provide guide services, with reservations required. **Glacier Guides** (406/387-5555 or 800/521-7238, https://glacierguides.com) leads day hikes, chalet overnights, and backpacking trips. **Waterton Outdoor Adventures** (The Tamarack, 214 Mount View Rd., 403/859-2379, www.hikewaterton.com) leads day hikes in Waterton Lakes National Park.

BACKPACKING

Glacier National Park's backpacking is unrivaled, with miles of well-marked scenic trails. Sixty-six designated backcountry campgrounds spread campers out to avoid crowds, and the permit system guarantees solitude. Go for popular trails such as Gunsight Pass, or head for something remote, like the Nyack-Coal Loop or Boulder Pass. Long-distance trekkers can tackle more than 100 miles (161 km) of Continental Divide Trail in 7-10 days. Find backpacking information, permit applications, advance reservations, trail status reports, and backcountry campsite availability online (www.nps.gov/glac). To speak with someone in person regarding conditions and routes, call the permit offices. Use hiker shuttles to create easy point-to-point routes.

Each backcountry campground has 2-7 sites, with four people allowed per site. All backcountry campgrounds have pit toilets (some with great views), community cook sites, and separate tent sites. No food, garbage, toiletries, or cookware should be kept in the tent sites. A bear pole, hanging bar, or bear-proof food storage boxes are in or near every cooking site. Many backcountry campsites do not allow fires; carry a lightweight stove for cooking. Take low-odor foods to avoid attracting bears, and practice Leave No Trace principles religiously.

Bring **backpacking gear** (tent, sleeping bag, pad, clothing, rain gear, topographic maps, compass or GPS device, first-aid kit, insect repellent, sunscreen, fuel, cooking gear, and stove) plus a 25-foot (7.6-m) rope for hanging food, a small screen or strainer for sifting food particles out of gray water, a one-micron or smaller filter for purifying water (tablets and boiling can also do the job), and a small trowel for emergency human waste disposal when a pit toilet is unavailable. Backpacking rental gear is available through **Glacier Guides** (406/387-5555, https://glacierguides.com) and **Glacier Outfitters** (406/219-7466, www.goglacieroutfitters.com).

Permits

Permits are required (adults $7 pp/night). Starting mid-March, the park service accepts online requests for **advance reservations** ($40 extra). You'll still need to pick up the physical permit the day before your trip and pay the per person fees. If you don't have an advance reservation, you can still nab a permit in person 24 hours prior to a trip. Current availability is updated frequently online (www.nps.gov/glac). If you have your heart set on a **specific route in July-August,** be in line by 6am at the **Apgar Backcountry Permit Office** (406/888-7859 May-Oct., 406/888-7800 Nov.-Apr., 7am-4:30pm daily May-Sept., 8am-4pm daily Oct.) or **St. Mary Visitor Center** (406/888-7800, daily late May-early Oct., backcountry permit desk 7am-4:30pm). You can also get permits in person at **Many Glacier Ranger Station, Two Medicine Ranger Station,** and **Polebridge Ranger Station.** During winter, permits are available at park headquarters by appointment (406/888-7800, Nov.-Apr.).

Guides

For guided backpacking, **Glacier Guides** (406/387-5555 or 800/521-7238, https://glacierguides.com) leads group trips that depart weekly for three, four, and six days. To avoid schlepping your own gear, hire a porter. The custom trips are the best option for families with kids.

CLIMBING

Glacier's peaks and off-trail scrambles are irresistible, but the park's crumbly sedimentary rock makes climbing risky. Loose handholds, wobbly footholds, rockfall, and unstable scree and talus slopes are hazardous. Each year, accidents and sometimes fatalities occur from falling while climbing. Only venture off-trail for climbing if you know the terrain and inherent risks. Do not attempt climbing in Glacier alone or without experience. Most ascents are actually scrambles, but still not for the inexperienced. For routes, J. Gordon Edwards's *A Climber's Guide to Glacier National Park* has been the bible, but Blake Passmore's several volumes of *Climb Glacier National Park* gives more detailed information for peak ascents, especially around Logan Pass.

Begin all off-trail adventures by registering at a ranger station or visitors center, and go prepared. Be aware of closures for bears and fragile vegetation, especially around Logan Pass. Check with visitors centers or ranger stations for the status, or call 406/888-7800. Always practice Leave No Trace principles. For emergencies, carry a cell phone along, but don't depend on its ability to work everywhere in the park. Be ready to self-rescue.

No commercial guiding outfitters operate climbing trips in Glacier. To hook up with climbers, **Glacier Mountaineering Society** (www.glaciermountaineers.com) offers volunteer-led climbs for members ($30), usually on weekends, and each summer the club packs one week in July full of climbs for Mountaineering Week.

Travel Tips

INTERNATIONAL BORDERS

Glacier National Park in the United States and Waterton Lakes National Park in Canada share an international boundary and combined designation as the world's first International Peace Park. For that reason, those who want to explore all parts of the joint park need to have appropriate travel documents.

Entering the United States

International travelers entering the United States must have passports. One exception applies to travelers from Canada and countries in the Western Hemisphere Travel Initiative, who may use a U.S. passport card, enhanced driver's license, or NEXUS card instead. Visas may also be required for some countries; check www.state.travel.gov for countries with visa waivers and visa applications. Except Canadians, international travelers entering the United States must have a current I-94 form ($6).

Entering Canada

International travelers entering Canada must

have passports. The one exception is travelers from the United States and Western Hemisphere Travel Initiative countries, who may use U.S. passport cards, enhanced driver's licenses, or NEXUS cards instead. Visas are not required for visitors from about 50 countries, including the United States. All others must apply for visas. Find the list of visa-exempt countries and visa requirements at www.cic.gc.ca.

Road Ports of Entry

A seasonal port of entry on Chief Mountain International Highway, **Chief Mountain border crossing** is only open daily mid-May-September (7am-10pm June-Labor Day, 9am-6pm May and Sept. after Labor Day). When it is closed, the daily year-round port of entry on Waterton-Glacier's east side is **Piegan-Carway** (7am-11pm) on U.S. 89 and Alberta Highway 2. The only west-side daily year-round port of entry is **Roosville** (open 24 hours) on U.S. 93 between Montana and British Columbia. It's 90 miles (145 km) from West Glacier, but on the direct route to Banff.

Goat Haunt, USA

A small summer-season port of entry at the south end of Waterton Lake, Goat Haunt is accessible only by boat or on foot across the mid-lake boundary. Because of the International Peace Park status, special regulations are in effect. For visitors in Canada traveling down Waterton Lake in private boats or on the tour boat, clearing U.S. Customs is not required, even though you cross the Canadian-U.S. border. At Goat Haunt, you can debark and freely wander around the International Peace Park Pavilion and the walkway along the beach. From Waterton, **hikers** walking the Lakeshore Trail to Goat Haunt or taking the tour boat to Goat Haunt to hike the trails there must report in electronically to U.S. Customs on the morning of your departure. You'll need appropriate **passports** or **passport cards.** Before hiking from Waterton or taking the boat to Goat Haunt, file trip plans at the CBP ROAM kiosks at the tour boat dock and other locations around town; a CBP ROAM app is also available for smartphones.

Visitors from countries other than Canada and the United States must have a current I-94 form or I-94W status to hike beyond Goat Haunt; these forms ($6) must be previously acquired at the Chief Mountain, Piegan-Carway, or Roosville border crossings. For further information on crossing from Canada into the United States, call the **Roosville Port of Entry** (406/889-3865).

For backpackers hiking into Canada, phone the **Canada Border Services Agency** (403/653-3535) when you reach the Waterton Townsite. You can also phone the agency for information in advance of your trip. Backpackers taking the Waterton boat will be given customs forms to fill out.

Customs

In general, Canada and the United States have similar customs laws: no plants, drugs, firewood, or live bait can cross the border. Some fresh meats, poultry products, fruits, and vegetables are restricted, as are firearms in Canada. Pets are permitted to cross the border with a certificate of rabies vaccination dated within 30 days prior to crossing. Bear sprays are considered firearms in Canada; they must have a U.S. Environmental Protection Agency-approved label to go across the border. For clarification, call the **Roosville Canadian customs office** (250/887-3413).

Money and Currency Exchange

Traveling to Waterton for a day or two doesn't require exchanging money. Waterton has no bank, but **The Tamarack** (214 Mount View Rd., 403/859-2378, www.hikewaterton.com, May-mid-Oct.) does offer money-exchange services for Canadian and U.S. currency only. Most stores and businesses in Waterton accept U.S. currency but give Canadian currency as change. Exchange rates vary by store; to receive the best exchange rates, use credit or debit cards.

For Canadians visiting Glacier or Flathead

Valley, some businesses accept Canadian currency. They are used to converting it, but credit and debit cards will receive the most accurate exchange rate. On Glacier's east side, the Native American Bank is in Browning.

For both Canada and the United States, smaller denominations ($20 and under) work best for short trips on either side of the border. International travelers should exchange currency at their major port of entry (Seattle, Vancouver, or Calgary).

TRAVELING SOLO

Plenty of people travel solo to Glacier, but hiking alone is not recommended due to bears and mountain lions. Nevertheless, some hikers still venture into the backcountry alone. If you're one of them, make lots of noise while hiking and brush up on your bear skills. Solo travelers looking for trail companions can join park naturalist hikes. For times and dates, check the park newspaper or online (www.nps.gov/glac). Solo travelers can also join guided group day hikes and backpacking trips with **Glacier Guides** (406/387-5555 or 800/521-7238, https://glacierguides.com) for a fee.

TRAVELING WITH CHILDREN

Children can find plenty of fun in Glacier and Waterton. The lakes, albeit chilly, offer lots of water play, and both parks have child-friendly trails. In Glacier, when the snow melts, Logan Pass has special interpretive signs with hand-cranked speakers geared toward kids, and in Waterton, the Townsite children's park has water-spray features.

Families with babies can rent gear such as cribs, day packs, car seats, and strollers from **Glacier Baby Outfitters** (406/318-5533, https://glacierbabyoutfitters.com). The company delivers equipment to Flathead Valley locations and West Glacier, but you can travel with it throughout the park. **Glacier Outfitters** (196 Apgar Loop Rd., 406/219-7466, www.goglacieroutfitters.com) rents baby backpacks and bicycle trailers in Apgar.

Kids will get more out of their park visit with a guidebook-journal designed specifically for children. *What I Saw in Glacier: A Kid's Guide to the National Park* is by Ellen Horowitz (Riverbend Publishing, 2017), a longtime park educator. The book also serves as a record of their trip. It's available from **Glacier National Park Conservancy** (406/892-3250, https://glacier.org).

Junior Ranger Program

In Glacier, kids can earn a Junior Ranger badge by completing self-guided activities in the *Junior Ranger Activity Guide*, available at all visitors centers. Most activities target ages 6-12 and coincide with a trip over Going-to-the-Sun Road. When kids return the completed newspaper to a visitors center, they are sworn in as Junior Rangers and receive Glacier National Park badges. Waterton has a comparable program with the *Parks Canada Xplorers Program*.

Interpretive Programs

The **Apgar Nature Center** in Apgar serves up educational kid fun during summer. Interpretive rangers lead hands-on activities, including talks and walks, to teach children about wildlife, geology, and habitats. Elsewhere in select locations, rangers lead special children's interpretive programs; consult the park newspaper or online (www.nps.gov/glac) for schedules. Waterton offers family geocaching activities (www.pc.gc.ca).

Hikes

For young kids, short hikes of 2-4 miles (3.2-6.4 km) round-trip work best; always pack water, snacks, and an extra layer for weather changes. On Going-to-the-Sun Road, go for **Avalanche Lake, Hidden Lake Overlook,** and **St. Mary and Virginia Falls.** In Many Glacier, hike to **Red Rock Lake** or take the boat across Swiftcurrent Lake and Lake Josephine to hike to **Grinnell Lake.** In Two Medicine, take the boat uplake to hike to **Twin Falls** or **Upper Two Medicine Lake.** In Waterton, climb the

Bear's Hump or walk around **Red Rock Canyon.**

TRAVELING WITH PETS

Pets are allowed in Glacier National Park, but only in limited areas: campgrounds, parking lots, and roadsides. They are not allowed on trails, beaches, off-trail in the backcountry, or at any park lodges or motor inns. When outside a vehicle or in a campground, pets must be on a leash or caged. Be kind enough to avoid leaving them unattended in a car anywhere. Be considerate of wildlife and other visitors by keeping your pet under control and disposing of waste in garbage cans.

Protection of fragile vegetation and prevention of conflicts with wildlife are two main reasons pets are not allowed on Glacier National Park trails; bears provide their own class of reasons. For pooch-walking purposes, you can head to the paved Apgar Bike Trail (2 mi/3.2 km), which allows pedestrians as well as pets (on leashes). Pets are permitted on trails in surrounding Flathead National Forest. Contrary to Glacier, Waterton permits dogs on leashes on its trails.

Find overnight kenneling in Flathead Valley. **Columbia Mountain Kennels** (531 Windy Acres Dr., Columbia Falls, 406/897-7197, https://columbiamountainkennels.com) is the closest. More choices are in Kalispell, Whitefish, and Bigfork.

SENIOR TRAVELERS

National parks, as well as lands run by the U.S. Fish and Wildlife Service, U.S. Forest Service, and Bureau of Land Management, offer a bargain for U.S. citizens or permanent residents over age 61: $80 buys the National Parks and Federal Recreational Lands Pass, valid for life. To purchase one, bring proof of age (state driver's license, birth certificate, or passport) in person to any national park entrance station. In a private vehicle, the card admits four adults in the vehicle, plus all children under age 16. This pass is not valid in Waterton, but seniors can get into the Canadian national park at a special rate.

The lifetime park pass also grants 50 percent discounts on fees for federally run tours and campgrounds; however, discounts do not apply to park concessionaire services like hotels, boat tours, and bus tours. Glacier's historic hotels do not give discounts to seniors, but some private lodging establishments surrounding the park do; ask to be sure.

TRAVELERS OF COLOR

Many Montanans simply have not been exposed to much racial diversity. The state is 90 percent white and 6 percent Indigenous American (seven reservations are home to 12 nations). Around 4 percent of the state's population include other ethnicities.

Glacier National Park draws people from all across the United States—from big, diverse cities to small-town rural America. But the makeup of Montana's population to the east and west of Glacier varies. To the west, Flathead Valley is about 93 percent white. On the east, where the Blackfeet Nation borders Glacier, including several towns with visitor services, the population is about 65 percent Indigenous American and 30 percent white.

Flathead Valley has a strong presence of **Love Lives Here** (https://loveliveshereflathead.org), an organization that's affiliated with the Montana Human Rights Network. The organization puts together educational programs and events in support of inclusivity. Love Lives Here acts as a local connection point to survey discrimination in the area and as a vehicle to report hate crimes.

LGBTQ TRAVELERS

In Montana, you won't find major hubs of gay bars or super-visible LGBTQ culture, but rather small pockets of people that are big fans of the outdoors. They hike, bike, camp, raft, and ski. While you will find many supportive people here, be aware that the state has conservative roots and some people unfamiliar with gender issues. Popular cultural terms and symbols are not ubiquitous, and may, in fact, refer here to something else; for instance, while you may see some rainbow colors of inclusivity, the word "rainbow" commonly refers to rainbow trout, one of Montana's game fish.

Two Flathead Valley resources to get you connected are the **Glacier Queer Alliance** (www.glacierqueeralliance.org) and **Love Lives Here** (https://loveliveshereflathead.org); both promote education, events, and inclusivity. The statewide organization is **Big Sky Pride** (www.bigskypride.com) based in Helena. Check with the **Pride Foundation** (https://pridefoundation.org/community-impact/initiatives/open-to-all/) for businesses in Montana that support inclusivity; find Kalispell in its own list while all other towns in Flathead Valley and the Glacier environs are listed under "Rural."

TRAVELERS WITH DISABILITIES

Visitors with mobility, hearing, and vision disabilities should consult Glacier's accessibility landing page (https://www.nps.gov/glac/planyourvisit/accessibility.htm). At visitors centers, you can pick up the Accessible Facilities and Services brochure, which contains the same information. The **Disabled Traveler's Companion** (www.tdtcompanion.com) also gives comprehensive information for traveling in Glacier.

Park Passes

Blind or permanently disabled U.S. citizens or permanent residents can get a free lifetime National Parks and Federal Recreational Lands **Access Pass** for access to all national parks and other federal sites. The pass admits the pass holder plus three other adults in the same vehicle; children under age 16 are free. Pass holders also get 50 percent discounts on federally run tours and campgrounds. Get these passes in person at entrance stations with proof of medical disability or eligibility for receiving federal benefits.

Park Facilities and Shuttles

Five **campgrounds** in Glacier reserve a couple sites each for wheelchair needs: Apgar, Fish Creek, Rising Sun, Sprague Creek, and Two Medicine. **Picnic areas** at Apgar, Rising Sun, and Sun Point also have wheelchair access, as do all **lodges** within the park boundaries, although they have a limited number of guest rooms that conform to Americans with Disabilities Act Accessibility Guidelines.

Other wheelchair-accessible sites include **boat docks** at Lake McDonald, Many Glacier, and Two Medicine as well as **evening naturalist programs** in Apgar Amphitheater, Lake McDonald Lodge Auditorium, Many Glacier Hotel Auditorium, Rising Sun Campground, and Two Medicine Campground. Most **parking lots** offer designated parking. **Shuttles** on the Sun Road have wheelchair ramps or lifts. Each shuttle can accommodate one wheelchair in a designated spot.

Park Trails

In McDonald Valley, the paved **Apgar Bike Trail** is mostly flat. Most accessible trails on Going-to-the-Sun Road have flat boardwalk and/or hard-packed surfaces: **Lower McDonald Falls, Trail of the Cedars**, and **Red Rock Point. Oberlin Bend Trail** has a sloped ramp and flat metal platform. The sloping paved **Logan Pass interpretive loop** has a ramp that may require assistance.

On the park's east side, **Running Eagle Falls Nature Trail** in Two Medicine and **Swiftcurrent Nature Trail** in Many Glacier have hard-packed surfaces. On Highway 2 on Glacier's south end, the **Goat Lick Overlook** has a flat boardwalk platform. In Waterton, people using wheelchairs can access paved flat surfaces of the **Linnet Lake Trail** and **Waterton Townsite Trail.**

While pet dogs are not permitted on Glacier's backcountry trails, **service dogs** are allowed. But due to bears, they are discouraged. With service dogs, be safe by sticking to well-traveled trails during midday.

Cell Phone Service and Internet Access

Cell-phone service and internet connectivity in Glacier is limited, thanks to high mountains that block reception. In general, plan to be out of reach while you travel inside the park, where service is unavailable on many roads, trails, campgrounds, picnic areas, and lodges. Internet is equally limited. Glacier offers a chance to sever the technological chain and sink into utter beauty. Only then can you notice the ascending trill of a Swainson's thrush and catch the dash of a grizzly.

FAQS: CELL PHONES

- **Where can I find service?** St. Mary, East Glacier, West Glacier, Apgar, Waterton, and Flathead Valley.

- **Where will I *not* find service?** Going-to-the-Sun Road, Logan Pass, U.S. 2, North Fork, Goat Haunt, Many Glacier, Two Medicine, and most trails in Glacier National Park.

- **Why did my call get dropped?** With only a few cell towers and service companies, alternate services get bumped during heavy use times.

- **How do I use an old-fashioned landline?** Pick up the phone and dial using a phone card. Phone cards are sold in camp stores inside the park.

- **What do I do if I get a flat tire and can't call AAA?** Flag down help and ask them to go to the nearest pay phone, ranger station, or visitors center.

- **What about an emergency while hiking or backpacking?** Be prepared to deal with emergencies yourself and self-rescue. If you can't, send someone for help to the nearest trailhead or ranger station.

MAPS AND PLANNERS

Get park maps that include Glacier and Waterton at entrance stations, visitors centers, ranger stations, and online (www.nps.gov/glac). These maps are perfect for driving tours and perhaps a short walk or two. For hiking trails, small-area brochure-type maps (Many Glacier, Lake McDonald, Two Medicine, Logan Pass, and St. Mary) are available free at ranger stations, visitors centers, and online. These do not have as much detail as topographic maps but can work in a pinch for day hikes on well-signed trails. Each year the National Park Service updates its *Glacier Vacation Planner,* a newspaper listing current information on campgrounds, roads, the park, visitors centers, border crossings, trails, and safety. The current edition is online.

For those heading into the backcountry on day hikes and backpacking trips, pick up a topographic map through **Glacier National Park Conservancy** (406/892-3250, https://glacier.org, $10-12). Order these ahead online or purchase them in Glacier at conservancy bookstores. Three **Trails Illustrated maps** are sold: the large Glacier map that includes Waterton, and the more detailed North Fork and Two Medicine maps. The **Day Hikes of Glacier National Park** map guide combines a topographic map with trail descriptions. The conservancy also sells the **Going-to-the-Sun Road Driving Guide** map that includes stops and interpretive details.

For more detailed maps, USGS maps are sold in the 7.5-minute series at Flathead Valley sporting goods stores or through the **U.S. Geological Survey** (888/275-8747, https://store.usgs.gov). These maps do not include Waterton. You can also download and print them free from **National Geographic** (www.natgeomaps.com).

For hiking Waterton, find the Gem Trek topographic map at the **Waterton Lakes Visitor Information Centre** (403/859-5133)

CELL PHONE ETIQUETTE

· Turn off ringers. Phone noise catapults park visitors from a natural experience back into the hubbub of modern life.

· If you must make a call, move away from campsites, beaches, and other visitors to avoid disrupting their experience.

· On trails, refrain from using phones in the presence of other hikers. Be considerate of other people in the backcountry and their desire to get away from it all.

FAQS: INTERNET ACCESS

· **Why doesn't Glacier offer public internet access?** Most of Glacier, including the ranger stations and campgrounds, does not have Wi-Fi. Isn't it better that the park spends its tight resources on wildlife research and needed facilities?

· **Where can I hook up to wireless internet?** Apgar and St. Mary Visitors Centers have public Wi-Fi. Inside park lodges offer limited Wi-Fi for overnight guests. Some private campgrounds and hotels in West Glacier, Apgar, East Glacier, St. Mary, and Waterton have wireless internet for guests. Waterton Townsite has limited free Wi-Fi and a stronger, fee-based Wi-Fi. At least one coffee shop or restaurant in West Glacier, East Glacier, Polebridge, and Waterton has public internet access. Contrary to Glacier National Park environs, internet is widely available in Flathead Valley at hotels, campgrounds, cafés, and libraries.

· **Do I need to prepare for limited internet access?** Yes! Download apps, maps, and anything you intend to stream before you arrive due to limited internet strength in the park.

or order online (www.gemtrek.com). The map shows roads, trails, and bike routes, and it adds trail descriptions for easy, moderate, and strenuous hikes. It also includes the eastern end of Akamina-Kishinena Provincial Park and the Goat Haunt area of Glacier.

River floaters can find river maps in the *Three Forks of the Flathead Float Guide* ($13 or download free online) at **Hungry Horse Ranger Station** (Flathead National Forest, 10 Hungry Horse Dr., Hungry Horse, 406/387-3800, www.fs.usda.gov/flathead). For maps and information about national forests and the Bob Marshall Wilderness Complex adjacent to the park, contact the **Hungry Horse Ranger Station.** For Helena-Lewis and Clark National Forest, call the **Rocky Mountain Ranger Station** (1102 Main Ave. NW, Choteau, 406/466-5341, www.fs.usda. gov/lewisclark).

PACKING FOR GLACIER COUNTRY

Northwest Montanans have a saying: "Wait five minutes ... the weather will change." Weather can fluctuate wildly within two days. Because snow can fall in August, **dress in layers.** Lightweight wicking synthetics, fleeces, and breathable waterproof or water-resistant fabrics are best. Bring gloves, a warm hat, and rain gear for cold snaps and a hat, sunscreen, and sunglasses for sun. Sturdy **walking shoes** or **hiking boots** work best on the rugged trails.

In Montana, dressing for dinner means putting on a clean shirt. **Casual attire** is the restaurant norm, as are hiking boots and river sandals. Cool weather brings out fleece rather than cashmere. Despite the Wild West heritage, cowboy hats and boots are only for wranglers.

Health and Safety

WILDLIFE
Bears

Glacier has the highest density of grizzly bears in the Lower 48, and black bears find likable habitat here, too. Food is the biggest bear attractant. Proper use, storage, and handling of food and garbage prevents bears from being conditioned and turning aggressive. With strict food and garbage rules, Glacier has minimized aggressive bear encounters, attacks, and both human and bear deaths.

Bears are dangerous around food, be it a carcass in the woods, a pack on a trail, or a cooler in a campsite. Protecting bears and protecting yourself starts with being conscious of food, including wrappers and crumbs. Gorp tidbits dropped along the trail attract wildlife, as do "biodegradable" apple cores chucked into the forest. Pick up what you drop and pack out all your garbage; don't leave a Hansel-and-Gretel trail for the bears.

Camp safely: Use low-odor foods, keep food and cooking gear out of sleeping sites in the backcountry, and store them inside your vehicle in front-country campgrounds. Every picnic table in the park has detailed explanations of how to camp safely in bear country stapled to them. For information on camping in bear country, pick up the *Waterton-Glacier Guide* and Glacier's *Backcountry Guide* at entrance stations, visitors centers, ranger stations, permit offices, or online (www.nps.gov/glac).

Hike safely: On trails, you'll hear jingle bells, sold in gift shops as bear bells. Locals call them "dinner bells," and many hikers hate them. While making noise best prevents surprising a bear, bells fail to carry sound the way a human voice does. To check their minimal effectiveness, see how close you get to hikers before you hear the ringing. Bear bells are best as a souvenir, not as a substitute for human noise on the trail in the form of talking, singing, hooting, and hollering. You may feel silly at first, but everyone does it.

Most hikers carry **pepper spray.** Its capsicum derivative deters bear attacks without injuring the bears or humans. Unlike insect repellents, do not use bear sprays on your body, in tents, or on gear; it is to be sprayed directly into a bear's face, aiming for the eyes and nose. Wind and rain may reduce its effectiveness. Small purse-size pepper sprays are too small to deter bears; buy an 8-ounce (237-ml) can. Practice how to use it, but still make noise on the trail. Carry it on the front of your pack where it is easily reached. If confronted with a bear, you won't have time to dig it out of your pack. Pepper spray is not allowed on airplanes unless it's in checked luggage, and only brands with U.S. Environmental Protection Agency labels can be carried into Canada. Federal law allows people who can legally carry **firearms** under federal, state, and local laws to bring their guns into Glacier (prohibited in most buildings), but discharging firearms in the park is illegal except when presented with "imminent danger."

Mountain Lions

These large cats rarely prey on humans, but they can, especially small kids. Making noise for bears will also help you avoid surprising a lion. Hike with others, and keep kids close. If you stumble on a lion, above all, do not run. Be calm, and group together to appear bigger. Look at the cat with peripheral vision rather than staring straight on, and back away slowly. If the lion attacks, fight back with everything: rocks, sticks, or kicking.

ENVIRONMENTAL CONCERNS
Water Hazards

Contrary to popular belief, bears are not the number-one cause of death in Glacier; rather it is drowning from falling. Be extremely cautious around lakes, fast-moving streams, and waterfalls, where slick moss and algae cover the rocks. Waters are swift, frigid, clogged with submerged obstacles, unforgiving, and sometimes lethal.

Giardia

Lakes and streams can carry parasites like *Giardia lamblia*. If ingested, it causes cramping, nausea, and severe diarrhea for up to six weeks. Avoid giardia by boiling water (for one minute, plus one minute for each 1,000 ft/305 m of elevation above sea level) or using a one-micron filter. Bleach also works (add two drops per quart and wait 30 minutes). Tap water in campgrounds, hotels, and picnic areas has been treated; you'll taste the chlorine.

Dehydration

Many first-time hikers to Glacier are surprised to find they drink more water than at home. Glacier's winds, altitude, and lower humidity can add up to a fast case of dehydration. It manifests first as a headache. While hiking, drink lots of water, even more than you normally would. With children, monitor their fluid intake.

Altitude

Some visitors from sea level locales feel the effects of altitude at high elevations like Logan Pass. Watch for lightheadedness, headaches, or shortness of breath. To acclimatize, slow down the pace of hiking and drink lots of fluids. If symptoms spike, descend in elevation as soon as possible. Altitude also increases UV radiation exposure: To prevent sunburn, use a strong sunscreen and wear sunglasses and a hat.

Ice and Snow

While glacial ice often looks solid to step on, it harbors unseen caverns beneath. Buried crevasses (large vertical cracks) are difficult to see, and snow bridges can collapse as a person crosses. Be safe by staying off the ice; even Glacier's tiny ice fields have caused fatalities. Steep-angled snowfields also pose a danger

from falling. Use an ice ax and caution, or stay off them. If you want to slide on the snow for fun, slide only where you have a safe run out away from rocks and trees.

PERSONAL HEALTH
Hypothermia

Insidious and subtle, exhausted and physically unprepared hikers are at risk for hypothermia. The body's inner core loses heat, reducing mental and physical functions. Watch for uncontrolled shivering, incoherence, poor judgment, fumbling, mumbling, and slurred speech. Avoid becoming hypothermic by staying dry. Don rain gear and warm moisture-wicking layers, rather than cottons that won't dry and fail to retain heat. Get hypothermic hikers into dry clothing and shelter. Give warm nonalcoholic and noncaffeinated liquids. If the victim cannot regain body heat, get into a sleeping bag with the victim, both stripped for skin-to-skin contact.

Blisters

Incorrect socks and ill-fitting shoes cause most blisters. Cotton socks absorb water from the feet while you're hiking and hold onto it, providing a surface for friction. Synthetic or wool-blend socks wick water away from the skin. To prevent blisters, recognize "hot spots" or rubs, applying moleskin or New-Skin to sensitive areas. In a pinch, slap duct tape on trouble spots. Once a blister occurs, apply blister bandages or Second Skin, a product developed for burns that cools blisters and cushions them. Cover Second Skin with moleskin to absorb future rubbing and secure the Second Skin.

Hantavirus

Hantavirus infection, with flu-like symptoms, is contracted by inhaling dust from deer mice droppings. Avoid burrows and woodpiles thick with rodents. Store all food in rodent-proof containers. If you find rodent dust in your gear, disinfect it with water and bleach (1.5 cups bleach to one gallon water). If you contract the virus, get immediate medical attention.

Mosquitoes and Ticks

Bugs can carry diseases such as West Nile virus and Rocky Mountain spotted fever. Protect yourself by wearing long sleeves and pants as well as using insect repellent in spring-summer, when mosquitoes and ticks are common. If you are bitten by a tick, remove it, disinfect the bite, and see a doctor if lesions or a rash appears.

HOSPITALS AND EMERGENCIES

For emergencies inside the park, call 406/888-7800. For emergencies outside the park, call 911. On Glacier's west side, the nearest hospitals are in Flathead Valley. **Kalispell Regional Medical Center** (310 Sunny View Ln., Kalispell, 406/752-5111) and the **North Valley Hospital** (1600 Hospital Way, Whitefish, 406/863-3500) are 35 minutes from West Glacier and can be up to 90 minutes from Logan Pass, depending on traffic. On Glacier's east side, **Blackfeet Community Hospital** (760 Blackweasel Rd., Browning, 406/338-6100) is 20 minutes from East Glacier and one hour from St. Mary.

Resources

Suggested Reading

DRIVING GUIDES

Schmidt, Thomas. *National Geographic Road Guide to Glacier and Waterton Lakes National Park*. Washington DC: National Geographic, 2004. A handy 93-page guide to driving the park's roads. Each section is complete with a map, nature notes, landscape features, and stops.

GEOLOGY

Ahlenslager, Kathleen. *Glacier: The Story Behind the Scenery*. Wickenburg, AZ: KC Publications, 1988. Color photos and text in this 48-page book tell the natural history of Glacier with an emphasis on geology.

Tomlin, Teagan. *Geology Along Going-to-the-Sun Road*. West Glacier, MT: Glacier Natural History Association, 2018. An easy-to-read guide for folks with no science background for a self-guided tour. Maps, stops, and diagrams describe the geologic phenomena on the historic highway, along with great photos showing rock formations.

GRIZZLY BEARS

Herrero, Stephen. *Bear Attacks: Their Causes and Avoidance*. Guilford, CT: The Lyons Press, 3rd edition, 2018. Somewhat sensationalized with attention to gory detail, Herrero's book paints a picture of the myriad reasons for bear attacks while also covering safety and how to avoid attacks. Not for light sleepers who plan to go into the backcountry. Herrero is one of the leading authorities on bear research.

McMillion, Scott. *Mark of the Grizzly*. Helena, MT: Falcon Press, 2nd edition, 2011. McMillion tells the stories behind 18 different grizzly bear attacks. He doesn't shy away from the gore, nor does he become preachy or judgmental, but he does examine each attack in detail to determine what we can learn about bears.

Olsen, Jack. *Night of the Grizzlies*. Moose, WY: Homestead Publishing, 1996. A true story of one night in 1968 when grizzlies killed two women in two different locations in Glacier's backcountry. These events altered park policies regarding food and garbage as well as bear management practices.

Schneider, Bill. *Bear Aware*. Helena, MT: Falcon Press, 4th edition, 2012. This handy 104-page book is packed with advice on how to hike safely in bear country. One section tackles bear myths, debunking them with facts.

WILDLIFE

Chadwick, Doug. *The Wolverine Way*. Ventura, CA: Patagonia Inc., 2012. Stories of the gluttonous creatures that epitomize wilderness, gleaned from research in Glacier.

Benson, David. *Glacier is for the Birds: A Trail Guide for the Birds of Glacier National Park*. Habitats for All Press, 2016. Written by a ranger-naturalist in Many Glacier and professor of biology at Marion University, this guide shows you where to spot 170 bird species along Glacier's trails.

Fisher, Chris, Don Pattie, and Tamara Hartson. *Mammals of the Rocky Mountains.* Edmonton, Alberta, Canada: Lone Pine Publishing, 2000. A Lone Pine Field Guide for 91 species of animals found in the Rocky Mountains—a breeze to use. Each animal has details on physical description, behavior, habitat, food, denning, range, and young. Similar species are described to point out differences for identification.

Harada, Sumio, and Karen Yale. *Mountain Goats of Glacier National Park.* Helena, MT: Farcountry Press, 2008. Harada has photographed mountain goats in Glacier for the past two decades; Yale chronicles their behavior.

HISTORY

Djuff, Ray, and Chris Morrison. *Glacier's Historic Hotels and Chalets: View with a Room.* Helena, MT: Farcountry Press, 2013. Loaded with historical photos, this quasi-coffee-table book tells the story behind each of Glacier Park's lodges and chalets, including the chalets that no longer exist. A great background read for anyone who falls in love with Glacier's historic lodges.

Guthrie, Carol. *All Aboard for Glacier: The Great Northern Railway and Glacier National Park.* Helena, MT: Farcountry Press, 2004. For train buffs, this is the history of the Great Northern Railway building up Glacier as a destination for its passengers.

Guthrie, C. W. *Glacier National Park: The First 100 Years.* Helena, MT: Farcountry Press, 2008. The official centennial book contains rich color and historical photos in its decade-by-decade waltz through Glacier's history.

Guthrie, C. W. *Going-to-the-Sun Road: Highway to the Sky.* Helena, MT: Farcountry Press, 2006. With historical photos and maps, Going-to-the-Sun Road takes shape

in this chronicle of the 20-year building of the National Historic Landmark.

Holterman, Jack. *Place Names of Glacier National Park.* Helena, MT: Riverbend Publishing, 2006. A list of 663 park names—how peaks, passes, lakes, rivers, and valleys in Glacier acquired their monikers.

INDIGENOUS PEOPLES

Grinnell, George Bird. *Blackfoot Lodge Tales.* Whitefish, MT: Kessinger Publishing, 2008. Grinnell, who negotiated the purchase of reservation land for the park, chronicles Blackfeet stories from his days in Glacier in the late 1800s.

Schultz, James Willard. *Blackfeet Tales of Glacier National Park.* Helena, MT: Riverbend Publishing, 2016. Original Blackfeet stories collected by Schultz in the late 1800s, including the history of Two Medicine, Cut Bank, St. Mary, Swiftcurrent, and Chief Mountain.

McClintock, Walter. *The Old North Trail: Life, Legends & Religion of the Blackfeet Indians.* CreateSpace Independent Publishing Platform, 2016. Adopted into the Blackfeet in 1886, Walter McClintock recorded his experiences living with the Blackfeet.

Thompson, Sally. *People Before the Park: The Kootenai and Blackfeet before Glacier National Park.* Helena, MT: Montana Historical Society Press, 2014. Thompson spent three decades working to construct Indigenous history in the Northern Rockies and then published their stories in this 220-page book.

NATURAL HISTORY

Kershaw, Linda, Andy MacKinnon, and Jim Pojar. *Plants of the Rocky Mountains.* Edmonton, Alberta, Canada: Lone Pine Publishing, 2nd edition, 2017. A Lone Pine Field Guide for eight types of flora found in the Rocky Mountains: trees, shrubs, wildflowers, aquatics, grasses, ferns, mosses, and lichens. Although the pictures are small, the detailed descriptions of appearance, season, and habitat help in identification. Notes on each of the 1,300-plus species given include fun tidbits on the origin of names and Native American uses.

Kimball, Shannon Fitzpatrick, and Peter Lesica. *Wildflowers of Glacier National Park and Surrounding Areas*. Kalispell, MT: Trillium Press, 2005. One of the best regional flower guides. Flowers are categorized by color, with big sharp photos allowing easy identification. Includes entries for trees, ferns, and grasses.

Rockwell, David. *Glacier: A Natural History Guide*. Helena, MT: Falcon Press, 2007. Contrary to the title, this is not a guidebook but a description of Glacier Park's natural history. Rockwell covers geology, glaciers, flora, fauna, fires, and human impact on the ecosystem in the best available in-depth natural history book on the park.

OUTDOOR RECREATION

Duckworth, Carolyn, ed. *Hiker's Guide to Glacier National Park* and *Short Hikes and Strolls in Glacier National Park*. West Glacier, MT: Glacier Natural History Association, 1996. Two books covering Glacier only, not Waterton. The hiker's guide contains 110 pages describing popular trails. *Short Hikes* is a 46-page book covering 16 favorite 1- to 4-mile (1.6- to 6.4-km) walks.

Edwards, J. Gordon. *A Climber's Guide to Glacier Park*. Helena, MT: Falcon Press, 2017. The definitive guide to mountaineering in Glacier National Park. Edwards pioneered many of the routes up Glacier's peaks and is considered the park's patron saint of climbing. Routes cover technical climbs and off-trail scrambles.

Good Monod, Stormy. *Day Hikes Around the Flathead*. Whitefish, MT: Flathead Guidebooks, 2018. A self-published book covering 120 day hikes with maps, route descriptions, distances, difficulty, and special emphasis on identifying dog-friendly trails.

Molvar, Erik. *Best Easy Day Hikes in Glacier and Waterton Lakes*. Helena, MT: Falcon Press, 2001. A roundup of day hikes in both Glacier and Waterton. At half the size of his hiking guidebook, this focuses only on day hikes, with emphasis on well-signed, less-strenuous trails.

Molvar, Erik. *Hiking Glacier and Waterton Lakes National Parks*. Helena, MT: Falcon Press, 5th edition, 2018. The most definitive trail guide for Glacier and Waterton Parks. Molvar gives detailed trail descriptions, including maps, for all the popular trails inside the parks. Routes cover day hikes, overnights, and extended backpacking trips. Hiker safety, campsite details, and fishing information are also included.

Molvar, Erik. *Hiking Montana's Bob Marshall Wilderness*. Helena, MT: Falcon Press, 2001. A detailed trail guide covering the Great Bear, Bob Marshall, and Scapegoat Wilderness areas. Trail descriptions include maps, elevation charts, and accurate information on how to find even the more difficult-to-locate trailheads.

Passmore, Blake. *Climb Glacier National Park*, vols. 1-5. Stevensville, MT: Stoneydale Press, 2011-2016. These illustrated guides provide climbing routes for peaks in the Logan Pass, Two Medicine, and central Glacier area. Color photos, maps, and GPS points identify routes.

Schneider, Russ. *Fishing Glacier National Park*. Helena, MT: Falcon Press, 2002. The most definitive fishing guide to Glacier. Schneider explains what flies to use to catch certain fish, where you'll catch arctic grayling or westslope cutthroat trout, and where you'll find nothing.

Internet Resources

GLACIER

Glacier National Park
www.nps.gov/glac
The official website for Glacier National Park. It provides information on park conditions, roads, campsites, trails, history, and more. Six webcams are updated every few minutes. In addition to trip planning information, the site includes downloadable maps, publications, and backcountry permit information as well as a Going-to-the-Sun Road status report, updated daily.

Glacier National Park Conservancy
https://glacier.org
The best resource for books, maps, posters, and cards on Glacier Park. Proceeds from book sales are donated to the park to support education, preservation, and research.

Northern Rocky Mountain Research Center
www.usgs.gov/centers/norock
The research center works under the U.S. Geological Survey. The website contains current research in Glacier on grizzly bears, glaciers, climate change, bighorn sheep, avalanches, and amphibians.

The Glacier Institute
www.glacierinstitute.org
An educational nonprofit park partner, the Glacier Institute presents programs for kids and adults in field settings taught by expert instructors. Field classes take place in Glacier as well as surrounding ecosystems.

Glacier National Park Volunteer Associates
https://gnpva.org
This nonprofit assists with historic preservation, education, and trail work. The organization looks for volunteers to help on projects ranging from a few days to summer-long.

National Park Service Reservation Center
www.recreation.gov
Fish Creek, Many Glacier, and St. Mary Campgrounds take reservations using this service.

Hike 734
www.hike734.com
Jake Bramante documented all of Glacier's 734 miles (1,180 km) of trail in 2011. You can look up specific trails by map to see photos, video, and blogs.

WATERTON

Waterton Lakes National Park
www.pc.gc.ca/en/pn-np/ab/waterton/index
The official website for Waterton. It contains basic park information on camping, hiking, and Parks Canada-operated services, but not the commercial services in Waterton Townsite.

National Park Service Reservation Center
https://reservation.pc.gc.ca
Log on to make reservations at Waterton Townsite's campground.

Waterton Chamber of Commerce
https://mywaterton.ca
The official website for Waterton Townsite contains dining, lodging, recreation, visitor services, and camping information for Waterton. Some services adjacent to the park are also included.

FLATHEAD VALLEY

Flathead Valley Convention and Visitors Bureau
www.fcvb.org

The Flathead Valley's tourism board covers info on Kalispell, Columbia Falls, Whitefish, Bigfork, Lakeside, Flathead Lake, and ski resorts. It covers recreation, lodging, dining, and special events.

Whitefish Convention and Visitors Bureau
https://explorewhitefish.com

The official travel website covering recreation, lodging, dining, and special events in the town of Whitefish and at Whitefish Mountain Resort.

MONTANA TRAVEL

Glacier Country
https://glaciermt.com

The official state travel website for northwest Montana. You can find lodging, dining, and activity information, and it's easy to navigate by activity or location.

Montana Travel
www.visitmt.com

The official travel website for Montana. You'll find access to the state's activities, lodging, dining, and recreation by location or activity.

Montana Department of Transportation
www.mdt.mt.gov

Travel advisories and road conditions for Montana. Glacier's interior roads are not yet included on the website; information on Going-to-the-Sun Road is sporadic. Check the park's website for the most accurate information.

Helena-Lewis and Clark National Forest
www.fs.usda.gov/main/hlcnf/home

Information on campgrounds, trails, fishing, cabin rentals, and other recreation, particularly for the Bob Marshall Wilderness.

Flathead National Forest
www.fs.usda.gov/flathead

Information on campgrounds, fishing, rafting, wilderness areas, cabin rentals, ski areas, trails, and other recreation. However, the recreation section is limited to specifics for trails.

Montana Fish, Wildlife, and Parks
fwp.mt.gov

Up-to-date fishing and hunting information, licenses, state park, and wildlife refuge details for Montana.

CANADA TRAVEL

Travel Alberta Canada
www.travelalberta.com

The province's official portal to Alberta resorts, parks, ski areas, festivals, events, cities, outdoor recreation, and touring. It's easy to navigate by location or activity to find what you want.

Alberta Road Reports
https://roadreports.ama.ab.ca

Check this site for road construction, advisories, and closures from the Alberta Motor Association.

British Columbia Transportation
www.drivebc.ca

Road reports update travel information, closures, construction, and weather for British Columbia. Webcams give you a firsthand look.

Akamina-Kishinena Provincial Park
bcparks.ca

Information on recreation, camping, and hiking in Akamina-Kishinena Provincial Park, adjacent to Waterton and Glacier. Maps are also available.

Index

List of Maps

Acknowledgments

A huge thank you goes out to the National Park Service for all of their work in Glacier. It's through their labors that we can enjoy such an impressive and fast-changing place.

Thanks also go to my parents for introducing me as a child to the outdoors and national parks. Our family expeditions for hiking, backpacking, camping, and skiing shaped a way of life for me. Those experiences and the exposure to nature are a priceless gift.

Without my hiking buddies, *Moon Glacier National Park* would not be. My hiker clan and backpacking girls accompany me on trails, providing laughter and joy.

Last, big thanks go to Leah Gordon for her editing work on the book, along with an outstanding photo wiz Darren Alessi and map guru Kat Bennett.

USA
NATIONAL
PARKS

THE COMPLETE GUIDE TO ALL
62 PARKS

BECKY LOMAX

Craft a personalized
journey through the
top National Parks in
the U.S. and Canada
with Moon!

ACADIA
NATIONAL PARK

HILARY NANGLE

ARCHES &
CANYONLANDS
NATIONAL PARKS

BANFF
NATIONAL
PARK

HIKE·CAMP
SEE WILDLIFE

ANDREW HEMPSTEAD

DEATH VALLEY
NATIONAL PARK

GLACIER
NATIONAL PARK

HIKING · CAMPING
LAKES & PEAKS

BECKY LOMAX

GRAND
CANYON

HIKE·CAMP
RAFT THE
COLORADO RIVER

TIM HULL

MOUNT RUSHMORE
& THE BLACK HILLS

Including the Badlands

LAURAL A. HOWELL

ROCKY
MOUNTAIN
NATIONAL PARK

HIKE·CAMP
SEE WILDLIFE

SEQUOIA &
KINGS CANYON

HIKING·CAMPING
WATERFALLS & BIG TREES

LEIGH BERNACCHI

In these books:

Coverage of gateway cities and towns

Suggested itineraries from one day to multiple weeks

Advice on where to stay (or camp) in and around the parks

MOON
GREAT SMOKY MOUNTAINS NATIONAL PARK
HIKING · CAMPING SCENIC DRIVES
JASON FRYE

MOON
JOSHUA TREE & PALM SPRINGS
JENNA BLOUGH

MOON
YELLOWSTONE & GRAND TETON
HIKE, CAMP, SEE WILDLIFE
BECKY LOMAX

MOON
YOSEMITE SEQUOIA & KINGS CANYON
ANN MARIE BROWN

MOON
ZION & BRYCE
W.C. McRAE & JUDY JEWELL

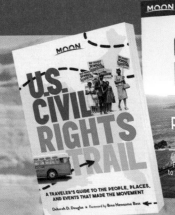

MOON
U.S. CIVIL RIGHTS TRAIL
A TRAVELER'S GUIDE TO THE PEOPLE, PLACES, AND EVENTS THAT MADE THE MOVEMENT
Deborah D. Douglas · Foreword by Bree Newsome Bass

MOON
the OPEN ROAD
50 BEST ROAD TRIPS in the USA
From Weekend Getaways to Cross-Country Adventures
JESSICA DUNHAM

MOON
Road Trip USA
25th ANNIVERSARY EDITION
CROSS-COUNTRY ADVENTURES ON AMERICA'S TWO-LANE HIGHWAYS
Jamie Jensen

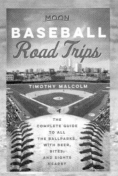

MOON
BASEBALL Road Trips
TIMOTHY MALCOLM
THE COMPLETE GUIDE TO ALL THE BALLPARKS, WITH BEER, BITES, AND SIGHTS NEARBY

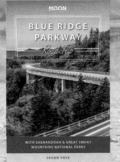

MOON
BLUE RIDGE PARKWAY Road Trip
WITH SHENANDOAH & GREAT SMOKY MOUNTAINS NATIONAL PARKS
JASON FRYE

MOON
CALIFORNIA
SAN FRANCISCO, YOSEMITE, LAS VEGAS, GRAND CANYON, LOS ANGELES, & THE PACIFIC COAST HIGHWAY
STUART THORNTON

MOON
NASHVILLE TO NEW ORLEANS Road Trip
NATCHEZ TRACE PARKWAY · MEMPHIS · TUPELO · MISSISSIPPI BLUES TRAIL
MARGARET LITTMAN

MOON
NEW ENGLAND Road Trip
BOSTON, ACADIA NATIONAL PARK, WHITE MOUNTAINS, BERKSHIRES, NEWPORT, AND CAPE COD
JEN ROSE SMITH

MOON
NORTHERN CALIFORNIA Road Trips
DRIVES ALONG THE COAST, REDWOODS, AND MOUNTAINS WITH THE BEST STOPS ALONG THE WAY
STUART THORNTON & KAYLA ANDERSON

MORE ROAD TRIP GUIDES FROM MOON

MOON
OREGON TRAIL
Road Trip

HISTORIC SITES, SMALL TOWNS, AND SCENIC LANDSCAPES ALONG THE LEGENDARY WESTWARD ROUTE

KATRINA EMERY

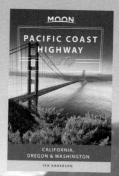

MOON
PACIFIC COAST HIGHWAY
Road Trip

CALIFORNIA, OREGON & WASHINGTON

IAN ANDERSON

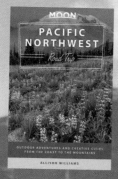

MOON
PACIFIC NORTHWEST
Road Trip

OUTDOOR ADVENTURES AND CREATIVE CITIES FROM THE COAST TO THE MOUNTAINS

ALLISON WILLIAMS

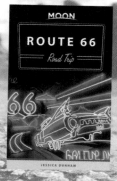

MOON
ROUTE 66
Road Trip

JESSICA DUNHAM

MOON
SOUTH FLORIDA & THE KEYS
Road Trip

WITH MIAMI, WALT DISNEY WORLD, TAMPA & THE EVERGLADES

JASON FERGUSON

MOON
SOUTHERN CALIFORNIA
Road Trip

DRIVES ALONG THE BEACHES, MOUNTAINS, AND DESERTS WITH THE BEST STOPS ALONG THE WAY

IAN ANDERSON

MOON
SOUTHWEST
Road Trip

LAS VEGAS, ZION & BRYCE, MONUMENT VALLEY, SANTA FE & TAOS, AND THE GRAND CANYON

TIM HULL

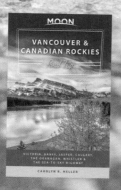

MOON
VANCOUVER & CANADIAN ROCKIES
Road Trip

VICTORIA, BANFF, JASPER, CALGARY, THE OKANAGAN, WHISTLER & THE SEA-TO-SKY HIGHWAY

CAROLYN B. HELLER

MOON
YELLOWSTONE TO GLACIER NATIONAL PARK
Road Trip

JACKSON HOLE, CODY, THE GRAND TETONS & THE ROCKY MOUNTAIN FRONT

CARTER G. WALKER

Get inspired for your next adventure

Follow @**moonguides** on Instagram or
subscribe to our newsletter at **moon.com**

#TravelWithMoon

MAP SYMBOLS

═════	Expressway	○	City/Town	✈	Airport	⚓	Golf Course
═════	Primary Road	◉	State Capital	✖	Airfield	🅿	Parking Area
═════	Secondary Road	✹	National Capital	▲	Mountain	⛩	Archaeological Site
┈┈┈	Unpaved Road	◉	Highlight	✦	Unique Natural Feature	⛪	Church
┈┈┈	Trail	★	Point of Interest				
┈┈┈	Ferry	●	Accommodation	🕊	Waterfall	⛽	Gas Station
━━━	Railroad	▼	Restaurant/Bar	▲	Park	◯	Glacier
═════	Pedestrian Walkway	■	Other Location	TH	Trailhead	▦	Mangrove
▭▭▭	Stairs	Λ	Campground	⛷	Skiing Area	▨	Reef
						▱	Swamp

CONVERSION TABLES

°C = (°F − 32) / 1.8
°F = (°C x 1.8) + 32
1 inch = 2.54 centimeters (cm)
1 foot = 0.304 meters (m)
1 yard = 0.914 meters
1 mile = 1.6093 kilometers (km)
1 km = 0.6214 miles
1 fathom = 1.8288 m
1 chain = 20.1168 m
1 furlong = 201.168 m
1 acre = 0.4047 hectares
1 sq km = 100 hectares
1 sq mile = 2.59 square km
1 ounce = 28.35 grams
1 pound = 0.4536 kilograms
1 short ton = 0.90718 metric ton
1 short ton = 2,000 pounds
1 long ton = 1.016 metric tons
1 long ton = 2,240 pounds
1 metric ton = 1,000 kilograms
1 quart = 0.94635 liters
1 US gallon = 3.7854 liters
1 Imperial gallon = 4.5459 liters
1 nautical mile = 1.852 km

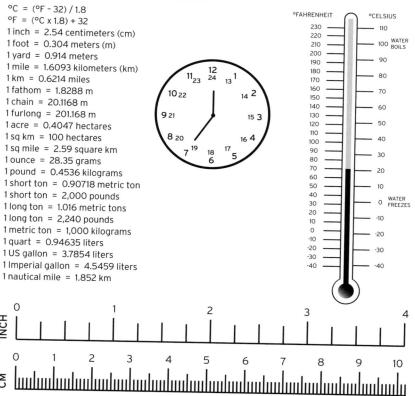

GLACIER NATIONAL PARK
Avalon Travel
Hachette Book Group
1700 Fourth Street
Berkeley, CA 94710, USA
www.moon.com

Editor: Leah Gordon
Graphics and Production Coordinator: Darren Alessi
Cover Design: Kimberly Glyder
Interior Design: Domini Dragoone
Moon Logo: Tim McGrath
Map Editor: Kat Bennett
Cartographers: Brian Shotwell, Stephanie Poulain, Kat Bennett
Indexer: Rachel Kuhn

ISBN-13: 9781640494374

Printing History
1st Edition — 2006
8th Edition — March 2021
5 4 3

Text © 2021 by Becky Lomax.
Maps © 2021 by Avalon Travel.
All photos © Becky Lomax except page 19 © Mountain Photography

Front cover photo: Mount Wilbur reflected in Swiftcurrent Lake at sunrise © America / Alamy Stock Photo
Back cover photo: Swiftcurrent Lake at sunrise in Many Glacier area © Donna Nonemountry | Dreamstime.com

Printed in China by RR Donnelley

Avalon Travel is a division of Hachette Book Group, Inc. Moon and the Moon logo are trademarks of Hachette Book Group, Inc. All other marks and logos depicted are the property of the original owners.